Faces in a Crowd:
The Individual Learner
in Multisection Courses

Carol A. Klee
Editor

Change in Style for the AAUSC Series
This volume introduces a change in style for the AAUSC series approved at the November 1993 Editorial Board and Executive Council meetings. Henceforth, this publication will follow the *Chicago Manual of Style* (Reference Style B). See pages 381–386 in this volume for details about preparing articles for submission.

Faces in a Crowd: The Individual Learner in Multisection Courses

Carol A. Klee
Editor

Heinle & Heinle Publishers
Boston, Massachusetts 02116, U.S.A.

Manufactured in the United States of America.

Heinle & Heinle Publishers is a division of Wadsworth, Inc.

ISBN 0-8384-63673
10   9   8   7   6   5   4   3   2

Contents

III. Policy and Curricular Implications

Contributors

AAUSC Syle sheet for Authors

Acknowledgments

I would like to take this opportunity to thank the many people who contributed to the production of this volume. Sally Sieloff Magnan, Series Editor, and Charles J. James, Managing Editor, provided help and excellent advice throughout the editing process. I also owe a special to debt of gratitude to the members of the Editorial Board who evaluated the manuscripts promptly and provided feedback that helped improve the quality of the submissions. In addition, I would like to thank the authors for their cooperation, often on very short notice, in producing the final version of their chapters. Holly Tucker of the University of Wisconsin deserves special acknowledgment for her help in designing the Style Sheet for the AAUSC series, which is included at the end of this volume.

This volume and series would not have been possible without the continued support of Heinle & Heinle Publishers, in particular publisher Stan Galek. I would also like to thank Elizabeth Holthaus, Director of Production, Pat Ménard, Editorial Director, and Laura Ferry, Project Manager, for guiding the manuscript through the production process.

Finally, a special word of appreciation is due to my family, Luis and Camille, for their patience and support throughout this project.

Carol A. Klee
Editor

Introduction

The focus of the fifth volume in the series of the American Association of University Supervisors, Coordinators, and Directors of Foreign Language Programs (AAUSC), Issues in Language Program Direction, is on the individual learner in multisection courses. During the past two decades an increasing amount of research has been dedicated to aspects of individual learners (cf. Skehan 1989) and has been accompanied by a focus on the needs of individual learners in curriculum development and instructional practice (cf. Nunan 1988; Tarone and Yule 1989).

For directors of large language programs, in which multisection courses are the norm, this change in focus presents new challenges. On the one hand, we are faced with the need to provide consistency and coherence across sections taught by instructors with varying degrees of talent, experience, and interest in language teaching in order to ensure that the courses in the program are well articulated and that students can proceed relatively seamlessly from one course to the next. On the other hand, we are faced with the reality that one curriculum and set of instructional practices does not fit all students or instructors. As Dekeyser (this volume) warns, "The streamlined curricula [in large language programs] (often designed to be teacher-proof) leave little room for the individual differences in aptitude level, aptitude profile, cognitive style, personality, motivational level, and motivational orientation that characterize the undergraduate population now more than ever before."

The contributions in this volume address this issue in a variety of ways, and many of them provide suggestions for directors of language programs who would like to attend better to individual differences in their multisection courses. Much of the work of the director of language programs in this regard involves sensitizing teaching assistants (TAs) to differences in individual learners and helping them find ways to assist learners with different needs and interests and varying strengths and weaknesses.

The volume is divided into three sections: the first section contains two articles that provide overviews of research on language anxiety and gender issues in second language classrooms; the second section comprises six research studies on learner variables; and the third section offers three articles that deal with the policy and curricular implications that accompany a focus on individual learners.

In the first article, "New Directions in Language Anxiety Research," Dolly Jesusita Young provides a comprehensive overview of language anxiety research, describing major research findings in the field and suggesting directions for future study. Since it has been shown that language anxiety negatively affects second language performance, as well as having a negative impact on language learning (at both the input and processing levels), Young discusses anxiety-reducing and coping strategies that directors of language programs should find useful in planning curriculum and designing TA workshops.

Lydie E. Meunier seeks to broaden our understanding of gender issues in a second language classroom by examining these issues from a sociolinguistic and anthropological perspective. Following a review of relevant first and second language research, she argues convincingly for the premise that "the socialization process undergone by L2 learners sets various types of preferential cognitive networks, and that gender-specific strategies in SLA [second language acquisition] may ultimately stem from nurture rather than nature, that is, from a possible sociolinguistic transfer out of native genderlects." She cautions instructors to be vigilant concerning gender bias in classroom interactions, pedagogical materials, classroom activities, and test design.

The next six articles are research studies of aspects of learner variables. Madeline Ehrman begins the section with a well-designed study that examines the weakest and strongest 2–4 percent of a large group of adult students in an intensive language training program at the Foreign Service Institute to determine how they compare in terms of such variables as language learning aptitude, demographics, preferred learning strategies, motivation and anxiety, and personality factors. Her results indicate that the usual definition of language learning aptitude should perhaps be broadened to include not only cognitive skills, but also various personality attributes that predispose learners "to impose their own structure on what they would otherwise experience as chaos."

Robert M. Dekeyser sets out to determine whether error correction shows a main effect on students' motivation and anxiety levels and an interaction effect with several individual characteristics. His results suggest that "individual variables should be taken into account when deciding how to react to errors during oral communication activities in the classroom" since error correction seems to help students with high previous achievement, high verbal aptitude, low anxiety, and low extrinsic motivation, and appears detrimental to the complementary groups. Dekeyser suggests that directors of language programs sensitize TAs to the interactions between error correction and individual differences and encourage individualized treatment within sections.

The purpose of M. Mahodi Alosh's study of the learning strategies used by successful students of Arabic during a three-year intensive summer program is to identify, describe, and classify the strategies used by successful students and determine whether there is a common denominator among the learners in terms of shared strategies. He points out the potential benefits of teaching students about learning strategies so that they can self-direct their learning more effectively and efficiently; this may be especially important in the less commonly taught language programs in which student enrollment is a constant concern.

Sadia Zoubir-Shaw and Rebecca L. Oxford examine gender differences in language learning strategies among university students studying French and find that women surpass men in the use of several strategy categories and use strategies that might be viewed as effective for language learning more frequently than men. They point out that knowing how students function can help instructors tailor instruction and provide workable instructional strategies for both males and females. They, like Alosh, emphasize the importance of teaching students to use more and better strategies.

Another contribution to research on gender differences in the second language classroom is the study by Christine M. Campbell and Victor M. Shaw. They analyze changes in anxiety felt by male and female postsecondary students before beginning a foreign language course and after sixty hours of instruction. Their results reveal a significant interaction between gender and the time of survey administration; the level of anxiety in male students rose significantly, while the level of language anxiety in female students dropped slightly. They recommend paying attention to gender differences in the classroom not only by making changes in teacher and student behavior, but also by changing the curriculum itself, providing specially designed courses for anxiety-ridden students so that they can learn ways to enhance their language learning.

In the final contribution in this section, Monika Chavez examines the complex relationship between students' curricular preferences and certain demographic variables (e.g., foreign travel, previous foreign language experience, chosen or intended major field of study, age, language learning success, and gender). Her results underline how difficult it can be for directors of language programs to take students' curricular preferences into account in program design.

The final section of the volume deals with policy and curricular implications resulting from attention to learner variables. The first article in this section, by Susan J. Weaver and Andrew D. Cohen, is based on the premise that language learning will be facilitated if students become more aware of the range of possible strategies that they can use throughout the language learning process. The authors take the perspective that the most efficient way to do this is by providing learning strategies instruction to students as part of the foreign language curriculum. They explain a variety of options for providing student-directed learning strategy instruction, present suggestions for developing in-service strategy training seminars for foreign language instructors, and conclude with a step-by-step approach to the design of strategy training programs.

The article by Ann Sax Mabbott is based on the premise that second language learning should be made universally available and that all students, including those who are labeled learning disabled, have the right to second language instruction. She argues against exempting such students from language requirements and provides suggestions for alternative methods of teaching and assessment that will aid them in their attempts to learn a second language. In addition, she provides material that directors of language programs will find useful when they organize TA workshops or seminars on the topic of assisting students labeled learning disabled to learn a second language.

In the final article in this volume, Cecilia Rodríguez Pino and Daniel Villa describe the development of a student-centered Spanish for Native Speakers (SNS) program at New Mexico State University that "aims to identify the individual speakers' instructional needs and his or her knowledge of Spanish and to design a curriculum that recognizes the diverse language abilities of all students and enriches those abilities." The principal goal of the program is the reversal of language shift in the community; thus, the spoken standard of the classroom reflects that of the students' community. The close connections between the SNS program and the community are maintained through classroom assignments that include ethnographic interviews, sociolinguistic surveys, and oral history interviews, all carried out by students who are expected to take an active role in their own language enrichment.

It is the editor's hope this volume will contribute to a better understanding of individual differences in the second language classroom and begin to help us distinguish the "faces in the crowd." Providing learner-centered instruction in multisection courses will continue to provide a challenge to directors of language programs; some of the contributions in this volume suggest ways in which the needs of individual learners can be better met, even in large language programs.

Carol A. Klee
Editor

Works Cited

Nunan, David. 1988. The Learner-Centred Curriculum. New York: Cambridge University Press.

Skehan, Peter. 1989. Individual Differences in Second-Language Learning. New York: Edward Arnold.

Tarone, Elaine, and George Yule. 1989. Focus on the Language Learner. New York: Oxford University Press.

Part I

Overviews of Research

New Directions in Language Anxiety Research

Dolly Jesusita Young
University of Tennessee

Introduction

In the last few decades we have seen an increase in the research on affective variables in second language (SL) acquisition (Gardner and MacIntyre 1993a). More recently the concept of *language anxiety* has gained increased visibility. The concept of anxiety in SL acquisition has achieved the status of a precise technical notion, in contrast to the general concept of anxiety prevalent in the research. Since the classic synthesis of research on anxiety and language learning written by Scovel (1978), there have been important advances in our understanding of the role of this concept; a wealth of more recent research is now available. The purpose of this chapter is to offer language department administrators, foreign language coordinators and instructors, and prospective teachers an overview of this new language anxiety research and to suggest directions for future research in this expanding field of study.

The new research discussed here provides both anecdotal and empirical evidence defining, describing, and establishing a paradigm for language anxiety. The new insights provided by this research dating from the mid-1980s to today advance our understanding of language anxiety and hence provide the basis for better informed program and pedagogical decisions. Whether we direct a language program or teach in one, we are all researchers seeking more effective and efficient ways to improve language learning.

Anxiety Definitions and Instruments

In most of the early studies on students' anxiety, researchers established the existence of anxiety in the second language classroom and investigated its effect on SL performance.[1] While some of this research suggested a relationship between anxiety and SL performance, other findings indicated no such relationship. Table 1 presents a sample of the early research on the effects of anxiety on language learning and performance; among other things, the table illustrates the contradictory results of many of these early studies. Within these studies, for example, anxiety was negatively correlated to one language skill but not another (Swain and Burnaby 1976; Tucker, Hamayan, and Genesee 1976); it was related to one foreign language but not another, and the direction of that relationship varied (Chastain 1975). In one study, the least proficient students scored the highest and lowest on an anxiety scale (Backman 1976). In another study, some anxiety actually enhanced learners' oral performance (Kleinmann 1977).

One problem with much of this research was that many of the studies had different goals, objectives, definitions, and conceptual schemata, rendering comparisons difficult. Some of the major issues making interpretation and generalization difficult included the following: whether the anxiety definition and the observable behaviors chosen to measure it were harmonious; whether the type of anxiety (e.g., state anxiety, trait anxiety, test anxiety, facilitative or debilitative anxiety, communication apprehension) was appropriate to the basic purpose of the study; and whether the research was designed to examine anxiety alone or several other variables as well, including motivation, personality, self-esteem, or whatever. In essence, most of this research did not adequately or consistently define anxiety, nor did it sufficiently explain how it was related to language learning.

MacIntyre and Gardner (1988) illustrated the wide variety of definitions of the concept "'anxiety" and their corresponding measurement (see Table 2 and Appendix). These various types of anxiety did not completely encompass the kind of anxiety experienced by language learners; as a result, more precise definitions and instruments were needed to identify and measure foreign language anxiety or specific aspects of it. Gardner developed a French Classroom Anxiety Scale (FCAS)—Revised (MacIntyre 1988), versions of which he used in early research and in many of his recent investigations (see Appendix for FCAS). Horwitz, Horwitz, and Cope (1986) developed the Foreign Language Classroom Anxiety Scale (FLCAS). Both scales have yielded data on their construct validity and/or reliability (Gardner and MacIntyre 1993b; Horwitz 1986).[2]

Table 1

Research on Anxiety and Foreign or Second Language Learning up to 1985

Researcher(s)	Language Setting	Population	Measures	Language Skill(s)	Comments
Backman (1976)	SLL	21 Venezuelan university students	Interest in foreign languages Need achievement Attitude toward native speakers Motivational intensity Instrumental orientation Integrative orientation	Placement test, aural comprehension, and teacher ratings of oral skills	The least proficient student scored the highest and lowest on the anxiety variable of the oral interview test.
Bailey (1983)	FLL	Language teachers learning a foreign language	Personal diaries		The following competitive learner characteristics may increase anxiety about language learning: outright self-comparisons to other students; emotional response to self-comparisons; a feeling of having to "outdo" other students; a preoccupation with grades and tests; a desire to please the teacher to meet his/her expectations or gain his/her approval.

Table 1 (cont.)

Research on Anxiety and Foreign or Second Language Learning up to 1985

Researcher(s)	Language Setting	Population	Measures	Language Skill(s)	Comments
Bartz (1974)	FLL	University students	Sixteen Personality Factors Questionnaire	Communicative competence oral/writing	Linguistic ability is best predictor of oral skill. Low anxiety Ss scored better in writing.
Brewster (1971)	FLL	392 male adult students at the Defense Language Institute	Sixteen Personality Factors Questionnaire	The Defense Language Aptitude Test, course grade with equal weight given to all four skills, and proficiency tests	Successful language learners had the following personality traits: persevering, intellectual, analytical, trusting, easy to get along with, adaptable, outgoing, resourceful, imaginative, creative, warm, and spontaneous.
Chastain (1975)	FLL	University students beginning French, German, or Spanish	Text Anxiety Scale and Taylor Manifest Anxiety Scale	Final Grade	Correlation between anxiety and final grade high in all 3 FL's, but direction of correlation not consistent within or across languages. Some anxiety had positive results.

| Clément, Gardner, & Smythe (1977) | SL | 304 10th and 11th grade francophone students learning English | English class anxiety
English use anxiety
Thirty-one additional affective variables | Final grade—oral English;
Final grade—written English | Learners who report little anxiety have the following characteristics: use English often, speak more than one language, are eager to learn English, and have strong English skills. |
| Clément, Gardner, & Smythe (1980) | SL | 223 francophone students learning English | Generalized interpersonalized anxiety
French classroom anxiety
English test anxiety
English use anxiety
English class anxiety
Self-rating of writing, understanding, reading, and speaking
Threat to ethnic identity
Behavioral intention of reenrolling in English
Sex
Degree of instrumentality
Degree of integrativeness
Attitude toward learning English
Attitude toward Americans
Frequency of English use
Motivational intensity
No. of years studying English
No. of years language spoken at home | Aural and reading comprehension
Grammatical knowledge
IQ
Standardized test scores of French
Standardized test scores of English | Students who perceived themselves as competent in reading, writing, and understanding also reported little anxiety in speaking. |

Table 1 (cont.)

Research on Anxiety and Foreign or Second Language Learning up to 1985

Researcher(s)	Language Setting	Population	Measures	Language Skill(s)	Comments
Dunkel (1949)	FLL	24 university students	Items on a psychological test	Latin placement exam	Conclusions suspect due to procedural weakness.
Gardner et al. (1976)	SLL	1,000 junior & senior high school students	Language aptitude Need achievement Ethnocentrism Interest in FL Parental encouragement Integrativeness Instrumentality Evaluative reactions to the learning situation Motivation, course grade	Depended on grade level; ranged from aural comprehension, to Canadian Achievement Test in French, to speech skills, to grades	Grade 7: $r = 32$ Grade 8: $r = 28$ Grade 9: $r = 33$ Grade 10: $r = 31$ Grade 11: $r = 43$ Anxiety increases with grade level.
Gardner et al. (1977)	SLL	192 university and high school students and teachers in a five-week intensive French program (beginning, intermediate, and advanced levels)	Need achievement Ethnocentrism French classroom anxiety French Canadian attitudes Interest in foreign languages Instrumental orientation Integrative orientation	Speech skills	Anxiety decreased when proficiency increased.

New Directions in Language Anxiety Research   9

				Parent encouragement to learn French Attitudes toward learning French Attitudes toward European French people Motivational intensity Desire to learn French Orientation index Behavioral intention to continue French Opportunity to use French outside school Evaluation of the French teacher's rapport, competence, inspiration Evaluation of the French course Difficulty of the French course Utility of the French course		
Kleinmann (1977)	SLL	39 ESL university students	Facilitating/debilitating anxiety		Speech skills	Students with facilitative anxiety did not avoid structures researchers predicted they would avoid.

Table 1 (cont.)

Research on Anxiety and Foreign or Second Language Learning up to 1985

Researcher(s)	Language Setting	Population	Measures	Language Skill(s)	Comments
Pimsleur et al. (1962)	FLL	Junior and senior high school students	Manifest Anxiety Scale	Intelligence and previous language experience	No difference in anxiety between average achievers and under achievers
Scott (1986)	FLL	Approximately 160 university students at beginning or intermediate levels of EFL	Affective responses to oral tests	Group or pair oral achievement tests of course material	Ss taking group tests were more nervous than Ss in pairs. Factor analysis showed anxiety as one of two factors affecting questionnaire answers.
Swain & Burnaby (1976)	SLL	Children	Items on a personality measure/teacher rating	French reading scores	$r = 69, p < 05$ (for immersion stu. only)
Tucker et al. (1976)	SLL	Junior high school students	French class anxiety	French reading scores	Significant negative correlation between reading and anxiety, but not between anxiety and oral French

| Westcott (1973) | FLL | High school students | Motivation, aptitude, peer influence, and test anxiety | Language | Anxiety not significantly related to learning French |
| Wittenborn et al. (1945) | FLL | University students enrolled in French or Spanish | Items on a self-report of study habits | Final grade | Negative correlation between anxiety and grade for French but not for Spanish |

Table 2

Definitions of Anxieties

Test Anxiety:

Drive Theory
> Drive theory is similar to Yerkes Dodson Law in which arousal could lead to greater information processing and enhanced performance; too much arousal, however, could lead to confusion, blocking out information, and decrements in performance.

Facilitating/Debilitating Anxiety
> Anxiety is not always negative. Anxiety that improves performance is called facilitative anxiety; anxiety that impairs performance is called debilitative anxiety.

State Anxiety
> State anxiety refers to an unpleasant emotional condition or temporary state.

Worry Emotionality
> Worry refers to cognition; emotionality refers to automatic reactions, such as trembling or perspiring. Worry impedes performance; emotionality does not.

Cognitive Attentional Theory
> Within this cognitive framework, anxiety is defined as a cognitive response marked by self-doubt, feelings of inadequacy, and self-blame.

Direction of Attention Hypothesis
> Task-irrelevant preoccupations represent cognitive interference. The difference between performance of high-anxiety and low-anxiety students is due to their attentional focus.

General Anxiety:

Communication Apprehension
> Communication apprehension is the fear or dread associated with communication with another individual or individuals.

Social Evaluative Anxiety
> Social evaluative anxiety refers to fear, tension, discomfort, or anxiety experienced by individuals in social situations. Eventually social evaluative anxiety leads to reduced social interactions and less participation in conversations.

Trait Anxiety
> Trait anxiety refers to a stable propensity to be anxious. Trait anxiety is a permanent personality feature.

Table 2 is taken from MacIntyre and Gardner 1988.

The development of such measures of anxiety specific to the language learning process, in addition to improved research designs, has led recently to significant insights into the phenomenon referred to today as "language anxiety."

The concept of language anxiety arose in the mid-1980s.[3] The following is a discussion of the language anxiety research from that time forward (see Table 3 for a summary of this research). While much of this language anxiety research has continued to examine the effects of anxiety on language learning and performance, some studies have expanded into investigations of related issues, including (1) theoretical models and frameworks of language anxiety in relation to other anxieties, (2) sources and characteristics of language anxiety through both quantitative and qualitative analyses, and (3) anxiety-reducing and coping strategies.

Effects of Anxiety on Language Learning and Performance

Most of the research on language anxiety suggests consistently that anxiety can negatively impact performance in the SL. Young (1986), for example, reported a statistically significant negative relationship between anxiety and student oral performance.[4] Madsen, Brown, and Jones (1991) found a negative relationship between anxiety and certain test types and grades. Trylong (1987) discovered that anxiety and course grades also exhibited a significant negative relationship. Results from a study by Gardner, Moorcroft, and MacIntyre (1987) indicated that French production of vocabulary and anxiety correlated negatively. Ely (1986) discovered a significant positive relationship between discomfort in the language class and unwillingness to volunteer answers and poor student performance. Gardner et al. (1987) reported a significant negative relationship between anxiety and standardized tests. Gardner and MacIntyre (1993b) found that among a broad spectrum of affective variables, language anxiety was the best predictor of language achievement and of learners' self-ratings of proficiency.

Most of the research on language anxiety reported above compared anxiety levels with such indicators as grades, oral test scores, teacher ratings, standardized tests, test types, vocabulary performance scores, self-ratings of proficiency, and the like. Anxiety, however, has manifested itself in other ways. A study by Steinberg and Horwitz (1986) was the first to induce anxiety and show its more subtle effects. The authors asked learners in two groups, an anxiety condition group and a nonanxiety condition group, to

Table 3

Research on Language Anxiety Since the Mid-1980s

Researcher(s)	Language Setting	Population	Measures	Language Skills/Ability	Comments
Campbell & Ortiz (1991b)	FLL	Beginning foreign language students at the Defense Language Institute	Foreign Language Class Anxiety Scale (FLCAS) Survey of attitudes specific to the foreign language classroom		Students were almost twice as anxious in their French class (speaking and listening) through the course as compared to the beginning of the course.
Ely (1986)	FLL	University students of first-year Spanish	Language class discomfort Language class risk-taking Language class sociability Strength of motivation Attitude toward the class Concern for grade Previous language study or background Language learning aptitude Classroom participation	Oral fluency Oral correctness Written correctness	Language class discomfort (i.e., anxiety) was a negative predictor of language class risk-taking and sociability. Language class risk-taking was a significant predictor of classroom participation. Class participation was a significant predictor of oral correctness (at one level).

| Ganschow, Sparks, Anderson, Javorsky, & Skinner (1994) | FLL | University beginning-level foreign language students | FLCAS | Modern Language Aptitude Test (MLAT) Language and memory tests: Foreign Language Screening Instrument Nelson-Denny Reading Test Test of Language Competence Wide Range Achievement Test—Revised Woodcock-Johnson Psychological Battery Woodcock Reading Mastery Test—Revised Writing sample | Researchers found a significant difference among high-anxious, average-anx., and low-anx. groups and tests of language competence. Results also indicated a significant difference among high, average, and low anx. students on the phonological measures, and a significant difference between high and low anx. on the FL screening instrument and on the MLAT. High anx. and low anx. were weaker at oral expression and listening comprehension. |

Table 3 (cont.)

Research on Language Anxiety Since the Mid-1980s

Researcher(s)	Language Setting	Population	Measures	Language Skills/Ability	Comments
Gardner, Day, & MacIntyre (1992)	SL	49 introduction-to-psychology students not currently taking French or who had not taken it	Motivational intensity Desire to learn French Attitudes toward learning French Integrative orientation Attitudes toward the learning situation French use anxiety French class anxiety Social desirability Communication apprehension	Vocabulary scores Viewing time	Researchers found significant negative correlations among anxiety and motivation and integrative motivation. Learners who were anxious about French also tended to be less motivated compared to those who were not anxious. Presence of video camera did not successfully induce anxiety in this study.
Gardner, Moorcroft, & MacIntyre (1987)	SL	University psychology students	State anxiety Trait anxiety French class anxiety French use anxiety Audience sensitivity Test anxiety Interpersonal anxiety Physical danger anxiety Novelty anxiety Daily routine anxiety	Word production Free speech quality	Not anxiety per se that seemed to produce anxiety but anxiety evoked by the task itself, particularly to a task with limited options.

| Gardner & MacIntyre (1993b) | SL | University-level French students with 5 years high school French | French class anxiety (Likert scale and semantic version) French use anxiety (Likert scale and semantic version) FLCAS Attitudes toward French Canadians Interest in foreign language Integrative orientation French course evaluation French teacher evaluation Motivational intensity Desire to learn French Attitudes toward learning French Instrumental orientation (Likert scale, single-item scale, and semantic versions for the above variables after anxiety measures) Orientation Index (rating of 4 items) Motivation Intensity (10 items, multip. choice) Identification measure with French Canadians | French grades French cloze test French word production French prose writing Objective French proficiency Four self-ratings of French proficiency: Cando Speaking Test Cando Understanding Test Cando Writing Test Cando Reading Test | Language anxiety was the best single correlate of self-ratings of proficiency and achievement. It correlated significantly with all achievement indices except grades. |

Table 3 (cont.)

Research on Language Anxiety Since the Mid-1980s

Researcher(s)	Language Setting	Population	Measures	Language Skills/Ability	Comments
Horwitz, Horwitz, & Cope (1986)	FLL	75 students enrolled in beginning-level Spanish classes at a large university	FLCAS		Significant levels of anxiety are experienced by language learners, particularly in response to their fears of not understanding all they hear, feeling less capable than other students, and making a mistake in the language.
Horwitz (1986)	FLL	University-level language learners	FLCAS State/Trait Anxiety Inventory Personal report of communication apprehension Fear of negative evaluation Test anxiety scale Self-rating of anxiety level		Foreign language anxiety can be distinguished from other anxiety constructs and can be reliably assessed.
Koch & Terrell (1991)	FLL	119 first- and second-year Spanish students at a large university	Questionnaire designed to assess student attitudes in the Natural Approach class		Most Natural Approach activities produced low levels of anxiety. Some of these activities, how-

					ever, produced some anxiety for a sizable minority. Of all the activities, only oral reports evoked anxiety for a large majority of students.
MacIntyre & Gardner (1989)	SL	Native English speakers enrolled in introduction-to-psychology courses	French class anxiety, English class anxiety, Trait anxiety, Computer anxiety, Test anxiety, Audience anxiety, French use anxiety	Paired associates (French–English noun pairs), Vocabulary test	Findings indicated higher anxiety levels for French class than math or English (which were similar).
MacIntyre & Gardner (1991a)	SL	Conversation, French adult classes	French use anxiety, French class anxiety, Personal report of communication apprehension, Fear of negative evaluation, Trait anxiety, State anxiety, Anxometers, Essay in which students were to write about an experience in using French skills during which they either felt very relaxed and confident or very anxious	Digit span test in native language and French, Thing category test in native language and French, Self-rating of ability to do specific tasks	The essays about an anxious event typically described a speaking task. Essays in which students described a confident/relaxed experience usually described a speaking or understanding task.

Table 3 (cont.)

Research on Language Anxiety Since the Mid-1980s

Researcher(s)	Language Setting	Population	Measures	Language Skills/Ability	Comments
MacIntyre & Gardner (1991b)	SL	University psychology students who had French in the 11th or 12th grade	French classroom anxiety English classroom anxiety Mathematics classroom anxiety General test anxiety Facilitating French test anxiety Debilitating French test anxiety Audience sensitivity Personal report of communication apprehension Fear of negative evaluation Trait anxiety French use anxiety Anxiety in novel situation Anxiety in routine situations Anxiety over physical danger Anxiety in interpersonal situations	Digit span test Thing category test in both English and French	Results indicate that language anxiety *can* be discriminated from other anxieties and that language anxiety *can* negatively impact cognitive processing of SL.

MacIntyre & Gardner (1994)	SL	First-year students of French at large university	Situations involving social evaluation State anxiety English categories anxometer French categories anxometer English digits anxometer French digits anxometer State anxiety measures (the anxometer)	Digit span test for input stage Pair associates learning task for processing stage Thing category test and self-description for output stage	Anxiety successfully induced by camera and at each of the stages anxiety correlated negatively with performance. Communicative tasks were much more anxiety producing than learning tasks.

Table 3 (cont.)

Research on Language Anxiety Since the Mid-1980s

Researcher(s)	Language Setting	Population	Measures	Language Skills/Ability	Comments
MacIntyre & Gardner (1994b)	SL	First-year French students at a large university	Input anxiety Processing anxiety Output anxiety French class anxiety French use anxiety FLCAS	Word span test Digit span test T-scope (identification of French words or English words) for input stage French achievement test Paragraph translation Paired associates learning for processing stage Thing category test Cloze test Self-description for output stage	Performance quality negatively correlated with anxiety; i.e., high anxious learners were less fluent, had less complex sentences, and had poorer pronunciation than low anxious students.
Madsen, Brown, & Jones (1991)	FLL	220 students enrolled in first- and second-year German courses at a major university	Affective Reaction Questionnaire (open-ended questions) designed to assess student reactions to the various test types	Test types: Dictation Oral questions Grammatical fill-ins Grammatical manipulations English to German translations	Researchers found significant differences in student reactions to test types. The dictation and true/false culture test types evoked the least amount of learner anxiety while the translation

Study	Measures	Sample	Results
	German to English translations True/false German culture		test type produced the most amount of anxiety. The reactions to the oral test format became more positive as students gained proficiency.
Mejias, Applbaum, Applbaum, & Trotter II (1991) FLL	Two versions of the Personal Report of Communication Apprehension (PRCA-24), one for speaking English and the other for speaking Spanish	429 college students enrolled in basic psychology and 284 high school students from grades 9 to 12 taking English	Communication apprehension was higher for Spanish-speakers (Mexican Americans) than English-speakers. There were higher communication apprehension scores for females than males. Spanish-speakers had highest communication apprehension scores when speaking English or Spanish, but experienced less communication apprehension in the dominant language than the SL. Communication apprehension increased the more formal the context became.

Table 3 (cont.)

Research on Language Anxiety Since the Mid-1980s

Researcher(s)	Language Setting	Population	Measures	Language Skills/Ability	Comments
Phillips (1992)	FLL	University-level third-semester French students	FLCAS Oral interviews	Oral exam Written exam Teacher-ranked global proficiency of students	Researcher found a significantly negative correlation between the FLCAS and oral exam scores. Students with higher levels of language anxiety said less, had few dependent clauses and French structures, and produced shorter communication units.
Price (1991)	FLL	15 "anxious" foreign language learners	Oral interviews (in the native language) over various aspects of anxiety, e.g., sources		Fear of public embarrassment greatest source of language anxiety.
Samimy & Rardin (forthcoming)	FLL	Graduate students majoring in TESOL or FLE	Reflection papers of students in Community Language Learning classes over a 6-year period		Anxiety was the one affective variable most frequently mentioned. Anxiety stemmed from past unsuccessful experiences in language

Study	Type	Subjects	Measures	Skills	Results
Steinberg & Horwitz (1986)	SLL	Spanish-speaking adults enrolled in ESL class	Test anxiety scale Multiple affect adjective checklist	Oral skills	A significant difference found between anxious group and nonanxious group for quality of response style. Responses of anxious group contained less interpretive information. Responses of nonanxious group were more interpretive and subjective.
Young (1986)	FLL	University-level students majoring in French, German, or Spanish	State anxiety inventory items on FLCAS Cognitive interference questionnaire A self-report of anxiety (on a Likert scale)	ACTFL's Oral Proficiency Interview (OPI) Communicative-oriented dictation test Self-appraisal of speaking proficiency	Students were more nervous during the OPI than during the dictation test, but no significant difference between OPI and anxiety once ability was controlled.

learning. Learners also mentioned a lack of anxiety or a reduction of it with Communicative Language Learning.

Table 3 (cont.)

Research on Language Anxiety Since the Mid-1980s

Researcher(s)	Language Setting	Population	Measures	Language Skills/Ability	Comments
Young (1990)	FLL	135 university-level Spanish students enrolled in first- and second-semester Spanish courses at a large university and 109 high school students taking first or second year Spanish	Questionnaire designed to identify in-class activities and instructor characteristics that evoke anxiety		Students expressed being more anxious when they were forced to speak in front of the class, when instructors practiced overt error correction, and when they came unprepared to class.

describe pictures that had been selected specifically for their ability to elicit interpretive and denotative speech. The more anxious learners offered less interpretive language than did learners in the nonanxiety condition group.

A few years ago, Phillips (1992) also investigated the relationship between anxiety and the quality of oral performance in the SL. She found statistically significant negative correlations between scores on the FLCAS and oral exam grades, and in addition found that students with higher levels of language anxiety said less and produced shorter communication units and fewer target structures and dependent clauses than the students who experienced low levels of anxiety. MacIntyre and Gardner (1994b) reported similar subtle effects of language anxiety on learners' output. MacIntyre and Gardner (1994b, p. 300) reported that "anxious students were judged to have lower Fluency, lower Sentence Complexity, and less of a French Accent."

Most of the studies discussed up to this point have examined the relationship between anxiety and some indicators of language *output*.[5] Recently, MacIntyre and Gardner (1991b) examined, from an information-processing perspective, the effects of language anxiety on *input*. In this study, anxiety was measured through a variety of anxiety-related tests (social evaluative anxiety, state anxiety, and language anxiety). The study showed that only language anxiety was associated negatively and significantly with French performance on the thing category test and a digit span test[6] in the SL versus the native language. These findings suggest language anxiety negatively affects the processing of language input. If anxiety affects input, this means that anxiety impedes a learner's ability to process *new* language. In other words, it hinders language acquisition.

In a later study, MacIntyre and Gardner (1994a) examined the effect of anxiety on language performance at three stages of learning: input, processing, and output. This is the second study to attempt to induce anxiety, in this case with the presence of a video camera. For each experimental group in this study, learners' anxiety increased with the presence of the camera and their corresponding performance at all three stages decreased. The researchers (1994a, p. 16) argued that "anxiety arousal at earlier stages of processing will create cognitive deficits that can be overcome only when the individual has an opportunity to recover the missing material, that is, return to the Input and/or Processing stages."

Knowledge of the debilitative effects of anxiety on learner performance is important for the design of pedagogical techniques to reduce negative emotions in SL learners and thereby increase the effectiveness and efficiency of SL learning. The contention that language anxiety can negatively affect language input is alarming in that it reduces what a learner can hope to process as usable "intake" from what the instructor provides.

A recent study has offered further insights into language anxiety. Sparks and Ganschow (1991)[7] contend that some learners experience high levels of anxiety as a consequence of foreign language learning problems that are rooted in the learners' native language skills. They examined the native language skills of unsuccessful SL learners or students who had managed to avoid taking a SL and found weak language-based factors in the native language, such as phonology and syntax, to be strong indicators of unsuccessful foreign language learning. The researchers posit that the latent native language difficulties of some learners may not have been detected over the years because of their ability to use compensatory strategies successfully in the native language. When these learners attempt to apply the same strategies in the SL situation, they are unsuccessful. Sparks and Ganschow urge the foreign language profession to investigate the native oral and written language skills of learners who are experiencing difficulty and anxiety in learning the foreign language.

To sum up research on the effects of language anxiety: (1) language anxiety negatively affects SL performance (learner grades, oral proficiency, standard test scores, self-ratings of proficiency, etc.); (2) language anxiety can also negatively impact language learning (input and processing of the SL); and (3) high levels of anxiety in the acquisition of language may stem from difficulties in native language skills.

Theoretical Models and Frameworks of Language Anxiety

In 1986 Horwitz, Horwitz, and Cope proposed three conceptual foundations underlying language anxiety. They contended that it is derived from (1) a form of communication apprehension, (2) worry over frequent testing in a language classroom (although they were not sure if this anxiety was specific to the types of tests found in language classes or was a general test anxiety), and (3) fear of negative evaluation (academic and personal). Since then, studies by Young (1990, 1991), MacIntyre and Gardner (1989, 1991c), and Gardner and MacIntyre (1993b) support the tenets advanced by Horwitz, Horwitz, and Cope (1986). The components that seem to receive the strongest support are those related to the communicative and social evaluative aspects of the theory. MacIntyre and Gardner (1991c, pp. 105–6) posit that "test anxiety, broadly defined, may be less important, though a rigorous investigation has yet to be made."

The research by MacIntyre and Gardner has made an impressive contribution to the theoretical framework of language anxiety. In one study, MacIntyre and Gardner (1991b) compare native English speakers' anxiety levels for French, English, and math classes. The French class produced significantly higher levels of anxiety than the other two classes. In another study (Gardner and MacIntyre 1993b), these researchers administered a repertoire of instruments to assess a variety of affective variables using several form types (i.e., Likert scale, single-item scale, semantic version) in addition to the FLCAS and various form-types of their French Class Anxiety Scale. Their findings support the conceptual distinctions among most of the variables, including language anxiety. These results support other studies of Horwitz (1986) and MacIntyre and Gardner (1989), which suggest that language anxiety is distinct from other types of anxiety.

From their review of the literature on the research methods and measures of language anxiety, MacIntyre and Gardner (1991c) have proposed the following hypothesis to explain language anxiety:

> During the first few experiences in the foreign language, anxiety plays a negligible role in proficiency since, even if anxiety is present, it is not the foreign language anxiety that has been discussed to this point. Anxiety experienced at this time would be based on trait anxiety, test anxiety, communication apprehension, novelty anxiety, etc., that are not necessarily specific to the language learning situation. Anxiety aroused in this context, as a result of early language experience, would best be called state anxiety. After several experiences with the second language context, the student forms attitudes that are specific to the situation—emotions and attitudes about learning a new language. If these experiences are negative, foreign language anxiety may begin to develop. As negative experiences persist, foreign language anxiety may become a regular occurrence and the student begins to expect to be nervous and perform poorly. (p. 110)

MacIntyre and Gardner cite a handful of studies that provide indirect support of their hypothesis (1991c, p. 110) and point out that in these studies "favorable experiences and increased achievement reduced anxiety" and "gains in proficiency resulted in students having reduced levels of foreign language anxiety" (p. 111).

Two studies by other researchers provide further evidence in support of MacIntyre and Gardner's hypothesis. Campbell and Ortiz (1991b) administered the FLCAS and their Survey of Attitudes Specific to the

Foreign Language Classroom to beginning adult foreign language learners at the Defense Language Institute. They found that students were almost twice as anxious in their foreign language class midway through the class as they were at the beginning of the course.

In an examination of reflection papers of different students in Community Language Learning (CLL) classes over a six-year period, Samimy and Rardin (1994) found that learners consistently stated that their language anxiety stemmed from past negative language learning experiences.

If we accept MacIntyre and Gardner's hypothesis, then it would be crucial that learners have favorable experiences in language learning early in the language learning process.

The research on theoretical models and frameworks of language anxiety is less extensive than the research on the effects of language anxiety on language learning and performance, but several critical concepts emerge from research in this area: (1) language anxiety is distinguishable from other types of anxiety and is situation-specific in much the same way as math anxiety or test anxiety is—in other words, it is particular to the language learning context; (2) the communicative and social aspects of language classes are the strongest components of language anxiety; (3) language anxiety may be the consequence of negative experiences in language learning.

Sources of Language Anxiety in Quantitative and Qualitative Research

Empirical research in language anxiety has more often than not taken the form of correlational studies (see Tables 1 and 3). While correlational studies have produced significant contributions to understanding the effects of language anxiety, qualitative methods of analysis can offer insights into language learners' anxiety that may often be undetected in a quantitative approach. Recent acknowledgment of the benefits of qualitative techniques (Glesne and Peshkin 1992; Nunan 1992) has sparked a growing body of qualitative research that analyzes the students' perspectives on anxiety in language learning.

Through interviews (Phillips 1992; Price 1991), open-ended questionnaires (Young 1991), and journals (Bailey 1983), language learners have offered their own perceptions of language anxiety. In addition, interviews with language specialists have provided an understanding of language anxiety from the language instructor's point of view (Young 1992). While early quantitatively oriented analyses had not provided consistent results regarding the negative effects of language anxiety, qualitative examinations have consistently reported that "students feel that anxiety *does* matter" (Phillips 1991, p. 2). Student voices tell us that certain aspects of language learning provoke anxiety. As Phillips (1991, p. 2) argues, "from a psychological perspective, then, the study of anxiety is important because what the students *believe* can affect their attitudes toward language class, language study in general, even the target culture." Moreover, student attitudes and feelings about language learning affect decisions to continue past the lower division requirements or to stop language study altogether.

Young (1991) examines the sources of language anxiety from an in-depth review of quantitative and qualitative research in this field (see also Horwitz and Young 1991). She identifies a number of primary sources of language anxiety. Some are associated with the learner, some with the teacher, and some with the instructional practice. Young classifies them as anxieties stemming from (1) personal and interpersonal anxieties, (2) role-related beliefs about language teaching, (3) instructor–learner interactions, (4) classroom procedures, and (5) language testing. The following outline of these categories includes examples for each category:

A. Anxiety stemming from personal and interpersonal anxieties
   1. low self-esteem
   2. competitiveness
   3. self-perceived low ability levels
   4. communication apprehension
   5. social anxiety (see Table 1)
   6. existential anxiety[8]
   7. lack of SL group membership
   8. learner beliefs about language learning
B. Anxiety stemming from role-related beliefs about language teaching
   1. that some intimidation of students is necessary
   2. that the instructor's role is to correct students constantly
   3. that the instructor cannot have students working in pairs because the class may get out of control
   4. that the instructor should be doing most of the talking and teaching
   5. that the instructor is like a drill sergeant
C. Anxiety stemming from instructor–learner interactions
   1. from the instructor's harsh manner of correcting student errors
   2. from students' fear of being incorrect in front of their peers

3. from students' concerns over how mistakes are perceived in the language class

D. Anxiety stemming from classroom procedures
   1. having students speak in the target language in front of the class
   2. giving frequent oral quizzes, listening comprehension in particular
   3. calling on students to respond orally and exclusively in the SL

E. Anxiety stemming from aspects of language testing
   1. test formats that evoke more anxiety than others, e.g., listening comprehension, translation from SL to English
   2. overstudying for hours only to find that the tests assess different material
   3. unfamiliar test tasks.

Young concludes that while instructors and learners can identify other sources of language anxiety, most of the evidence suggests that the sources are interrelated and may be, in part, a result of unnatural classroom procedures, such as correcting every student mistake, intimidating students, and believing that the teacher should be doing most of the talking. She calls for future research to document this contention.

Students repeatedly report oral communicative tasks (speaking) as the strongest source of language anxiety (Horwitz et al. 1986; Phillips 1991, 1992; Young 1990, 1991, 1992). Another source of anxiety identified by MacIntyre and Gardner is the task type. In their study (1994a), they ask students to complete two tasks. Students take a "thing category test" that limits what students are permitted to say (see footnote 5). Only words that are appropriate to a particular category are correct. Students experienced more anxiety performing the thing category test than a free speech task. In the free speech situation students had more options; it was not as if there were specific "appropriate" answers. Students were allowed to repeat themselves, repair misstarts, circumlocute, and talk about tangential information. They could, in other words, make use of different strategies in completing the task and thereby alleviate some of their anxiety.

In this study by MacIntyre and Gardner (1994a), it appears that learners were allowed to use the kind of strategic competence that Canale and Swain (1980) identified in their model of communicative competence. The difference in anxiety levels in this study may be explained by the circumstance that the nonconstrained task is similar to real-life expectations for language use (where strategic competence can facilitate communication), while the constrained (only-one-right-answer) task is more related to the "rules" of the classroom environment, that is, the often artificial constraints of language use in classroom practices.

To sum up the research on sources of language anxiety, we can conclude that (1) quantitative data consistently indicates that learners experience anxiety in language learning; (2) language anxiety can stem from a variety of sources; (3) speaking and the conditions under which learners speak are the strongest sources of language anxiety; (4) learners can experience increases in anxiety when they are required to complete oral tasks with limited options versus more open-ended oral tasks.

Anxiety-Reducing and Coping Strategies

While a wealth of anxiety-reducing and coping strategies are overtly described in a number of studies (Campbell and Ortiz 1991a; Cope Powell 1991; Crookall and Oxford 1991; Foss and Reitzal 1988; Kennedy Vande Berg 1993; Young 1991), few of these have been empirical studies that have actually tested the effectiveness of anxiety-reducing strategies.

Young (1991) offers a variety of anxiety-reducing strategies for the categories of sources she identifies in her review of the literature. Some of them originate from first identifying the source of anxiety and then making recommendations for removing or neutralizing that source. For example, if students say that direct and overt error correction produces anxiety, then we can expect that indirect error correction (modeling) would reduce language anxiety. Other suggestions come from the students themselves, from such sources as their diary entries, open-ended questionnaire comments, and oral interviews. And finally, a handful of suggestions are derived from researchers' conclusions over ways to reduce language anxiety. The following outline summarizes Young's (1991) suggestions.

A. Personal and interpersonal anxieties
   1. Have students recognize their irrational beliefs or fears through tasks/group work/games that serve this purpose.
   2. Suggest that highly anxious students participate in some form of supplemental instruction, e.g., a support group, tutoring, a language club.
   3. Suggest students do relaxation exercises and practice self-talk.
   4. Discuss periodically with students reasonable commitments for successful language learning.
B. Role-related beliefs about language teaching
   1. Develop a sensitivity toward your role as a language teacher, which includes being more of a facilitator than a drill sergeant.

2. Beliefs about language learning are often reflected in teacher behavior; use videotaping or reciprocal class visits to facilitate the identification and discussion of assumptions about language learning.

3. Complete the Beliefs about Language Learning Inventory (a questionnaire designed to identity beliefs about language learning). The results of this measure offer instructors insights into notions, sometimes erroneous ones, about language learning that they bring to the classroom and pass on to students.

4. Become involved in language teaching workshops and language teaching research for insights into current teaching practices and approaches and for setting realistic expectations of what students should be able to do at a particular level of language instruction.

C. Instructor–student interactions

1. Give students more positive feedback.
2. Help students develop more realistic expectations.
3. Maintain a good sense of humor.
4. Try to adopt an attitude that mistakes are part of language learning and will be made by everyone.
5. Try to be friendly, relaxed, and patient.
6. Offer students correct feedback though modeling, rather than overcorrection.
7. Emphasize the importance of conveying meaning as much as grammatical accuracy.

D. Classroom procedures

1. Emphasize more small group and pair work.
2. Personalize language instruction.
3. Tailor activities to the affective needs of the learner—e.g., have students practice their role-plays in groups before presenting them to the class.

E. Aspects of language testing

1. Test what you teach in the context of how you teach it.
2. Provide pretest practice of test-item types.
3. Award points for conveyance of meaning and not just for grammatical accuracy.

One recent empirical study (MacIntyre and Gardner 1991a) reveals a strategy that could help students enhance their self-confidence, and as a result reduce their anxiety over SL skills. In this study students were asked to write an essay either about an experience in which they were nervous or one in which they were relaxed in using their French skills. Those students who wrote about a positive experience expressed "more confidence while those writing an anxious essay showed less confidence with their language skills" (p. 303). MacIntyre and Gardner (1991a, p. 303) conclude that "conceivably, students taught to emphasize their own successful experiences in the second language would come to perceive themselves as more proficient language learners, increasing their self-confidence" and reducing their language anxiety.

In the study mentioned before where MacIntyre and Gardner (1994b) examined learner anxiety levels at three different stages (input, processing, and output), they found that "the combined effects of language anxiety at all three stages may be that, compared with relaxed students, anxious students have a smaller base of second language knowledge and have more difficulty demonstrating the knowledge that they do possess" (p. 301). Interestingly, however, in the processing stage, anxious students were able to overcome their anxiety if they were given sufficient time to study.

Other suggested anxiety-reducing strategies are linked to the language teaching methods. Koch and Terrell (1991) report that most activities in the Natural Approach are affectively oriented in that they attempt to produce comfort rather than anxiety. Young (1993) offers evidence to support their findings.

In Samimy and Rardin's (1994) examination of the reflection papers of students in Community Language Learning (CLL) classes over a six-year period, learners reported a lack of anxiety or a reduction in it with CLL. Students also mentioned increased motivation and a favorable change in attitude toward the SL culture with CLL.

Computerized discussions also seem to be a promising way to reduce learners' anxieties. In computerized class discussions, students participate in a real-time electronic conversation in the classroom. The real-time, synchronous discussion eases learners' fear of error correction and allows students freedom of expression with anonymity. Beauvois (1992) examined the affective responses of language learners to classroom discussions on the computer and found that students repeatedly reported this type of activity as less anxiety-provoking than oral discussions in class.

To sum up the research in the area of anxiety-reducing and coping strategies, we observe the following: (1) some suggestions for reducing language anxiety stem from research on the sources of language anxiety, others come from students' voices in questionnaires or interviews, and still others from researchers' conclusions about how to reduce anxiety; (2) there are few empirical studies that investigate the effectiveness of anxiety-reducing strategies; (3) there may be some concrete practices that instructors, students, and administrators can adopt to help alleviate language anxiety, such as giving students ample time to complete processing tasks, assigning them tasks that highlight positive language learning experiences, or supplementing oral discussions with class discussion on the computer.

Directions for Future Language Anxiety Research

While we have experienced an increase in research on language anxiety, we have recognized it as a vital component of SL acquisition only in the last ten years, and are therefore still in the process of understanding the concept. Continued research is necessary if we are to build a sound theoretical model of language anxiety. For example, we need empirical investigations to test MacIntyre and Gardner's hypothesis that language anxiety occurs as a result of negative experiences in language learning. We need to know more about what those negative experiences are and how we can prevent or mitigate them.

It would be useful to examine more closely the relationship between test anxiety and language anxiety and the relationship among language anxiety and other affective variables, such as self-esteem, motivation, and risk taking. We need to investigate whether there are differences in language anxiety on the basis of minority and majority language groups, as suggested with communication apprehension in Mejías et al. (1991). In addition, further research is needed that investigates whether anxiety indeed decreases with language proficiency.

Research is also needed to explain further the contradictory findings of earlier anxiety research and to resolve several other important issues: (1) the role and effect of language anxiety on the processing of language input; (2) the relationship between language proficiency and language anxiety; (3) further sources of language anxiety; and (4) the effectiveness of anxiety-reducing and coping strategies.

Research yet to be undertaken, but that needs to be included in this call for research, includes inquiries into the relationship between anxiety and the following: (1) learners' cognitive styles as opposed to instructors' cognitive styles; (2) teacher and student personalities; (3) learner cognitive styles and global versus analytically oriented language textbooks; and (4) the degree of learners' literacy in the native language and SL speech. The concept of language anxiety would also be clarified by an examination of its relation to other psychological phenomena particular to language learning, such as Guiora's (1972) language ego and Clarkes's (1976) theory of cultural assimilation.

Other areas of inquiry might include the relationship between anxiety and age, gender, grade levels, and type of language learning experience (intensive vs. regular language classes). Furthermore, we would benefit from knowing something about the relationship between SL anxiety and native language forensics and the differences between SL anxiety and L3, L4 anxiety.

Conclusion

This decade will most assuredly witness a continued interest in research on affective variables in SL acquisition because we now know that cognitive and linguistic aspects alone do not make up a complete picture of the language learning process. My hope is that this synthesis of research will offer interested professionals the insights they need to make well-informed curricular and research decisions. If our goal is to increase student motivation and increase the effectiveness of SL learning, then understanding language anxiety will lead us closer to that goal.

Notes

1. Over thirty years ago, Robert Gardner was one of the first to examine the role of anxiety in language learning. In his investigations of affective variables in language learning, Gardner often assessed anxiety as one affective variable among others.

2. Other instruments used to measure aspects of anxiety in the language learning process include the Survey of Attitudes Specific to the Foreign Language Classroom (Campbell and Ortiz 1991a) and Young's (1990) Student Reactions to In-Class Activities.

3. The actual term "language anxiety," as used in this chapter, first appeared in print in the volume edited by Horwitz and Young (1991).

4. Once ability was accounted for, however, anxiety was not significant, suggesting that less proficiency results in more anxiety. But MacIntyre and Gardner (1991c, p. 108) point out that these results deserve reconsideration because the particular analysis used in the study "ignores the difficulty of interpreting the residualized scores used in

partial correlation." If they are correct, then there was indeed a significant negative relationship between anxiety and students' oral proficiency scores.

5. See MacIntyre and Gardner (1991c).

6. The thing category test was in essence a vocabulary test. Students were, for example, asked to name everything that could be found in a refrigerator. The digit span test required students to hear a string of single-digit numbers at a rate of one per second and to write them down as soon as they heard them.

7. Also see Sparks, Ganschow, Javorsky, Pohlman, and Patton (1992) and Ganschow et al. (1994).

8. Jennybelle Rardin defines existential anxiety as a profound type of anxiety *inherently* built into the language learning process, particularly for adolescent and adults, that "touches the core of one's self-identity, one's self-image." According to her, the learner's train of thought is somewhat as follows: "If I learn another language, I will somehow lose myself; I, as I know myself to be, will cease to exist" (quoted in Young 1992, p. 68).

Works Cited

Backman, Nancy. 1976. Two Measures of Affective Factors as They Relate to Progress in Adult Second-Language Learning. *Working Papers in Bilingualism* 10: 100–122.

Bailey, Kathleen M. 1983. Competitiveness and Anxiety in Adult Second Language Learning: Looking At and Through the Diary Studies. In *Classroom Oriented Research in Second Language Acquisition,* edited by Herbert W. Seliger and Michael H. Long, 67–102. Rowley, MA: Newbury House.

Bartz, Walter M. 1974. A Study of the Relationship of Certain Factors with the Ability to Communicate in a Second Language (German) for the Development of Communicative Competence. Ph.D. diss., Ohio State University.

Beauvois, Margaret Healey. 1992. Computer-Assisted Classroom Discussion in the Foreign Language Classroom: Conversation in Slow Motion. *Foreign Language Annals* 25: 455–63.

Brewster, Elizabeth S. 1975. Personality Factors Relevant to Intensive Audiolingual Foreign Language Learning. Ph.D. diss., University of Texas.

Campbell, Christine M., and Jose A. Ortiz. 1991a. Helping Students Overcome Foreign Language Anxiety. In Horwitz and Young, 153–68.

————. 1991b. Toward a More Thorough Understanding of Foreign Language Anxiety. In *Focus on the Foreign Language Learner,* edited by Lorraine A. Strasheim, 12–24. Lincolnwood, IL: National Textbook.

Canale, Michael, and Merrill Swain. 1980. Theoretical Bases of Communicative Approaches to Second Language Teaching and Testing. *Applied Linguistics* 1: 1–47.

Chastain, Kenneth. 1975. Affective and Ability Factors in Second Language Learning. *Language Learning* 25: 153–61.

Clarke, Mark A. 1976. Second Language Acquisition as a Clash of Consciousness. *Language Learning* 26: 377–89.

Clément, R., Robert C. Gardner, and P. C. Smythe. 1977. Motivation Variables in Second Language Acquisition: A Study of Francophones Learning English. *Canadian Journal of Behavioral Science* 9: 123–33.

————. 1980. Social and Individual Factors in Second Language Acquisition. *Canadian Journal of Behavioral Science* 12: 293–302.

Cope Powell, Jo Ann. 1991. Foreign Language Classroom Anxiety: Institutional Responses. In Horwitz and Young, 169–76.

Crookall, David, and Rebecca L. Oxford. 1991. Dealing with Anxiety: Some Practical Activities for Language Learners and Teacher Trainees. In Horwitz and Young, 141–50.

Dunkel, Harold B. 1947. The Effect of Personality on Language Achievement. *Journal of Educational Psychology* 38: 177–82.

Ely, Christopher M. 1986. An Analysis of Discomfort, Risktaking, Sociability and Motivation in the L2 Classroom. *Language Learning* 36: 1–25.

Foss, Karen A., and Armeda C. Reitzel. 1988. A Relational Model for Managing Second Language Anxiety. *TESOL Quarterly* 22: 437–54.

Ganschow, Leonore, Richard L. Sparks, Reed Anderson, James Javorsky, Sue Skinner, and Jon Patton. 1994. Differences in Language Performance among High-, Average-, and Low-Anxious College Foreign Language Learners. *Modern Language Journal* 78: 41–55.

Gardner, Robert C., J. B. Day, and Peter D. MacIntyre. 1992. Integrative Motivation, Induced Anxiety, and Language Learning in a Controlled Environment. *Studies in Second Language Acquisition* 14: 197–214.

Gardner, Robert C., R. N. Lalande, R. Moorcroft, and F. T. Evers. 1987. Second Language Attrition: The Role of Motivation and Use. *Journal of Language and Social Psychology* 6: 29–47.

Gardner, Robert C., and Peter D. MacIntyre. 1993a. A Student's Contributions to Second-Language Learning, Part 2: Affective Variables. *Language Teaching* 26: 1–11.

————. 1993b. On the Measurement of Affective Variables in Second Language Learning. *Language Learning* 43: 157–94.

Gardner, Robert C., R. Moorcroft, and Peter D. MacIntyre. 1987. *The Role of Anxiety in Second Language Performance of Language Dropouts.* Research Bulletin No. 657. London, Ontario: University of Western Ontario.

Gardner, Robert C., P. C. Smythe, R. Clément, and L. Gliksman. 1976. Second Language Learning: A Social-Psychological Perspective. *Canadian Modern Language Review* 32: 198–213.

Gardner, Robert C., P. C. Smythe, and G. R. Grunet. 1977. Intensive Second Language Study: Effects on Attitudes, Motivation, and French Achievement. *Language Learning* 27: 243–61.

Glesne, Corrine, and Alan Peskin. 1992. *Becoming Qualitative Researchers.* White Plains, NY: Longman.

Guiora, Alexander A. 1972. Construct Validity and Transpositional Research: Toward an Empirical Study of Psycho-Analytic Concepts. *Comprehension Psychiatry* 13: 139–50.

Horwitz, Elaine K. 1986. Preliminary Evidence for the Reliability and Validity of a Foreign Language Anxiety Scale. *TESOL Quarterly* 20: 559–62.

Horwitz, Elaine K., Michael B. Horwitz, and Jo Ann Cope. 1986. Foreign Language Classroom Anxiety. *Modern Language Journal* 70: 125–32.

Horwitz, Elaine K., and Dolly J. Young, eds. 1991. *Language Anxiety: From Theory and Research to Classroom Implications.* Englewood Cliffs, NJ: Prentice-Hall.

Kennedy Vande Berg, Camille. 1993. Managing Learner Anxiety in Literature Courses. *French Review* 67: 27–36.

Kleinmann, Howard. 1977. Avoidance Behavior in Adult Second Language Acquisition. *Language Learning* 27: 93–107.

Koch, April, and Tracy D. Terrell. 1991. Affective Reactions of Foreign

Language Students to Natural Approach Activities and Teaching Techniques. In Horwitz and Young, 109–26.

MacIntyre, Peter D. 1988. The Effects of Anxiety on Foreign Language Learning and Production. M.A. thesis, University of Western Ontario, London, Ontario.

MacIntyre, Peter D., and Robert C. Gardner. 1988. *The Measurement of Anxiety and Applications to Second Language Learning: An Annotated Bibliography.* Research Bulletin No. 672. London, Ontario: University of Western Ontario. Washington DC: ERIC Clearinghouse on Languages and Linguistics (ERIC Document Reproduction Service, No. ED 301 040, 39p.).

————. 1989. Anxiety and Second Language Learning: Toward a Theoretical Clarification. *Language Learning* 39: 251–75.

————. 1991a. Investigating Language Class Anxiety Using the Focused Essay Technique. *Modern Language Journal* 75: 296–304.

————. 1991b. Language Anxiety: Its Relationship to Other Anxieties and to Processing in Native and Second Language. *Language Learning* 41: 513–34.

————. 1991c. Methods and Results in the Study of Anxiety and Language Learning: A Review of the Literature. *Language Learning* 41: 85–117.

————. 1994a. The Effects of Induced Anxiety on Three Stages of Cognitive Processing in Computerized Vocabulary Learning. *Studies in Second Language Acquisition* 16: 1–17.

————. 1994b. The Subtle Effects of Language Anxiety on Cognitive Processing in the Second Language. *Language Learning* 44: 283–305.

Madsen, Harold S., Bruce B. Brown, and Randall L. Jones. 1991. Evaluating Student Attitudes toward Second Language Tests. In Horwitz and Young, 65–86.

Mejías, Hugo, Ronald L. Applbaum, Susan J. Applbaum, and Robert T. Trotter. 1991. Oral Communication Apprehension and Hispanics: An Exploration of Oral Communication Apprehension among Mexican American Students in Texas. In Horwitz and Young, 87–97.

Nunan, David. 1992. *Research Methods in Language Learning.* New York: Cambridge University Press.

Phillips, Elaine M. 1991. Anxiety and Oral Competence: Classroom Dilemma. *French Review* 65: 1–14.

———. 1992. The Effects of Language Anxiety on Students' Oral Test Performance and Attitudes. *Modern Language Journal* 76: 14–26.

Pimsleur, Paul, Ludwig Mosberg, and Andrew L. Morrison. 1962. Student Factors in Foreign Language Learning. *Modern Language Journal* 46: 160–70.

Price, Mary Lou. 1991. The Subjective Experience of Foreign Language Anxiety: Interviews with Anxious Students. In Horwitz and Young, 101–8.

Samimy, Keiko, and Jennybelle Rardin. 1994. Adult Language Learners' Affective Reactions to Community Language Learning: A Descriptive Study. *Foreign Language Annals* 27: 379–90.

Scott, M. L. 1986. Student Affective Reactions to Oral Language Tests. *Language Testing* 3: 99–118.

Scovel, Thomas. 1978. The Effect of Affect on Foreign Language Learning: A Review of the Anxiety Research. *Language Learning* 28: 129–42.

Sparks, Richard, and Leonore Ganschow. 1991. Foreign Language Learning Differences: Affective or Native Language Aptitude Differences. *Modern Language Journal* 75: 4–16.

Sparks, Richard, Leonore Ganschow, James Javorsky, Jane Pohlman, and John Patton. 1992. Identifying Native Language Deficits in High- and Low-Risk Foreign Language Learners in High School. *Foreign Language Annals* 25: 403–18.

Steinberg, Faith S., and Elaine K. Horwitz. 1986. Anxiety and Second Language Speech: Can Conditions Affect What Students Choose to Talk About? *TESOL Quarterly:* 131–36.

Swain, Merrill, and Barbara Burnaby. 1976. Personality Characteristics and Second Language Learning in Young Children: A Pilot Study. *Working Papers in Bilingualism* 2: 115–28.

Trylong, V. L. 1987. Aptitude, Attitudes and Anxiety: A Study of Their Relationships to Achievement in the Foreign Language Classroom. Ph.D. diss., Purdue University.

Tucker, Richard, Else Hamayan, and Fred H. Genesee. 1976. Affective, Cognitive, and Social Factors in Second Language Acquisition. *Canadian Modern Language Review* 32: 214–26.

Westcott, D. B. 1973. Personality Factors Affecting High School Students Learning a Second Language. Ph.D. diss., University of Texas.

Wittenborn, J. R., R. P. Larsen, and R. L. Mogil. 1945. An Empirical Evaluation of Study Habits for College Courses in French and Spanish. *Journal of Educational Psychology* 36: 449–74.

Young, Dolly J. 1986. The Relationship between Anxiety and Foreign Language Oral Proficiency Ratings. *Foreign Language Annals* 19: 439–45.

———. 1990. An Investigation of Students' Perspectives on Anxiety and Speaking. *Foreign Language Annals* 23: 539–53.

———. 1991. Creating a Low-Anxiety Classroom Environment: What Does the Language Anxiety Research Suggest? *Modern Language Journal* 75: 426–37.

———. 1992. Language Anxiety from the Foreign Language Specialist's Perspective: Interviews with Krashen, Omaggio, Terrell, and Rardin. *Foreign Language Annals* 25: 157–72.

Young, Dolly J., and Rebecca L. Oxford. 1993. Attending to Learner Reactions to Introductory Spanish Textbooks. *Hispania* 76: 593–605.

Appendix

Anxiety Measures—References[1]

Affect Adjective Checklist

Zuckerman, M. 1960. The Development of an Affect Adjective Check List for the Measurement of Anxiety. *Journal of Consulting Psychology* 24: 457–62.

Attitude toward the Language Class

Ely, C. M. 1986. An Analysis of Discomfort, Risktaking, Sociability, and Motivation in the L2 Classroom. *Language Learning* 36: 1–25.

Classroom Anxiety Scale—revised by MacIntyre

MacIntyre, P. D. 1988. The Effects of Anxiety on Foreign Language Learning and Production. Master's thesis, University of Western Ontario.

Concern for Grade

Ely, C. M. 1986. An Analysis of Discomfort, Risktaking, Sociability, and Motivation in the L2 Classroom. *Language Learning* 36: 1–25.

Debilitating Anxiety Scale

Alpert, R., and R. N. Haber. 1960. Anxiety in Academic Achievement Situations. *Journal of Abnormal and Social Psychology* 61: 207–15.

Facilitating Anxiety Scale

Alpert, R., and R. N. Haber. 1960. Anxiety in Academic Achievement Situations. *Journal of Abnormal and Social Psychology* 61: 207–15.

Fear of Negative Evaluation

Watson, D., and R. Friend. 1969. Measurement of Social-Evaluative Anxiety. *Journal of Consulting and Clinical Psychology* 33: 448–57.

The Fear Thermometer

Walk, R. D. 1956. Self Ratings of Fear in a Fear-Invoking Situation. *Journal of Abnormal and Social Psychology* 52: 171–78.

French Class Anxiety Scale

Gardner, R. C. 1985. *Social Psychology and Second Language Learning: The Role of Attitudes and Motivation.* London: Edward Arnold.

French Use Anxiety Scale (R. C. Gardner)

Gliksman, L. 1981. Improving the Prediction of Behaviours Associated with Second Language Acquisition. Ph.D. diss., University of Western Ontario.

Foreign Language Classroom Anxiety Scale

Horwitz, E. K., M. B. Horwitz, and J. Cope. 1986. Foreign Language Classroom Anxiety. *Modern Language Journal* 70: 125–32.

Language Class Discomfort

Ely, C. M. 1986. An Analysis of Discomfort, Risktaking, Sociability, and Motivation in the L2 Classroom. *Language Learning* 36: 1–25.

Language Class Risk-Taking

Ely, C. M. 1986. An Analysis of Discomfort, Risktaking, Sociability, and Motivation in the L2 Classroom. *Language Learning* 36: 1–25.

Language Class Sociability

Ely, C. M. 1986. An Analysis of Discomfort, Risktaking, Sociability, and Motivation in the L2 Classroom. *Language Learning* 36: 1–25.

Personal Report of Communication Apprehension (PRCA)—College

McCroskey, J. C. 1970. Measures of Communication-Bound Anxiety. *Speech Monographs* 37: 269–77.

PRCA—Ten (Grade 10 students), PRCA—Seven (Grade 7 students)

McCroskey, J. C. 1970. Measures of Communication-Bound Anxiety. *Speech Monographs* 37: 269–77.

PRPSA

McCroskey, J. C. 1970. Measures of Communication-Bound Anxiety. *Speech Monographs* 37: 269–77.

PRCA—Long Form, PRCA—Short Form

McCroskey, J. C. 1978. Validity of the PRCA as an Index of Oral Communication Apprehension. *Communication Monographs* 45: 192–203.

Social Avoidance and Distress Scale

Watson, D., and R. Friend. 1969. Measurement of Social-Evaluative Anxiety. *Journal of Consulting and Clinical Psychology* 33: 448–57.

Speech A/Trait Scale (Sample Items)

Lamb, D. H. 1972. Speech Anxiety: Towards a Theoretical Conceptualization and Preliminary Scale Development. *Speech Monographs* 39: 62–67.

Speech A/State Scale (Sample Items)

Lamb, D. H. 1972. Speech Anxiety: Towards a Theoretical Conceptualization and Preliminary Scale Development. *Speech Monographs* 39: 62–67.

The S-R Inventory of General Trait Anxiousness

Endler, N. S., and M. Okada. 1975. A Multidimensional Measure of Trait Anxiety: The S-R Inventory of General Trait Anxiousness. *Journal of Consulting and Clinical Psychology* 43: 319–29.

Strength of Motivation

Ely, C. M. 1986. An Analysis of Discomfort, Risktaking, Sociability, and Motivation in the L2 Classroom. *Language Learning* 36: 1–25.

Suinn Test Anxiety Behavior Scale

Suinn, R. M. 1969. The STABBS, a Measure of Test Anxiety for Behavior Therapy: Normative Data. *Behaviour Research and Therapy* 7: 335–39.

Taylor Manifest Anxiety Scale

Taylor, J. A. 1953. A Personality Scale of Manifest Anxiety. *Journal of Abnormal and Social Psychology* 48: 285–90.

Test Anxiety Scale

Sarason, I. G., and V. J. Ganzer. 1962. Anxiety, Reinforcement, and Experimental Instructions in a Free Verbalization Situation. *Journal of Abnormal and Social Psychology* 65: 300–307.

Writing Apprehension Measure

Daly, J. A., and M. C. Miller. 1975. The Empirical Development of an Instrument to Measure Writing Apprehension. *Research in the Teaching of English* 9: 242–49.

Note 1. Appendix taken from MacIntyre and Gardner 1988.

Native Genderlects and Their Relation to Gender Issues in Second Language Classrooms: The Sex of Our Students as a Sociolinguistic Variable

Lydie E. Meunier
University of Tulsa

Introduction

Sociolinguistic and anthropological research on native genderlects can offer dependable findings to help us understand gender issues in second language (L2) development in their full complexities. The debate concerning the role of nature, "system-internal" factors, versus the role of nurture, "system-external" factors, in the learning process is an old one. Today this debate has reached the area of gender issues in first and second language development. More specifically, this chapter will address the following question: Are gender-specific communicative patterns in L2 development genetically predetermined or are they acquired within a given social interactive external system? To date, SLA researchers have essentially addressed gender differences in L2 development as stemming from "system-internal" factors, such as learning styles and cognitive approaches. This chapter will discuss gender issues in L2 development from the broader view of sociolinguistic and anthropological studies. The narrowing down of gender issues to "system-internal" factors falsely depicts gender specificity in SLA as a "natural," and thus unchangeable, gender-specific cognitive process.

The purpose of this chapter is to add a new perspective to the discussion by underlining the premise that the socialization process undergone by

L2 learners sets various types of preferential cognitive networks, and that gender-specific learning strategies in SLA may ultimately stem from nurture rather than nature, that is, from a possible sociolinguistic transfer out of native genderlects. More specifically, this chapter aims to provide a better understanding of genderlect development in first language acquisition as well as a better understanding of the role that native genderlects can play in L2 development. The comprehension of gender differences in first language use is, indeed, a precondition for a better interpretation of gender issues observed in L2 acquisition. Keeping this in mind, this chapter will report findings about genderlects in first language communication before addressing the issue of gender differences and gender-specific communicative competence in a second language. Research reveals that gender-specific interactional patterns noticed in L2 acquisition tend to reflect interactional patterns that commonly take place across and between genders in first language use. The presence of gender-linked sociolinguistic native patterns in L2 interaction suggests that communicative competence in a foreign language (FL) may be prone to sociolinguistic transfers from native genderlects. L2 studies also reveal that traditional values related to gender-specific societal roles are still part of today's hidden curricula in L2 instruction, and that gender differences are more strongly emphasized in an instructional environment than in society. Implications for research in L2 studies are highlighted throughout. Recommendations for L2 instruction are given in the conclusion.

Native Genderlects

Outcome of the Socialization Process

The American sociolinguist Labov (1966) and the British anthropologist Trudgill (1972) paved the way to the study of genderlects in Western societies. Their studies consistently indicated that women used a more standard language than did men, regardless of their socioeconomic level, age, or race. Their studies were often interpreted to mean that this gender difference was the result of early childhood socialization processes (Lakoff 1975; Goodwin 1980; Malz and Borker 1982; Cameron 1992). Girls are encouraged and rewarded for using "elegant" language whereas boys are allowed more flexibility and roughness in language use. As Lakoff (1975, p. 6) notes, "Rough talk is discouraged in little girls more strongly than in little boys, in whom parents may often find it more amusing than shocking." Cameron (1992, p. 73) also points out that children's activities shape various styles of speech:

"Boys tend to play in large groups organized hierarchically; thus they learn direct, confrontational speech. Girls play in small groups of 'best friends,' where they learn to maximize intimacy and minimize conflict." Lever (1978) observed the playground activities of fifth-grade children and also interviewed them. She found that boys organized competitive team games with specific rules and goals, whereas girls played games in smaller groups involving repeated rituals and greater cooperation than boys. Lever (1978) also observed that when girls were involved in team games, they were likely to ignore the rules, whereas boys were very careful to adhere to them.

Other studies that have been conducted regarding the use of vernacular styles across genders (Cheshire 1982; Coates 1986; Milroy 1980) show that males tend to use a more vernacular style than females. This difference has often been interpreted as a sign of females' greater desire to conform to societal norms. Yet this interpretation may stem from a sexist view that traditionally stresses the idea that females are naturally more dependent than males. When considered from a historical perspective, the difference in the use of vernacular styles across genders can be explained differently. Keeping in mind that languages have evolved from vernacular forms, today's nonstandard styles are often the avant-garde of the next generation's standard language. As such, speaking nonstandard forms is an expression of both freedom and creative power in which females were not allowed to participate. If one assumes that nonstandard forms are lacking in elegance when spoken by a woman, we are faced with the illocutionary force of prohibition. What is usually perceived as compliance to societal forms on the part of females is in essence the result of "a long social imprisonment" while men use the "powerful language" of creation (Spender 1980).

Social Status, Language, and Interruptions

Lakoff (1975) further claims that women are denied access to the "powerful" style that characterizes not only the male's linguistic creativity but also the male's authority. More recent research (Cameron 1992) indicates that gender-specific linguistic differences lead to gender-specific conversational strategies. Keeping in mind that a linguistic exchange is the result of the relationship between interlocutors, and that males and females have disparate social statuses, conversational patterns between males and females have been found to reflect social inequalities existing between them (Stern 1994). Historically, this interactive pattern was reinforced by sociolinguistic practices during biblical times when a wife had to address her husband in the manner of a slave addressing his master, or a subject addressing his king (Daly 1991, p. 159). This implied that a man could also address his wife in the manner of a master addressing his slave and a king addressing his subject, that is, by using a clear rhetoric of authority. Today, conversational dominance by males is not as extreme, but it is still inherent to male-specific discourse and has become the focus of some interesting sociolinguistic research.

Zimmerman and West (1975) and West and Fenstermaker (1993) investigated mixed-gender conversations and linguistic inequality in gender-specific styles. Thirty-one conversations were taped in public places such as libraries, coffee shops, drug stores, and the University of California. The data were composed of eleven mixed-gender conversations, ten male-only, and ten female-only conversations. The findings indicated significant differences between same-gender pairs and mixed-gender pairs regarding the use of overlaps and interruptions. Overlaps were defined as an act of anticipating the end of a sentence spoken by an interlocutor while articulating it with a topic-related response. An interruption, on the other hand, was considered as a violation of turn-taking rules whereby topical disarticulation is flagrant. Results showed that all the overlaps were caused by male speakers and that 96 percent of the interruptions resulted from men interrupting women. Interestingly, men rarely interrupted each other; they primarily used interruptions when speaking to women. Women used fewer overlaps with men than with women due to the fact that men tended to perceive overlaps as interruptions. As Steinem (1991, p.302) notes, "Male interruptions of women bring less social punishment than female interruptions of men." Zimmerman and West (1975) and West and Fenstermaker (1993) observed that in mixed-gender conversations men tended to infringe on women's right to speak. The studies also found that as a result of male interruptions, women tended to be more silent than men. Silent periods in single-gender pairs averaged 1.35 seconds, while they averaged 3.21 seconds in mixed-gender groups. Interestingly, the illocutionary act of silence was also defined as clearly gender-specific. Females have been observed to fall silent after male interruptions, indicating their powerlessness, while males primarily used silence preceding minimal responses such as "Yeah," indicating, according to Zimmerman and West (1975) and West and Fenstermaker (1993), a lack of interest in the interlocutor's topic, denying women the right to control the topic of conversation. West (1984) has shown that male interruptions apply even when females have a higher social status. Her study was conducted among male and female doctors interacting with patients.

West (1984, p. 92) found that "[w]hereas male physicians (as a group) initiated 67% of all interruptions relative to their patients' 33%, female physicians (as a group) initiated only 32% of interruptions relative to their patients' 68%." West (1984) notes:

> In our society, Hughes observes, the auxiliary characteristics that have emerged around the status "physician" are "white," "Protestant" and "male." Hence, when persons assuming the powerful status of physician are not properly equipped with whiteness, Protestantism or maleness, there tends to be what Hughes terms a "status contradiction"—or even a "status dilemma. . . ." The "lady doctor" is a case in point, the adjective "lady" (or "woman" or "female") serving to underscore the presumed maleness of the status "Physician. . . ." The dilemma is likely to ensue over whether to treat them [lady doctors] as members of the social category "women" or as members of the profession "physician." (p. 98)

Amount of Talk

Silence and talkativeness are another interesting aspect of gender-specificity in conversational strategies due to the fact that women are often believed to talk more than men. This widespread belief, however, has been unanimously disconfirmed by anthropologists. In an experiment where males and females were asked to describe three pictures, males were found to speak an average of 13 minutes per picture as opposed to females who spoke only an average of 3.17 minutes (Swacker 1975). Further research showed that men talk more than women in public settings but are less involved in private talks (Coates 1986; Eakins and Eakins 1978; Spender 1980; Steinem 1991). Researchers who have investigated the issue have indicated that public settings are considered as a ground for competitiveness by men, hence the greater amount of talk by men in public. Women have been shown to talk more in private with female friends about topics often considered trivial and unimportant by men. Coates (1986, p. 103) remarks, "The fact that topics such as sports, politics, and cars are seen as 'serious' while topics such as childbearing and personal relationships are labeled 'trivial' is simply a reflection of social values that define what men do as important, and conversely what women do as less important." As a result, men end up using a great deal of silence in privacy. Yet this private silence has been analyzed as an act of denying conversation topics which, according to males, are uninteresting (Aries 1976, 1987; Spender 1980).

Harmony and Competitiveness

Anthropological studies based on observations and interviews of couples indicate that females are more likely to adjust to a male interlocutor, asking questions and introducing numerous "male-specific topics" until males end up accepting a conversation (Aries 1976, 1987; Coates 1986; Spender 1980). Steinem (1991, p. 305) observes that "[s]ubjects introduced by males in mixed groups are far more likely to 'succeed' than subjects introduced by women." Once males decide to speak on a topic, they end up talking as experts, holding the center stage of the conversation. Wittig (1992) interpreted this control of conversation topics as a result of males primarily using language for competitive rather than for relational purposes:

> For most women, the language of conversation is primarily a language of rapport: a way of establishing connections and negotiating relationships. . . . For most men, talk is primarily a means to preserve independence and negotiate and maintain status in a hierarchical social order. This is done by exhibiting knowledge and skill, and by holding the center stage through verbal performance such as story telling, joking, or imparting information. (p. 77)

Jones (1980) observed that women are more likely to discuss interrelational topics and to personalize conversations, a discursive style that males satirically define as gossiping. Males have been found to keep their distance from relational and human issues by reducing them to theories and abstractions (Aries 1976; Steinem 1991; Swacker 1975; Tannen 1990). As Steinem (1991) notes,

> Lecturers often comment, for instance, that women in an audience ask practical questions about their own lives, while men ask abstract questions about groups or policies. When the subject is feminism, women tend to ask about practical problems. Men are more likely to say something like, "But how will feminism impact the American family?" (p. 305)

In mixed-gender interactions Steinem's (1991, p. 302) study implies that men talk more than women and that talkativeness is not an exclusive female trait: "The uncomfortable truth seems to be that the amount of talk by women has been measured less against the amount of men's talk than against the expectations of female silence." In other words, a talkative woman talks as much as a man.

Assertiveness

In the light of anthropological findings, mixed-gender conversations are considered by some as crosscultural in nature, with men and women speaking different genderlects (Tannen 1990). The primary difference between these genderlects is that females speak to maintain harmony and strong relationships, as well as to keep conversations open, whereas males use more assertiveness and insistence. Women, for instance, have been observed to speak in a more tentative way than men, using more tag questions and more questions in general (Coates 1986; Holmes 1988). The use of such language patterns was explained by Holmes (1988) as follows: tag questions are an indication of females being more polite and more suggestive (since they are less assertive) than males. Lakoff (1975) viewed such language patterns as a sign of "insecurity" or "approval seeking." Fishman (1980) explained such patterns in terms of "skillful strategies" to engage men in talk.

The language used by females seems to stem from oppressive structures whereby women addressed men as their masters (Daly 1991). Politeness, although positively valued today, was once a sign of humility. The primary function of politeness was to signal the status difference between inferiors and their superiors. Since females historically addressed their husbands with reverence, this socially sanctioned form of obeisance may explain why females are often found to be more polite in anthropological studies. However, since the relation between language and gender is also context-dependent (Tannen 1992), the way politeness can be used in modern society lost some of its historical function. Brown's observations (1990) in a Tenejapan court indicated that women could also use politeness in a sarcastic way and as such show more confrontation than reverence. Nonetheless, whether sarcastic or not, the truth remains that women used more polite forms than men do, and that women most likely learned confrontational strategies using the language forms they inherited throughout history.

Regarding the use of compliments, Johnson and Roen (1992) conducted a study on peer reviews of graduate students' papers. Their study indicated that male compliments were functionally more ideational (reflecting an actual evaluation, i.e., the language of the expert) and that women demonstrated a complimenting discourse that was functionally more interpersonal (making the interlocutor feel good, i.e., the language of solidarity).

Summary

This first section summarized research in gender-specific conversational styles in mixed-gender interaction. Coates (1986, p. 117) concluded that "[t]he differences between the competitive, assertive male style and the cooperative supportive female style mean that men will tend to dominate in mixed-gender interaction." Research to date indicates that men tend to control topics of conversation and to interrupt women. Women tend to raise more questions and to give minimal responses to maintain harmonious exchanges. Men talk more, contrary to what is commonly believed, and are more likely to use a vernacular style in private, while females use a standard and polite language. These conclusions, however, should be considered with caution since language use also varies according to situational conditions. Yet the fact remains that anthropologists consistently observe gender-specific patterns for conversational interaction and that, as such, males and females are considered to be part of separate speech communities (Tannen 1990) and to use different genderlects.

In the next section, I will address gender issues in L2 communication and interaction. More specifically, gender-specific patterns in L2 use will be investigated to assess if communicative competence in a foreign language is affected by gender-specific native behaviors related to L1 use.

Gender Differences and Communicative Competence in L2

Communicative interaction between two human beings varies a great deal according to the interlocutors' ethnic background, personality, cognitive style, and/or sex. In other words, in addition to grammatical and textual competence, everyone has a developed sense of language appropriateness, which is also referred to in some circles as "pragmatic" or "sociolinguistic competence." We know when to speak, how to adjust our speech to a specific situation, what to talk about, and when to remain silent. Recent communicative approaches in FL teaching are based on the premise that using language in social interactions increases students' individual capacity, a system defined by Vygotsky (1978) as "the zone of proximal development." This zone, however, varies for every language student due to the individual's personal characteristics. The study of these individual differences traditionally focuses on motivation, anxiety level, learning styles, and cognitive strategies. Gender differences, however, constitute a rather recent field of research.

Gender Difference and L2 Acquisition

Ho (1987, p. 127), in a study investigating psychological factors contributing to individual differences in FL skills, found that gender was the "single variable with the most predictive power." The predictor domain was composed of verbal intelligence, personality, attitude, and gender variables. Personality variables were considered to "predict achievement . . . only on occasions, [leading the researcher to] conclude that personality factors were quite unreliable or trivial as predictors" (Ho 1987, p. 128). Ho (1987, p. 127) noted that "[f]emales were superior to males (at the .05 level of significance) in the expressive skills, writing and especially speaking: like in the Western culture, Chinese males prefer to manipulate facts and data as opposed to expressing themselves on personal matters." Ho's study was conducted among 230 first-year students at the University of Hong Kong using an English proficiency test and a battery of psychology tests translated into Chinese. The psychology test was based on six constructs: rigidity, authoritarianism, dogmatism, conformity, fatalism-superstition, and belief stereotypy. The results of the psychology tests indicated that authoritarianism, belief stereotypy, and dogmatism had negative effects on the acquisition of FL skills, and that the other psychological constructs did not show significant correlation with language results. Since females obtained superior results, it could also be speculated that females were less authoritative and dogmatic than males. However, this issue was not directly examined by Ho.

In the light of anthropological studies reviewed in the first part of this chapter, it can be speculated that females feel more at ease than males with language activities in which students are requested to speak or write about themselves and others. Such activities typically take place at the novice and intermediate levels of FL classes and may not particularly appeal to male students. So-called content-based discussions that are based on scholarly disciplines (Krueger and Ryan 1993), the type of discussion males seem to prefer (Coates 1986; Eakins and Eakins 1978; Spender 1980; Steinem 1991), could be designed for classroom use in addition to commonly practiced interpersonal activities. In a content-based approach, language is acquired through studying other subject matters as opposed to speaking about personal issues. By mixing activity types, both males and females may be more equally motivated. Interestingly, a study (Meunier-Cinko 1993) investigating mixed- and same-gender dyads during a computer-based activity in French indicated that males and females tend to focus their attention on particular types of information. The females in this study learned significantly more vocabulary pertaining to descriptions, while the males learned more cultural facts. This result accords with findings in gender studies which indicate that females are more sensitive to information pertaining to story characters and their life-styles, whereas men pay more attention to facts that do not involve them personally

(Coates 1986; Holmes 1992; Tannen 1990). Even more interesting, Meunier-Cinko's (1993) study indicated that in mixed-gender groups females tended to acquiesce to male factual preferences and to lower their interest in the descriptive texts of the software, whereas males did not show any such adjustment. The female trend to adjust to masculine preference has been described in previous research as a process of immasculination which, according to Schweickart (1986), is particularly acute in universities, an interesting issue that deserves further investigation.

Effect of the Interlocutor's Gender on Communication

Pearson and Lee (1992) investigated the effects of native/nonnative speakers' status and gender and found that the gender of interlocutors was the primary factor influencing the structure and content of the discourse. Their study was conducted at Pennsylvania State University. Four graduate students acted as typical student direction-seekers. Two of them were nonnative speakers (NNSs) of English from China and Japan, and two were native speakers (NSs) of English, with a male and a female in each group. The four volunteer students asked a sample of two hundred (one hundred male, one hundred female) U.S. native English-speaking university students for directions from a single location on campus at similar times of day. Communication patterns indicated that the gender of both the direction-seeker and the direction-giver influenced the structure and content of the discourse. Female direction-givers paused to check the comprehension of their interlocutor more often than did male direction-givers. Female direction-seekers, whatever their status, were given more directives, were addressed with a more complex vocabulary, and received more parenthetical remarks from both male and female direction-givers. The NS/NNS status affected only greetings and leave-takings. It was observed that NNSs were addressed with longer leave-takings.

Markham (1988) examined the double effect of gender and perceived expertise of a speaker on the recall of orally presented material by ESL university-level students. About one hundred ESL students were assigned to one of the study's treatment conditions: (1) presentation of a passage by a male speaker who was not introduced, (2) presentation of a passage by a female speaker who was not introduced, (3) presentation by an "expert" male speaker, and (4) presentation by an "expert" female speaker ("expert" meant that the presentation was preceded by a fictitious introduction of the speaker's alleged expertise; all presenters were actors). Students recalled more idea units from the presentation of the "nonexpert" male speaker than from the presentation of the "nonexpert" female speaker. Similarly, more idea units were recalled from the expert male speaker than from the expert female speaker. Interestingly, expert females were listened to more closely than nonexpert females, whereas no difference was found in the attention given to both expert and nonexpert males. An even more disturbing finding indicated that both female and male subjects listening to the male speakers scored higher than when listening to the female speaker. This suggests that males as well as females perceive expertness as a male attribute. According to Markham (1988), both males and females have been conditioned to abide by deeply engraved sexist conventions.

This finding clearly indicates that the gender of FL instructors is likely to have an unexpected effect on L2 development, one issue that remains to be empirically researched.

The Hidden Curriculum

Tannen (1992, p. 144) underlines the danger of "trying to understand how speakers use language without considering the context. The same linguistic means can both express power or solidarity depending on the context." A number of studies (Davies and Meighan 1975; Ehrman and Oxford 1989; Ho 1987; Liski and Puntanen 1983; Oxford, Nyikos, and Ehrman 1988; Powel 1986; Scarcella and Oxford 1992) have examined the classroom context and have found that gender-specific interactional patterns in conversations may indicate that schools foster distinct gender-specific behaviors. The influence of teachers' tacit and covert expectations, often based on stereotypical roles, is what Davies and Meighan (1975) call the "hidden" or "covert" curriculum, as opposed to the official and overt curriculum. The "hidden curriculum" is defined as "those concepts of learning in schools that are unofficial, unintentional, or undeclared consequences of the way in which teachers organize and execute teaching and learning" (p. 171). To date, the effects of hidden curricula are still believed to counteract the goals of the civil rights legislation written for the prevention of ethnic and gender discrimination (Fennema 1987; Holmes 1989; Sunderland 1992).

Sunderland (1992) studied ESL classrooms and found that the generic "he" is still often used by teachers and in teaching materials. ESL books are characterized as follows: (1) there are very few female characters; (2) stereotypes in gender roles are greater than stereotypes in society regarding professions (females tend to be of lower-status occupations), age (females are younger), actions (females are relatively inactive), relationships (females tend to be confined to conventional roles); (3) in most of the mixed-gender dialogues, males speak first and lead conversations (females being only responders). According to Sunderland (1992, p. 86), "[U]nconscious influence of female characters who play restricted social, behavioral, and linguistic roles does not suggest cognitive and communicative empowerment for female learners. . . . It is more likely to hinder than facilitate their learning." This observation, however, has not to my knowledge been empirically examined.

Amount of Talk by Males and Females in L2 Classrooms

Similarly, in an investigation of EFL classes, Holmes (1989) transcribed taped lessons and found that teachers of mixed classes paid more attention to male students, and that, as a result of this extra attention, male students got more speaking practice and more feedback. Holmes's investigation of ESL classes also indicated that adult male students both answered and questioned the teacher more, thus getting more speaking practice. The same study indicated that in mixed-gender group work, male students spoke more and took longer turns than females, who primarily gave feedback to the males' statements. These observations tend to echo the finding in anthropological studies that during childhood males are encouraged to speak more in public settings than females are (Coates 1986; Eakins and Eakins 1978; Spender 1980; Steinem 1991). Considering that classrooms are public settings, the connection between Holmes's finding and anthropological studies raises the issue of a possible sociolinguistic transfer in FL classrooms. Sunderland (1992, p. 89) observes: "One message both teacher–learner and learner–learner interaction can carry, then, is that women and girls are discoursally if not socially marginal in the foreign language classroom."

A study involving 698 university students learning EFL (Liski and Puntanen 1983) supported the fact that males liked holding the center stage in FL classrooms, to the point that they got better grades. However, Liski and Puntanen also found that the accuracy of the language males used was lower than that of females. The testees' performance was evaluated during oral interviews by noting errors under four categories: pronunciation, grammatical structure, lexis, and language use. The language production of female students was considered better than that of male students, yet males were considered better at language use.

Clearly, Liski and Puntanen's (1983) study of ESL mirrors studies in English as a native language reported in the first section of this chapter, namely, that female speakers tend to use a higher proportion of standard forms than male speakers. Mention was also made that in spite of the fact that women are linguistically more formal than males, male speakers make more frequent contributions than females in formal contexts. As a result, males end up getting more status enhancement than females, the equivalence of better grades in a FL classroom (Coates 1986; Holmes 1992). Clearly, the possible effect of the "hidden curriculum" in FL instruction should be acknowledged as a serious factor affecting not only classroom communication and interaction, but also FL proficiency and academic results as a whole.

Gass and Varonis (1985) give additional support to the contention that FL conversational pairs often demonstrate unequal interactive partnership. In a one-way task, males are more likely to signal their lack of understanding than females. Females are more likely to show their lack of understanding in same-gender pairs. In a two-way task, however, females tended to express their lack of understanding more, although not as much as males in mixed-gender pairs. The authors suggest that women feel less confident in signaling a lack of understanding when interacting with men. In a later study, Gass and Varonis (1986) further noticed differences between men and women in the amount they participated in conversations. This time, the authors noticed a greater amount of dynamic interaction in mixed-gender groups than in same-gender groups. Gass and Varonis (1986) also found major gender-specific differences in interactional patterns:

> What we have seen in this study is a situation of unequal partnership. Men took greater advantage of the opportunities to use the conversation in a way that allowed them to produce a greater amount of "comprehensible output," whereas women utilized the conversation to obtain a greater amount of comprehensible input. . . . If it is the case that in same-sex dyads there is less negotiation, then this might provide an opportunity to share information to a greater extent. In contrast, in mixed-sex dyads there is a greater amount of negotiation that provides an opportunity for a greater amount of language focus. Thus, the advantages provided by different dyadic arrangements depend on the purpose of the interaction itself. (p. 349)

Similarly, Pica, Holliday, and Lewis (1991) investigated conversational patterns in NS–NNS interactions. Their study indicated interesting patterns:

> Male and female NNSs made and received a comparable number of opportunities to request L2 input and modify interlanguage output during interaction with female NSs, but during interaction with male NSs, these opportunities were significantly lower for female than for male NNSs. (p. 343)

Pica et al.'s results may be further interpreted in the light of anthropological studies reported in the first part of this chapter (Steinem 1991; Tannen 1992; West 1984; Zimmerman and West 1975). Language interventions requested in their study could have been perceived by students as interruptions or overlaps. Mention was made, indeed, that through the socialization process, females have subconsciously learned to make a minimal use of interventions perceived as interruptions by males. If, in addition, females are NNSs and males NSs, males end up with a double advantage, that is, both linguistic and sociolinguistic. Clearly, a socially gender-specific acquired behavior can have a significant impact not only on L2 communication and interaction, but also on L2 development itself if active participation is inhibited by the way a partner behaves or is perceived.

Overall, the above-mentioned findings lead to interesting and very important questions: (1) Is there an actual transfer of gender-specific communication patterns from L1 to L2? (2) If this is the case, can gender-specific linguistic patterns, acquired through first language development, be controlled in a L2 classroom? (3) How can instructors account for gender-related discourse patterns transferred from L1 to L2 and more specifically during L2 oral evaluations?

Target Language and Target Genderlects

The degree of integration into the target language culture has been explained in terms of "social" and "psychological" distance: the greater the social and psychological distance perceived by learners between their native culture and the target language culture, the smaller the degree of accommodation and acculturation, and the lower the level of L2 proficiency. Likewise, the smaller the social and psychological distance, the better the L2 proficiency (Beebe 1985; Schumann 1978; Tarone 1979). Adamson and Regan (1991) showed that the same theory applies for "subcultures" within cultures. Studies in anthropology have indicated, for instance, that sociolects and genderlects are marked by the use of distinct patterns in grammar, phonology, and vocabulary (Coates 1986). Keeping this in mind, genderlects as well as other sociolects are offered to ESL learners as various types of target language in addition to the standard language. Adamson and Regan (1991) investigated whether female and male NNSs would adopt gender-linked sociolinguistic norms. And, indeed, they found that both male and female NNSs accommodated to gender-related sociolinguistic patterns. They found that nonnative females naturally related to native females by adopting their speech patterns, as did nonnative males with native males. These conclusions were reached by studying the pronunciation of the gerundive final "ing" in English: "ing" had been determined to be pronounced /in/ by middle-class native males, and pronounced /iñ/ by middle-class native females (Trudgill 1983; cited in Adamson and Regan 1991). Results among ESL learners showed that nonnative males were more likely to accommodate to the native male community by adopting their pronunciation of the final "ing," while nonnative females were more likely to accommodate to the sociolinguistic norms of the native females by adopting their pronunciation of the final "ing." These conclusions were all the more interesting because NNSs shared the same linguistic background. With this in mind, considering that FL programs are more and more team-taught, it would be interesting to investigate the gender-specific linguistic impact that instructors may have in cases of mixed-gender teams. Would female students develop language patterns similar to those used by the female instructor? Would male students develop language patterns similar to those used by the male instructor? Would such phenomena take place in an instructional environment at all?

Gender-Specific Learning Strategies

Ehrman and Oxford's (1989) study of the FL learning strategies of seventy-nine adult learners indicated that females excelled at strategies used to establish and convey meaning (i.e., guessing meaning from context; finding alternative ways, such as circumlocutions and synonyms; and expressing meaning in conversation). Ehrman and Oxford also indicated that language used among women was based on establishing connections: females reported more authentic language use "searching for and communicating meaning" (p. 7). Likewise, females used more social learning strategies, such as requests for clarification, asking questions, circumlocutions, and the like, than did males. Yet Gass and Varonis (1985) indicated that females were more likely to use social learning strategies with female partners than with male partners. According to Ehrman and Oxford (1989, p. 8), this profile of the female FL student showed that females generally prefer intuition to sensing and feeling to thinking as defined by the Myers-Briggs Type Indicator:

> [A] person with a preference for sensing perception sees the world in a practical and factual way. An intuitor is likely to be aware first of relationships. . . . A preference for thinking judgments results in impersonal, objective cause-and-effect criteria. Judgments made on feeling grounds are made on the basis of personal or social values and automatically take into account personal relationships and the feelings of others. (Myers 1986; cited in Erhman and Oxford 1989, p. 3)

Clearly, females and males not only tend to have different gender-related personality profiles, but gender-related personality profiles also tend to be related to gender-specific learning strategies. Thus mixed-gender group activities in the FL classroom are likely to cause communication difficulties.

Politzer (1983) has also found that females used more social learning strategies in L2 classes than males. Likewise, females often showed more interest in social activities and were much less aggressive than males in cooperative activities. A related study conducted among students learning French (Lee 1986) indicated that more female than male students reacted favorably to the practice of short French conversations in class. Writing about oneself or a personal activity in French was also an activity preferred by female students. Male students, on the other hand, had a preference for playing games due to the competitive nature of such activities. At this point, we cannot help but notice the connection that exists between this study and studies reported in anthropological research (Cameron 1992; Lever 1978). Interactive behaviors observed in Politzer's (1983) FL classrooms seem to reflect the children's early team activities during which boys behave competitively while girls interact on a more friendly basis.

In a recent book dealing with FL pedagogy, *The Tapestry of Language Learning* (Scarcella and Oxford 1992), FL professionals are cautioned to be aware of the gender-difference issue in the L2 classroom:

> Men and women, in general, have distinct different communications styles, and these styles include different modes of listening. Men often listen for facts and information, while women frequently listen for underlying intentions and feelings. This is definitely true for U.S. culture and most Western Hemisphere societies. . . . Teachers [must] help their students—female and male—to focus on the nature of the listening task and to be flexible in what they notice and take into their consciousness. They help students go beyond any culturally-induced gender stereotypes for listening and communicating. . . . Teachers who aid all students in using appropriate listening strategies can assist students in breaking out of gender-bound limitations. (p. 148)

Studies in gender differences and listening skills (Bacon 1992; Bacon and Finneman 1992) indicate that females use more global strategies (e.g., top-down processing, such as trying to think in the target language, using advance organizers, listening to known words and cognates, inferring meaning from context) and that males use more local strategies (e.g., bottom-up processing, such as linear processing, understanding of every word, reliance on English). Around one thousand university-level students (Bacon and Finneman 1992) and an additional fifty university-level students

(Bacon 1992) had to listen to two radio broadcasts in Spanish. Students were asked to report on their comprehension strategies immediately after listening to the text. These postlistening reports were first given in writing (Bacon and Finneman 1992), then orally (Bacon 1992). After reporting on their thinking processes, students were asked to give a recall protocol followed by a series of questions about noticed affective reactions while listening. Besides showing clear strategic patterns in gender-specific listening strategies (i.e., top-down strategies for females and bottom-up strategies for males), women also showed more affective responses than men. But overall, none of the cognitive or affective factors were found to have a negative impact since males and females showed an equal level of comprehension. In the light of such a result, Bacon (1992, p. 176) concludes that "it would be wrong to apply a generic set of strategies in classroom" since male and female recall protocols were of a similar quality.

Boyle (1987) has also investigated gender differences in listening vocabulary, using students at the Chinese University of Hong Kong as his subjects. Male Chinese students of English were found superior to females on the comprehension of heard vocabulary. Boyle mentions that these results confirmed previous studies showing that native male speakers were superior to women in listening to vocabulary. This study, however, has two major limitations that could put the conclusions into doubt. First, words to be understood were given in a paradigm, completely disconnected and out of context. Thus the study may be cited for a lack of ecological validity. When communicating with other people, we are rarely asked to understand lists of disconnected vocabulary: words are usually context-embedded. Second, in the light of gender-specific comprehension strategies (Ehrman and Oxford 1989; Nyikos 1990; Oxford, Nyikos, and Ehrman 1988; Politzer 1983), the vocabulary test was obviously biased for men's strategies. If we keep in mind that females tend to use more top-down processes than males (Bacon 1992; Bacon and Finneman 1992; Ehrman and Oxford 1989), females clearly tend to rely more on context in order to comprehend language. Because males use more bottom-up processes, males may be superior listeners in a task that does not require much top-down process. As Nyikos (1990, p. 275) observed, "[W]omen recall vocabulary significantly better under one study condition and men most successfully under another."

Nyikos (1990) investigated the use of associative memory among students learning German. One memorization strategy was assigned to each of four groups: a rote memorization group, a color-only group (using a color code for vocabulary), a picture-only group (associating pictures with words), and a color-plus-picture group (associating both a picture and a color with each word). Results indicate that males and females did not differ in the rote memorization group. However, men outscored women using the color-plus-picture memorization strategy. Women had better results in the picture-only and color-only groups. These results were consistent with research in cognitive psychology that has found that males are better in associative visual spatial tasks (Halpern 1986), while females are more global and intuitive in their approach, showing more sensitivity to colors and to art than to associated details. According to Nyikos (1990, p. 273), memorization strategies stem from gender-specific schemata acquired during the learners' childhood: "Factors in the socialization of the sexes must be recognized as exerting a strong influence on memorization processes. It follows that in verbal learning tasks, men and women end up diverging radically in what they accept as salient retrieval clues."

It is not clear, however, whether learning styles stem from nurture or nature, or whether nurture has an impact on nature, and/or vice versa. Oxford (1993) observes that brain hemispherity may explain gender differences in learning strategies:

> Springer and Deutsch (1989) assert that in men, compared to women, the left hemisphere is more lateralized (specialized) for verbal activity and the right hemisphere is more lateralized for abstract or spatial processing; women use both the left and the right hemispheres for verbal and spatial activity. In women as compared to men, part of the corpus callosum (the bundle of brain fibers linking the left and the right hemispheres) is bigger in relation to overall brain weight, allowing more information to be exchanged between the two hemispheres, thus lending strength to the possibility that women have more integrated brain function than men. (p. 69)

This theory of gender-specific lateralization process is related to studies in cognitive psychology (Cheng 1985; Rumelhart and Norman 1978; Spolsky 1988) which indicate that series of stimulus reinforcement (nurture) set various types of preferential cognitive networks among people (nature). Therefore, considering that series of social stimuli (also called the socialization process) are different for men and women, the development of gender-specific preferential cognitive networks may cause the brain to shape differently as a result of a gender-specific lateralization process stemming from gender-specific social reinforcement. In other words, women may not be *born* women; they may be *made* women. The same assumption would apply for men. This hypothesis lends itself to longitudinal and correlational neurological and neurolinguistic studies investigating the impact of the socialization process on brain shape and cognitive approaches. Such a study may enlighten us with regard to the origins of gender-specific learning strategies, that is, whether they ultimately stem from nature or nurture.

Are Females Better Language Learners?

In discussions dealing with gender differences in language learning, many people ask why researchers bother investigating gender differences in language learning since everyone knows that women are better language learners than men. This observation is so widespread that the issue is worth investigating. If the general belief is true that females are better language learners—and eventually FL learners—than males, then it should be documented with empirical research.

Ehrman and Oxford (1989) have challenged the common belief that females tend to reach a higher level of L2 proficiency because they have a greater aspiration for social approval. They hypothesized that women demonstrated a more integrative motivation when learning a FL than men because their native communicative style was more socially based than the style of men. Men, on the other hand, were hypothesized to demonstrate a more instrumental motivational orientation; that is, they were learning a FL in order to be more competitive professionally. Some research has, in fact, already been conducted (Ludwig 1983) to investigate such hypotheses. The findings indicate that a majority of male students signed up for FL classes because they believed them to be useful (instrumental motivation), whereas female students were more likely to register for FL classes because they were interested in the target language culture and planned to travel and live in the target language country (more closely related to integrative motivation). Differences between genders, however, were not statistically significant, and further research needs to be conducted regarding gender-specific motivations for learning a FL.

The psychological literature reports small but consistent gender differences in performance on cognitive tests involving language and mathematics (Maccoby and Jacklin 1974; Hyde 1981; Lips 1989). Lips (1989), for example, notes:

> By the onset of adolescence, girls tend to outperform boys on a variety of language-related tasks, whereas boys tend to outscore girls on mathematics tests and test of visual–spatial ability. Despite the small size of these differences and the wide individual variation among children, the differences have sometimes been cited as evidence that girls and boys are naturally suited for different kinds of tasks and should prepare for

different kinds of work. . . . Because the differences are so small, the argument misses the point. For example, Hyde (1981), making the initial assumption that a person would have to be in the top 5 percent of the range of spatial abilities to be qualified for a profession such as engineering, calculated that, if spatial ability were the only determining factor, the ratio of males to females in such professions would be 2 to 1. Since the ratio of men to women in engineering has never been less than 20 to 1, gender differences in spatial ability could conceivably explain only a small part of the male dominance of the engineering professions. (p. 206)

Lips's work indicates that cognitive tests are inconclusive and cannot be considered as reliable placement tests—although they are often used this way—and that such tests are actually used to reinforce stereotypical roles. Lips's analysis (1989) also shows that the socialization process begins long before children enter school and that results on cognitive tests reflect, to a greater extent, nurture rather than nature. Similarly, cognitive tests have been found to reflect teaching practices and parental expectations. Thirty-three second-grade teachers were observed during instruction and found to spend more time teaching reading to girls and teaching mathematics to boys (Leinhardt, Seewald, and Engel 1979). Similarly, a large-scale study focusing on first graders in Baltimore indicated that girls and boys enter school with gender-specific ideas of what is important (Entwisle, Alexander, Pallos, and Godigan 1987). Generally, girls were concerned with obeying rules and good behavior, whereas boys wanted to be able to do well in arithmetic. Interestingly, the same study indicates that African-American parents give fewer gender stereotypic messages to their daughters than European-American parents do: African-American girls and boys did not show any significant differences in preferences and achievement tests, whereas European-American girls and boys did. In a similar study conducted by Stables (1990), over 2,300 pupils aged thirteen to fourteen in seven mixed-sex and six single-sex British schools were asked to rank their school subjects in terms of liking and perceived importance. Stables (1990) found that:

> The polarization of subject interest between the sexes is greater in mixed than in single-sex schools, at least in relation to Physical Sciences and Modern Languages . . . [where] boys are more affected than girls by the presence of the opposite sex in terms of science interest, suggesting that they may be more prone to sex-role stereotyping than the girls in this respect. (p. 225)

In Stables's study, single-gender educated boys rated high on drama, biology, and languages, whereas boys in mixed schools enjoyed physics and sciences more. Similarly, physics was better liked by girls in single-sex schools than by girls in mixed-gender schools. Modern languages were preferred by both single-gender educated boys and girls. Clearly, Stables's study did not lead to any conclusive evidence regarding the superiority of females in language learning.

A report published in London by the Center of Information on Language Teaching and Research (Powel 1986) was based on a meta-analysis of numerous British investigations in FL classes and gender differences. The results gathered from this study were also inconclusive: "Where differences [in language results] do occur [between males and females], they are seldom statistically significant" (Powel 1986, p. 42). As a matter of fact, sex-linked polarization of subject preferences was found to fade out in single-gender schools, where male students were as good in foreign languages as female students and female students were as good as males in mathematics (Loulidi 1989; Powel 1986), which confirms Stables's (1990) observation mentioned above. Loulidi (1989) found that gender-related hidden curricula are not as acute in the absence of the opposite sex. These studies led to the conclusion that "female superiority in FL is a myth" (Powel 1986, p. 42). What is not a myth, however, is that societal stereotypes affect the students' attitude toward a particular subject matter. As Fennema (1987, p. 329) has observed, "The stereotyping of subjects by learners can affect performance. Children choose tasks they identify as sex-appropriate. . . . [T]he unstated goals of education have included training males and females for the separate and not equal spheres of men's and women's lives." Fennema (1987) mentions that civil rights legislation originally written for the protection of ethnic groups was amended to prohibit sex discrimination as well. Something that civil rights legislation does not account for, however, is that hidden values are still generating sex (as well as racial) discrimination. Fennema (1987) observed that females and males performed at about the same level in every subject area in elementary schools, but that females became better at languages and males became better at mathematics in the later elementary years because of a hidden but nevertheless systematic tracking process. Differences in enrollment are due to the pressure of stereotypical sex roles imposed by tacit or apparent values. Fennema surmised that affective factors stemming from an internal belief system play a significant role in academic success: "Achievement in an 'inappropriate' domain is perceived as a failure to fulfill one's sex-role identity" (p. 341).

Other studies have indicated that learning atmosphere could affect language results. For example, Powel (1986) found that males studying a FL perform better under pressure and in a competitive environment as opposed to females, who perform better when not under pressure. Cross (1983), on the other hand, explains gender differences on the basis of the teacher's gender. In Cross's study, boys perform better than girls, and differences are explained as follows: "The teaching of modern languages is largely in the hands of female teachers. In the schools investigated here, the language departments enjoyed a more balanced staffing, with comparatively more young male teachers in evidence [than in most schools]" (Cross 1983, p. 159).

Summary and Conclusions

The research conducted to date underlines the fact that gender-specific patterns of behavior are relevant factors and important sociolinguistic variables in FL classrooms. More specifically, gender-specific behavior seems to be fostered mostly in mixed-gender groups and schools. This chapter established that females are not better L2 learners than males, contrary to what is commonly believed. Instead, this chapter underlined the strong impact a hidden curriculum can have in shaping gender-specific motivations and attitudes in learning foreign languages. Studies reviewed in this chapter caution us against the use of old and reedited classroom materials that tend to reflect stronger stereotypes than those that actually exist in society. Mention was also made of the fact that gender-specific personalities and cognitive styles play a significant role in the way students learn a FL. Females and males tend to have a gender-related personality profile which in turn tends to be connected to gender-specific learning strategies. Studies have shown that females are often most comfortable with affective and social meaning, as well as with top-down strategies, whereas males tend to prefer referential, factual, and information-oriented discourse, as well as bottom-up strategies. In the light of both anthropological and L2 studies, I am led to hypothesize that cognitive differences between males and females do not stem exclusively from inherently natural and static neurolinguistic preferential networks: the socialization process undergone by L2 male and female learners, whether at home or at school, past or present, may play a much stronger role in the shaping of cognitive networks than previously admitted. Indeed, there is every reason to believe that nurture may very well affect and shape nature to the point where males and females end up developing different cognitive styles.

On the subject of classroom communication and interaction, studies indicate that males tend to speak in classrooms more than females, and that females tend to listen more and to use shorter statements. Findings in L2 development tend to echo findings in first language use, and suggest a possible transfer from the students' respective genderlect in the native language to the target language. This hypothetical transfer from the native genderlect is already supported by recent research that indicates the tendency of males and females to adopt gender-specific linguistic markers and sociolinguistic communicative patterns while using the target language. To date, gender studies have essentially focused on student populations. Yet this chapter raised the importance of gender differences and group dynamics in L2 classrooms where the hidden curriculum of instructors and teaching material can have a serious effect on the attitude and motivation of both males and females vis-à-vis foreign languages.

These conclusions enable me to make some recommendations for L2 instruction. One very important suggestion is vigilance. Instructors have to remain on the *qui vive* and make sure to readjust possible interactional imbalances when males tend to intervene too often in whole-class and group discussions. This can be done by encouraging female students to initiate more responses during whole-class activities, in order to reestablish a balance in conversational turn-taking. During group exchanges instructors should make it a point to check that students feel comfortable and speak more or less equally with their partners. Mixed-gender groups may need to be closely monitored, and eventually some students may need to be reassigned to a new partner. Instructors also need to pay attention to their students' reactions vis-à-vis the types of activities used in class. A sensitive commitment to our students implies that we recognize our students' personalities, possibly by organizing more than one activity at the same time. Relatively short multiple activity sessions, during which students may be allowed to choose the most appealing game, discussion, and so on, may have an unexpected positive effect. This, of course, remains to be empirically tested. Mention was made earlier in this chapter, for instance, that content-based activities may be more appealing to male students than to female students, and that females may be more at ease with activities in which students are requested to speak or write about themselves and others. Activities based on either bottom-up or top-down strategies are also likely to be attended to differently by males and females. During such activities male and female students working together may not necessarily disagree. If interacting in a spirit of mutual respect, they may also assist each other and help each other both to build on personal strengths and to expand into less preferred learning approaches. Yet research still needs to determine whether mutual assistance is more likely to take place in male-only groups, female-only groups, or in mixed-gender groups. Research is also needed to determine whether a positive group dynamic helps to go beyond socially acquired gender-specific learning strategies.

Since activities differ in nature and since there seems to be a gender-specific preference for certain activity types, caution is also required in test design. Tests are composed of "activities" and may eventually lead to gender bias if activity selection is not done cautiously. One way to avoid gender bias in exams, besides avoiding the use of sexist language and of gender-specific schemata, is to pretest the format of some of the activities that may lend themselves to a potential bias. Such pretests can be done through the evaluation or observation of the students' comfort and language outcome while going through such activities during a lesson. Because communication is the goal of today's language teaching, if students happen to feel uncomfortable with communicative and open-ended formats, extra practice will be needed until all students, females and males, feel comfortable with communicative activities.

Another very important recommendation hinges on our ability to detect the subconscious or hidden values we as instructors may have. We may have a conscious image of ourselves but still accidentally convey hidden societal values internalized during our own childhoods. Gender-related, hidden values are often detected among instructors, both females and males, who tend to praise and call more on male students than on female students, or who refer to males as "men" and to females as "girls" in spite of their similar age. In order to become aware of possible gender-biased language use, or of gender-biased sociolinguistic behavior, a colleague, or even a friend from the outside, could be asked to attend some classes and to look specifically for possible gender biases in the way we instructors interact with our students. Videotaping a sample of lessons for the purpose of a self-analysis would also be a valuable approach. Yet the perspective of someone else may lead to a more comprehensive analysis, since it is always possible for the individual involved to remain blind to possible gender biases.

Finally, classroom material also has to be carefully selected not solely on the basis of the underlying pedagogical philosophy, the organization of lessons, and the activity types of a textbook, but also after very close scrutiny for a possible hidden agenda. Gender bias can be detected by sampling dialogues and finding out whether males are primarily leading conversations and whether females are primarily responders. Gender bias can also be detected in the way females are represented in dialogues, pictures, and drawings, for example, females who are younger than males and confined to traditionally female roles. To date, avoiding the use of sexist language has been the main area of effort toward creating less biased textbooks. Yet hidden values and sexist ideas may still unintentionally occur both in dialogues and activities, not only in the way gender-specific roles are presented, but also in the ways males and females interact from a sociolinguistic perspective in written and oral dialogues. This implies that in addition to textbooks, ancillaries such as audiotapes, videos, software, workbooks, and so on require very close scrutiny.

For further recommendations and insights on gender issues, *Gender in the Classroom: Power and Pedagogy* (Gabriel and Smithson 1990) is a valuable reference, providing an interesting analysis of the dynamics that stem from gender differences in classroom communication and interaction, although not directly related to L2 instruction.

Instructors concerned with the influence of gender on L2 acquisition often lack the necessary research to support or even understand the interactional behaviors and learning patterns that take place in their classrooms. The goal of this chapter was to fill in this gap. Now that they have been enlightened by the results of dependable studies reported in this chapter, instructors can pursue further research. Such research should include:

1. more studies to investigate how activity types are perceived by female and male students;

2. further research on mixed- and same-gender group activities;

3. more attention to gender-related motivations;

4. investigation into the possible effects of the instructor's gender and perceived expertise in L2 classrooms;

5. attention to the attitude of instructors, whether female or male, toward female and male students;

6. surveys of classes taught by mixed-gender teams to find out if female and male students accommodate linguistically to the target language spoken by either female or male instructors;

7. more studies that investigate how females are presented in FL teaching material across languages—to date, studies of this type have only been conducted in ESL;

8. finally, close scrutiny of gender-related sociolinguistic transfer from L1 to L2. These are only a few suggestions to expand gender studies beyond the single issue of learning styles and learning strategies in L2 use.

This chapter highlighted the fact that gender issues should be addressed from multiple angles. The impact on L2 use of the socialization process undergone by our students, as well as the effects of the instructional context and hidden curriculum, deserves to be thoroughly investigated in addition to cognitive factors, in order to comprehend gender differences in their full complexities.

Works Cited

Adamson, H. D., and Vera M. Regan. 1991. The Acquisition of Community Speech Norms by Asian Immigrants Learning English as a Second Language. *Studies in Second Language Acquisition* 13: 1–22.

Aries, Elizabeth. 1976. Interaction Patterns and Themes of Male, Female, and Mixed Groups. *Small Group Behaviour* 7: 7–18.

———. 1987. Gender and Communication. In *Sex and Gender,* edited by P. Shaver and C. Hendrick, 27–36. Newbury Park, CA: Sage.

Bacon, Susan M. 1992. The Relationship between Gender, Comprehension, Processing Strategies, Cognitive and Affective Response in Foreign Language Listening. *Modern Language Journal* 76: 160–78.

Bacon, Susan, and Michael Finneman. 1992. The Identification of Gender Differences in University Foreign Language Students in Relation to General Language-Learning Beliefs Dealing with Authentic Input. *Language Learning* 42: 471–95.

Beebe, Leslie M. 1985. Choosing the Right Stuff. In *Input in Second Language Acquisition,* edited by S. M. Gass and C. G. Madden, 404–14. Rowley, MA: Newbury House.

Boyle, Joseph P. 1987. Sex Differences in Listening Vocabulary. *Language Learning* 37: 273–84.

Brown, Penelope. 1990. Gender, Politeness, and Confrontation in Tenejapa. *Discourse Processes* 13: 123–41.

Cameron, Deborah. 1992. *Feminism and Linguistic Theory.* New York: St. Martin's Press.

Cheng, Paul. W. 1985. Restructuring versus Automaticity: Alternative Accounts of Skill Acquisition. *Psychological Review* 92: 214–23.

Cheshire, John. 1982. *Variation in an English Dialect.* Cambridge: Cambridge University Press.

Coates, Jennifer. 1986. *Women, Men and Language: A Sociolinguistic Account of Sex Differences in Language.* London: Longman.

Cross, David. 1983. Sex Differences in Achievement. *System* 11: 159–62.

Daly, Mary. 1991. "I Thank Thee Lord, That Thou Has Not Created Me a Woman." In *The Gender Reader,* edited by E. Ashton-Jones and G. A. Olson, 158–61. Boston: Allyn and Bacon.

Davies, Lynn, and Roland Meighan. 1975. A Review of Schooling and Sex Roles. *Educational Review* 27: 165–78.

Eakins, Barbara W., and Gene Eakins. 1978. *Sex Differences in Human Communication.* Boston: Houghton Mifflin.

Ehrman, Madeline, and Rebecca L. Oxford. 1989. Effects of Sex Differences, Career Choice, and Psychological Type on Adult Language Learning Strategies. *Modern Language Journal* 73: 1–13.

Entwisle, Doris R., Karl L. Alexander, Aaron L. Pallas, and Doris Gadigan. 1987. The Emergent Academic Self-Image of First Graders: Its Response to Social Structure. *Child Development* 58: 190–206.

Fennema, Elizabeth. 1987. Sex-Related Differences in Education: Myths, Reality, and Interventions. In *Educators' Handbook: A Research Perspective,* edited by V. Richardson-Koehler and D. C. Berliner, 329–47. New York: Longman.

Fishman, Pamela. 1980. Conversational Insecurity. In *Language: Social Psychological Perspectives,* edited by H. Giles, W. P. Robinson, and P. M. Smith, 134–58. Oxford, UK: Pergamon Press.

Gabriel, Susan L., and Isaiah Smithson, eds. 1990. *Gender in the Classroom: Power and Pedagogy.* Urbana, IL: University of Illinois Press.

Gass, Susan, and Evangeline M. Varonis. 1985. Task Variation and NNS/NNS Negotiation of Meaning. In *Input in Second Language Acquisition,* edited by S. M. Gass and C. G. Madden, 149–61. Rowley, MA: Newbury House.

———. 1986. Sex differences in NNS/NNS Interactions. In *Talking to Learn: Conversation in Second Language Acquisition,* edited by Richard Day, 327–51. Rowley, MA: Newbury House.

Goodwin, Marjorie. 1980. Directive-Response Speech Sequences in Girls' and Boys' Task Activities. In *Women and Language in Literature and Society,* edited by S. McConnel-Ginet, R. Borker, and N. Furman, 210–29. New York: Praeger.

Halpern, Diane F. 1986. *Sex Differences in Cognitive Abilities.* Hillsdale, NJ: Erlbaum.

Ho, David Y. 1987. Prediction of Foreign Language Skills: A Canonical and Part Canonical Correlation Study. *Contemporary Educational Psychology* 12: 119–30.

Holmes, Janet. 1988. Paying Compliments: A Sex-Preferential Politeness Strategy. *Journal of Pragmatics* 12: 445–65.

————. 1989. Stirring Up the Dust: The Importance of Sex as Variable in the ESL Classroom. Paper presented at the Australian Teachers of English to Speakers of Other Languages (ATESOL) 6th annual Summer School, Sydney, Australia.

————. 1992. Women's Talk in Public Context. *Discourse and Society* 3: 131–50.

Hyde, Janet. 1981. How Large Are Cognitive Gender Differences? *American Psychologist* 36: 892–901.

Johnson, Donna M., and Duane H. Roen. 1992. Complimenting and Involvement in Peer Reviews: Gender Variation. *Language in Society* 21: 27–57.

Jones, Deborah. 1980. Gossip: Notes on Women's Oral Culture. *Women's Studies International Quarterly* 3: 193–98.

Krueger, Merle, and Frank Ryan, eds. 1993. *Language and Content: Discipline- and Content-Based Approaches to Language Study.* Lexington, MA: D. C. Heath.

Labov, William. 1966. *The Social Stratification of English in New York City.* Washington, DC: Center for Applied Linguistics.

Lakoff, Robin. 1975. *Language and Woman's Place.* New York: Harper and Row.

Lee, Barbara. 1986. French Is Hard Because It's a Different Language. *British Journal of Language Teaching* 24: 71–76.

Leinhardt, Gaea, Andrea Seewald, and M. Engel. 1979. Learning What's Taught: Sex Differences in Instruction. *Journal of Educational Psychology* 71: 432–39.

Lever, Janet. 1978. Sex Differences in the Complexity of Children's Play and Games. *American Sociological Review* 43: 471–83.

Lips, Hilary. 1989. Gender-Role Socialization: Lessons in Femininity. In *Women: A Feminist Perspective,* edited by Jo Freeman, 197–216. Mountain View, CA: Mayfield.

Liski, Erkki, and Simon Puntanen. 1983. A Study of the Statistical Foundations of Group Conversation Tests in Spoken English. *Language Learning* 33: 225–46.

Loulidi, Rafik. 1989. Is Language Learning Really a "Female Business"? *Modern Languages: Journal of the Modern Language Association* 70: 201–8.

Ludwig, Jeannette. 1983. Attitudes and Expectations: A Profile of Female and Male Students of College French, German, and Spanish. *Modern Language Journal* 67: 216–27.

Maccoby, Eleonor E., and Carol N. Jacklin. 1974. *The Psychology of Sex Differences.* Stanford, CA: Stanford University Press.

Malz, Daniel N., and Ruth A. Borker. 1982. A Cultural Approach to Male–Female Miscommunication. In *Language and Social Identity,* edited by John J. Gumperz, 196–216. Cambridge: Cambridge University Press.

Markham, Paul L. 1988. Gender Differences and the Perceived Expertness of the Speaker as Factors in ESL Listening Recall. *TESOL Quarterly* 22: 397–406.

Meunier-Cinko, Lydie E. 1993. Cooperative CALL and Gender Differences. In *The Selected Proceedings of the Computer Assisted Learning and Instruction Consortium 1993 Annual Symposium on "Assessment,"* edited by F. L. Borchardt and E.M.T. Johnson, 107–11. Durham, NC: Duke University Press.

Milroy, Lesley. 1980. *Language and Social Networks.* Oxford, UK: Basil Blackwell.

Myers, Isabel B. 1986. *Introduction to Type.* Palo Alto, CA: Consulting Psychologists Press.

Nyikos, Martha. 1990. Sex-Related Differences in Adult Language Learning: Socialization and Memory Factors. *Modern Language Journal* 74: 273–87.

Oxford, Rebecca L. 1993. Instructional Implications of Gender Differences in Second/Foreign Language (L2) Learning Styles and Strategies. *Applied Language Learning* 4: 64–94.

Oxford, Rebecca L., and Madeline Ehrman. 1988. Psychological Type and Adult Language Learning Strategies: A Pilot Study. *Journal of Psychological Types* 16: 22–32.

Oxford, Rebecca L., Martha Nyikos, and Madeline Ehrman. 1988. *Vive la différence?* Reflections on Sex Differences in Use of Language Learning Strategies. *Foreign Language Annals* 21: 321–29.

Pica, Theresa, Lloyd Holliday, and Nora Lewis. 1991. Language Learning through Interaction. What Role Does Gender Play? *Studies in Second Language Acquisition* 13: 343–76.

Pearson, Bethyl A., and Samuel K. Lee. 1992. Discourse Structure of Direction Giving: Effects of Native/Nonnative Speaker Status and Gender. *TESOL Quarterly* 26: 113–27.

Politzer, Robert. 1983. Research Notes: An Exploratory Study of Self-Reported Language Learning Behaviors and Their Relation to Achievement. *Studies in Second Language Acquisition* 6: 54–68.

Powel, Bob. 1986. Boys, Girls, and Languages. Eric Doc. No. ED276253.

Rumelhart, David, and Daniel Norman. 1978. Accretion, Tuning, and Restructuring: Three Modes of Learning. In *Semantic Factors in Cognition,* edited by J. Dotton and R. Klatzky, 134–67. Hillsdale, NJ: Erlbaum.

Scarcella, Robin, and Rebecca L. Oxford. 1992. *The Tapestry of Language Learning. The Individual in the Communicative Classroom.* Boston: Heinle & Heinle.

Schumann, John H. 1978. *The Pidginization Process.* Rowley, MA: Newbury House.

Schweickart, Patrocinio. P. 1986. Reading Ourselves: Toward a Feminist Theory. In *Gender and Reading,* edited by E. A. Flynn and P. P. Schweickart, 31–62. Baltimore: Johns Hopkins University Press.

Spender, Dale. 1980. *Man Made Language.* London: Routledge and Kegan.

Spolsky, Bernard. 1988. Bridging the Gap: A General Theory of Second Language Learning. *TESOL Quarterly* 22: 377–96.

Springer, Sally P., and Georg Deutsch. 1989. *Left Brain, Right Brain.* New York: Freeman.

Stables, Andrew. 1990. Differences between Pupils from Mixed- and Single-Sex Schools in Their Enjoyment of School Subjects and in Their Attitudes to Science and to School. *Educational Review* 42: 221–30.

Steinem, Gloria. 1991. Men and Women Talking. In *The Gender Reader,* edited by E. Ashton-Jones and G. A. Olson, 299–312. Boston: Allyn and Bacon.

Stern, Daniel N. 1994. The Sense of Verbal Self. In *The Women Language Debate,* edited by C. Roman, S. Juhasz, and C. Millwe, 199–215. New Brunswick, NJ: Rutgers University Press.

Sunderland, Jane. 1992. Gender in the EFL Classroom. *ELT Journal* 46: 81–91.

Swacker, Marjorie. 1975. The Sex of the Speaker as a Sociolinguistic Variable. In *Language and Sex,* edited by B. Thorne and N. Henley, 35–49. Rowley, MA: Newbury House.

Tannen, Deborah. 1990. *You Just Don't Understand.* New York: Ballantine Books .

———. 1992. Rethinking Power and Solidarity in Gender and Dominance. In *Text and Context: Cross-Disciplinary Perspectives on Language Study,* edited by C. Kramsch and S. McConnell-Ginet, 135–47. Lexington, MA: D. C. Heath.

Tarone, Elaine. 1979. Interlanguage as Chameleon. *Language Learning* 29: 181–91.

Trudgill, Peter. 1972. Sex, Covert Prestige, and Linguistic Change in the Urban British English of Norwick. *Language in Society* 1: 88–104.

———. 1983. *On Dialect.* Oxford, UK: Basil Blackwell.

Vygotsky, Lev S. 1978. *Mind in Society: The Development of Higher Psychological Processes.* Cambridge, MA: Harvard University Press.

West, Candace. 1984. When the Doctor Is a "Lady": Power, Status, and Gender in Physician–Patient Encounters. *Symbolic Interaction* 7: 87–106.

West, Candace, and Sarah Fenstermaker. 1993. Power, Inequality, and the Accomplishment of Gender: An Ethnomethodological View. In *Theory on Gender: Feminism on Theory,* edited by Paula England, 151–74. Hawthorne, NY: Aldine de Gruter.

Wittig, Monique. 1992. *The Straight Mind.* Boston: Beacon Press.

Zimmerman, Don, and Candace West. 1975. Sex Roles, Interruptions, and Silences in Conversation. In *Language and Sex: Difference and Dominance,* edited by B. Thorne and N. Henley, 105–29. Rowley, MA: Newbury House.

Part II

Research Studies on Learner Variables

Weakest and Strongest Learners in Intensive Language Training: A Study of Extremes

Madeline Ehrman
Foreign Service Institute

Introduction

Many language training programs seek to select students. For example, they may seek the fastest learners for accelerated training or the weakest for remedial training or even for exclusion from training programs. In addition, even in the more usual situation—classes with a range of performance levels—it is often helpful to understand what characterizes the weakest and strongest learners in order to maximize their strengths and minimize their weaknesses. This study looks at the weakest and strongest 2–4 percent of a large group of adult students in a federal language training program to see how they can be characterized in terms of a wide range of individual difference variables often addressed in the literature of second language acquisition.[1] Although the subjects were not university students, nearly all were at least college graduates and thus may in some ways be similar to university students, especially those in majors that lead to careers in foreign affairs (e.g., international relations or foreign language and culture).

The students described here are drawn from a much larger sample in use for a multivariate study in progress that is examining the effects of individual differences on student achievement in intensive language training at the Foreign Service Institute (FSI), the training branch of the U.S. Department of State. Variable categories in the study include language learning aptitude, demographics, preferred learning strategies, motivation and anxiety, and personality factors.

Review of Literature

A number of individual difference categories are proving of interest in second language classrooms. These include language aptitude, age, sex, motivation, anxiety, self-esteem, tolerance of ambiguity, risk taking, language learning strategies, and language learning styles. Among the last named are often included personality type factors. Much detailed information on individual differences is available in the work of Ehrman (1990 1994), Ehrman and Oxford (1990 and in press), Galbraith and Gardner (1988), Oxford (1992), Oxford and Ehrman (1993, in press), and Skehan (1989). Although these variable categories are treated separately below, most of the cited findings indicate complex interrelationships among them.

Aptitude

Several tests have been devised to attempt to measure language learning aptitude; these have been of particular interest to government agencies and others who want to select students for training. The oldest of these is the Modern Language Aptitude Test (MLAT; Carroll and Sapon 1959; research summarized in Carroll 1990); it is still used by a number of universities and by at least one government agency. The U.S. Department of Defense agencies have developed their own language aptitude measures; their validity appears to be comparable to the MLAT, according to a personal communication (1993) from James Child a testing expert in the Department of Defense. Another such test commonly used for adolescents and children is the Pimsleur Language Aptitude Battery (described in Skehan 1989). Although some have suggested that such measures—developed for audiolingual language teaching—are incompatible with less structured, highly communicative language teaching approaches (see Parry and Stansfield 1990), at least one study shows that in fact the validity of the MLAT remains essentially unchanged since it was developed, despite substantial changes in training methodology (Ehrman and Oxford, in press).

Age

Most studies find that age is related to language learning success, generally finding that younger learners do better with respect to critical periods, type of input, and certain affective and sociocultural features (Oxford 1992; Schleppegrell 1987; Singleton 1989). However, one study of the same sample examined for this research showed that for a group of adults between roughly twenty-five and forty-five, the correlation of younger age with speaking and reading proficiency was only about .30—enough to be worthy of mention, but far from sufficient to be a selection factor for training (Ehrman and Oxford, in press).

Sex

Many studies in various parts of the world have found some advantages for females over males for use of conscious language learning strategies (Oxford, in press) and for listening skills (Larsen-Freeman and Long 1991). Oxford, Nyikos, and Ehrman (1988) cite a number of works that found that females tend to perform better than males in language classrooms. However, the correlations from the current FSI study (Ehrman and Oxford, in press) show no significant relationship between sex and end-of-training proficiency in a wide range of languages. (This finding suggests that sex differences found so far may be related to moderating variables such as education level, career choice, or interests, since the sample is generally homogeneous by sex on these variables.)

Motivation

Countless publications have addressed motivation and have found it to be a key variable in language learning success. Most readers are likely to be familiar with the distinction between instrumental (career-oriented) motivation and integrative (cultural-merging) motivation for language learning (Au 1988; Gardner 1985a; Horwitz 1990; Oxford and Shearin 1994). Additional investigation has added more variables to be considered in evaluating motivation, including need for achievement, fear of failure and possibly even fear of success in the language classroom, self-efficacy, and attribution of locus of control to personal effort versus outside factors like fate or society (Oxford and Shearin 1994). These authors note that motivation is related to expectancy of success and the value students place on such success, and that goals must be clear, challenging, and reachable, with feedback on goal achievement; in addition, mode of instruction also affects motivation (e.g., mastery learning may be more motivating than norm-referenced learning). The field of industrial-organizational psychology distinguishes between motivation due to extrinsic rewards and the intrinsic motivation that is activated by skilled teaching; the latter is thought to be more powerful than external rewards (Beck 1990). Extrinsic motivation may be similar to Gardner's (1985a) instrumental motivation, while intrinsic motivation may well encompass much of Gardner's integrative motivation as well as other motivations such as a desire to feel self-efficacy.

Anxiety

Language anxiety appears in a variety of forms—avoidance, face-saving humor, physical activity, psychosomatic symptoms—and has been shown to be deleterious among university students (Horwitz and Young 1991). Indeed, Horwitz (1990) suggests that in the language learning environment all anxiety is likely to be debilitating because language learning is such a complex and emotionally involved process. Others (e.g., Brown 1987) suggest that some degree of anxiety can actually be helpful for language learning. The correlation findings for the population reported on in this study confirm the latter view, at least for high-functioning adults (Ehrman and Oxford, in press).

Tolerance of Ambiguity and Risk Taking

Ely (1989) describes tolerance of ambiguity as acceptance of confusing situations and lack of clear lines of demarcation. Ehrman (1993) describes it in Piagetian terms as the ability not only to let new information in, but to hold contradictions in mind while they are integrated into new conceptual frameworks. She operationalizes tolerance of ambiguity through the concept of ego boundaries, readdressing Giora's (1972) concept of "language ego," showing a complex relationship between ego boundaries and learning success. Other studies have found that tolerance of moderate levels of ambiguity is related to persistence in language learning (Chapelle 1983; Naiman, Fröhlich, and Stern 1975) and frequency of use of certain learning strategies (Ehrman and Oxford 1989, 1990; Ely 1989). Risk taking is linked to tolerance of ambiguity, in that tolerance of ambiguity appears to lead to willingness to take some risks in language learning; and risk taking is an essential for progress (Beebe 1983; Brown 1987; Ely 1986; Stevick 1976).

Language Learning Strategies

There appears to be agreement among a number of authors that language learning strategies can be described as specific behaviors or techniques used by learners to increase their language growth (Cohen 1990; O'Malley and Chamot 1990; Oxford 1990; Wenden 1991; Wenden and Rubin 1987); they are selected in the light of the task, the goals, the curriculum, and the individual's personality and stage of learning (Ehrman 1989; Ehrman and Oxford 1990; Oxford 1990; Skehan 1989). The ability to use the right strategies at the right time appears to be more important than sheer number of strategies (Vann and Abraham 1989); hence language learning research has focused on cognitive and metacognitive learning strategies such as language practice or hypothesis formation (cognitive) or planning and evaluating one's study (metacognitive) (Oxford 1990).

Language Learning Styles

Language learning styles are the general approaches students use to learn or that affect their response to variations in curriculum or teaching technique (Ehrman 1990; Oxford 1992; Oxford, Ehrman, and Lavine 1991). One common distinction is analytic versus global (Schmeck 1988): analytic students tend to like to work within clear categories and to analyze components of language, whereas global students are likely to prefer conversation to rule learning and practice (Oxford, Ehrman, and Lavine 1991; Schmeck 1988). Another common category is sensory channel preference for learning activities; the usual distinctions are visual, auditory, and kinesthetic. Reid (1987) showed differences for ESL students' sensory preferences by national origin—for example, Asian learners tended to prefer visual input.

Within the category of learning style come personality preference variables. One common measure of such variables has a very rich history of use in educational settings: the Myers-Briggs Type Indicator (MBTI; Lawrence 1984). Its four dimensions are extraversion-introversion, sensing-intuition, thinking-feeling, and judging-perceiving (Myers and McCaulley 1985). Although it has seemed natural to speculate that the best learners would be extraverts because of their willingness to speak out and interact (Brown 1987), findings by Busch (1982) failed to confirm this hypothesis, and some recent research (Ehrman 1989; Ehrman and Oxford 1990, in press) indicates that introverts are not disadvantaged, at least in the small, long-term intensive classes characteristic of FSI. *Intuitive learners,* who tend to prefer abstract, random, future-oriented learning, seek generalizations and meaning; they are often bored by concrete, step-by-step learning. On the other hand, *sensing learners* find facts intrinsically interesting, may be less interested than intuitives in underlying principles, and tend to prefer concrete, sequential learning. *Thinking-oriented students* prefer logical and impersonal processing, whereas *feeling-oriented learners* want to make most forms of learning personal and grounded in relationships. *Judgers* seek closure, product, and a clear external structure; *perceivers* may resist external structure, be less oriented to meeting requirements, and may respond favorably to the relatively unstructured aspects of communicative methodology (Ehrman and Oxford 1989, 1990).

Although learners are likely to learn best initially when at least some attention is paid to their stylistic "comfort zone," those who can eventually use strategies not necessarily related to their preferred styles appear to be at an advantage; indeed, some level of versatility seems to be prerequisite to effective learning at some times (Ehrman 1989; Ehrman and Oxford 1990; Oxford and Ehrman, in press; Oxford, Ehrman, and Lavine 1991).

Methodology

Sample

The 15 very weak and the 27 very strong FSI students whose characteristics are addressed here were drawn from a subsample of 770 FSI students who had completed training. The subsample in turn was taken from a complete sample to date of over 1,200 students entering intensive long-term language training. For the 770-person subsample, the mean age was thirty-nine (SD 9) and the educational level averaged between B.A. and M.A. The sample was 55 percent male; the median number of languages previously studied was two. Most of the group (71 percent) were from the Department of State, while 10 percent were from the Department of Defense, 8 percent were from the U.S. Information Agency, 7 percent were from the Agency for International Development, and the rest (4 percent) were from other government agencies like the Department of Agriculture, the Department of Commerce, and the Drug Enforcement Agency. Of the total sample, 83 percent were employees, and 17 percent were spouses or college-age children. Of the dependents, 84 percent were female. English was the native language of 99 percent of the students. These students spent an average of twenty weeks in full-time intensive training, with a range of eight to forty-four weeks. Slightly less than one-third each were learning Spanish (29.6 percent) or French (28.5 percent). In order of numbers of students, the other thirty-two languages studied were Italian, Portuguese, Chinese, Arabic, Russian, Thai, Turkish, Hebrew, German, Dutch, Urdu, Indonesian, Burmese, Polish, Romanian, Serbo-Croatian, Greek, Japanese, Korean, Czech, Danish, Hindi, Bengali, Afrikaans, Finnish, Norwegian, Bulgarian, Cantonese, Lao, Swahili, Swedish, and Tagalog. Median end-of-training scores were S-2 R-2. (Scores are discussed in "Measures of Student Language Proficiency," below.)

Filter Variables

The extreme student groups were designated by two dichotomous filter variables, one for the weak students versus all others, and one for the strong students versus all others. Both variables were determined through a combination of difficulty of language category, number of weeks of study, and end-of-training speaking score (EOTS). Language categories are established on the basis of relative difficulty for English speakers to learn; normal maximum training lengths differ among categories as follows: Category 1 (Western European languages), twenty-four weeks; Category 2 (Swahili, Indonesian, Malay), thirty-six weeks; Category 3 (all others except Category 4), forty-four weeks; Category 4 (Arabic, Chinese, Japanese, Korean), eighty-eight weeks. There were so few students studying Category 2 languages in the sample that this category was excluded in this study. EOTS is the score from the FSI end-of-training interactive proficiency test, which is described below under "Instrumentation."

Weak Student Variable

Cases were selected if start-of-training speaking score was S-0 or S-0+ (beginners) *and* end-of-training speaking proficiency score (EOTS) < 1, *and:*

Category of Language	Number of Weeks >
1	16
3	30
4	36

Strong Student Variable

Cases were selected if start-of-training speaking score was S-0 or S-0+ (beginners) *and:*

Category of Language	Number of Weeks	End-of-Training Speaking
1	> 20	3+
1	< 18	3
3	> 36	3+
3	< 24	3
4	> 36	2+
4	< 26	2

Numbers of Strong and Weak Students

The numbers of extremely weak and strong subjects in the results cited below vary because not every participating student completed every instrument. Thus both total numbers of those for whom end-of-training data and any given instrument are available vary, as do the numbers of extreme (strong or weak) students whose scores are available for each instrument. Some of the N's are low but are included because they are at least suggestive and appear to be consistent with trends indicated for other instruments.

The very strong students represent about 3.5–4 percent of their various subsamples; the weak students represent about 2–3 percent of their respective subsamples. The difference in proportions is attributable to two factors. The first is an artifact of the cutting scores for number of weeks of training and level of end-of-training speaking proficiency that were used in the formulas given above for selecting members of each category. The second reflects the reality that a certain amount of screening of students takes place before they are ever sent to training: students with a poor track record in language learning or with poor MLAT scores may never be selected for training in the first place.

Individual Difference Variables

Data Collection

Data collection was done through questionnaires. Students were asked to complete a biographical data form and between one and seven aptitude, learning strategies, and learning styles instruments, based on a random-sampling procedure.[2] No measures were repeated. Instruments are described below under the heading "Instrumentation."

All students were asked to take the MBTI in either the short version (Form G) or its longer version (Form J, with the Type Differentiation Indicator [TDI] scoring system) at the beginning of their training. Many of them also completed one or more of the following: the Strategy Inventory for Language Learning (SILL, $N = 262$), the Hartmann Boundary Questionnaire (HBQ, $N = 233$), the National Association of Secondary Schools Principals Learning Styles Profile (LSP, $N = 276$), the Modern Language Aptitude Test (MLAT, $N = 282$), and the Affective Survey ($N = 163$). Many of those who had completed their training by July 1993 ($N = 770$) also had end-of-training proficiency ratings in speaking and reading, as well as faculty ratings on overall effectiveness as learners, effort, and other factors. The number of students with complete end-of-training data differ from instrument to instrument.

Almost all students took the MBTI, and many had MLAT scores on record when they entered training. The other instruments were administered on a random-sample basis. That is, student identification codes were selected at random to choose students who would receive one, two, or three questionnaires in addition to the MBTI. The number for the MBTI (TDI) is much larger than the others because it was also administered at the beginning of training to all French and Spanish students entering the classes beginning about each month from October 1991 through September 1992.

Instrumentation

The Affective Survey. The Affective Survey is a 114-item instrument developed by Madeline Ehrman and Rebecca Oxford (1991) based on the general ideas and in some instances adapted items from a variety of surveys and scales by Gardner (1985b), Campbell (1987), Horwitz (1985), Horwitz, Horwitz, and Cope (1986), and others. The authors recognized that no single survey or scale covered all the important affective (emotional and motivational) areas related to language learning success. The Affective Survey contains three parts: motivation (extrinsic, intrinsic, desire to use the language, and effort), beliefs about self as a language learner, and anxiety (as related to public performance, language use with native speakers, making errors, comprehension, self-esteem, competition, tests, outcomes, and general comfort-discomfort with language learning). The Affective Survey also has the option of a "negativity scale," which indicates to what degree a person agrees with negatively worded items about motivation and anxiety. The Cronbach alpha internal consistency reliability for the Affective Survey is .74, and the standardized item alpha is .82.

The Hartmann Boundary Questionnaire. (HBQ; Hartmann 1991). The HBQ was developed for research with sleep disorders and nightmares, using a psychoanalytic theoretical base. It is intended to examine the degree to which individuals separate aspects of their mental, interpersonal, and external experience through "thick" or "thin" psychological boundaries. Its 146 items address the following dimensions: sleep/dreams/wakefulness, unusual experiences, boundaries among thoughts/feelings/moods, impressions of childhood/adolescence/adulthood, interpersonal distance/openness/closeness, physical and emotional sensitivity, preference for neatness, preference for clear lines, opinions about children/adolescents/adults, opinions about lines of authority, opinions about boundaries among groups/peoples/nations, opinions about abstract concepts, plus a total score for all twelve of the above scales. Hartmann has found women and younger people to score consistently "thinner" than men and older people. Cronbach alpha reliability for the HBQ is .93, and theta reliabilities for subscales fall between .57 and .92 (Hartmann 1991).

The National Association of Secondary Schools Principals' Learning Style Profile. (LSP; Keefe and Monk 1986; Keefe, Monk, Letteri, Languis, and Dunn 1989). The LSP is a 125-item composite measure composed of many different approaches to measuring learning style. The main subscales are cognitive skills (analytic, spatial, categorization, sequential processing, detail memory, discrimination), perceptual response (i.e., sensory preferences: visual, auditory, emotive/kinesthetic), orientations (persistence, verbal risk taking, manipulative), study time preferences (early morning, late morning, afternoon, evening), and environmental context for learning (verbal vs. spatial, posture, light, temperature, mobility, and grouping). Cronbach's alpha for the subscales ranged from .47 to .76, with an average of .61. Test–retest reliabilities were .36 to .82 after ten days and somewhat lower after thirty days. Concurrent validity of the LSP's analytic subscale with the Group Embedded Figures Test was .39, $p < .002$. Concurrent validity of the perceptual response subscales of the LSP with the Edmonds Learning Style Identification Exercise was .51–.64, $p < .002$. Many of the environmental context subscales of the LSP correlated with Dunn and Dunn's Learning Style Inventory, .23–.71, $p < .04$–.002.

The Myers-Briggs Type Indicator. (MBTI; Myers and McCaulley 1985), Form G. This instrument is a 126-item, forced-choice, normative, self-report questionnaire designed to reveal basic personality preferences on four scales: extroversion-introversion (whether the person obtains energy externally or internally); sensing-intuition (whether the person prefers to take in information in a concrete/sequential or an abstract/random way); thinking-feeling (whether the person likes to make decisions based on objective logic or on subjective values); and judging-perceiving (whether the person prefers rapid closure or a flexible life). Internal consistency split-half reliabilities average .87, and test–retest reliabilities are .70–.85 (Myers and McCaulley 1985). Concurrent validity is documented with measures of personality, vocational preference, educational style, and management style (.40–.77). Construct validity is supported by many studies of occupational preferences and creativity.

The Type Differentiation Indicator. (TDI; Saunders 1989). The TDI is a scoring system for a longer and more intricate 290-item form (MBTI, Form J) that provides data on the following subscales for each of the four MBTI dimensions: extraversion-introversion (gregarious-intimate, enthusiastic-quiet, initiator-receptor, expressive-contained, auditory-visual); sensing-intuition (concrete-abstract, realistic-imaginative, pragmatic-intellectual, experiential-theoretical, traditional-original); thinking-feeling (critical-accepting, tough-tender, questioning-accommodating, reasonable-compassionate, logical-affective); and judging-perceiving (stress avoider-polyactive, systematic-casual, scheduled-spontaneous, planful-open-ended, methodical-emergent). The TDI includes seven additional scales indicating a sense of overall comfort and confidence versus discomfort and anxiety (guarded-optimistic, defiant-compliant, carefree-worried, decisive-ambivalent, intrepid-inhibited, leader-follower, proactive-distractible), plus a composite of these called "strain." Each of the Comfort-Discomfort subscales also loads on one of the four type dimensions; for example, proactive-distractible is also a judging-perceiving subscale. There are also scales for type-scale consistency and comfort-scale consistency. The reliability of twenty-three of the twenty-seven TDI subscales is greater than .50, an acceptable result given the brevity of the subscales (Saunders 1989).

The Modern Language Aptitude Test. (MLAT; Carroll and Sapon 1959). This is the classic language aptitude test, with 146 items. The manual describes its five parts: I—number learning (memory, auditory alertness); II—phonetic script (association of sounds and symbols), III—spelling clues (English vocabulary, association of sounds and symbols); IV—words in sentences (grammatical structure in English); and V—paired associates (memorizing words). The MLAT was correlated .75 with the Defense Language Aptitude Battery (Peterson and Al-Haik 1976) and .67 with the Primary Mental Abilities Test (Wesche, Edwards, and Wells 1982)—the latter suggesting a strong general intelligence factor operating in the MLAT. Split-half reliabilities for the MLAT are .92–.97, depending on the grade or age. For college students, validity coefficients are .18–.69 for the long form of the MLAT and .21–.68 for the short form. For adult students in intensive language programs, validity coefficients are .27–.73 for the long form and .26–.69 for the short form (Carroll and Sapon 1959). In this sample, almost all (95 percent) of the MLAT scores were current, that is, administered within the last three years. This study used the long form.

Strategy Inventory for Language Learning. (SILL; Oxford 1989). This eighty-item questionnaire was developed between 1985 and the present and has been used with over 5,700 language learners in many countries. The SILL asks students to react to a series of strategy descriptions (e.g., "I make associations between new material and what I already know") in terms of how often they use the strategies (always or almost always, generally, sometimes, generally not, never or almost never). In studies worldwide, the

SILL's reliability using Cronbach's alpha is .93 to .98, with an average of .95, and it has been shown to be a valid, significant predictor or correlate of language proficiency and achievement.

End-of-Training Learning Activity Questionnaires. Two questionnaires were distributed at the end of training. One, developed by Lucinda Hart-Gonzalez , Nikolaus Koster, Gisela Gonzales, and Madeline Ehrman at FSI, addresses various activities reported by a "snapshot" of FSI students for study on their own, without a teacher (Hart-Gonzalez 1991). Its thirty-six items ask the student to (1) assess the utility of the activity on a scale of "not useful, somewhat useful, very useful" and also (2) to estimate the approximate number of hours spent weekly on it. The other was developed by Madeline Ehrman and Frederick Jackson at FSI based on knowledge of frequent classroom events and on student end-of-training comments about their language learning experience. Its seventy items ask students to assess on the same Likert-type scale as the self-study questionnaire the utility of selected classroom events in the areas of conversation, pronunciation, grammar study, listening practice, reading practice, vocabulary study, classroom structure, and role of the teacher. Because it has taken a long time to amass a sufficient number of these two questionnaires for analysis (departing students are less likely to turn in questionnaires than those still in training that we can pursue), reliability and validity studies remain to be done. In fact, the present report is a first contribution to evaluation of their validity.

Measures of Student Language Proficiency. At the end of training, FSI students are given proficiency assessments resulting in ratings ranging from 0 to 5 for speaking (including interactive listening comprehension) and for reading. For example, R-3 means reading proficiency level 3. S-2 means speaking proficiency level 2. The ratings are equivalent to the ILR/ACTFL/ETS guidelines that originated at FSI and have been developed over the years by government agencies. (These guidelines are detailed by Omaggio Hadley 1989). FSI usually aims at end-of-training proficiency ratings of S-3 R-3 for full-time training, comparable to ILR Professional Proficiency or ACTFL Superior-Level Proficiency. Reliability studies have shown that government agencies have high interrater reliability for proficiency ratings within a given agency, but that the standards are not always the same at every agency; thus raters at different government agencies do not have as high an interrater reliability as raters at the same agency. Proficiency ratings are thus considered reliable indicators of the level of language performance of an individual student *within* an agency

(Clark 1986). Descriptive statistics for performance in terms of end-of-training proficiency are provided in Table 2 in Appendix 1. "Plus" scores (indicating, e.g., proficiency between S-2 and S-3) were coded as .5; thus, for example, a score of S-2+ was coded 2.5.

Faculty Rating Questionnaire.   After training was complete, faculty were asked to rate students on how they compared overall with other FSI students known, on observed language learning aptitude, motivation, effort, and observed anxiety. Data were collected by interview in order to get a rich texture of comments as well as quantitative data. In order to achieve reliability, interviewers were trained and asked to follow the format of the questionnaire.

Self-Report as an Issue in This Study

Self-report is sometimes viewed as suspect because of possible "social desirability response bias" (SDRB), that is, a tendency to answer in a way that would show the respondent to be in some socially acceptable way a "good person." The Affective Survey, HBQ, LSP, MBTI/TDI, and SILL are all self-report instruments and so are subject to questions of SDRB. Through instrument design, range of response in this sample, and precautions taken in the administration of the instruments, an effort was made to hold SDRB to a minimum in this study. (This problem is discussed in greater detail in Ehrman and Oxford, in press.)

Data-Analysis Procedures

To test for internal consistency within the sample, an 855-member subsample including the 770 subjects addressed in this investigation was divided randomly into two subsamples. The means were compared for the 135 variables of the entire project, using t-tests. With the exception of four variables, there was no difference between the means of the two subsamples; that is, they were essentially alike. The four significantly different means were within the range of chance at the .05 level, indicating that the two subsamples can be considered equivalent.

Each of the two variables derived from the formulas for finding the weakest and strongest learners was used to compare means for the various individual difference variables through a one-way analysis of variance using SPSS for Windows Version 5.0.1, through the "Compare Means" procedure. Results were considered significant at the .05 level; some were designated as near significant if the significance level was between .05 and

.099; and a few were listed as suggestive if their significance level fell between .10 and .17. These subsignificant results were included because the number of extremely weak and strong students was so small that a moderate increase in the N could well make the results significant and because they tended to pattern with other results that reached significance.

For correlational results referred to in this chapter, the analysis of choice was Spearman's rho on SAS, a correlation statistic usually used for rank-order data. When used with interval or ratio data, Spearman's rho provides a more conservative result than Pearson product-moment correlations. Since some of the measures involved ordered data with uneven intervals, and other measures involved equal-interval data, it seemed preferable to use the most conservative correlation coefficient (Spearman's rho) that could be used consistently with all the data. However, a check to see if there was a difference between Pearson's r and Spearman's rho revealed only very few small differences, all nonsignificant. All tests of correlational significance were two-tailed. Correlations of at least .20 are reported. Though .20 is low, findings at this level are reported so that later research can further examine them with other populations.

For all statistical tests reported in this study, the acceptable significance level was set at $p < .05$ level.

Results

This report of results is organized by a set of questions about each group of students. Each question is answered first for the weakest students, then for the strongest. The questions are:

What are they like (demographically and in personality)?
How do they feel (motivation and anxiety)?
What are their abilities?
What do they do to learn (strategies)?
How do their teachers rate them?

Details of number of subjects, means and standard deviations for the criterion group and the remainder of the sample, F-statistics, degrees of freedom, and significance levels are provided in Table 1 (Weakest Students) and Table 2 (Strongest Students) in Appendix 1. These data are therefore not ordinarily provided in the following text, unless required to make a special point.

What Are They Like?

Weakest Students

These students have significantly less previous language learning experience than other students, in terms of number of languages previously studied. There are no gender differences at the significant, near-significant, or suggestive levels.

On the HBQ, while most of the differences were not statistically significant, the general direction was for the weakest students to show thicker ego boundaries on every one of the HBQ categories and on both HBQ factors. Those results reaching significance include Factor II (external boundaries), preference for sharp edges in images, neat and orderly surroundings, clear lines of authority in organization, and total HBQ score. All but the total score (which includes both internal and external items) are in the external boundary group.

On the MBTI, the weakest students show a preference for taking in information through sensing: these people prefer practical, sequential, fact-oriented learning, with little need to make inferences or design aspects of their own training. On the TDI scoring system, which provides subscales for each of the main MBTI scales plus seven comfort-discomfort scales, weakest students significantly report themselves as pragmatic (vs. intellectual).

Strongest Students

These students show highly significant superiority in education level, in number of languages previously studied, and for highest speaking and reading scores in previously learned languages, relative to those who are not in this group. They also tend to be quite a bit younger (by about six years) than all other students and markedly younger than the weakest students (by nearly ten years). As in the case of the weakest learners, there is no difference with respect to gender.

The HBQ does not distinguish the strongest learners as clearly as it marks off the weakest ones. Only one HBQ category, a preference against neatness and order in the external world (thin), characterizes the strongest group. In contrast with the weakest students, who reported thicker ego boundaries on every category, whether significant or not, the strongest learners were much less consistent; there is no apparent pattern to the categories that have higher (thin) and lower (thick) means for this group relative to all the others.

On the MBTI, the only significant categories for strongest students were on two TDI subscales, where they reported themselves as more imaginative (vs. realistic) and more emergent (vs. methodical). The former is a sensing-intuition subscale, and the students reported themselves on the intuitive pole; the latter is a judging-perceiving subscale, and the students reported themselves on the perceiving pole.

Thus we see that weaker students are less experienced language learners; have thicker ego boundaries, especially with respect to the outer world; and prefer sensing perception to gather information. In contrast, the strongest students tend to be younger than other students, are advantaged with respect to previous learning, reject neatness and order in their surroundings, and report themselves as more imaginative (intuition) and emergent (perceiving) on the MBTI. There are no gender differences.

How Do They Feel?

Weakest Students

There are no significant or near-significant results for the weakest students on the Affective Survey. Faculty ratings for observed motivation and anxiety do not distinguish them either.

Strongest Students

These students report lower intrinsic and overall motivation levels. On the other hand, they tend to endorse significantly fewer negatively phrased items, both in general and with respect to items probing various forms of anxiety. A combination of motivation and anxiety totals that is interpreted as indicating overall emotional arousal level is significantly lower for the strongest students than for all others. Teacher reports do not distinguish them by observed anxiety level, but they are viewed by their teachers as having been significantly more extrinsically motivated than their classmates.

What Are Their Abilities?

Weakest Students

On the main measure of language ability in this study, the MLAT, the weakest students performed strikingly worse than their classmates and did so to a high level of significance on all the MLAT subscales as well as on its total and the scaled Index Score. The most distinguishing score was the Index (T-score), which represents the entire performance of the student on the MLAT; the weakest students did worse than other students to a highly significant degree. Of the subscales, those on which these students did particularly poorly were Parts III and IV. Part III tests both English vocabulary level and the ability to sort peculiar sound-related spellings. Part IV tests sensitivity to English structural nuances at the sentence level. In addition, the weakest students were significantly less adept at simultaneous visual processing on the LSP, showing less ability to match a stimulus to a whole image of which it is a part.

Strongest Students

Although the MLAT separated the strongest students from the rest, it did so less clearly than it did for the weakest students. Again, the Index appears to distinguish the strongest students, as it did the weakest, but Parts IV (English sentence structure) and V (rote memorization) provided no discrimination for this group, and Parts I, II, and III had a weaker effect (measured both by significance level and by F-statistic) for the strongest students than for the weakest ones. None of the LSP ability scales were distinctive for the strongest students.

What Do They Do to Learn?

Weakest Students

Too few students in this group turned in the SILL and the end-of-training questionnaires on self-study and classroom activities for meaningful analysis.

Strongest Students

There is more information available about how the strongest students learned, and even more about what they believed not helpful. On the SILL, they reported significantly more use of techniques to enhance memory. None of the results on the end-of-training questionnaire about self-study activities were significant.

An additional end-of-training questionnaire asked about the relative utility of various activities that take place in the classroom. The strongest students reported significantly more utility to constant correction by the teacher of their pronunciation (and conversely significantly less usefulness to teacher's withholding correction in the interests of communication). Otherwise they considered a variety of activities less useful: group work with other students, a regular routine to lessons, learning grammar patterns in context, translation into English when reading, and target-language word games.

How Do Their Teachers Rate Them?

Weakest Students

The weakest students were rated substantially lower on both an overall scale that compares them with other FSI students the faculty member has known and on a scale of observed language learning aptitude. Where the median percentile ratings for the whole sample are 60 and 58, respectively, the weakest students have median scores of 34 and 32, respectively.

Strongest Students

Conversely, the strongest students were rated as both better students overall and in terms of observed aptitude. Their median ratings were 92 and 87, respectively.

Summary of Results

Table 3 in Appendix 2 summarizes the findings of this study. We see that the weakest learners relative to all other learners in the sample appear to be characterized by fewer resources (previous language learning experience and awareness of use of learning strategies), lower tolerance of ambiguity (as manifested in the HBQ and the MBTI), and much lower cognitive aptitude. The strongest learners relative to all others seem to be characterized by more resources from the beginning of their training, including higher level of education, more language learning experience, and a tendency to use learning strategies associated with independence. They tend to display signs of more tolerance of ambiguity, reveal greater tested cognitive aptitude, and may exhibit more emotional stability under the stress of intensive language training.

Discussion

Student Characteristics

The lack of previous experience characterizing weakest students and the presence of previous experience reported by the strongest suggest a "Matthew Effect" ("to those who have more shall be given"). However, the direction of causality is difficult to ascertain. Certainly, it is likely that those who have learned more languages before and to a higher level of proficiency have learned how to learn. On the other hand, it is also common for those who find learning easy to gravitate to more learning of the same kind; foreign languages and international affairs should be no exception, so ability may also play a role from the beginning for the strongest students' involvement with language learning.

Most other studies have found that it is better to be younger, but such findings receive only limited confirmation here. Much more interesting is the fact that the mean age of the strongest 4–5 percent of learners is thirty-four, much older than those normally thought to be likely to learn languages. While not everyone can be a superstar, it is interesting to note further that the mean age of the entire sample, almost all of whom succeed in learning foreign languages to a high degree of proficiency in a rather short time, is thirty-nine, and roughly two-thirds of these generally successful students fall between the ages of thirty and forty-eight.

This study confirms other findings from the Language Learning Profiles Project that there is no gender difference in learning success (e.g., see Ehrman 1993, 1994). I interpret them as further supporting the statement made above in the literature review that the gender differences found in other populations may be more the result of moderating variables like education level, interests, career choice, socialization, and so on, than anything inherent to males or females (see also Meunier, this volume).

The relationship between thickness of ego boundaries on the HBQ and membership in weakest or strongest student groups is consistent with the correlational findings that are cited in Ehrman (1993) and Ehrman and Oxford (in press). These indicate that thicker ego boundaries are somewhat related to lower success rates for the sample as a whole and suggest a particular importance of external boundaries over internal boundaries in the learning of language and culture. Correlations between the HBQ categories and speaking and reading proficiency are low—in the 20s and 30s. The present findings suggest that any effect of this aspect of personality is greater for the weaker students and attenuated in the middle and top; hence the low correlations. In other words, thick boundaries may be more detrimental than thin ones are helpful. Since thick boundaries can mean that information is never taken into the learner in the first place, and moreover that if it is, such information may not be integrated with other knowledge, this relative effect of thick boundaries is not too surprising (see Ehrman, 1993, for extensive discussion of this question).

In particular, one factor on the HBQ distinguishes both weak and strong students from the rest of the students: relative preference for neatness and order. Perhaps the weakest students' strong need for various kinds of order and clarity among categories, including sharp edges in visuals and clear lines of authority, may hinder their ability to cope with the inconsistencies and lack of immediate closure entailed by communicative classrooms. In contrast, the active rejection of neatness and order by the strongest learners may suggest that too much prestructuring of material would get in their way. Other educational research findings indicate that this may be the case (Snow 1989).

The MBTI findings for weakest learners suggest a student who wants to learn only what is necessary, without the need to go beneath the surface of the material presented in class. Earlier findings showed that sensing students were most comfortable in structured, well-defined learning situations that required little in the way of making inferences or what-if imagining (Ehrman 1989; Ehrman and Oxford 1990). The subscale results are consistent with this picture: pragmatic people tend to be characterized by the words "executive, applied interests, things" in contrast to intellectual ones: "scholarly, knowledge for its own sake, words" (Saunders 1989, p. 6). Similarly, realistic people are described as "sensible, matter-of-fact" as opposed to "ingenious, enjoys play of imagination" (Saunders 1989, p. 6). Since many sensing students with the same preferences do very well in language training (hence the low correlations in Ehrman and Oxford, in press), it is likely that the key is some kind of moderating variable. Ehrman (1989) and Ehrman and Oxford (1990) suggest that the key is flexibility in adapting to different styles of teaching and cite a case of an extremely successful sensing learner who said that "intuitive-type" activities like round-robin storytelling were hard for him but that he found ways to adapt. Ehrman (1993) attempts to trace the source of the flexibility to the tolerance of ambiguity construct, operationalized at least in part by the HBQ.

Strongest learners show a tendency toward intuition (on one TDI subscale) and toward perceiving (on the MBTI main scale and on one TDI subscale). Intuitive and perceiving students enjoy abstractions, like to work out underlying systems (especially if intuitive and thinking), tend to use learning strategies characterized by the use of meaning, are often responsive to discovery learning procedures, and may experience boredom with routine and thus welcome some unpredictability in their learning experiences (Ehrman and Oxford 1989, 1990). In most work on the MBTI, intuition and perceiving are moderately correlated in the .30s and .40s range (Myers and McCaulley 1985); in the present sample they are correlated at .40 (Ehrman 1994), so the appearance of both together as strongest learner characteristics is not surprising (strongest learners prefer perceiving nearly significantly, $F = 3.3548$, $df = 751$, $p = .0675$, $N = 25$ out of 657 and significantly prefer the emergent [perceiving] pole of the methodical-emergent subscale). More surprising is the fact that judging does not appear along with sensing for the weakest learners, perhaps because the orderly study habits that judgers tend to prefer (Ehrman 1989) may compensate for some of these weakest learners' cognitive shortcomings. The continuous score means for weakest learners do fall more in the judging direction, at 88 as compared to 93 for all others, though at a non-significant level. (MBTI continuous scores below 100 indicate extraversion, sensing, thinking, and judging.)

Other investigations of this sample have revealed a relatively strong correlation between thick ego boundaries and MBTI sensing, thinking, and judging, and conversely between thin ego boundaries and MBTI intuition, feeling, and perceiving (Ehrman, 1993). These relationships appear in the present data as well: weak students are characterized by thick ego boundaries on a variety of categories and by sensing. In turn, strongest students have thin (external) ego boundaries on one HBQ subscale and sub-significantly tend to prefer perceiving as well as the significantly differentiating intuitive and perceiving poles on two TDI subscales.

Affective Factors

It is not surprising that the instructors of the strongest students tend to see them as more motivated than their classmates and that these students tend to have a relatively low level of negativity about their language study, though the direction of causality is uncertain for both findings. (In other words, do students succeed because they like what they are doing, or do they like what they are doing because they are succeeding?)

Much more unexpected is the consistently lower degree of motivation across the board reported by the strongest students relative to the rest of the students in the sample. To attempt an explanation for this paradoxical-seeming finding, we can turn to the significantly lower overall affective arousal level reported by these students as well, although it correlates positively with speaking proficiency in general at .32 $p < .0001$ (see Ehrman and Oxford, in press). It is possible that in these results this group of students displays a relative coolness and resistance to the pressures of intensive language training; the strongest students may be those who respond to this normally stressful situation with more than usual emotional stability.

FSI students contrast in one significant area with university students. Horwitz and her colleagues (Horwitz 1990; Horwitz, Horwitz, and Cope 1986; Horwitz and Young 1991) found that the most debilitating form of anxiety for her students was that related to speaking in class. In contrast, the FSI correlational data (Ehrman and Oxford, in press) show that such anxiety is facilitating (i.e., correlates with higher EOT proficiency). Although the results in this study were nonsignificant, there was a difference in the means between strongest and other students that was clearly in the direction of more anxiety about speaking in class for the former, consistent with the correlational findings. I have speculated that the difference has to do with what the anxiety is about: FSI students tend to compete for "air time" in class, perhaps driven by the fact that the end-of-training speaking test on which pay and advancement depend consists entirely of oral interaction at an advanced level. University grades often depend less on such evaluations.

Abilities

As mentioned above in the literature review, the MLAT appears to maintain roughly the same validity coefficient (about .50) for both the audio-lingual training in fashion when it was developed and the largely communicative training in use in most FSI programs today (Ehrman and Oxford, in press). The results reported here indicate that it is especially discriminating for students at the lowest end of the achievement continuum, but that it can also distinguish the best performers as well, though less dramatically. (Note that the weak student mean Index score is 43 vs. 63 for the rest; thus the weakest are about two standard deviations below the FSI mean of 62. The strong student mean Index score is 68 vs. 61 for the rest, or about two-thirds of a standard deviation above the FSI mean of 62.)

These findings are consistent with the informal observations of language training supervisors at FSI over the years to the effect that the MLAT appears to be more useful at the extremes of ability than in the middle of the range. The importance of Part IV to differentiating the weakest learners is consistent with findings in universities, where students needing language waivers have been shown to be particularly weak on this subscale (Gajar 1987; Ganschow, Sparks, Javorsky, Pohlman, and Bishop-Marbury 1991). Parts III and IV were the MLAT subscales having the strongest correlations with speaking and reading proficiency in the present sample. Interestingly, both of these subscales have to do with subtleties of English language proficiency in vocabulary and sentence structure, respectively, thus possibly suggesting that some related form of language aptitude may also affect first language proficiency level when opportunity to learn is more or less equal.

Speculation elsewhere suggests that part of what makes the MLAT valid across methodologies is the fact that it in part tests the ability to deal with unexpected input, part of a tolerance of ambiguity construct (Ehrman, 1993). If in fact tolerance for ambiguity—usually defined as an aspect of personality—is an important contributor to success on the MLAT, we have here an interesting intermixture of personality and aptitude. A link between personality and aptitude, at least as tested by the MLAT, is also reflected in the correlations between the MLAT Index and MBTI intuition and the intuition pole of the TDI subscale pragmatic-intellectual, at .28 p < .0001 and .39 p < .0001, respectively. We have seen that the sensing-intuition scale and the pragmatic-intellectual subscale also play a role in characterizing the extreme groups in the present study.

The relative inferiority of the weakest students on the LSP simultaneous processing variable suggests that these step-by-step, analytic rather than global students may have a disadvantage in processing holistically. This weakness may interfere with their ability to cope with language when it goes beyond linear, discrete-point processing.

Learning Strategies and Techniques

Unfortunately, too few of the weakest students turned in the end-of-training questionnaires about their learning activities for analysis. On the SILL, university students have tended to be differentiated by strategy use (Oxford and Ehrman, in press). In contrast, the SILL does not appear to distinguish among FSI learners. The absence of significant FSI results on the SILL might suggest that weakest students are not aware of any special patterns of strategy use. They may react with a kind of scattershot approach that tries anything that might work but without clear rationale, as was suggested for less adept university students (Vann and Abraham 1989). The low rate of return of the end-of-training questionnaires may reflect an overall lower level of interest in the program at the end of training. Many students who have found the language learning experience frustrating simply want to complete it as fast as possible and not dwell on it.

The strongest students appear to be significantly characterized by use of techniques related to enhancing memory and making use of instructor feedback about pronunciation. Such learners appear to take a pragmatic approach to making use of teacher feedback and maximizing at least one form of cognitive processing of what they learn. However, strongest students describe themselves as doing less of a wider range of activities than their classmates. Many of these activities are related to study alone (though at the same time, they do not find group work useful). This constellation of characteristics may be consistent with a tendency to introversion (with intuition) on the part of top achievers that appeared in a chi-square analysis of type tables (Ehrman, 1994). Their rejection of routine lessons is possibly consistent with their preference for perceiving on the MBTI. Correlations for the two end-of-training questionnaires, not yet reported elsewhere, suggest that proficiency in both speaking and reading is related to use of a variety of unstructured input situations, especially those that involve interaction with native speakers, and that such proficiency is negatively linked to techniques that reduce risk (e.g., not moving on until a grammar point is mastered, strict routine in lessons, or making the teacher responsible for one's learning). Thus, these strong students seem to reject a number of the more limiting items that are negatively correlated with proficiency, whereas they appear to derive value from relatively independent internal manipulation of the language (e.g., hypothesis generation, mnemonics, internalizing feedback). As more questionnaires become available from the weakest students in the latest group now in training, it will be interesting to see if they tend to endorse as useful the lower risk techniques that were rejected by the strongest and were negatively correlated with proficiency.

Teacher Ratings

The differential teacher ratings for overall quality as a student and observed aptitude provide no surprises. It may be worth notice that the strongest students are more clearly rated high than the weakest students are rated low, at least in terms of significance level. Perhaps this is a result of a charitable mind-set on the part of the faculty, who in general found it easier to rate students high than low; indeed, the sample median for overall quality as a student is the 60th percentile and the 58th for observed aptitude, suggesting either a volunteer effect in the sample, a lenient view by teachers, or both. (An attempt was made to eliminate volunteer effect to the degree possible by strongly encouraging all entering students in a cohort to participate in the research project, but it could not be eliminated altogether, since students could opt not to participate.)

Toward a Broadened Definition of Language Learning Aptitude

There are a number of ways in which these findings are of interest. First, they seem to support the importance of tolerance of ambiguity as a key to language learning, at least in FSI classrooms. This concept is realized through the HBQ, the MBTI, possibly the LSP simultaneous processing variable, and preference for or rejection of various learning strategies. Tolerance of ambiguity and the construct of MLAT-tested learning aptitude maintain their differentiating power despite the homogenizing influences of student preselection and strenuous efforts to find every way to help students reach their training goals once they are at FSI. (It is rare that students are dropped from training for poor performance; instead it is more likely that their training will be extended, within limits.)

By adding support to the centrality of tolerance of ambiguity, these two variable types also contribute to a model of learning that relates achievement to personality variables, beginning at the deepest level with the ego boundary distinction between thick and thin, which in turn is generally manifested by the MBTI categories (see Figure 1). These in turn may represent an approach to learning in which a particular track is favored; for example, a preference for MBTI feeling may be related to a learning track that maximizes interpersonal relations. Certain learning strategy categories are likely to be especially characteristic of one of the tracks; for instance, "judging students" often favor a well-organized and scheduled study approach. Most learners use several or all of the four tracks, but many especially favor one or two. We have seen that an apparently cognitive variable, MLAT performance, also appears to have a link to personality through the tolerance of ambiguity construct and the relative success of certain personality types on the MLAT.

These findings clarify correlational findings that were weak (in the .20 range) but appeared to be patterned, especially for the personality variables (Ehrman and Oxford, in press). The fact that some of the features showing up weakly in the correlations, particularly personality variables, are much stronger at the extremes suggests some sort of nonlinear relationship for which correlations are not the best measure.

Yet another important point is the role of tested language learning aptitude. The MLAT certainly differentiates the extreme learners from their classmates, and it is the most powerful of the variables used. It continues to retain its power in programs in which the role of rote learning has been greatly reduced from the time the MLAT was developed; perhaps the ability to manage unfamiliar and contradictory input leads both to success in communicative classrooms and to high scores on the MLAT. The MLAT may be the best of the differentiators in this study because it requires the examinee to cope with the unfamiliar on tasks that at least partially simulate language learning tasks, whereas personality inventories are asking about general life preferences, and strategy inventories do not

Figure 1

A Four-Track Model of Learning

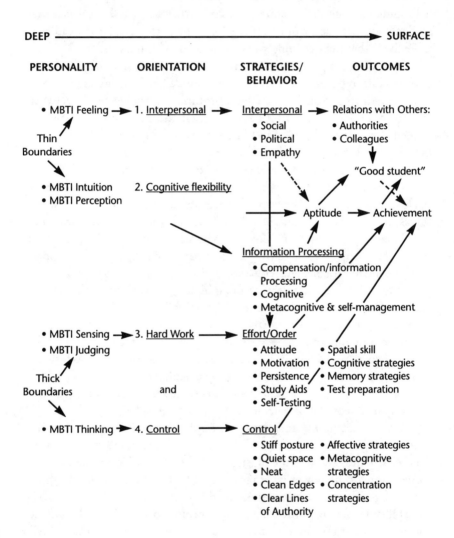

Reprinted with permission of Georgetown University Press, Ehrman 1993, p. 353.

address how the strategies are used but only whether the student is aware of using them. The significant correlations between the MLAT and the HBQ, though not strong (between .21 and .33), are consistent across HBQ and MLAT subscales (Ehrman, 1993) and with the present findings. Those between the MLAT and the MBTI are particularly telling for the sensing-intuition scale and most of its subscales, where they are significantly correlated with the intuition pole, with a range of .20 to .39. Again these are not strong, but they are consistent (Ehrman, 1994) both with each other and with the results of the present study.

The ability to learn strategically is receiving increasing attention. Important elements of strategic learning include the ability to connect new knowledge with existing knowledge, the ability to organize and elaborate it cognitively rather than simply add it to a single string of data, and to access appropriate learning strategies automatically (Jones, Palincsar, Ogle, and Carr 1987). The links between the MLAT and personality variables suggest a role for the disposition to use one's cognitive resources in ways that go beneath the surface and that establish elaborated knowledge structures. Those who are open to new material, can manage contradictions, treat their perceptions of input as hypotheses to be tested, are interested in meaning, and find ways to link new input with previous knowledge structures are advantaged in managing the highly complex tasks involved in learning a new language and culture rapidly and to a high degree of proficiency.

Thus perhaps we can broaden the usual definition of language learning aptitude to include not only the cognitive skills most clearly tested by the MLAT, but the kinds of personality attributes that predispose learners to tolerate ambiguity, to process data in elaborative ways, and to impose their own structure on what they would otherwise experience as chaos. The weakest students appear to be overwhelmed by the chaos they encounter; the strongest meet it head on, may even embrace it to a degree (MBTI perceiving), and find ways both to assimilate it to their existing schemata and to accommodate their schemata to what they select as the important elements of their experience.

The strongest learners are indeed differentiated by this nexus of personality and tested aptitude, but the weakest ones are much more clearly delineated. Perhaps this is because FSI students, at least, tend to be already selected for ability to use cognitive processing strategies of the sort that lead to success in learning even before they come to language training, so those who use these strategies even more adeptly will stand out from the main group less than those who have not developed these cognitive skills do. In any event, it may be that although students may favor one or more of the four MBTI tracks in Figure 1, some level of ability to operate on track 2 (cognitive flexibility) is essential to success in FSI classrooms.

Conversely, the role of motivation appears to work in the opposite direction. FSI students—weak, average, and strong—tend to be highly motivated, almost to a fault (Ehrman 1990). The affective advantage the strongest learners show may be a result of an extra ability to manage their feelings, shown in their cooler approach to the task on the Affective Survey.

Conclusions

We have seen a combination of individual difference factors that appears to differentiate extremely weak and strong learners in intensive language training. There are, however, cautions to be heeded in applying these findings.

Although a capacity to impose personal structure on chaos seems to be important, some of the influence may go the other way: that is, FSI curricula and classroom techniques have evolved over the years to meet the requirements of a certain type of student who tends to achieve well. Students in this sample appear to be quite similar to their colleagues who have entered in the past, so they doubtless benefit from training that has been developed to fit their predecessors. In other words, it may not be only that the set of aptitude attributes is characteristic of all good classroom learners; instead or in addition, FSI classrooms may have at the same time adapted to a certain profile of learner, thus increasing the advantages of those who most tend to have the features of the profile. We do not know yet to what degree the aptitude nexus that emerged from these data would advantage learners in other classroom milieux, let alone language learning in natural settings.

Needless to say, when FSI students are the subject of this kind of report, we must always ask how well we can generalize from them to the students in other classrooms. FSI students are older, better educated, generally high-functioning, and intensely motivated. They are relatively experienced learners and have already shown an interest in other languages and cultures by their very career choices. On the other hand, perhaps the combination of tested aptitude and personality that works well in FSI language training also would make the stronger students into the kind of good learner in high school and college language classes who would be attracted to a career involving other languages and cultures. Thus, the traits described in this study might well also characterize better and weaker language learners elsewhere.

Like most research studies, this report leaves work yet to be done. Statistical tests other than one-way analysis of variance (e.g., multiple ANOVA) could be done. The same study should be undertaken for reading proficiency, though based on other findings for speaking and reading from this sample, the differences can be expected to be relatively minor. The two end-of-training learning activity questionnaires need validation, and a larger number of them will permit analysis of both questionnaires for both learner extremes. Changes in the formulas used to establish the two filter variables (strongest students and weakest students) might change the results. At some point, it would be useful to examine interaction effects as well as main effects.

Perhaps the most important caution is one against overgeneralizing to individuals. The fact that one personality style, for instance, appears to have a statistical advantage in a certain learning situation does not mean that others cannot learn in that situation, and learn well. Statistics address trends, but do not describe an individual's drive, maturity, intelligence, or coping skills. Furthermore, statistics like these may be highly population- and situation-specific, thus adding weight to the need for replication and investigation of external validity.

Nevertheless, this relatively simple study has provided evidence of the value of looking at a variety of individual differences in understanding learning success and failure, at least among FSI adult students. It has led to an effort to expand the definition of language learning aptitude to include personality dispositions that interact with cognitive processing. Such findings will be even more valuable when related to variations in teacher personality and teaching techniques.

Notes

1. This report owes much to the efforts of the staff of the FSI Language Learning Profiles Project, in particular Lucinda Hart-Gonzalez, Stephanie Lindemann, Gisela Gonzales, and Frederick Jackson, all of whom contributed to it in multiple ways. Dr. Hart-Gonzalez, Ms. Lindemann, and Julie Thornton of the Center for the Advancement of Language Learning made valuable comments on the first draft. The material herein does not represent the policy of the U.S. Department of State: it is the responsibility of the author alone.

2. One group of students ($N = 60$) took all the measures. Subsequent groups were given the biographic data questionnaire and the MBTI/TDI

plus from one to three of the SILL, the HBQ, and the LSP. This was done in order to reduce the burden of questionnaires. Although the Affective Survey was given only to the first group in this sample, it has been used for later samples not reported here, and the results confirm the findings that are reported here.

Works Cited

Au, S. Y. 1988. A Critical Appraisal of Gardner's Socio-Psychological Theory of Second-Language (L2) Learning. *Language Learning* 38: 75–100.

Beck, R. C. 1990. *Motivation: Theories and Principles*. 3d ed. Englewood Cliffs, NJ: Prentice-Hall.

Beebe, Leslie M. 1983. Risk-Taking and the Language Learner. In *Classroom-Oriented Research in Second Language Acquisition*, edited by Herbert W. Seliger and Michael H. Long, 39–65. Rowley, MA: Newbury House.

Brown, H. Douglas. 1987. *Principles of Language Learning and Teaching*. 2d ed. Englewood Cliffs, NJ: Prentice-Hall.

Busch, Michael. 1982. Introversion-Extraversion and the EFL Proficiency of Japanese Language Students. *Language Learning* 32: 109–32.

Campbell, Christine. 1987. Survey of Attitudes Specific to the Foreign Language Classroom. Unpublished ms, Defense Language Institute, Monterey, CA.

Carroll, John B. 1990. Cognitive Abilities and Foreign Language Aptitude: Then and Now. In Parry and Stansfield, 11–29.

Carroll, John B., and Stanley M. Sapon. 1959. *Modern Language Aptitude Test*. New York: Psychological Corporation.

Chapelle, Carol A. 1983. The Relationship between Ambiguity Tolerance and Success in Acquiring English as a Second Language in Adult Learners. Ph.D. diss., University of Illinois at Champaign-Urbana.

Clark, John. 1986. *A Study of the Comparability of Speaking Proficiency across Three Government Language Training Agencies*. Washington, DC: Center for Applied Linguistics.

Cohen, Andrew D. 1990. *Language Learning: Insights for Learners, Teachers, and Researchers*. New York: Newbury House/Harper and Row.

Ehrman, Madeline E. 1989. *Ants and Grasshoppers, Badgers and Butterflies: Quantitative and Qualitative Investigation of Adult Language Learning Styles and Strategies.* Ann Arbor, MI: University Microfilms International.

————. 1990. Owls and Doves: Cognition, Personality, and Learning Success. In *Linguistics, Language Teaching, and Language Acquisition: The Interdependence of Theory, Practice, and Research,* edited by J. E. Alatis, 413–37. Washington, DC: Georgetown University Press.

————. 1993. Ego Boundaries Revisited: Toward a Model of Personality and Learning. In *Strategic Interaction and Language Acquisition: Theory, Practice, and Research,* edited by J. E. Alatis, 330-362. Washington, DC: Georgetown University Press

————. 1994. The Type Differentiation Indicator and Adult Language Learning Success. *Journal of Psychological Types* 30: 10-29.

Ehrman, Madeline E., and Rebecca L. Oxford. 1989. Effects of Sex Differences, Career Choice, and Psychological Type on Adults' Language Learning Strategies. *Modern Language Journal* 73: 1–13.

————. 1990. Adult Language Learning Styles and Strategies in an Intensive Training Setting. *Modern Language Journal* 74: 311–27.

————. 1991. *Affective Survey.* Arlington, VA: Foreign Service Institute.

————. In press. Cognition Plus: Correlates of Language Learning Success. *Modern Language Journal.*

Ely, Christopher. 1986. An Analysis of Discomfort, RiskTaking, Sociability, and Motivation in the L2 Classroom. *Language Learning* 36: 1–25.

————. 1989. Tolerance of Ambiguity and Use of Second Language Learning Strategies. *Modern Language Journal* 22: 437–45.

Gajar, Anna. H. 1987. Foreign Language Learning Disabilities: The Identification of Predictive and Diagnostic Variables. *Journal of Learning Disabilities* 20: 327–30.

Galbraith, Vicki, and Robert C. Gardner. 1988. *Individual Difference Correlates of Second-Language Achievement: An Annotated Bibliography.* London, Ontario: University of Western Ontario.

Ganschow, Lenore, Richard L. Sparks, James Javorsky, Jane Pohlman, and Andrea Bishop-Marbury. 1991. Identifying Native Language Difficulties among Foreign Language Learners in College: A "Foreign" Language Disability? *Journal of Learning Disabilities* 24: 530–41.

Gardner, Robert C. 1985a. *Social Psychology and Second Language Learning: The Role of Attitudes and Motivation.* London: Edward Arnold.

_____. 1985b. Motivation Questionnaire. Unpublished ms. produced for use in the Language Skill Change Project, Defense Language Institute, Monterey, CA.

Guiora, Alexander A. 1972. Construct Validity and Transpositional Research: Toward an Empirical Study of Psycho-Analytic Concepts. *Comprehension Psychiatry* 13: 139-50.

Hart-Gonzalez, Lucinda. 1991. Self-Study Strategies Used by FSI Students. Unpublished report, Foreign Service Institute, Arlington, VA.

Hartmann, Ernest. 1991. *Boundaries in the Mind: A New Psychology of Personality.* New York: Basic Books.

Horwitz, Elaine K. 1985. Using Student Beliefs about Language Learning and Teaching in the Foreign Language Methods Course. *Foreign Language Annals* 18: 333–40.

_____. 1990. Attending to the Affective Domain in the Foreign Language Classroom. In *Shifting the Instructional Focus to the Learner,* edited by Sally S. Magnan, 15–33. Middlebury, VT: Northeast Conference on the Teaching of Foreign Languages.

Horwitz, Elaine K., Michael B. Horwitz, and J. Cope. 1986. Foreign Language Classroom Anxiety. *Modern Language Journal* 70: 125–32.

Horwitz, Elaine K., and Dolly J. Young. 1991. *Language Learning Anxiety: From Theory and Research to Classroom Implications.* Englewood Cliffs, NJ: Prentice-Hall.

Jones, B. F., Annemarie S. Palincsar, Donna M. Ogle, and Eileen G. Carr. 1987. *Strategic Teaching and Learning: Cognitive Instruction in the Content Areas.* Alexandria, VA: Association for Supervision and Curriculum Development.

Keefe, James W., and John S. Monk. 1986. *Learning Style Profile Examiner's Manual.* Reston, VA: National Association of Secondary School Principals.

Keefe, James W., and John S. Monk, with Charles A. Letteri, Martin Languis, and Rita Dunn. 1989. *Learning Style Profile.* Reston, VA: National Association of Secondary School Principals.

Larsen-Freeman, Diane, and Michael Long. 1991. *An Introduction to Second Language Acquisition Research.* Oxford: Oxford University Press.

Lawrence, Gordon. 1984. A Synthesis of Learning Style Research Involving the MBTI. *Journal of Psychological Type* 8: 1–15.

Myers, Isabel B., and Mary H. McCaulley. 1985. *Manual: A Guide to the Development and Use of the Myers-Briggs Type Indicator.* Palo Alto, CA: Consulting Psychologists Press.

Naiman, Neil, Maria Fröhlich, and H. H. Stern. 1975. *The Good Language Learner.* Toronto: Ontario Institute for Studies in Education.

Omaggio Hadley, Alice. 1993. *Teaching Language in Context.* 2d ed. Boston: Heinle & Heinle.

O'Malley, J. Michael, and Anna Uhl Chamot. 1990. *Learning Strategies in Second Language Acquisition.* Cambridge: Cambridge University Press.

Oxford, Rebecca L. 1989. *Strategy Inventory for Language Learning.* Alexandria, VA: Oxford Associates.

———. 1990. *Language Learning Strategies: What Every Teacher Should Know.* New York: Newbury House/Harper and Row.

———. 1992. Who Are Our Students? A Synthesis of Foreign and Second Language Research on Individual Differences. *TESL Canada Journal* 9: 30–49.

———. In press. Gender Differences in Language Learning Styles and Strategies: A Review of Existing Research. *Applied Language Learning.*

Oxford, Rebecca L., and Madeline E. Ehrman. 1993. Second Language Research on Individual Differences. In *Annual Review of Applied Linguistics,* edited by William Grabe, 188–205. Cambridge: Cambridge University Press.

———. In press. Language Learning Strategies: Correlates and Outcomes for Adult Language Learners System.

Oxford, Rebecca L., Madeline E. Ehrman, and Roberta Z. Lavine. 1991. Style Wars: Teacher–Student Style Conflicts in the Language Classroom. In *Challenges in the 1990s for College Foreign Language Programs,* AAUSC Issues in Language Program Direction, edited by Sally S. Magnan, 1–25. Boston: Heinle & Heinle.

Oxford, Rebecca L., Martha Nyikos, and Madeline E. Ehrman. 1988. *Vive la différence?* Reflections on Sex Differences in Use of Language Learning Strategies. *Foreign Language Annals* 21: 321–29.

Oxford, Rebecca L., and Jill Shearin. 1994. Expanding the Theoretical Framework of Language Learning Motivation. *Modern Language Journal* 77: 12–28.

Parry, Thomas, and Charles W. Stansfield. 1990. *Language Aptitude Reconsidered.* Englewood Cliffs, NJ: Prentice-Hall.

Petersen, C. R., and A. R. Al-Haik. 1976. The Development of the Defense Language Aptitude Battery (DLAB). *Educational and Psychological Measurement* 36: 369–80.

Reid, Joy M. 1987. The Learning Style Preferences of ESL Students. *TESOL Quarterly* 21: 87–111.

Saunders, David. 1989. *Type Differentiation Indicator Manual: A Scoring System for Form J of the Myers-Briggs Type Indicator.* Palo Alto, CA: Consulting Psychologists Press.

Schleppegrell, Mary. 1987. *The Older Language Learner.* Washington, DC: ERIC Clearinghouse on Languages and Linguistics.

Schmeck, Ronald. R. 1988. *Learning Strategies and Learning Styles.* New York: Plenum Press.

Singleton, David. 1989. *Language Acquisition: The Age Factor.* Clevedon on Avon, UK: Multilingual Matters.

Skehan, Peter. 1989. *Individual Differences in Second Language Learning.* London: Edward Arnold.

Snow, Richard. E. 1989. Aptitude–Treatment Interaction as a Framework for Research on Individual Differences in Learning. In *Learning and Individual Differences,* edited by Philip E. Ackerman, Robert J. Sternberg, and Robert Glaser, 13–59. New York: W. H. Freeman.

Stevick, Earl W. 1976. *Memory, Meaning, and Method: Some Psychological Perspectives on Language Learning.* Rowley, MA: Newbury House.

Vann, Roberta, and Roberta Abraham. 1989. Strategies of Unsuccessful Language Learners. Paper presented at the annual meeting of Teachers of English to Speakers of Other Languages, San Francisco.

Wenden, Anita L. 1991. *Learner Strategies for Learner Autonomy: Planning and Implementing Learner Training for Language Learners.* Englewood Cliffs, NJ: Prentice-Hall.

Wenden, Anita L., and Joan Rubin. 1987. *Learner Strategies in Language Learning.* Englewood Cliffs, NJ: Prentice-Hall.

Wesche, Marjorie, Henry Edwards, and Winston Wells. 1982. Foreign Language Aptitude and Intelligence. *Applied Psycholinguistics* 3: 127–40.

Appendix 1

Table 1

Data on Weakest Students

Category	Nonweakest Students			Weakest Students			F	df	Significance
	N	Mean	(SD)	N	Mean	(SD)			
Biographic Data									
No. previous languages	674	1.7	(1.3)	15	1.0	(1.7)	7.1502	687	.008
Hartmann Boundary Questionnaire (Higher scores indicate thinner boundaries.)									
Factor II (External)	165	128.9	(19.8)	3	98.3	(18.5)	6.9881	166	.009
Prefer sharp edges	165	33.1	(7.4)	3	24.7	(5.0)	3.8414	166	.05
Prefer neat, orderly	165	19.8	(6.1)	3	12.3	(4.7)	4.4820	166	.04
Prefer clear authority	165	24.8	(4.6)	3	17.7	(1.5)	7.309	166	.008
Total boundary score	165	246.9	(39.9)	3	187.7	(1.5)	6.5579	166	.01
Myers-Briggs Type Indicator									
Sensing-intuition	738	103.4	(29.9)	15	88.3	(29.0)	3.7513	751	.05
Pragmatic-intellectual	676	6.2	(2.7)	13	4.3	(3.4)	6.4318	687	.01
Affective Survey None									
Learning Styles Profile									
Simultaneous visual processing	199	4.3	(1.1)	3	3.0	(0)	4.3550	200	.04
Modern Language Aptitude Test									
Part I	292	36.5	(9.1)	4	24.5	(6.5)	6.8524	294	.009
Part II	292	24.7	(4.5)	4	18.5	(3.5)	7.3634	294	.007
Part III	292	28.3	(9.9)	4	11.0	(8.6)	12.1415	294	.0006
Part IV	292	28.0	(7.5)	4	15.3	(5.3)	11.4289	294	.0008
Part V	292	19.3	(5.3)	4	11.5	(4.7)	8.7868	294	.003
Total Score	292	136.7	(27.5)	4	80.8	(24.6)	16.3881	294	.0001
Index Score	339	62.7	(10.5)	6	43.2.	(10.8)	20.5548	343	.0000
Strategy Inventory for Language Learning None									
Faculty Ratings None									

Note: End-of-training questionnaires on preferred self-study and classroom activities had too few respondents from the weakest student group to be included here.

Abbreviations used in Table 1: Factor I (HBQ)—Internal boundaries refer to relationships internal to the individual; Factor II (HBQ)—External boundaries refer to relationship to outer vs. inner world; HISP—Highest speaking proficiency in previously studied language; MLAT Part I—number learning; Part II—phonemic transcription; Part III—English vocabulary in scrambled spellings; Part IV—sensitivity to English sentence structure; Part V—paired associates: vocabulary learning; Index Score—T-score based on total.

Table 2

Data on Strongest Students

Category	Nonstrongest Students N Mean (SD)			Strongest Students N Mean (SD)			F	df	Signif-icance
Biographic Data:									
Education level	645	3.3	(1.1)	27	4.1	(1.2)	13.3136	670	.0003
No. previous languages	637	1.6	(1.0)	26	2.3	(0.7)	10.0750	661	.002
HISP	331	2.2	(1.1)	21	3.2	(1.0)	17.0908	350	.0000
HIRD	325	2.3	(1.1)	21	3.5	(0.9)	23.0790	344	.0000
Age	584	39.4	(9.3)	27	33.7	(7.9)	9.6396	609	.002
Hartmann Boundary Questionnaire (Higher scores indicate thinner boundaries)									
Prefer neat, orderly	153	19.5	(6.3)	9	23.7	(5.0)	3.8905	160	.05
Myers-Briggs Type Indicator									
Realistic-imaginative	575	5.7	(3.2)	21	7.2	(2.9)	4.5036	594	.03
Methodical-emergent	575	3.2	(2.5)	21	4.6	(2.8)	6.0914	594	.01
Affective Survey									
Intrinsic motivation	92	109.0	(13.2)	7	92.6	(36.8)	7.1201	97	.009
Overall motivation	92	212.4	(23.2)	7	190.7	(32.0)	5.4036	97	.02
Endorse neg. items	92	129.8	(13.8)	7	118.4	(9.8)	4.5077	97	.04
Endorse neg. anx. items	92	117.3	(12.8)	7	106.6	(9.1)	4.7010	97	.03
Gen'l affectve arousal	92	588.9	(32.4)	7	559.3	(38.2)	5.3086	97	.02
Learning Styles Profile None									

Table 2 continued

Data on Strongest Students

Category	Nonstrongest Students			Strongest Students			F	df	Signif-icance
	N	Mean	(SD)	N	Mean	(SD)			
Modern Language Aptitude Test									
Part I	224	35.0	(9.7)	14	40.5	(4.9)	4.4395	236	.04
Part II	224	24.3	(4.7)	14	27.2	(2.8)	5.2765	236	.02
Part III	224	26.9	(10.2)	14	32.8	(7.0)	4.5701	236	.03
Total Score	224	132.2	(29.6)	14	151.2	(13.8)	5.7291	236	.02
Index Score	269	60.9	(11.2)	19	68.2.	(5.9)	7.8286	286	.006
Strategy Inventory for Language Learning									
Memory strategies	166	2.7	(0.6)	11	3.1	(0.4)	6.5273	175	.01
End-of-Training Self-Study Activities Questionnaire None									
End-of-Training Classroom Activities Questionnaire									
Group work	63	2.0	(0.7)	5	1.2	(0.5)	5.1948	66	.03
Reg. lesson routine	74	2.3	(0.7)	6	1.7	(0.8)	4.8305	78	.03
Gramm. patt. in context	77	2.4	(0.7)	7	1.7	(0.5)	7.1121	82	.009
Trans. into Eng. for rdg	77	2.5	(0.6)	7	1.9	(0.7)	6.6371	82	.01
FL word games	46	2.1	(0.87)	2	1.0	(0)	4.4678	46	.04
Reg. pronunc. correctn	76	2.3	(0.7)	7	2.9	(0.4)	4.4039	81	.04
Tchr not avoid correctn	78	1.7	(.07)	7	1.0	(0)	6.0057	83	.02
Faculty Ratings									
Extrinsic motivation	254	0.3	(0.7)	16	1.1	(1.2)	16.0680	268	.0001

Abbreviations used in Table 2: Factor I (HBQ)—Internal boundaries refer to relationships internal to the individual; Factor II (HBQ)—External boundaries refer to relationship to outer vs. inner world; HIRD—Highest reading proficiency in previously studied language; HISP—Highest speaking proficiency in previously studied language; MLAT Part I—number learning; Part II—phonemic transcription; Part III—English vocabulary in scrambled spellings; Part IV—sensitivity to English sentence structure; Part V— paired associates: vocabulary learning; Index Score—T-score based on Total.

Appendix 2

Table 3
Summary of Results

Weakest Students	Strongest Students
Less language learning experience	Younger More language learning experience Higher education level (hence more use of learning strategies?)
Thick ego boundaries (inferred as low tolerance of ambiguity)	Rejection of neatness and order (thin direction) may indicate somewhat higher tolerance of ambiguity and be manifested in:
MBTI sensing preference, e.g., sequential, preorganized, concrete, and discrete-point learning	MBTI weak preferences for imaginative and emergent learning, e.g., more random, unplanned, or ambiguous learning.
(Tolerance for ambiguity as defined through the HBQ and the MBTI may be less an advantage to the strongest students than its lack is a disadvantage to the weakest.)	
	Less affectively aroused (motivation, anxiety)
	Less negative about learning Subsignificant anxiety about classroom
Substantially lower cognitive aptitude (2 SD) as measured on the MLAT.	More cognitive aptitude (ca. .6–.7 SD). as measured on the MLAT.
	Tend to use SILL memory strategies. Less time spent on study activities in general. Use resources (feedback, explanations) but do not want to be routinized; tend to be independent learners and use deep processing of new material.

Affective Outcomes of Error Correction: An Aptitude–Treatment Interaction Study

Robert M. DeKeyser
University of Pittsburgh

Introduction

Many universities and colleges have introduced or reintroduced a foreign language requirement during the last fifteen years, following the report of President Carter's Commission on Foreign Language and International Studies in 1979 and the publication of *A Nation at Risk* by the National Commission on Excellence in Education in 1983. The results of these new requirements, however, leave much to be desired. Many students take a foreign language for one year in order to fulfill the requirement, and thereafter quickly lose whatever tenuous skills they may have had at the end of that year. Others are genuinely interested in becoming proficient in a second language, but are turned off by certain aspects of the methodology or the institutional setup, both aimed at channeling large groups of students through the required year of course work. As a result, in terms of language study, we are no less a "nation at risk" than in 1983.

Streamlined foreign language curricula (often designed to be teacher-proof) leave little room for the individual differences in aptitude level, aptitude profile, cognitive style, personality, motivational level, and motivational orientation that characterize the undergraduate population now more than ever before. And yet foreign language education can only serve the nation if it serves the individual student, that is, if individual students are enabled to capitalize on their strengths and to compensate for their weaknesses in order to reach a maximum level of achievement.

One of the main problems facing directors of foreign language programs who would like to individualize their course offerings with these goals in mind, or at least cater to different groups by varying the teaching methodology of the many first-year sections taught in parallel, is that it is very hard to introduce any kind of variation into the curriculum without jeopardizing its streamlined character. The latter is seen as important to maintain proper oversight and quality control, and to ensure seamless transitions from one term to another, regardless of what section the student was in. Therefore, the most realistic candidates for individualization among the many methodological variables are those that do not imply any changes in scheduling, grammatical syllabi, evaluation techniques, or teacher training, but that can be implemented in the various sections while leaving these larger administrative frameworks intact.

A promising teaching variable from that point of view is error correction. Whether and how errors will be corrected during classroom communication in the foreign language is largely independent of other methodological options such as the nature of the syllabus, grammatical structures to be taught and their sequencing, or the choice of a textbook. Moreover, it is a variable that has drawn much attention both from theoreticians interested in the role of "negative evidence" in second language acquisition in formal contexts, and from teachers who struggle with the decision of when and how to correct their students on a daily basis, torn as they are between the desire to provide these students with some opportunities for unhampered communication in the foreign language and the perceived need to instill a minimal amount of linguistic competence in the narrow sense of morphosyntactic correctness.

The debate in the professional literature about whether error correction reduces the number of errors has both a theoretical and an empirical component, but neither has yielded any clear conclusions that could be applied to the practice of error correction. On the one hand, the theoretical arguments about the near-absence and the futility of error correction in first language acquisition and naturalistic second language acquisition may not apply to instructed second language acquisition; on the other hand, the empirical literature contains almost no reference to error correction during oral communicative activities in the classroom, while the research available on correction of written work is very inconsistent. (See DeKeyser 1993 for a detailed overview.)

While the inconsistency of the few existing studies may be due in part to methodological inadequacies, it is also likely that individual differences are a contributing factor, in the sense that the treatment that is better for certain students may be worse for others. Individual differences, especially aptitude, motivation, and anxiety, play a strong role both in instructed and naturalistic second language acquisition (see Carroll 1981; Krashen 1981; Gardner 1985; and especially the overview in Skehan 1989), and in spite of the small amount of research carried out on the interaction of these individual differences with teaching methodology, a number of findings exist that show the potential of research on such aptitude–treatment interactions (Skehan 1989, chap. 7). Some studies have yielded results that are very promising from the point of view of those who administer large programs; Wesche (1981), in particular, has shown how the efficiency of the teaching of French in the Canadian Public Service was improved by judicious matching of different instructional methods with different student profiles (relative degrees of analytical ability, memory, and preferred sensory modality).

However, only one aptitude–treatment interaction study mentioned in Skehan (1989) deals with error correction, that of Carroll and Spearritt (1967), which is based on data collected during a single class period. Since the differences in error treatment coincide with differences in the sequencing of information, and because of problems with the statistical analysis, "it does not appear that any conclusions can be drawn" (Cronbach and Snow 1977, p. 201).

Given this dearth of research in the second language field on aptitude–treatment interaction in general, and on the interaction of error correction with individual differences in particular, I set out to conduct a study on the latter, with linguistic as well as affective outcome variables. The linguistic outcomes were reported in DeKeyser (1993); this chapter presents the affective outcomes.

The Study

Background

Affective variables such as motivation and anxiety usually appear as predictor variables in studies of individual differences, or as mere covariates in studies on teaching variables. They are seldom selected as an outcome variable (probably because language proficiency is the most obvious objective of language instruction, and therefore most research tends to assess how well this goal was met), even though affective outcomes can be equally or more important in the long run. They largely determine whether the student will keep enrolling for foreign language courses once the foreign language requirement has been met, and may therefore be a better indicator of ulti-mate achievement than achievement or proficiency at the end of the first year are. They may also play a big role in the way the student approaches future learning tasks, for example, by focusing on accuracy or fluency, by risk taking or risk avoiding, by seeking out contact with native speakers, or by not making any such effort.

Two studies describe students' preferences about error correction. Chenoweth, Day, Chun, and Luppescu (1983) showed that their group of 418 students (all Asian) was overwhelmingly in favor of error correction by their native-speaking friends in informal contexts, regardless of gender, school, or nationality (except for the Korean respondents, whose opinions were divided). Cathcart and Olsen (1976) surveyed the attitudes of 188 students of different nationalities toward ESL teachers' corrections, and also found that the vast majority of students wanted to be corrected "all the time" (including during conversation), especially for "pronunciation and grammar" (p. 45) errors rather than for "vocabulary and word order errors" (Cathcart and Olsen 1976), even though native speakers tend to find the latter kinds more irritating (cf. Politzer 1978). A comparison with a teacher survey showed that "students wish to be corrected more than teachers feel they should be" (Cathcart and Olsen, 1976, p. 52).

Except for gender and nationality, no individual difference variables seem to have been scrutinized systematically for any possible effect on the desirability of error correction from the student's point of view; the literature only contains some vague references to taking the student's personality into account. Therefore, in the present study, I not only looked at affective out-comes of treatments with or without error correction, but also investigated the interaction between these treatments and individual difference variables, including aptitude, motivation, anxiety, and previous achievement.

Hypotheses

It was hypothesized that error correction would show both a main effect on the students' motivation and anxiety levels and an interaction effect with several individual characteristics.

Main Effects

Motivation has been the object of a considerable amount of research in the field of second language acquisition, but most of it concerns the social-psychological variables of integrative and instrumental motivation (e.g., Gardner 1985; Gardner and McIntyre 1991). It can be argued that for most *foreign* language learners, especially in a monolingual environment, and in contexts where the language is required, educational-psychological variables play a more important role (see also Crookes and Schmidt 1991); that is, extrinsic motivation, what Reber (1984, p. 37) describes as "motivation that originates in factors outside of the individual . . . by rewards and/or punishments administered by outside forces" is what really counts. It was hypothesized for this study that error correction would contribute to extrinsic motivation, because error correction would be a constant reminder to the students of what is expected of them, at least in terms of formal accuracy.

Anxiety, at least in the sense of foreign language classroom anxiety (Horwitz and Young 1991), was also hypothesized to increase as a result of error correction: frequent negative feedback on task performance is likely to increase the amount of psychological pressure resulting from that task. The constant feedback that characterized the audiolingual method, for instance, was probably the main reason why it was experienced as a high-pressure teaching method by most students.

Interaction Effects

It was further hypothesized that the effect of error correction on *anxiety* would depend on the students' level of initial anxiety, extrinsic motivation, previous achievement, and aptitude. Students who have a high anxiety level or strong extrinsic motivation to begin with are likely to suffer from increased anxiety levels if they receive frequent negative feedback. On the other hand, students with a high aptitude level or students who, for whatever reason, tend to be high achievers, are less likely to experience such pressure. No interaction effects on *extrinsic motivation* were hypothesized.

More formally stated, the following hypotheses were tested in this study:

Hypothesis 1: Main effect of error correction on posttreatment anxiety. A higher level of anxiety exists for the group with error correction than for the group without.

Hypothesis 2: Main effect of error correction on posttreatment extrinsic motivation. A higher level of extrinsic motivation exists for the group with error correction than for the group without.

Hypothesis 3: Interaction effect on posttreatment anxiety between error correction and initial anxiety. For students with high initial anxiety levels, posttreatment anxiety will be higher with error correction than without. For students with low initial anxiety, there will be no such effect.

Hypothesis 4: Interaction effect on posttreatment anxiety between error correction and initial extrinsic motivation. For students with high initial levels of extrinsic motivation, posttreatment anxiety levels will be higher with error correction than without; for students with low initial extrinsic motivation, there will be no such effect.

Hypothesis 5: Interaction effect on posttreatment anxiety between error correction and verbal aptitude. For students with low aptitude levels, posttreatment anxiety will be higher with error correction than without; for students with high aptitude levels, there will be no such effect.

Hypothesis 6: Interaction effect on posttreatment anxiety between error correction and previous achievement. For students with low previous achievement, posttreatment anxiety will be higher with error correction than without; for students with high previous achievement, there will be no such effect.

Hypothesis 7: No interaction effects on posttreatment extrinsic motivation exist between error correction and individual difference variables.

Subjects

The subjects of this study were thirty-five Dutch-speaking high school seniors learning French as a second language in the Dutch-speaking part of Belgium.[1] Roughly equal numbers of male and female students were involved. All had had three or four hours of French per week for at least six years. Their instruction had always had a fairly strong focus on form, but all classroom communication was in French, and communicative exercises without focus on form (such as discussion of readings, debates, skits, and problem-solving activities) were frequent. Exams and tests were typically strongly form-focused. None of the students reported any substantial out-of-class contact with French, and most students said they never used French at all.

Treatments

The treatments lasted a full school year. The subjects belonged to two classes (of nineteen and sixteen students, respectively) and had different teachers. For scheduling reasons, it was impossible to study two classes taught by the same teacher. The two teachers used the same thematically organized textbook, and constantly consulted with each other to make sure that they would spend the same amount of time on the same activities. Both teachers were female; they were of the same age and had received their teacher training at the same institution a few years earlier. They had identical social backgrounds, and both were rather authoritarian. One teacher was asked to correct mistakes as frequently and explicitly as possible, including during oral communicative activities; the other was asked to avoid error correction as much as possible (i.e., during communicative activities, and when the students did not explicitly ask for feedback on a specific sentence). Most error correction concerned morphosyntax. The teachers were not asked to focus on any particular constructions, in order not to confound error correction with an increase of attention to specific forms. In fact, they were not even told what specific constructions were to be tested for the study (see below for those constructions).

Both classrooms were regularly observed to assess whether the teachers were implementing the treatments as foreseen; ten class periods were audiotaped by this author, and transcribed and analyzed in Debeuf (1988), a descriptive study of interaction patterns, which used the same classroom corpus recorded for the present study. This analysis confirmed that the treatments were implemented as intended. The ratio of error corrections to the total number of negotiations of meaning (e.g., comprehension checks, clarifications requests, self-repetitions) was much greater for the class *with* than for the class *without* error correction (188/505 vs. 18/296), while the total number of noncorrective interactions was roughly similar in the two classrooms (278 vs. 318). Moreover, in the class "without" error correction, in all but one of the eighteen cases the teacher provided immediate correction in an inconspicuous fashion, without explicitly saying "No," "Wrong," or anything of the kind, and without making the student self-correct. As a result, the difference between this sort of error correction and a cooperative restatement of what the interlocutor has said, as may happen in a native–native interaction, is difficult to perceive. The error treatment in the other class was quite conspicuous; usually the teacher would indicate that an error had been made and try to get the student to apply the relevant rule, but sometimes the teacher would correct the error herself.

Instruments

Aptitude was defined in this study as grammatical sensitivity and operationalized as a component of a Dutch-language verbal aptitude battery. This component, called "Functions of Words" (Drenth and van Wieringen 1969), is a validated and normed adaptation of "Words in Sentences," Part IV of Carroll and Sapon's (1959) *Modern Language Aptitude Test* (MLAT). While using only this component is a narrow operationalization of the concept of language learning aptitude, it was adequate for this study, which dealt only with morphosyntax, and not with vocabulary, pronunciation, or spelling, for which other parts of the MLAT may be more relevant.

Extrinsic motivation was operationalized as follows. While questionnaires exist in the literature for both integrative/instrumental motivation in second language learning and for extrinsic motivation in general, none exists for extrinsic motivation in second language learning. I wrote six Likert scale–type items, which were then randomly distributed within a questionnaire along with items measuring a number of other affective variables. A factor analysis of these six motivation items was performed on the results from sixty-two students in a pilot study, and only the items that clustered into the predicted factor were kept; as a result, five items were left (internal consistency: Cronbach's alpha = .78).

In order to measure *French class anxiety,* I took advantage of a questionnaire developed by Gardner and his collaborators (Gardner 1985, p. 179). The five items from this questionnaire, in free Dutch translation, were factor-analyzed along with ten items measuring attitude toward the norm, and all five clustered into the same factor. The internal consistency (Cronbach's alpha) for the resulting anxiety scale was .88.

Let us now turn to the linguistic variables, which in this chapter are only used as pretest variables (for the analysis of the linguistic outcomes of the experiment, see DeKeyser 1993). *Proficiency* was assessed by means of three oral communication tasks with a native interlocutor. These three tasks were a twelve-to-fifteen-minute interview, a picture-description task of about the same length, and a storytelling task of about five to six minutes. Great care was taken to ensure that these tasks would be communicative, that is, that the learners would feel they had to convey a number of ideas and not just do a language exercise. Therefore, the interview centered around their plans for further study after graduating from high school, a decision they would have had to discuss with outside counselors around that time; the picture-description task made sure they would convey detailed information by requiring them to describe a picture to the native speaker, who then drew it according to their instructions without seeing it; and the storytelling task, based on a video mime sketch, was made demanding by telling the students that after they had finished, the native speaker, who had not seen the mime sketch, would be asked to decide which one of several very similar stories the student had seen.

Finally, in order to measure *grammatical achievement,* I designed a test that would measure monitored knowledge of French grammar.[2] A fill-in-the-blank test seemed preferable to other formats, such as multiple choice or a grammaticality judgment task, because it is less likely to engage the student in a variety of strategies for answering that have nothing to do with his or her linguistic knowledge, and because it is a format with which the students were more familiar. The test consisted of sixty items corresponding to six problems of French grammar; the items were presented in scrambled order. The six grammar problems were: (1) the use of the subjunctive after *vouloir;* (2) the use of the imperfect indicative in the subordinate clause of a present conditional (counterfactual) sentence; (3) the reduction of the partitive article after an adverb expressing a quantity; (4) the use of the auxiliary in the compound tenses of the verb *aller;* (5) the use of *il y a* and the corresponding forms in various tenses with the meaning of "there is/there are"; and (6) the formation of the regular adverb, that is, the adverb formed by adding *-ment* to the feminine form of the adjective. The problems were chosen because: (1) they represent different levels of difficulty (numbers 1 and 2 being the most difficult); (2) they represent very different aspects of morphosyntax so as to be reasonably representative of French grammar as taught in high school; and (3) they are easy to test within the format described.

Procedures

The aptitude test and the affective variable questionnaire were group-administered during a regular classroom period; together they took a full fifty-minute period. The written grammar test was also given to one class at a time and took almost a full period.

The oral tests were individual; students came to the school library during free periods between classes. As the length of the test varied somewhat from student to student, and to avoid practical complications, only one student was scheduled per class period. Students were interviewed first, and then shown the video. Immediately after viewing, they told the story they had seen. Finally, they were given the picture to describe, and were asked to begin describing it after about one minute. The students were not told about the exact purpose of the study, but they were informed that it was "part of a bigger project aimed at improving the teaching of French in high school."

The recordings of the three oral tasks were given to three native speakers of French, who rated them for fluency and accuracy on a scale of 1 to 20 (since the judges were educated native speakers of French, but not social scientists, I decided to use the 1–20 scale that is most commonly used for academic testing in France). The judges listened to a sample tape (recorded in the same school, but not part of this study) together with the researcher, discussed the various errors and dysfluencies, and agreed on a rating. They were then given the tapes to be rated, along with written instructions to listen to the tapes twice, once for fluency and once for accuracy, and to randomize the order of the tapes between the two listening sessions in order to avoid influence of one rating on the other. They took these written instructions home along with the tapes. Interrater reliability coefficients (calculated by means of Ebel's method of estimating reliability by the intraclass correlation; that is, essentially the average of correlations between the judges) were .90 for accuracy and .92 for fluency.

Results

Table 1 presents the descriptive statistics for the two criterion variables and the individual difference variables for the two groups. The scores for the grammar tests are percentages correct; the scores for the oral accuracy and fluency tests are raw scores out of 60 (20 × 3 raters); for grammatical sensitivity the raw scores on the test are given, and for motivation and anxiety the sum of the relevant questionnaire items are given. As there are too many variables here to test for significant pretreatment differences between

Table 1

Means and Standard Deviations for All Variables

| | Class without Correction | | Class with Correction | |
	Mean	SD	Mean	SD
Individual difference variables:				
Written grammar pretest	.71	.08	.77	.12
Oral fluency pretest	37.40	6.82	37.47	7.34
Oral accuracy pretest	33.43	6.45	34.28	6.77
Grammatical sensitivity	29.56	4.05	30.63	6.18
Initial anxiety	17.64	5.72	18.19	6.87
Initial extrinsic motivation	23.21	3.40	25.65	2.37
Criterion variables:				
Final anxiety	17.79	7.05	18.26	7.26
Final extrinsic motivation	22.86	4.07	22.39	3.24

the two groups by means of simple t-tests, a MANOVA (multiple analysis of variance) was performed on the six individual difference variables together (see Siegel 1990). No significant difference between the two groups was found (Hotelling's $T^2 = .28; p = .47$).

The seven hypotheses were tested by means of an ANCOVA (analysis of covariance) program (see SPSS 1988, p. 617, comment 3) that allows testing for the effect of the grouping variable (in this case, error correction), the individual difference variable (previous achievement, grammatical sensitivity, motivation, and anxiety), and their interaction; the latter is essentially a test of the parallelism of the regression lines for the two groups. The results of these analyses are presented in Table 2.

As Table 2 makes clear, only one covariate was used at a time. Using all the individual difference variables as covariates at the same time would have

Table 2

Significance of Group Differences and of Relationships between Criterion Measures and Individual Difference Variables

	F for group	p	r	F for regression	p	F for interaction	p
Criterion Variable: Anxiety							
Independent variables:							
Grammatical sensitivity	0.05	.005	-.31	.05	.833	8.81	.006
Written grammar pretest	.22	.642	-.59	10.07	.004	.08	.782
Oral accuracy pretest	.01	.936	-.32	3.17	.086	.00	.991
Oral fluency pretest	.01	.942	-.24	1.76	.195	.01	.904
Initial anxiety	.69	.414	.81	29.42	.000	.58	.455
Initial extrinsic motivation	5.94	.022	.03	.48	.497	6.23	.019
Criterion Variable: Extrinsic Motivation							
Independent variables:							
Grammatical sensitivity	1.67	.207	.17	2.20	.149	1.88	.181
Written grammar pretest	2.19	.150	-.11	1.52	.228	2.15	.153
Oral accuracy pretest	.05	.869	.17	.88	.358	.05	.816
Oral fluency pretest	.27	.610	.16	.91	.349	.33	.568
Initial anxiety	.00	.999	.14	.38	.544	.01	.913
Initial extrinsic motivation	1.39	.250	.56	13.20	.001	1.08	.308

provided a stronger test of the main effects, but the number of subjects does not provide enough statistical power for such an analysis. It appears from Table 2 that the main effect was almost never significant, except for anxiety as the dependent variable with grammatical sensitivity or extrinsic motivation as covariates. It should be noted, however, that the main effect only *appears* to be significant where the interaction effect is significant. In fact, when there is an interaction effect between the grouping variable and the covariate, the analysis of covariance does not yield valid results for the main effect. It can be concluded, therefore, that the main effect is not significant; the two instances where it appears to be are an artifact of the interaction between the grouping variable and the covariate. Thus, Hypotheses 1 and 2 could not be confirmed. Hypothesis 3 (interaction effect between error correction and initial anxiety) could not be confirmed either.

Hypothesis 4 (interaction between error correction and initial extrinsic motivation) *was* confirmed ($p = .019$): for students with high initial extrinsic motivation, posttreatment anxiety levels were higher with error correction than without. For students with low initial extrinsic motivation, there is no such effect; there is even an effect in the opposite direction (see Figure 1).

Hypothesis 5 (interaction between error correction and verbal aptitude in the sense of grammatical sensitivity) was also confirmed ($p = .006$): students with low aptitude levels show higher posttreatment anxiety with error correction than without; students with high aptitude levels show no such effect. For the latter group there is even an effect in the opposite direction (see Figure 2).

Hypothesis 6 (interaction between error correction and previous achievement) was not confirmed. No interaction effects were found between error correction, on the one hand, and pretreatment written grammar test scores, oral accuracy, or oral fluency on the other hand.

Hypothesis 7 (no interaction between error correction and individual difference variables with extrinsic motivation as dependent variable) was confirmed: no significant interaction effects of this kind were found.

Conclusions and Implications

This study found no main effects for error correction. Contrary to what was hypothesized, error correction did not lead to significantly higher levels of anxiety or extrinsic motivation in members of the group that was corrected compared to the group that did not receive error correction.

For extrinsic motivation, no interaction effects were found either. For anxiety, interaction effects were found between error correction on the one hand, and grammatical sensitivity and extrinsic motivation on the other hand. These interaction effects could explain the lack of a main effect, given that the effects of the treatment for the high-aptitude versus the low-aptitude students appear to cancel each other out (see Figure 1). The same can be said for the low-motivation versus the high-motivation students (see Figure 2).

Combining the findings of this article with those of DeKeyser (1993), a more complete picture now emerges. Error correction appears to have no generalizable effect on linguistic or affective outcomes. For both types of outcomes, however, interaction effects do obtain: with previous achievement

Figure 1

Interaction between Error Correction and Extrinsic Motivation with Anxiety as Dependent Variable

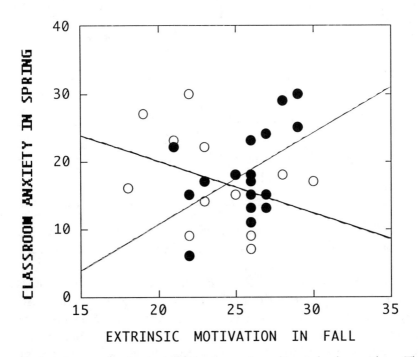

Black circles represent the class with error correction, white circles those without. The line that goes down from right to left is the regression line for the students with error correction; the one that goes down from left to right is the regression line for those without.

Figure 2

Interaction between Error Correction and Grammatical Sensitivity with Anxiety as Dependent Variable

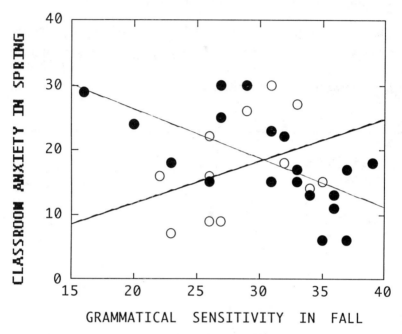

Black circles represent the students with error correction, white circles those without. The line that goes down from left to right is the regression line for the students with error correction; the line that goes down from right to left is the regression line for those without.

and anxiety for grammar knowledge as the outcome variable, with extrinsic motivation for oral proficiency as the outcome variable, and with grammatical sensitivity and extrinsic motivation for anxiety as the outcome variable.

These findings have to be treated with caution for several reasons. First, this was a quasi-experimental study: even though the teachers had very similar backgrounds, and even though the two treatments were found to be identical except for the variable of error correction, a teacher effect cannot be excluded with complete certainty. Second, the number of students studied was small ($N = 35$). Third, the study was carried out in a

Horwitz, Elaine, and Dolly Young. 1991. *Language Anxiety: From Theory and Research to Classroom Implications.* Englewood Cliffs, NJ: Prentice-Hall.

Krashen, Stephen D. 1981. Aptitude and Attitude in Relation to Second Language Acquisition and Learning. In *Individual Differences and Universals in Language Learning Aptitude,* edited by Karl C. Diller, 155–75. Rowley, MA: Newbury House.

National Commission on Excellence in Education. 1983. *A Nation at Risk: The Imperative for Educational Reform.* Washington, DC: U.S. Government Printing Office.

Politzer, Robert L. 1978. Errors of English Speakers of German as Perceived and Evaluated by German Natives. *Modern Language Journal* 62: 253–61.

President's Commission on Foreign Language and International Studies. 1979. *Strength through Wisdom. A Critique of U.S. Capability.* Washington, DC: U.S. Government Printing Office.

Reber, Arthur S. 1984. *The Penguin Dictionary of Psychology.* London: Viking.

Sharwood Smith, Michael. 1991. Speaking to Many Minds: On the Relevance of Different Types of Language Information for the L2 Learner. *Second Language Research* 7: 118–32.

Siegel, Andrew F. 1990. Multiple t Tests: Some Practical Considerations. *TESOL Quarterly* 24: 773–75.

Skehan, Peter. 1989. *Individual Differences in Second-Language Learning.* London: Edward Arnold.

SPSS. 1988. *SPSS-X User's Guide.* 3d ed. Chicago: SPSS.

Wesche, Marjorie Bingham. 1981. Language Aptitude Measures in Streaming, Matching Students with Methods, and Diagnosis of Learning Problems. In *Individual Differences and Universals in Language Learning Aptitude,* edited by Karl C. Diller, 119–54. Rowley, MA: Newbury House.

Teachers Turned Learners: How Do They Learn?

M. Mahodi Alosh
Ohio State University

Introduction

The purpose of this study is to describe the learning strategies that a group of successful learners used while studying Arabic over three intensive summers at the Arabic Language and Culture Institute offered by Ohio State University and funded by the National Endowment for the Humanities. The subjects of this study are full-time teachers of foreign languages or social studies at American secondary schools selected from among the participants in that institute. In order to situate this study in the proper perspective, a discussion of research in learning strategies is in order.

Overview

Disenchantment with the search for the perfect method for delivering instruction to learners of second and foreign languages has led to a growing focus on the learner. Classroom procedures have become more learner-centered, and curricula have been developed in which the learner is the focus of activity (Nunan 1988). Interest has also shifted from *what* learners learn to *how* they learn (Oxford 1990), thus creating a new emphasis on the *process* rather than the *product* of learning. Among the learner variables that have been explored by different researchers over the past two decades or so are attitudes, motivation, cognitive style, and learning strategies.

Research in learning strategies began to receive increasing attention in the 1970s and 1980s. Stern's (1975) seminal study of good language learners was followed by others, both enriching and focusing this new direction of research (see Oller and Richards 1973; Rubin 1975; Naiman, Frölich, Stern, and Todesco 1978; Bialystok 1979; Pimsleur 1980; Stevick 1981; Politzer and McGroarty 1985; Oxford 1986; Chamot, O'Malley, Küper, and Impink-Hernandez 1987). These and other endeavors attempted to identify, classify, and describe the techniques or routines used by learners consciously or subconsciously in order to learn. Stevick (1989), for example, analyzed in detail oral interviews with seven successful foreign language learners to describe strategies those learners used and strategies they did not use. Raimes (1985), using the opposite approach, examined the behaviors of *unskilled* second language writers; she believed their strategies to be as informative and revealing as those of good learners.

Features of Language Learning Strategies

Researchers in language learning and cognitive psychology have used different terms (e.g., procedures, cognitive processes, ways, techniques, tactics, conscious plans, routines, operations, and learning skills) to refer to what learners do and the procedures they employ in order to organize and facilitate their learning. These procedures may be affective, cognitive, or communicative. However, as O'Malley and Chamot (1990) note, the focus in language acquisition research is on *learning* strategies, which are cognitive operations that enhance learning. Wenden (1987, p. 7) regards these different designations as an indication of the "elusive nature of the term."

In her model of second language learning, Bialystok (1978) recognized four categories of learning strategies: inferencing, monitoring, formal practicing, and functional practicing. Each type of strategy is activated according to task requirements, since each of these strategy types is associated with a specific type of knowledge. In her model, three distinct types of knowledge are represented: implicit linguistic knowledge, explicit linguistic knowledge, and general knowledge of the world. In this manner, Bialystok's model accounts for all kinds of language learning, both formal and informal. It should be noted, however, that the three types of knowledge are activated by what she terms *processes,* while input, knowledge stores, and output are linked together by other operations she calls *optional strategies.*

Wenden (1987, pp. 7–8) does not provide a concise, straightforward definition of strategies. Instead, she advances six criteria that seem typical of language learning behaviors:

1. Specific *actions* or *techniques* (e.g., repeating or remembering a rule, listening to a TV program).

2. *Observable* (e.g., asking a question) and *nonobservable* (e.g., making a mental comparison) behaviors.

3. *Problem-oriented strategies* (i.e., facilitating the acquisition, storage, retrieval, or use of information).

4. The fourth criterion includes two kinds of behaviors: (A) Behaviors that contribute *directly to learning.* This criterion is divided into three subcategories: what learners do to *control* or *transform* incoming knowledge (e.g., guessing from context), to *retrieve* and *use* this knowledge (e.g., practice), and to *regulate* learning (e.g., noting if one understands). (B) Behaviors that contribute *indirectly to learning.* This category represents what is known as communication and social strategies (e.g., use of circumlocution and gestures; creating opportunities to learn and use the language).

5. *Conscious versus subconscious* (i.e., automatic) behaviors.

6. Behaviors *amenable to change.*

Oxford (1990, p. 9) lists twelve features of language learning strategies that reflect a number of assumptions she holds about language learning, language use, and the nature of learning strategies. She defines learning strategies as "specific actions taken by the learner" and claims that they are problem-oriented and contribute to the main goal, which is communicative competence. They support learning both directly and indirectly and are not always observable, but are often conscious. They can be taught and are flexible. She believes that learning strategies involve many aspects of the learner, not just the cognitive aspect. She also maintains that awareness of learning strategies allows learners to become more self-directed by making them conscious of the purpose of their learning and the steps they take to make it happen.

One can easily see the overlap between the two classifications of Wenden and Oxford. Both of them put learning strategies in perspective with regard to second language learning. Further, Oxford envisions a new role for the teacher that involves the ability to identify learners' strategies, train learners to master new learning strategies, and help them become more independent. She notes that strategies are influenced by a variety of factors. The generality of this feature makes her model account for almost any learner and learning factors, including age, gender, ethnicity, cognitive style, and task requirements.

Classification of Learning Strategies

Definitions of learning strategies have tended to be of an elusive, vague nature, which has made some researchers refrain from using the word *strategy* altogether (e.g., Stevick 1989). Thanks to efforts by Rubin (1975), Stern (1975), Wenden (1987), O'Malley and Chamot (1990), and Oxford (1990), among others, we now have a much better understanding of learning strategies. Not only have these researchers and theorists identified and described a variety of learning strategies, but they have also classified them into categories. A brief description of these similar, yet distinct, classifications will help put the present study in perspective.

O'Malley and Chamot (1990) and Chamot (1987) classify learning strategies into three categories: metacognitive, cognitive, and social affective (see Figure 1). Metacognitive strategies are not directly related to learning, though they are believed to enhance it. They involve planning for a learning activity, monitoring it, and evaluating its success. Cognitive strategies, on the other hand, affect learning directly by manipulating the input, transforming it into new, permanent knowledge that can be stored in long-term memory. These researchers list four metacognitive strategies, eight cognitive strategies, and three social affective strategies.

Rubin (1987) adopts a classification similar to that of O'Malley and Chamot. However, she identifies an additional group of communication strategies used by language learners, and maintains that while cognitive and metacognitive strategies contribute directly to learning, communication strategies lead to learning only indirectly. It must be noted that Rubin's communication strategies may be loosely equivalent to Canale and

---

Figure 1

O'Malley and Chamot's (1990) Typology of Strategies

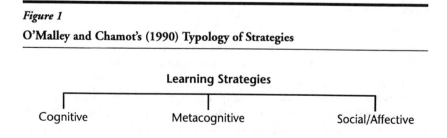

Swain's (1980) strategic competence. Rubin (1987, p. 26) explains that learners resort to these strategies "due to the fact that their communication ends outrun their communication means." Further, she adds that social strategies have no direct effect on learning, since their use only provides learners with the opportunity to practice their language. Thus, her conceptualization of the relationship between the different categories of strategies is rather different from that of O'Malley and Chamot. While O'Malley and Chamot see metacognitive strategies as indirect contributors to learning, Rubin considers them to be equally important to learning, the same as cognitive strategies. Her scheme may be represented as in Figure 2.

Oxford (1990) provides a sophisticated, detailed hierarchy of strategies, which basically divides learning strategies into direct and indirect strategies (see an adapted version in Appendix 1). Direct strategies include memory, cognitive, and compensation strategies. Indirect strategies, on the other hand, include metacognitive, affective, and social strategies (see Figure 3). Oxford enumerates a number of strategies for each subcategory, which she in turn subdivides into more precise strategies, yielding a total of sixty-two specific strategies. It is interesting to note that cognitive strategies are classified as direct, whereas metacognitive strategies are considered indirect, in consonance with O'Malley and Chamot's (1990) classification. The category Oxford labels as compensation strategies (e.g., guessing and overcoming limitations) resembles what Rubin (1987) describes as communication strategies. She cautions, however, that there is still disagreement about the number of strategies that may exist, their definitions, and the demarcation lines that separate them.

Figure 2
Rubin's (1987) Classification of Strategies

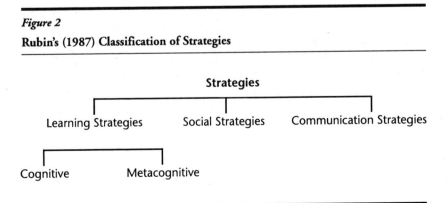

Figure 3

Outline of Oxford's (1990) Classification of Strategies

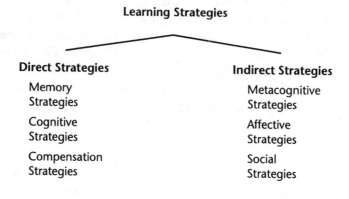

Learning Strategies

Direct Strategies	**Indirect Strategies**
Memory Strategies	Metacognitive Strategies
Cognitive Strategies	Affective Strategies
Compensation Strategies	Social Strategies

Additions to Oxford's original sixty-two strategies were made later on the basis of the informants' descriptions in this study of the actions they performed in order to learn or enhance their learning. A total of twenty-four additional strategies have been integrated into Oxford's paradigm, keeping unchanged her basic classification into six major categories (see Appendix 1).

Description of the Study

This study is based on personal accounts elicited from informants learning Arabic in order to explore the ways in which they organized and facilitated their learning. The aim was to find out what learning strategies they used to aid their learning of Arabic and how effective these strategies were according to the informants' perception. At the time of this study, the informants were learning Arabic at the Arabic Language and Culture Summer Institute[1] offered by Ohio State University and funded by the National Endowment for the Humanities. Part of the data was initially collected during the second year of the institute in the summer of 1992, and the other part was collected a year later while the informants were overseas during the third year of the institute toward the end of the summer session. The data were derived from a survey, from oral interviews with the informants, and from required daily journals which they kept throughout the third summer session.

Purpose and Objectives

The research reported in this chapter was primarily based on Stevick's (1989) work on learning strategies used by successful learners. It was also inspired by the work done by Rubin (1987), Chamot (1987), Wenden (1987), O'Malley and Chamot (1990), and particularly Oxford (1990). This research was guided by four general questions borrowed from Wenden (1987) with slight modifications to fit this study. These questions, she maintains, have consistently been used in research on mental processes in cognitive science. The questions are:

1. What do successful learners of Arabic do to learn?
2. How do these learners manage their learning in and out of class?
3. What do they know about the different aspects of their Arabic learning process?
4. How can their learning skills be developed and refined?

This study had two specific objectives. The first of these objectives was to identify, describe, and classify the strategies used by the informants, who were identified as successful language learners on the basis of their academic achievements and on their performance in class, on tests, and in modified oral proficiency interviews. The other objective was to determine whether there is a common denominator among the informants in terms of shared strategies.

Informants

The nine informants who participated in this study were drawn from a group of thirty-seven non-native speakers of Arabic, all of whom were American secondary and high school teachers of foreign languages and social studies.[2] These teachers participated in the Arabic Language and Culture Summer Institute where they studied Arabic language and culture intensively for up to three summers (1991–1993). Eight of the informants were foreign language teachers, and one was a social studies teacher. Eight of them studied Arabic for three summers, and one studied it for two summers only. The sample comprises six females and three males. As noted above, the informants were selected on the basis of their successful performance on tests and in the classroom. For comparison purposes, another sample of nine less successful participants was drawn from the same population. This second sample is not used in this study in any way other than comparing its scores on the survey with those of the informants who constitute the first sample.

Instruments for Data Collection

According to Cohen (1987), data derived from verbal reports are divided into three categories. The first category includes *descriptions* by informants of what they do, which are based on their beliefs of the way in which they learn languages. The second category is *self-observation*, which is inspection of language behavior during the process of learning (introspection) or after it has occurred (retrospection). The third category is termed *self-revelation*. It involves revealing the process as it is in progress, such as in think-aloud techniques. Cohen notes that a given report may include more than one type of data; this is substantiated by the reports obtained for this study. The data in this study fit in the first category where informants describe the processes they think they use in order to learn, and also in the second category where they describe learning processes right after they have occurred. Although the instruments have not been designed to elicit descriptions of processes as they occur, there were instances when informants engaged in what resembled a think-aloud technique. During the interview, they seemed to relive a specific learning experience or relearn a specific item while they were describing the process. The interviews, however, primarily contained retrospective accounts of the participants' learning experiences.

Three instruments were used. The first one was a Likert-style survey on learning strategies administered in the summer of 1992 to thirty-seven institute participants, including the nine informants in this study (see Appendix 2). The survey was an adaptation of Oxford's (1990, pp. 283–91) survey designed for speakers of English learning a new language. The purpose of the adapted version, which consists of an inventory of eighty-four language learning strategies divided into six categories (see Figure 3), was to obtain information about the processes that the institute participants used in describing their learning of Arabic.

The second instrument was a daily language learning journal that was required of the informants as part of their course requirements in the summer of 1993 (see instructions for writing the journal in Appendix 3). The journals, which were written in English (the first language of the informants), covered five weeks of intensive language learning, both formally in the classroom and informally with the people in the target culture (e.g., in taxicabs, on the street, with shopkeepers). The journals were later analyzed to identify learning strategies.

The third instrument was oral interviews conducted individually in English by the present investigator during the final week of the five-week intensive summer session of 1993. Each interview lasted between twenty and thirty minutes. The informants were asked questions designed to elicit the strategies they used or thought they used. The questions were adapted mainly from Stevick (1989) and were consistently used in a conversational fashion, allowing the informants as much time as they needed to respond (see Appendix 4 for a list of the questions asked in the interview). Some informants did produce extensive, uninterrupted chunks of discourse, describing what they did or characterizing their learning styles. The interviews were later transcribed and analyzed for learning strategies.

Criticism and Justification of Verbal Self-Reports

As the result of researchers' embrace of behavioristic principles earlier this century and their increasing reliance on observable and quantifiable data, the validity of verbal self-reports through introspection was called into doubt or dismissed as unreliable data in studies about the learning process. Cohen (1987) states that the principal objection to such data is that they cannot provide accurate representations of mental processes because language learning occurs at an unconscious level and is therefore inaccessible. Seliger (1983), for example, wonders whether the informant is reporting about unconscious mental processes or about the product of these processes. O'Malley and Chamot (1990, p. 96) criticized studies that used verbal reports for assuming "a high degree of isomorphism between verbal reports and underlying mental processes." McLaughlin (1987) maintains that whether the processes are conscious or unconscious, the data collected from verbal reports would still be unreliable.

Stevick (1989, p. xii) acknowledges these concerns about the validity of verbal reports as sources of usable data on the grounds that the data are not accounts of what the informants actually did, but of what they *thought* they did. Nevertheless, he thinks that data yielded by oral interviews "can be of real and legitimate interest to students of second language learning" (p. xii). He lists five reasons for using verbal self-report data:

1. They are data about what the informants said, though perhaps not data about what they did. In either case, they are data to be accounted for as "sources for conjecture about learning" (p. xii).

2. They are statements that may fit or challenge a second language learning theory and thus may either support or lead to the modification of a given theory.

3. They are consistent with the expectations of many teachers.

4. They serve for student teachers as models of personalities with which they can match abstract ideas.

5. They make prospective teachers aware of the diversity among learners.

Naiman et al. (1978) believe that only through verbal self-reports is it possible to obtain access to strategies not overtly observable. Cohen (1987) maintains that verbal reports about effective strategies are helpful in learner training, but he points out that they should be limited to reports on conscious strategies only. He (1987, p. 36) reports that such data now "enjoy modified support of a respectable group of cognitive psychologists." However, he cautions that they must be collected with care. Ericsson and Simon (1980, p. 247) contend that verbal reports, if they are carefully elicited and interpreted, serve as "a valuable and thoroughly reliable source of information about cognitive processes."

Data Analysis

The data were obtained in two different ways. First, in the survey, the respondents used a scale of 1 to 5 to assess various statements regarding the frequency of their strategy use. Then the average of each one of the six categories of strategies (see Figure 3 and Appendix 1) was calculated by dividing the sum of the items' ratings in that category by the number of items. Second, in the transcripts of the oral interviews and in the journals, the different strategies were first identified and then classified according to the six categories. Most informants made frequent statements about actions that represented one specific strategy used in different situations or contexts. This multiple mention of strategy use was taken into account as an estimate of the degree of use of a particular strategy. The occurrences were then tallied and considered as frequencies of the use of these strategies.

As noted above, by the time the data had been analyzed, a number of additional strategies was identified and integrated into the inventory of strategies originally compiled by Oxford (1990). These additional strategies were gleaned from the informants' descriptions of what they had done in order to learn new information from language input or to facilitate the retrieval of items they had learned before. The bulk of the additional strategies that were identified in the data were in the categories of memory, cognitive, and metacognitive strategies (see Appendix 1). These categories were also used overall more often by the informants than the other three categories.

Table 1

Averages of Strategy Use by Informants in Each Category

Informant Strategy:	1	2	3	4	5	6	7	8	9	Overall
Memory	3.2	2.5	4.3	2.8	3.7	3.4	3.0	3.8	4.3	3.4
Cognitive	3.5	4.1	3.7	3.7	4.0	3.9	3.0	3.4	4.1	3.7
Compensation	4.6	4.3	4.2	2.4	3.8	4.3	3.6	3.9	3.6	3.9
Metacognitive	4.2	3.8	4.6	3.4	4.4	3.1	4.5	4.0	4.7	4.1
Affective	4.0	3.3	4.4	1.7	4.4	2.6	4.0	3.3	3.9	3.5
Social	4.2	3.7	5.0	2.9	4.9	3.0	5.0	4.0	4.4	4.1
Overall average	4.0	3.6	4.4	2.8	4.2	3.4	3.8	3.7	4.2	3.8

Results

There are basically two types of data: one type is derived from Likert-type scales in the survey and the other made up of frequencies derived from the interviews and journals; each type will be presented separately. The analysis of the survey data reveals variability among the nine informants with regard to their usage of learning strategies despite the fact that they belong to the same proficiency level. As Table 1 reveals, although these informants are at approximately the same level of proficiency (Intermediate High), they use different learning strategies in varying degrees. The data in Table 1 represent averages of use by each informant of learning strategies in the six categories of strategies: memory, cognitive, compensation, metacognitive, affective, and social strategies.

Overall usage of strategies by each informant indicates variation in strategy use among the informants, with a range of 1.7 to 5.0 out of 5 and an average of 3.8. The highest individual average is 4.4 and the lowest is 2.8, as shown in Table 1. These individual averages were obtained by calculating the sum of averages of each category for each informant and dividing the sum by six (the number of categories). While there is evidence of variability among the informants, the informants' overall use of strategies is rather high on the scale as illustrated by the graph in Figure 4.

Nonetheless, an examination of the scores of the nine less successful institute participants who make up the second sample and who come from the same larger group from which the first sample in this study was drawn is surprising in light of previous studies that clearly differentiated between

Figure 4

Variation in Overall Strategy Use Among Informants

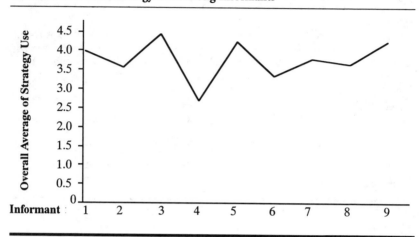

successful and less successful language learners. As Table 2 demonstrates, their scores do not differ appreciably from those of the informants in this study, who were identified as the most successful learners in the institute. The range within the overall individual averages of the less successful participants is 1.4 to 5.0, which suggests slightly greater variability than what exists among the successful informants. However, the combined average of the nine less successful participants is 3.6, which is virtually identical to the average of the more successful group of informants. By comparing strategy use of the two groups, illustrated in Figure 5, one can easily see that both successful and less successful learners follow patterns of usage that are relatively similar. The reason for this unexpected result probably lies in the fact that the sample is too small to show any differences. A recent study by Oxford and Burry-Stock (1993) shows high reliability of

Table 2

Overall Averages of Strategy Use by Less Successful Institute Participants

Participant	1	2	3	4	5	6	7	8	9
Overall Average	4.3	3.4	2.9	3.5	3.7	3.6	3.7	3.2	4.0

Figure 5

Strategy Use by Successful and Less Successful Institute Participants

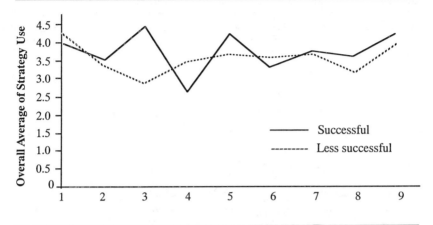

this instrument (Strategy Inventory for Language Learning) and provides evidence of this survey's validity in predicting language proficiency across several ethnic groups around the world.

Another possible reason for the inability of the survey instrument to discriminate between the two groups in this study resides perhaps in the participants' perceptions when they filled out the survey. They might have indicated what they thought they should have done in order to learn better or to enhance their learning, rather than what they actually did.

The other two instruments (the oral interview and the language learning journal) describe the informants' actions when they learn from a different perspective. The information contained in them is specific to actions in which the informants have actually engaged while attempting to perform a particular learning task. The key difference between these two instruments and the survey lies in the fact that the survey items were selected for the informants, whereas the information in the journals and in the interviews were selected and produced by the informants themselves.[3]

By taking a closer look at the informants' use of particular categories in the other two instruments (e.g., the journal and the interview), overall variability is confirmed by variability on specific categories. Let us consider, as an example, the percentages of use of memory, cognitive, and metacognitive strategies by each informant, since they are the most heavily

Table 3

Percentages of Memory, Cognitive, and Metacognitive Strategy
Use by Individual Informants in Journals and Interviews

Informant	%JM	%JC	%JMC	%IM	%IC	%IMC
1	27.31	31.57	26.31	20.00	40.00	0.00
2	37.50	12.50	50.00	15.78	31.57	21.05
3	30.00	20.00	30.00	5.26	73.68	10.52
4	31.70	43.90	17.07	27.27	59.09	4.54
5	36.36	13.63	36.36	37.56	40.62	12.50
6	21.42	42.85	25.00	16.66	40.90	27.27
7	14.28	20.00	60.00	21.21	39.39	24.24
8	25.00	50.00	8.33	25.00	37.50	25.00
9	0.00	38.46	53.84	36.36	27.27	9.09

Legend: J: journal; I: interview; M: memory; C: cognitive; MC: metacognitive

used strategies in this study. Table 3 shows a range of 0 to 37 percent in the use of memory strategies reported in the language learning journals, 12 to 50 percent in cognitive strategies, and 8 to 60 percent in metacognitive strategies. Similarly, usage of these categories in the interviews ranges from 5 to 38 percent in memory strategies, 27 to 74 percent in cognitive strategies, and 0 to 27 percent in metacognitive strategies.

In the oral interviews, the informants collectively made a total of 238 statements, describing various strategies. The majority of these strategies fall into the category of cognitive strategies. They account for 43.3 percent of all strategies mentioned by the informants. The second most commonly used strategies are memory strategies, with 21.8 percent of the total number. Metacognitive strategies come next with 17.6 percent. The use of the other two categories of compensation, affective and social strategies, ranges between 2.5 per cent and 9.2 percent of the total. These figures are listed in Table 4.

The other set of data was obtained from the analysis of the language learning journals that were kept daily by the informants throughout the five-week intensive summer session. Most of the informants had almost instant access to their notebooks to write down descriptions of what they did in order to learn or retrieve language information. Those who delayed

Table 4

Frequencies and Percentages of Strategies Reported by the Informants in Oral Interviews for Each Category

Category	Frequency	Percent
Memory strategies	52	21.8%
Cognitive strategies	103	43.3%
Compensation strategies	13	5.5%
Metacognitive strategies	42	17.6%
Affective strategies	6	2.5%
Social strategies	22	9.2%
Total	238	100%

this process until after instruction ended provided their descriptions retrospectively. Analysis of these data yielded a total of 188 strategies (see Appendix 3 for guidelines on writing the journals). The data from the journals reveal a trend of strategy usage similar to what is reported in the oral interviews. Despite differences in the frequency of strategy usage in the two instruments within each category, the informants used strategies in the same categories more often than in other categories. For instance, the three most heavily used categories of strategies in the journals are metacognitive, cognitive, and memory strategies, at 33.5, 31.9, and 24.5 percent, respectively. All three account for 89.9 percent of the total percentage of usage. The frequencies and percentages of strategy use as reported in the language learning journals are listed in Table 5.

It is interesting to compare the informants' verbal reports of strategy use derived from the last two instruments, namely, the oral interviews and the language learning journals. As the graph in Figure 6 shows, the informants display similar patterns of strategy usage in spite of differences in the reported frequency of usage across the two instruments. They consistently employ memory, cognitive, and metacognitive strategies at much higher frequencies than they do the other three categories. There are, however, differences in the frequency of use of cognitive and metacognitive strategies as reported in the oral interviews.

There is an apparent similarity in the patterns of strategy usage reported in the informants' journals and identified in the interviews. This similarity may be attributable to the fact that the two instruments encourage intensive

Table 5

**Frequencies and Percentages of Strategies Reported by the
Informants in Language Learning Journals for Each Category**

Category	Frequency	Percent
Memory strategies	46	24.5%
Cognitive strategies	60	31.9%
Compensation strategies	3	1.6%
Metacognitive strategies	63	33.5%
Affective strategies	8	4.3%
Social strategies	8	4.3%
Total	188	100%

retrospection although they are used in conjunction with two different modalities (speaking vs. writing).

Discussion

With regard to differences in the degree of strategy use by the informants across the six categories, it may well be that level of proficiency and type of strategy are unrelated factors for participants in this study. Differences in the frequency of usage of specific strategies are consistent with Chamot's (1987) finding that cognitive and metacognitive strategies are the most used strategies by subjects in her study. It is not clear, however, why affective and social strategies are so underutilized; certainly, the informants in the present study were aware of the importance of these factors to learning. Perhaps the intensity of the course made them unconsciously focus almost exclusively on direct strategies, such as cognitive strategies. Also, the learning environment during the first two summers may have had an impact on the way they approached learning, since their learning experience was almost totally limited to the classroom the first summer and to classroom and tutoring sessions during the second summer.

Despite the fact that this study is mainly task-free, the informants did relate strategy use to specific learning tasks. The strategies of grouping, repeating, associating, and placing words in context were often related to learning vocabulary, whereas the strategies of structured reviewing, using formulas and patterns, analyzing, reasoning deductively and inductively, and synthesizing linguistic items were associated with learning grammar. Getting the idea quickly and using linguistic and other clues were used mostly in association with reading tasks. In addition to talking to oneself, recombining, communicating with native speakers, and monitoring pronunciation, two social strategies, those of asking for clarification and cooperating with peers, were used often with reference to speaking.

One informant described how she recalled vocabulary by using an association strategy: "I visualize the passport (referring to its picture in the textbook). . . . For some reason, I can sometimes recall in what unit or what part of the book that I learned the vocabulary in." Another used this strategy: "I learn most of my vocabulary from context." Another one made use of an inherent feature of Arabic morphology to figure out the meaning of words: "If a word sounds like another word in some way, then chances are good with Arabic that they have some common meanings." Two other informants found out that making flashcards helped them to write, to remember, and to focus. Yet another one used patterns to identify words: "I looked for prefix and suffix patterns."

Figure 6

Comparison of Strategy Use by the Informants as Reported in the Oral Interviews and the Language Learning Journals

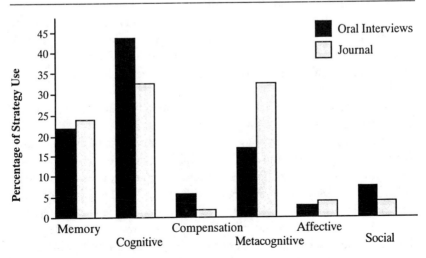

Almost all the informants exhibited a fair amount of sophistication in their use of metalanguage, not only in describing actions they performed in order to learn the new language, but also in describing the systems of the languages they know and that of the new language. One informant maintained that listening first helped him with his production. Another informant put it in this manner: "The first thing is to train the ear and the second thing is that you have to break the habits of a lifetime of speaking other languages where the organs of speech are not forced to produce these sounds." Another informant claimed that she was a firm believer in what she called "germination time," meaning that the best way to learn was to be introduced to a topic at a high level of generality, let it percolate in the mind for some time, then be provided with the details and the opportunity to apply the newly acquired ability.

Perhaps one of the major benefits gained from examining learning strategies is the development of increased sensitivity to learners' perspectives regarding their learning. The first step toward developing such a sensitivity may be for teachers to examine their own learning strategies. Several participants in the institute, upon taking the language learning strategies survey, said that the new knowledge they had gained had made them better learners *and* teachers.

A Taxonomy of Strategies Used by the Informants in This Study

Based on statements made by the informants in the oral interviews and in their language learning journals, a taxonomy of strategies that they had actually used can be developed. This taxonomy, the subject of Appendix 1, is based on the classification originally compiled by Oxford (1990) and then expanded in this study by adding strategies reported by the informants (note that an asterisk denotes an added or a modified item). The number of occurrences of each strategy mentioned in the journals and oral interviews appears on the right.

The modified taxonomy used as a frame of reference in this study consists of a total of seventy specific strategies, including forty-six original strategies contributed by Oxford and twenty-four additional strategies identified in the present data and integrated into the original classification (note that not all Oxford's strategies are listed in Appendix 1; only those reported by the informants are included). The majority of the added strategies are low-frequency strategies, though one of them (communicating with native speakers), at twenty-three occurrences, has the highest frequency in the data.

The additional strategies have a total of eighty-two occurrences and account for 19 percent of total strategy use.

Limitations of the Study

The relatively small sample size and the type of learner the informants represent may preclude generalizations to other learner populations. Cognitively, however, the results may be applicable to a wide spectrum of learners since there is no empirical evidence to substantiate significant differences in cognitive processes across different types of learners. Another possible limitation might result from differences in the types of data elicited from the survey on the one hand and from the two self-report instruments on the other. Further, data pertinent to cognitive styles were excluded from the analysis in this study, not for lack of interest but because these are personality traits that do differ from individual to individual, and therefore are not as amenable for utilization by other learners. Almost all informants described one or more of their cognitive styles in the three instruments.

Implications and Conclusion

The findings in this study reiterate what many studies in language acquisition have postulated about the learning process. Learners' minds, or their language learning faculties, are not like empty vessels to be filled up with new linguistic information. Rather, learners receive language input and process it differentially, applying various strategies; their choice of strategy is influenced by a host of factors, including context, language task requirements, linguistic information, time available for language "germination," and several more. An examination of the informants' use of metacognitive strategies implies that some learners do plan for and manage their learning. This fact should be accounted for in the learning materials and the manner in which learning and instruction are conducted.

One major benefit that can be gleaned from studies in language learning strategies is the potential for providing autonomous, or self-directed, learning. If foreign language programs, especially those in the less commonly taught languages, in which student enrollment is a significant administrative concern, can systematically train students to self-direct their learning effectively and efficiently, then these programs would succeed in addressing two major concerns: minimizing attrition and, at the same time, meeting the diverse needs of students. Such language programs, particularly

Arabic ones, are unlikely to create a section for "general language learning" and a special one for "academic language learning." The need for both is obvious, especially within departments that have graduate degree programs. Autonomous learning would certainly meet some of these needs, where learners in the same section can follow different tracks, based on their program needs. Care, however, should be taken to avoid some of the pitfalls of individualized instruction as practiced in American schools in the 1970s and 1980s, which may be summarized in two major concerns: a possible lack of systematic interaction in the language on the part of the students with other students and with an instructor, and the possibility of not providing each student with strategic sophistication to enable them to manage their learning successfully.

Notes

1. The institute was offered on the campus of Ohio State University in the summers of 1991 and 1992, and in Amman, Jordan, in the summer of 1993.

2. The 1992 institute had a group of seven native-speaker participants. One of their roles was to act as resource persons and tutors to the non-native-speaker participants.

3. This idea was suggested by James Coady.

Works Cited

Bialystok, Ellen. 1978. A Theoretical Model of Second Language Learning. *Language Learning* 28: 69–83.

———. 1979. The Role of Conscious Strategies in Second Language Proficiency. *Canadian Modern Language Review* 35: 372–94.

Canale, Michael, and Merrill Swain. 1980. Theoretical Bases of Communicative Approaches to Second Language Teaching and Testing. *Applied Linguistics* 1: 1–47.

Chamot, Anna U. 1987. The Learning Strategies of ESL Students. In Wenden and Rubin, 71–83.

Chamot, Anna U., J. Michael O'Malley, L. Küper, and M. V. Impink-Hernandez. 1987. *A Study of Learning Strategies in Foreign Language Instruction: First Year Report.* Rosslyn, VA: Interstate Research Associates.

Cohen, Andrew D. 1987. Student Processing of Feedback on Their Compositions. In Wenden and Rubin, 57–69.

Ericsson, K. Andres, and Herbert A. Simon. 1980. Verbal Reports on Data. *Psychological Review* 87: 215–51.

McLaughlin, Barry. 1987. *Theories of Second Language Teaching.* London: Edward Arnold.

Naiman, Neil, Maria Fröhlich, H. H. Stern, and Angie Todesco. 1978. *The Good Language Learner.* Toronto: Institute for Studies in Education.

Nunan, David. 1988. *The Learner-Centered Curriculum.* Cambridge: Cambridge University Press.

Oller, John, and Jack Richards, eds. 1973. *Focus on the Learner: Pragmatic Perspectives for the Language Teacher.* Rowley, MA: Newbury House.

O'Malley, J. Michael, and Anna U. Chamot. 1990. *Learning Strategies in Second Language Acquisition.* Cambridge: Cambridge University Press.

Oxford, Rebecca L. 1986. Development of a New Survey and Taxonomy for Second Language Learning. Paper presented at the fourth annual conference on Learning Strategies, LaGuardia Community College, LaGuardia, NY.

_____. 1990. *Language Learning Strategies: What Every Teacher Should Know.* New York: Newbury House/Harper and Row.

Oxford, Rebecca L., and Judith A. Burry-Stock. 1993. Language Learning Strategies as Measured Around the World by the *Strategy Inventory for Language Learning.* Paper presented at the National Council on Measurement in Education, Atlanta.

Pimsleur, Paul. 1980. *How to Learn a Foreign Language.* Boston: Heinle & Heinle.

Politzer, Robert, and Mary McGroarty. 1985. An Exploratory Study of Learning Behaviors and Their Relationship to Gains in Linguistic and Communicative Competence. *TESOL Quarterly* 19: 103–23.

Raimes, Ann. 1985. What Unskilled ESL Students Do as They Write: A Classroom Study of Composing. *TESOL Quarterly* 19: 229–58.

Rubin, Joan. 1975. What "the Good Language Learner" Can Teach Us. *TESOL Quarterly* 9: 41–51.

_____. 1987. Learner Strategies: Theoretical Assumptions, Research History and Typology. In Wenden and Rubin, 15–30.

Seliger, H. W. 1983. The Language Learner as Linguist: Of Metaphors and Realities. *Applied Linguistics* 4: 179–91.

Stern, H. H. 1975. What Can We Learn from the Good Language Learner? *Canadian Modern Language Review* 31: 304–18.

Stevick, Earl. 1981. Learning a Foreign Language: The Natural Ways. In *On TESOL 81,* edited by M. Hines and W. Rutherford, 1–10. Washington, DC: TESOL.

———. 1989. *Success with Foreign Languages: Seven Who Achieved It and What Worked for Them.* Hempstead, UK: Prentice-Hall International.

Wenden, Anita. 1987. Conceptual Background and Utility. In Wenden and Rubin, 3–13.

Wenden, Anita, and Joan Rubin, eds. 1987. *Learner Strategies in Language Learning.* London: Prentice-Hall International.

Appendix 1
Frequencies of Strategies Used in Oral Interviews and Journals

Direct Strategies

   I. *Memory Strategies*   Number of occurrences

      Creating mental linkages

Grouping	6
Associating/elaborating	15
Placing new words into a context	18

      Applying images and sounds

Using imagery	21
Semantic mapping	2
Using key words	1
Representing sounds in memory	4
Using diagrams and charts*	2
Mental mapping*	1

      Reviewing well

Structured reviewing	15
Forcing recall of items*	4

Employing action
   Using mechanical techniques   3
Memorizing by rote (taking in unanalyzed chunks)*   4
Recording language data in writing*
   Recording verbs*   2
   Recording nouns*   1
   Recording grammar notes*   1

II. *Cognitive Strategies*

Practicing
   Repeating   21
   Formally practicing with sounds and writing systems   22
   Recognizing and using formulas and patterns   12
   Recombining   3
   Practicing naturalistically (communicatively)   12
   Talking to oneself*   2
   Using technology (computer-assisted learning)*   4
   Creating alternative patterns*   1
Receiving and sending messages
   Getting the idea quickly   5
   Using resources for receiving and sending messages   2
Analyzing and reasoning
   Reasoning deductively   4
   Reasoning inductively*   7
   Using resources   1
   Analyzing expressions   18
   Relating new information to prior knowledge   3
   Analyzing contrastively (across languages)   10
   Translating   2
   Transferring (using prior linguistic knowledge to assist comprehension and production)   6
   Classifying and categorizing*   7
   Synthesizing linguistic items   4

Monitoring pronunciation*	1
Self-evaluating	7
Verifying items picked up informally*	2

V. *Affective Strategies*

Encouraging yourself

Making positive statements	8
Rationalizing difficulties and problems*	1
Reaffirming self-confidence to oneself*	2

Taking your emotional temperature

Writing a language learning diary	1
Realizing your limitations	2

VI. *Social Strategies*

Asking questions

Asking for clarification or verification	4
Asking for correction	3

Cooperating with others

Cooperating with peers	10
Cooperating with proficient users of the new language	1

Empathizing with others

Developing cultural understanding	5
Becoming aware of others' thoughts and feelings	5
Total	**431**

• *Based on Oxford's (1990) classification of learning strategies.*
• *An asterisk denotes an added or modified item.*

Appendix 2

Foreign Language Learning Strategies

Name: _____   Date: _____

Instructions
The following statements are related to your experience in learning Arabic. Please read each statement and rate it in terms of how true the statement is in reflecting *what you actually do* when you are learning Arabic, not in terms of what you think you should do or what other people do. There are no right or wrong answers, since people learn differently. To rate each statement, circle the appropriate number. Number 1 means that the statement is very rarely true of you—that is, the behavior described is never or rarely used—and 5 denotes high frequency or constant use of that behavior. Also, on the next line, rate the degree to which each statement is embedded in the instructional activities to which you have been exposed, using the same scale. Instructional strategies include presentation techniques, activities involving student interaction in class, and out-of-class writing activities. Please use the back of each sheet for your comments on particular items, marking each comment with the number of that item.

Please return this form and the worksheet. You may keep the Profile and the Key.

When learning a new word . . .	Never		Most Often		

1. I group new vocabulary items based on type of word (i.e., nouns; similarity; greetings; opposites).　　　　　　　　　　　　　　　　　1　2　3　4　5
   How much is this behavior embedded in instructional strategies?　　　　　　　1　2　3　4　5

2. I relate new language information to concepts already in memory (i.e., associations between two things, e.g., bread and butter, or multiple things, i.e., semantic maps).　　　　1　2　3　4　5
   How much is this behavior embedded in instructional strategies?　　　　　　　1　2　3　4　5

	Never			Most Often	

3. I put the new word in a sentence so that I can remember it. 1 2 3 4 5
How much is this behavior embedded in instructional strategies? 1 2 3 4 5

4. I associate the sound of the new word with the sound of a familiar word. 1 2 3 4 5
How much is this behavior embedded in instructional strategies? 1 2 3 4 5

5. I use rhyming to remember a new word.
How much is this behavior embedded in instructional strategies? 1 2 3 4 5

6. I remember the word by making a clear mental image of it or by drawing a picture. 1 2 3 4 5
How much is this behavior embedded in instructional strategies? 1 2 3 4 5

7. I visualize the spelling of the new word in my mind. 1 2 3 4 5
How much is this behavior embedded in instructional strategies? 1 2 3 4 5

8. I use a combination of sounds and images to remember the new word. 1 2 3 4 5
How much is this behavior embedded in instructional strategies? 1 2 3 4 5

9. I list all the other words I know that are related to the new word and draw lines to show relationships. 1 2 3 4 5
How much is this behavior embedded in instructional strategies? 1 2 3 4 5

10. I remember where the new word is located on the page, or where I first saw or heard it. 1 2 3 4 5
How much is this behavior embedded in instructional strategies? 1 2 3 4 5

11. I use flashcards with the new word on one side and the definition of other information on the other. 1 2 3 4 5

	Never			Most Often	
How much is this behavior embedded in instructional strategies?	1	2	3	4	5
12. I physically act out the new word.	1	2	3	4	5
How much is this behavior embedded in instructional strategies?	1	2	3	4	5

When learning new material . . .

	Never			Most Often	
13. I review often.	1	2	3	4	5
How much is this behavior embedded in instructional strategies?	1	2	3	4	5
14. I schedule my reviewing so that the review sessions are initially close together in time and gradually become more widely spread apart.	1	2	3	4	5
How much is this behavior embedded in instructional strategies?	1	2	3	4	5
15. I go back to refresh my memory of things I learned much earlier.	1	2	3	4	5
How much is this behavior embedded in instructional strategies?	1	2	3	4	5
16. I write down the new words, using transliteration (i.e., Roman characters).	1	2	3	4	5
How much is this behavior embedded in instructional strategies?	1	2	3	4	5
17. I do not write down the new words, but rather try initially to memorize them and use them orally.	1	2	3	4	5
How much is this behavior embedded in instructional strategies?	1	2	3	4	5
18. I say or write new expressions repeatedly to practice them.	1	2	3	4	5
How much is this behavior embedded in instructional strategies?	1	2	3	4	5
19. I imitate the way native speakers talk.	1	2	3	4	5
How much is this behavior embedded in instructional strategies?	1	2	3	4	5
20. I read a story or a dialogue several times until I can understand it.	1	2	3	4	5

	Never			Most Often	

How much is this behavior embedded in instructional strategies?	1	2	3	4	5
21. I revise what I write in Arabic to improve my writing.	1	2	3	4	5
How much is this behavior embedded in instructional strategies?	1	2	3	4	5
22. I practice the Arabic sounds and alphabet.	1	2	3	4	5
How much is this behavior embedded in instructional strategies?	1	2	3	4	5
23. I use idioms and other routines in Arabic.	1	2	3	4	5
How much is this behavior embedded in instructional strategies?	1	2	3	4	5
24. I use familiar words in different combinations to make new sentences.	1	2	3	4	5
How much is this behavior embedded in instructional strategies?	1	2	3	4	5
25. I initiate conversations with classmates in Arabic.	1	2	3	4	5
How much is this behavior embedded in instructional strategies?	1	2	3	4	5
26. I watch TV shows or movies or listen to the radio in Arabic.	1	2	3	4	5
How much is this behavior embedded in instructional strategies?	1	2	3	4	5
27. I try to think in Arabic.	1	2	3	4	5
How much is this behavior embedded in instructional strategies?	1	2	3	4	5
28. I attend and participate in out-of-class events where Arabic is spoken.	1	2	3	4	5
How much is this behavior embedded in instructional strategies?	1	2	3	4	5
29. I read for pleasure in Arabic.	1	2	3	4	5
How much is this behavior embedded in instructional strategies?	1	2	3	4	5
30. I write personal notes, messages, letters, or reports in Arabic.	1	2	3	4	5

	Never		Most Often		

How much is this behavior embedded in instructional strategies? 1 2 3 4 5

31. I skim the reading passage first to get the main idea; then I go back and read it more carefully. 1 2 3 4 5
How much is this behavior embedded in instructional strategies? 1 2 3 4 5

32. I seek specific details in what I hear or read. 1 2 3 4 5
How much is this behavior embedded in instructional strategies? 1 2 3 4 5

33. I use reference materials, such as glossaries or dictionaries, to help me use Arabic. 1 2 3 4 5
How much is this behavior embedded in instructional strategies? 1 2 3 4 5

34. I take notes in class in Arabic. 1 2 3 4 5
How much is this behavior embedded in instructional strategies? 1 2 3 4 5

35. I make summaries of new language material. 1 2 3 4 5
How much is this behavior embedded in instructional strategies? 1 2 3 4 5

36. I apply general rules to new situations when using Arabic. 1 2 3 4 5
How much is this behavior embedded in instructional strategies? 1 2 3 4 5

37. I find the meaning of a new word by dividing the word into parts which I understand. 1 2 3 4 5
How much is this behavior embedded in instructional strategies? 1 2 3 4 5

38. I look for similarities and contrasts between Arabic and my first language. 1 2 3 4 5
How much is this behavior embedded in instructional strategies? 1 2 3 4 5

39. I try to understand what I have heard or read without translating it word-for-word into my first language. 1 2 3 4 5

	Never				Most Often

How much is this behavior embedded in
instructional strategies? 1 2 3 4 5

40. I am cautious about transferring words or
concepts directly from my language to Arabic. 1 2 3 4 5
How much is this behavior embedded in
instructional strategies? 1 2 3 4 5

41. I look for patterns in Arabic. 1 2 3 4 5
How much is this behavior embedded in
instructional strategies? 1 2 3 4 5

42. I use inductive reasoning (generalize from
instances). 1 2 3 4 5
How much is this behavior embedded in
instructional strategies? 1 2 3 4 5

43. I develop my own understanding of how the
language works, even if sometimes I have to
revise my understanding based on new
information. 1 2 3 4 5
How much is this behavior embedded in
instructional strategies? 1 2 3 4 5

44. When I do not understand all the words I
read or hear, I guess the general meaning by
using any clue I can find, for example, clues
from the context or situation. 1 2 3 4 5
How much is this behavior embedded in
instructional strategies? 1 2 3 4 5

45. I read without looking up every unfamiliar word. 1 2 3 4 5
How much is this behavior embedded in
instructional strategies? 1 2 3 4 5

46. In a conversation, I anticipate what the other
person is going to say based on what has been
said so far. 1 2 3 4 5
How much is this behavior embedded in
instructional strategies? 1 2 3 4 5

47. If I am speaking and cannot think of the right
expression, I use gestures or switch back to
my own language momentarily. 1 2 3 4 5

	Never		Most Often		

How much is this behavior embedded in
instructional strategies?   1   2   3   4   5

48. I ask the other person to tell me the right
    word if I cannot think of it in a conversation.   1   2   3   4   5
    How much is this behavior embedded in
    instructional strategies?   1   2   3   4   5

49. When I cannot think of the correct expression
    to say or write, I find a different way to
    express the idea; for example, I use a synonym
    or describe the idea.   1   2   3   4   5
    How much is this behavior embedded in
    instructional strategies?   1   2   3   4   5

50. I make up new words if I do not know the
    right ones.   1   2   3   4   5
    How much is this behavior embedded in
    instructional strategies?   1   2   3   4   5

51. I direct the conversation to a topic for which
    I know the words.   1   2   3   4   5
    How much is this behavior embedded in
    instructional strategies?   1   2   3   4   5

52. I preview the language lesson to get a general
    idea of what it is about, how it is organized,
    and how it relates to what I already know.   1   2   3   4   5
    How much is this behavior embedded in
    instructional strategies?   1   2   3   4   5

53. When someone is speaking Arabic, I try to
    concentrate on what the person is saying and
    put unrelated topics out of my mind.   1   2   3   4   5
    How much is this behavior embedded in
    instructional strategies?   1   2   3   4   5

54. I decide in advance to pay special attention to
    specific language aspects; for example, I focus
    on the way native speakers pronounce
    certain sounds.   1   2   3   4   5
    How much is this behavior embedded in
    instructional strategies?   1   2   3   4   5

	Never				Most Often

55. I try to find out all I can about how to be a
better language learner by reading books or
articles, or by talking to others about how
to learn.   1   2   3   4   5
How much is this behavior embedded in
instructional strategies?   1   2   3   4   5

56. I arrange my schedule to study and practice
the new language consistently, not just when
there is the pressure of a test.   1   2   3   4   5
How much is this behavior embedded in
instructional strategies?   1   2   3   4   5

57. I arrange my physical environment to promote
learning; for instance, I find a quiet,
comfortable place to review.   1   2   3   4   5
How much is this behavior embedded in
instructional strategies?   1   2   3   4   5

58. I organize my language notebook to record
important language information.   1   2   3   4   5
How much is this behavior embedded in
instructional strategies?   1   2   3   4   5

59. I plan my goals for language learning, for
example, how proficient I want to become or
how I might want to use the language in the
long run.   1   2   3   4   5
How much is this behavior embedded in
instructional strategies?   1   2   3   4   5

60. I plan what I am going to accomplish in
language learning each day or each week.   1   2   3   4   5
How much is this behavior embedded in
instructional strategies?   1   2   3   4   5

61. I prepare for an upcoming language task by
considering the nature of the task, what I
have to know, and my current language skills.   1   2   3   4   5
How much is this behavior embedded in
instructional strategies?   1   2   3   4   5

	Never			Most Often	

62. I clearly identify the purpose of the language activity; for instance, in a listening task, I might need to listen for the general idea or for specific facts.   1 2 3 4 5
How much is this behavior embedded in instructional strategies?   1 2 3 4 5

63. I take responsibility for finding opportunities to practice Arabic.   1 2 3 4 5
How much is this behavior embedded in instructional strategies?   1 2 3 4 5

64. I actively look for people with whom I can speak Arabic.   1 2 3 4 5
How much is this behavior embedded in instructional strategies?   1 2 3 4 5

65. I try to notice my language errors and find out the reasons for them.   1 2 3 4 5
How much is this behavior embedded in instructional strategies?   1 2 3 4 5

66. I learn from my mistakes in using Arabic.   1 2 3 4 5
How much is this behavior embedded in instructional strategies?   1 2 3 4 5

67. I evaluate the general progress I have made in learning the new language.   1 2 3 4 5
How much is this behavior embedded in instructional strategies?   1 2 3 4 5

68. I talk to myself in Arabic to practice the language.   1 2 3 4 5
How much is this behavior embedded in instructional strategies?   1 2 3 4 5

69. I try to relax whenever I feel anxious about using Arabic.   1 2 3 4 5
How much is this behavior embedded in instructional strategies?   1 2 3 4 5

70. I make encouraging statements to myself so that I will continue to try hard and do my best in language learning.   1 2 3 4 5

	Never		Most Often		

How much is this behavior embedded in
instructional strategies? 1 2 3 4 5

71. I actively encourage myself to take wise risks
in language learning, such as guessing meaning
or trying to speak, even though I might make
some mistakes. 1 2 3 4 5

How much is this behavior embedded in
instructional strategies? 1 2 3 4 5

72. I give myself a tangible reward when I have
done something well in my language learning. 1 2 3 4 5

How much is this behavior embedded in
instructional strategies? 1 2 3 4 5

73. I pay attention to physical signs of stress that
might affect my language learning. 1 2 3 4 5

How much is this behavior embedded in
instructional strategies? 1 2 3 4 5

74. I keep a private diary or journal where I write
my feelings about language learning. 1 2 3 4 5

How much is this behavior embedded in
instructional strategies? 1 2 3 4 5

75. I talk to someone I trust about my attitudes
and feelings concerning the language learning
process. 1 2 3 4 5

How much is this behavior embedded in
instructional strategies? 1 2 3 4 5

76. If I do not understand, I ask the speaker to
slow down, repeat, or clarify what was said. 1 2 3 4 5

How much is this behavior embedded in
instructional strategies? 1 2 3 4 5

77. I ask other people to verify that I have
understood or said something correctly. 1 2 3 4 5

How much is this behavior embedded in
instructional strategies? 1 2 3 4 5

78. I ask other people to correct my pronunciation. 1 2 3 4 5

How much is this behavior embedded in
instructional strategies? 1 2 3 4 5

	Never				Most Often
79. I work with other language learners to practice, review, or share information.	1	2	3	4	5
How much is this behavior embedded in instructional strategies?	1	2	3	4	5
80. I have a regular language learning partner.	1	2	3	4	5
How much is this behavior embedded in instructional strategies?	1	2	3	4	5
81. When I am talking with a native speaker, I try to let him or her know when I need help.	1	2	3	4	5
How much is this behavior embedded in instructional strategies?	1	2	3	4	5
82. In conversation with others in Arabic, I ask questions in order to be as involved as possible and to show that I am interested.	1	2	3	4	5
How much is this behavior embedded in instructional strategies?	1	2	3	4	5
83. I try to learn about the culture of the place where the new language is spoken.	1	2	3	4	5
How much is this behavior embedded in instructional strategies?	1	2	3	4	5
84. I pay close attention to the thoughts and feelings of other people with whom I interact in Arabic.	1	2	3	4	5
How much is this behavior embedded in instructional strategies?	1	2	3	4	5

Based on Oxford (1990).

Worksheet

Name: _____

1. In each blank, copy the number you circled for each item that describes behaviors (i.e., 1, 2, 3, 4, or 5), *excluding* the number on the next line concerning embedded instructional strategies.

2. Total each column and put the result on the line marked "Sum."

3. Divide each Sum by the number under "Sum" to provide an average for each column. Round each average to the nearest tenth (3.36 ➙ 3.4). Your average for each part should be between 1.0 and 5.0.

4. Calculate overall average by adding up all the Sums and dividing by 84, which should also be between 1.0 and 5.0.

5. When the Profile of results is distributed, transfer the averages for each part to the respective parts of the Profile to obtain an interpretation of your results.

Part A	Part B	Part C	Part D	Part E	Part F	Total of Sums
1. ___	18. ___	44. ___	52. ___	69. ___	76. ___	A. _____
2. ___	19. ___	45. ___	53. ___	70. ___	77. ___	B. _____
3. ___	20. ___	46. ___	54. ___	71. ___	78. ___	C. _____
4. ___	21. ___	47. ___	55. ___	72. ___	79. ___	D. _____
5. ___	22. ___	48. ___	56. ___	73. ___	80. ___	E. _____
6. ___	23. ___	49. ___	57. ___	74. ___	81. ___	F. _____
7. ___	24. ___	50. ___	58. ___	75. ___	82. ___	
8. ___	25. ___	51. ___	59. ___		83. ___	
9. ___	26. ___		60. ___		84. ___	
10. ___	27. ___		61. ___			
11. ___	28. ___		62. ___			
12. ___	29. ___		63. ___			
13. ___	30. ___		64. ___			
14. ___	31. ___		65. ___			
15. ___	32. ___		66. ___			
16. ___	33. ___		67. ___			
17. ___	34. ___		68. ___			
	35. ___					

Part A	*Part B*	*Part C*	*Part D*	*Part E*	*Part F*	*Total of Sums*
36. ___						
37. ___						
38. ___						
39. ___						
40. ___						
41. ___						
42. ___						
43. ___						

Sum ___   Sum ___   Sum ___   Sum ___   Sum ___   Sum ___   Sum ___

%17 = ___   %26 = ___   %8 = ___   %17 = ___   %7 = ___   %9 = ___   %84 = ___

Overall Average _____

Profile of Results on the Language Learning Strategies

This profile will summarize your results on language learning strategies and will show the kinds of strategies you use in learning a new language, specifically Arabic. Please note that there is no best average scores for each part, since people learn languages differently.

To complete this profile, transfer your averages from the Worksheet. *You may keep this form.*

Part	What Strategies Are Covered	Your Average on This Part
A.	*Remembering More Effectively:* Grouping; making associations; placing new words into a context to remember them; using imagery sounds, sound-and-image combinations, actions, etc.; reviewing in a structured way; going back to review earlier material.	_____
B.	*Using Your Mental Processes:* Repeating; practicing with sounds and writing systems; using formulas and patterns; recombining familiar items in new ways; practicing the new language in a variety of new situations; involving the four skills (listening, speaking,	

reading, and writing); skimming and scanning
to get the idea quickly; using reference resources;
taking notes; summarizing; reasoning deductively
(applying general rules) and inductively
(generalizing from instances); analyzing
expressions; analyzing contrastively via
comparisons with another language; looking
for language patterns; adjusting your understanding according to new information. _____

C. *Compensating for Missing Knowledge:* Using
all possible clues to guess the meaning of what
is heard or read in the new language; trying
to understand the overall meaning and not
necessarily every single word; finding ways to
get the message across in speaking and writing
despite limited knowledge of the new language,
for instance, using gestures, switching to your
own language momentarily, using a synonym
or description, coining new words. _____

D. *Organizing and Evaluating Your Learning:*
Overviewing and linking with material you
already know; deciding in general to pay
attention; deciding to pay attention to specific
details; finding out how language learning
works; arranging to learn (schedule, environment, notebook); setting goals and objectives;
identifying the goal of a language task; finding
practice opportunities; noticing and learning
from your errors; evaluating your progress. _____

E. *Managing Your Emotions:* Lowering your
anxiety; encouraging yourself through positive
statements; taking risks wisely; rewarding
yourself; noting physical stress; keeping a
language learning diary; talking to someone
about your feelings/attitudes. _____

F. *Learning with Others:* Asking questions for
clarification or verification; asking for correction;
cooperating with peers; cooperating with
proficient users of the new language; developing

cultural awareness; becoming aware of others'
thoughts and feelings.   _____

YOUR OVERALL AVERAGE   _____

Key to Understanding Your Averages

What These Averages Mean to You

1. The overall average indicates how frequently you use language learning
   strategies in general.

2. The averages for each part show which groups of strategies you tend to
   use the most in learning a new language, such as Arabic.

Optimal use of language learning strategies depends on age, personality,
stage of language learning, purpose for learning the language, previous
experience, and other factors (Figure 7).

Figure 7

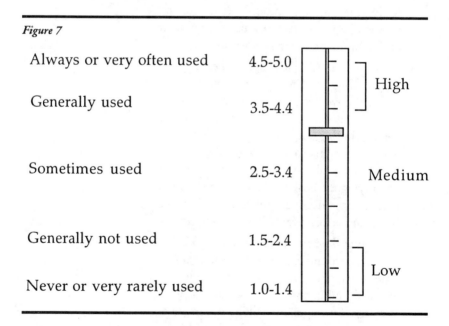

Always or very often used	4.5-5.0	High
Generally used	3.5-4.4	
Sometimes used	2.5-3.4	Medium
Generally not used	1.5-2.4	
Never or very rarely used	1.0-1.4	Low

If you want, you can make a graph of your averages to see how high or low
you are on a given part. Place dots that represent your averages of the different parts and draw bars (Figure 8).

Figure 8

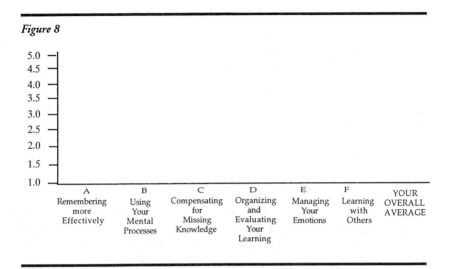

| | A Remembering more Effectively | B Using Your Mental Processes | C Compensating for Missing Knowledge | D Organizing and Evaluating Your Learning | E Managing Your Emotions | F Learning with Others | YOUR OVERALL AVERAGE |

Appendix 3
Guidelines for Writing the Language Learning Journal

The language learning journal is a sort of introspection/retrospection in the process of your learning Arabic in formal and informal settings, reflecting your conscious and subconscious actions that have led or failed to lead to learning. As you reflect on particular language items or structural aspects of the language, describe how you have learned them; which activities or devices have helped or have not helped; what would you have done alternatively; or which course of action you would like instruction to have taken. In short, the focus of the journal should be on your *own* learning styles and strategies.

Naturally, every person has different, rather unique, styles and strategies, and this uniqueness should, of course, be represented in the language learning journal. In a learning situation, for example, learners may be deliberate or impulsive; and they may tolerate the ambiguity of the new language or have no tolerance for it. Describe in English these and other personal traits and show how they have impacted your learning; which ones have facilitated learning and which ones have impeded it. For example, some people say they learn through the ear; others say they learn through the eye. Point out whether you are aurally or visually oriented and explain how this has contributed, positively or negatively, to learning. Describe the devices and strategies you have used to remember words or to learn structural relationships. Indicate whether you have a personal involvement in Arabic language and culture and to what degree. Have you benefited from contact with native speakers? Why or why not? Given the limited opportunity in the classroom for interaction with instructor, tutor, or fellow participants, do you seek or invent an occasion to speak Arabic? If the opportunity to speak the language is not available, what do you do to develop this skill further? Do you speak to yourself, for instance? These are only a small sample of language learning strategies used for illustration, and your journal should not be in any way limited to them. Look very closely into your cognitive, psychological, and emotional disposition toward this enterprise and identify and isolate the elements that you think have significantly interacted with the process of learning (again, negatively or positively). The point is to describe not only how well you have learned something, but also how you failed to learn certain aspects as well.

Since the purpose of writing this journal is to describe what you think you do in order to learn a particular item or structure, it is imperative that these thoughts be recorded immediately on a daily, continuous basis. Have a notebook ready at your side at all times so that you can jot down these thoughts quickly as they occur to you.

Appendix 4
Selected Questions Asked in the Oral Interviews

1. Do you learn through the eye or through the ear?
2. Do you have to systematize the language input or do you simply take it in?
3. Do you relate the input of the new language to other languages you know?
4. What do you do to produce the new sounds of the language?
5. Are you a good mimic?
6. Which works better for you, creating your own system of the new language and modifying it regularly, or studying the system in the textbook?
7. What do you do to learn vocabulary?
8. What do you do to create your own grammatical system of the new language?

9. Is it necessary for you to learn and master one point at a time in grammar or vocabulary?

10. When you listen to the new language or read it, is it only the sounds and letters on which you focus?

11. Do you have to identify with the speakers of the language in order to learn it well?

12. Do you see a pattern in the language input?

13. Do you visualize the sounds?

14. Do you seek or create opportunity to use the language?

Gender Differences in Language Learning Strategy Use in University-Level Introductory French Classes: A Pilot Study Employing a Strategy Questionnaire

Sadia Zoubir-Shaw,
University of Alabama
Rebecca L. Oxford,
University of Alabama

Introduction

Foreign or second language (L2) learning strategies are specific actions, behaviors, steps, or techniques that students use—often consciously—to improve their own progress in internalizing, storing, and using the L2 (Oxford 1990a, 1990b; Rigney 1978). Gender differences appear very frequently in the use of various L2 learning strategies; women report employing a number of strategies significantly more often than men.

This chapter explores the phenomenon of gender differences in L2 strategy use by reviewing previous research and by presenting a new pilot study of strategies employed in introductory French classes at the university level. In this investigation, we take a strategy-by-strategy view as well as examining whole clusters of strategies. This is the first time that French classes have been specifically targeted for such a close look at strategy use. This study is also important because its results are compared to a number of published and unpublished investigations on gender differences in strategy use.

Strategies are the tools for the kind of active, self-directed involvement that is necessary for developing L2 communicative ability (O'Malley and Chamot 1990; Wenden and Rubin 1987). For example, Suzanne's seeking out conversation partners, Mikhail's grouping and labeling words that are related, Lidia's giving herself encouragement through positive self-talk, Ashraf's using gestures to stay in a conversation when a needed word is unknown, Gustav's learning words by breaking them down into parts, Feng-jie's drawing "semantic maps" with lines and arrows pictorially showing the linkages between new words according to their meaning, and Lazlo's guessing meanings from context are all strategies. L2 learning strategies like these are very important, because research has repeatedly shown that the conscious, "tailored" use of such strategies is related to language achievement and proficiency (Cohen 1990; O'Malley and Chamot 1990; Oxford 1989; Oxford and Burry 1993; Skehan 1989; Wenden and Rubin 1987).

Techniques often used for assessing students' L2 strategies include informal observation, formal observational rating scales, informal or formal interviews, group discussions, think-aloud procedures, language learning diaries, dialogue journals between student and teacher, open-ended narrative-type questionnaires, structured questionnaires of strategy frequency, and even computer tracking. This chapter focuses on one type of strategy assessment, a questionnaire, used to discern gender differences in strategy use in introductory French classes. The chapter is organized as follows: review of relevant research, research questions, methodology, results, and implications.

Review of Relevant Research

This review covers strategies of more and less effective L2 learners and gender differences in strategy choice.

Strategies of More and Less Effective L2 Learners

Strategies of More Effective L2 Learners

Early researchers tended to make lists of strategies and other features presumed to be essential for all "good L2 learners." For instance, Rubin (1975) offered the following list of characteristics of such learners: they use guessing willingly and accurately, have a strong drive to communicate, are often uninhibited and willing to make mistakes, focus on form by looking for patterns and analyzing, take advantage of all practice opportunities, monitor their own speech and that of others, and pay attention to meaning. Naiman, Fröhlich, and Todesco (1975) developed a list of strategies used by good L2 learners, and remarked that such good learners learn to think in the language and address the affective aspects of language learning. In 1975 Stern also offered his first set of strategies of good L2 learners, and in 1983 published another list.

L2 research has supported the effectiveness of using certain L2 learning strategies and has shown that successful language learners often use strategies in an orchestrated fashion. Here are some of the main findings:

1. *Use of appropriate language learning strategies often results in improved proficiency or achievement overall or in specific skill areas* (see Chamot and Kupper 1989; Cohen 1990; O'Malley and Chamot 1990; Oxford and Burry 1993; Oxford and Crookall 1989; Oxford, Park-Oh, Ito, and Sumrall, 1993a, 1993b).

2. *Successful language learners tend to select strategies that work well together in a highly orchestrated way,* tailored to the requirements of the language task (Chamot and Kupper 1989; Vann and Abraham 1989).

3. *Cognitive strategies (e.g., translating, analyzing, taking notes) and metacognitive strategies (e.g., self-evaluating, planning, organizing) are often used together,* supporting each other (Oxford and Crookall 1989).

4. *Social and affective strategies are far less frequently observed,* probably because these behaviors are not as carefully studied and also because learners are not familiar with paying attention to their own feelings and social relationships as part of the L2 learning process (Oxford 1990b).

Strategies of Less Effective L2 Learners

Three points of view exist in studies about the strategies of less effective L2 learners. It may be that each one of the three is true for at least some less effective learners. Some of these learners might be very limited in the number and quality of their strategies (Nyikos 1987), others might be unaware of their strategies and thus unable to describe them (Nyikos 1987), and still others might use large numbers of strategies that lack coherence (Lavine and Oxford, forthcoming; Vann and Abraham 1989).

Gender as an Influence on Choice of L2 Learning Strategies

Gender might be one of the most important influences on the choice of L2 learning strategies (Oxford 1993a, 1993b). Other factors include motivation, cultural background, type of task, age, L2 learning stage, learning style (analytic/global, random/sequential), personality type (extroverted/introverted, intuitive/sensing, thinking/feeling, judging/perceiving), sensory preference, and ambiguity tolerance (for descriptions of all these, see Oxford 1989).

Gender Differences in Social and Linguistic Development

According to many studies (Maccoby and Jacklin 1974), females show greater interest than males in social activities, prefer "gentle" interaction more than aggressive interaction, and are more cooperative and less competitive than males. A meta-analysis by Hyde and Linn (1986) showed substantive gender differences in aggression (both verbal and physical), amounting to .5 standard deviation, with males more aggressive than females. Even in early childhood, girls establish intense, nurturing, empathic relationships in pairs and triads, while boys travel in larger groups characterized by dominance-aggression hierarchies; these patterns continue through adulthood (Gilligan 1982; Maccoby and Jacklin 1974). Females are more likely than males to show a continuing need for approval and a desire to please others through good grades and social behavior (Nyikos 1990). They also smile and laugh significantly more than males (Hyde and Linn 1986).

Developmental differences in verbal skill are sometimes very strong (Halpern 1986). In the native language (L1), girls usually say their first words and learn to speak in sentences earlier than do boys. This produces an initial "rate advantage" (Larsen-Freeman and Long 1991). Later on, women often speak in longer, more complex sentences than men and score higher than men on tests of spelling, grammar, and perceptual speed. Boys have a far greater frequency of disabilities in learning, reading, and speaking than do girls. On verbal ability tests and reading tests, females on the average surpass males, particularly from age eleven on, according to most studies (Cahn 1988; Gage and Berliner 1975; Maccoby and Jacklin 1974; Slavin 1988). Compared with men's L1 or native speech, women's L1 speech in many parts of the world shows more empathy, concern, politeness, encouragement of other speakers, negotiation, detail remembering, uncertainty, questioning behavior, and grammaticality (Kramarae 1981; Lakoff 1975; Tannen 1986, 1990). Men use more verbal expressions of power and aggression, adversarial-argumentative style, interruption, ridicule, analytical critique, and discouragement of other speakers (Belenky, Clinchy, Goldberger, and Tarule 1986; Tannen 1986, 1990). Anthropologists Brown and Levinson and sociologists Giles and Tajfel attribute such L1 differences to socialization, with special reference to the subordinate role of women in economic and political spheres (for details, see Kramarae 1981; Thorne, Kramarae, and Henley 1983).

Gass and Varonis (1986) studied the conversational behavior of L2 learners. Men dominated conversations, but women initiated more "negotiations of meaning," trying to understand and communicate clearly. In learning an L2, males and females sometimes show different levels of skill, especially in listening (Eisenstein 1982; Farhady 1982).

Gender Differences in Strategy Use of Native English Speakers Learning Other Languages

Table 1 shows the statistically significant results of studies of gender differences in L2 strategy use for native speakers of English learning other languages. For ease of comparison, results of our own study (described later in this chapter) are included in Table 1 along with findings from other studies.

Oxford, Nyikos, and Ehrman (1988) were the first to publish a review of studies involving gender differences in L2 learning strategies. At that time, among over eighty investigations of L2 learning strategies, only four considered gender differences. The first of the four studies was by Politzer (1983), who employed his own strategy inventory with 90 American students learning French, Spanish, or German. Politzer reported that female college students used social strategies for L2 learning significantly more often than their male peers—an unexplained difference that might be related to gender differences in social orientation. In another study discussed in the 1988 review, Ehrman and Oxford (1989) used the Strategy Inventory for Language Learning (SILL; published in Oxford 1990b) with seventy-nine adults in an intensive foreign language learning setting, the Foreign Service Institute of the U.S. Department of State. The range of languages learned was very large. Those authors found that females, compared with males, reported significantly more frequent use of L2 learning strategies in four factor-analytic categories: general study strategies, strategies for negotiating meaning, self-management strategies, and functional practice strategies. The third of the four studies was by Oxford and Nyikos and was published the next year (1989). The researchers used the SILL with 1,200 university students, each of whom was learning one or more of these languages: French, Spanish, German, Russian, and Italian. These investigators

Table 1

Significant Gender Differences in Strategy Use of Native Speakers of English Learning Other Languages

Date	Researcher(s)	Languages Learned	Strategies Females Use More Than Males	Strategies Males Use More Than Females
1983	Politzer	French, German, Spanish	Social strategies	None
1989	Ehrman & Oxford	Many	General study strategies Strategies for negotiating meaning Self-management strategies Functional practice strategies	None
1989	Oxford & Nyikos	French, German, Spanish, Italian, Russian	Formal rule-based strategies General study strategies Conversational input-elicitation strategies	None
1987	Nyikos	German	*After strategy training:* Color-only memory strategies	*After strategy training:* Color-plus-picture memory strategies
1993a, 1993b	Oxford, Park-Oh, Ito, & Sumrall	Japanese	Cognitive strategies Social strategies Affective strategies	None
Forth.	Lavine & Oxford	Spanish	*Strategy categories:* Cognitive strategies Memory strategies Social strategies Affective strategies	*Strategy categories:* None

Year	Authors	Language		
1990, 1991	Brecht, Davidson, & Ginsberg	Russian (in Russia)	*Specific strategy:* Trying out new vocab. learning techniques	*Specific strategies:* Thinking about my progress; Judging success of a particular strategy
			None	Social strategies; Affective strategies; *Strategy categories:* Learning from various activities
1994	Zoubir-Shaw & Oxford	French	*Strategy categories:* Learning conjugations; Learning grammar structures/rules; Learning from context; *Specific strategies:* Using color-coded cards for gender; Using pink and blue for gender; Using other colors for gender; Using flash cards; Using lists organized in grammatical classes; Accepting rules at face value; Reviewing from textbook material	*Specific strategies:* Concentrating more on oral communication than structures; Being impeded by not knowing the meaning of a word (neg. strat.); Reviewing from test material only (neg. strat.); Not comparing and accepting rules as a separate system (neg. strat.); Looking for the general meaning, idea, or theme

found that female students, contrasted with males, used L2 learning strategies in three of five factor-analytic categories significantly more often: formal rule-based strategies, general study strategies, and conversational input-elicitation strategies. The gender differences found in the second and third studies might be associated with women's social skills, stronger verbal skills (including pattern usage), and greater conformity to academic and linguistic norms. The final study in the 1988 review was by Nyikos (1987), who discovered significant gender differences among 135 university students in using memory strategies for German vocabulary learning. Nyikos used her own strategy assessment instrument for this study. After training in the use of these strategies, men outperformed women in the color-plus-picture combination, which Nyikos postulated was potentially related to men's putatively greater visual–spatial acuity. However, women surpassed men in the color-only condition, which Nyikos theorized was explained by women's greater interest in color (often as a social attractor).

Using an L2 learning strategy questionnaire adapted from the SILL, Oxford et al. (1993a, 1993b) discovered gender-difference trends among 107 high school students studying Japanese by satellite. Females tended to use a number of cognitive strategies, social strategies, and affective strategies (such as positive self-talk and relaxing) more often than did males. Gender differences were not as strong in metacognitive, compensation, and memory strategies. Males in this study, as in others, did not surpass females in strategy use in any of the main strategy categories. Females also outperformed males in terms of motivation and Japanese language achievement. Likewise, Lavine and Oxford (forthcoming) found gender differences in learning strategy use via the diaries of forty-two Spanish language students at the university level. Several of the general strategy-category differences favored women, and none favored men. For instance, significantly more females than males used cognitive, memory, social, and affective strategies, though the percentage differences were not large. In terms of specific strategies rather than overall categories, the strategy of trying out new techniques for vocabulary learning was used significantly more often by women than men. However, some gender differences favoring males were seen for two specific evaluation-related strategies.

Interestingly, in the only research conducted on informal language development of American students in the target country, Brecht, Davidson, and Ginsberg (1990, 1991) found some of the expected gender differences to be reversed. American male college students on study-abroad programs in Russia (learning Russian as a second language) were more likely to improve their proficiency, more likely to use social and affective strategies, and more likely to employ a broader range of strategies than women. Brecht et al. suggest that the greater aggression of the male students allowed them greater access to the foreign culture and to strategy-using opportunities.

Gender Differences in Strategy Use of Learners of English as a Second or Foreign Language

Table 2 illustrates statistically significant gender differences in strategy use among learners of ESL or EFL around the world.

Tran (1988), using his own strategy-assessment instrument, studied gender differences in English language acculturation and learning strategies among Vietnamese adults over age forty in the United States. Contrary to most research, Tran found that females had more L2 learning problems and that males were more likely than females to use a variety of L2 learning strategies to improve their English skills. Possibly, age and cultural gender-role differences influenced these results. In contrast, employing a sample of five hundred ESL learners in Australia, Willing (1988) discovered significant gender differences in frequency of use of L2 learning strategies, mostly favoring women.

Bedell (1993) used a Chinese translation of the SILL with a sample of 353 mostly high-achieving EFL students from several mainland Chinese postsecondary institutions to determine language learning strategy use. Bedell found that seventeen strategies showed significant gender differences, with fifteen favoring greater use by females (mostly strategies requiring patience and attention to detail) and the other two by males. Examining the SILL's six strategy categories, Bedell found that females were significantly more likely than males to use compensation strategies and memory strategies; no significant gender differences favored males as users of particular strategies. The picture was somewhat different when Bedell contrasted males and females on the nine factors from a Varimax factor analysis. Females significantly surpassed males in the use of compensation strategies (factor 3), memory strategies (factors 5 and 6), and metacognitive strategies (factor 2). Men did not score higher than women on many of the factors, but for those factors on which they did score higher—functional practice-productive strategies (factor 1) and formal practice and affective/emotional strategies (factor 7)—the difference was strong.

Yang (1992, 1993) used a Chinese SILL translation with 505 Taiwanese EFL students, most of whom were in their first year of university studies. She discovered significantly more frequent use of social strategies

Table 2

Significant Gender Differences in Strategy Use of Nonnative Speakers of English Learning English as a Second or Foreign Language

Date	Researcher(s)	ESL vs. EFL	Strategies Females Use More Than Males	Strategies Males Use More Than Females
1988	Tran	ESL Vietnamese	Not cited	Many
1988	Willing	ESL Mixed	Learning many new words Learning by seeing Learning by doing Learning by talking to friends	Writing in notebook Learning by cassettes
1993	Bedell	EFL Chinese	*Strategy categories:* Compensation strategies Social strategies *Factor-analytic strategy categories:* Compensation strategies Memory strategies Metacognitive strategies *Specific strategies:* Organizing a notebook Reading several times Skimming then reading Concentrating on speaker Revising a written piece	*Strategy categories:* None *Factor-analytic strategy categories:* Functional practice-productive strategies Formal/affective strategies *Specific strategies:* Applying general rules Finding practice opportunities
1992	Yang	EFL Chinese	Social strategies	None
1991	Chang	ESL Chinese	None	None

Year	Author	Group		
1991	Noguchi	EFL Japanese	In general	None
1992	Dreyer	ESL Afrikaans	Social strategies Metacognitive strategies	None
1991	Green	ESL/EFL Puerto Ricans	Metacognitive strategies Social strategies	None
1993	Green & Oxford	ESL/EFL Puerto Ricans	*Strategy categories:* Memory strategies Metacognitive strategies Affective strategies Social strategies	*Strategy categories:* None
			Specific strategies: Using flash cards Reviewing often Learning words by location Skimming then reading Making summaries Using gestures Trying to find out about language-learning process Thinking about my progress Giving myself a reward Noticing my tension Asking for slower speech or repetition Asking for correction Asking for help	*Specific strategies:* Watching TV or movies in English

Table 2 (cont.)

Date	Researcher(s)	ESL vs. EFL	Strategies Females Use More Than Males	Strategies Males Use More Than Females
Forth.	Frumina, Khasan, Leaver, & Oxford	EFL Russians	Memory strategies (general stream) Cognitive strategies Metacognitive strategies Affective strategies Social strategies	None
Forth.	Frumina, Khasan, Leaver, & Oxford	EFL Russians (advanced [IB] stream)	Memory strategies Metacognitive strategies Affective strategies	Cognitive strategies Compensation strategies

among the women compared with the men. Chang (1991) is the only researcher who has studied strategy use by Chinese students who has not found any significant gender differences. Using a Chinese translation of the SILL with fifty mainland and Taiwanese students who were studying ESL at the University of Georgia, Chang found that gender did not influence strategy use. Noguchi (1991) used a Japanese language strategy questionnaire derived from the SILL to assess the learning strategy use of 174 junior high students learning third-year EFL. Overall, Noguchi found that girls reported more frequent use of a greater variety of language learning strategies than boys. Dreyer (1992), examining 305 South African university EFL students whose native language is Afrikaans, found significant differences between males and females in strategy use on the SILL. A significant gender difference in overall use of learning strategies was identified between males and females, with females having the higher average strategy use. Females showed significantly more frequent use of most strategy groups for which they were tested, especially the categories of social and metacognitive strategies.

Green (1991) used the SILL with 213 prebasic, basic, and intermediate English students at the University of Puerto Rico in Mayaguez. This can be considered a "hybrid" ESL/EFL environment. Like ESL students, the Puerto Ricans have strong English input all around them, but like EFL students they do not have to use English for daily survival. In terms of strategy categories, females surpassed males in metacognitive and social strategy use; males did not use any strategy category more often than females. In a larger study with the same instrument at the same university, Green and Oxford (1993) studied the strategy use of 374 prebasic, basic, and intermediate English students. Memory, metacognitive, affective, and social strategies were used significantly more often by women than by men. Cognitive and compensation strategies showed no significant gender differences. Specific strategies employed more often by women were using flash cards, reviewing often, learning words by location, skimming before reading text, making summaries, using gestures, trying to find out about language learning processes, thinking about one's own progress, giving oneself a reward, noticing tension, asking for slower speech or repetition, asking for correction, and asking for help. The only strategy that men used significantly more than women was watching TV or movies in English.

Frumina, Khasan, Leaver, and Oxford (forthcoming) used the SILL to examine the learning strategies of 152 university-level Russian students learning EFL. These students were in two "streams": the general stream and the international baccalaureate (IB) stream (the latter being more accelerated). Within the general stream, significant gender differences repeatedly occurred for five out of six strategy categories, in each case with women surpassing men in reported frequency of strategy use: memory, cognitive, metacognitive, affective, and social. In the IB stream, however, women used strategies more frequently than men in the categories of memory, metacognitive, and affective strategies, but men used cognitive and compensation strategies more often than women.

Possible Causes of These Gender Differences

Socialization within cultures is one of the main causes of many of these gender differences (Bedell 1993; Crawford and Gentry 1989; Dunn 1991; Eccles 1989; Jacklin 1983; Nyikos 1990; Slavin 1988). However, Moir and Jessel (1991) argue that "brain sex" (anatomical difference in heterosexual male and female brains) causes some of the observed differences. Gender differences in brain lateralization/hemisphericity have been noted, with greater nerve linkages in the corpus callosum between right and left hemispheres for females than males (Springer and Deutsch 1989) and for homosexual males than heterosexual males (Associated Press 1992; Elias 1992). Furthermore, verbal functioning was found by Kimura (1985) to be more diffuse in women than in men, which is probably a sign of hemispheric differences. Probably any gender differences in development of social behavior and cognition arise from an intricate, not fully understood interaction of socialization and physiology. Keeping these previous results in mind, we now turn to the current study, starting with research questions.

Research Questions

1. Do gender differences exist in French language learning strategies among university students?
2. If so, what differences are there?
3. How can those differences be explained?

Methodology

Sample

The sample used in this pilot investigation consisted of twenty-five adults (thirteen females and twelve males) attending an intensive introductory

French class (French 103) aimed at fulfilling a core curriculum requirement. The course was equivalent to a review of first-year French (101 and 102). The class met five times a week for a fifty-minute class period, and the three-month semester was almost completed at the time of the questionnaire. Respondents were American university students aged eighteen to twenty-two with a minimum background of two years of high school foreign language study. All voluntarily agreed to respond to the questionnaire.

Instrument

The questionnaire used in this study (see Appendix) is the Romance Language Learning Strategy Questionnaire created by the first author. In this sixty-item questionnaire, respondents were asked to circle a response for each of the statements (strategy descriptions). Choices were recorded on a separate answer sheet.

Several of the items on the questionnaire were similar in content or nature to items on the SILL (Oxford 1990b), while others were specifically developed and applied to Romance languages. This leads to our assertion of content validity, because items were systematically chosen to represent the spectrum of introductory Romance language learning strategies likely to be used. This spectrum included strategies that could be considered positive, that is, facilitative of effective learning; but it also included a few strategies that were not so positive, since these too are among the strategies students often use. The SILL, which donated to the current questionnaire some strategy ideas as well as the response format, is noted for its high reliability (Cronbach alpha internal consistency coefficients in the .90s), as well as its predictive validity and concurrent validity in relation to language proficiency and achievement, learning styles, motivation, and career choice (for details, see Oxford and Burry 1993).

For each item there were five possible choices:

1. Never or almost never true of me
2. Generally not true of me
3. Somewhat true of me
4. Generally true of me
5. Always or almost always true of me

The sixty items were distributed among nine categories representing different dimensions corresponding to target tasks students face during the language learning process. The nine dimensions were:

Part A: Developing learning strategies—seven items
Part B: Learning gender—eight items
Part C: Learning conjugations—three items
Part D: Learning new words—nine items
Part E: Learning grammar structures/rules—twelve items
Part F: Learning from context—seven items
Part G: Learning from various activities—seven items
Part H: Learning from errors—three items
Part I: Learning from reviewing—four items

Data-Collection Procedures

All data were gathered at the end of the fall semester, three weeks before the final exam, and were uncontaminated by any strategy training by the teacher. The data-collection period was chosen so that students could have developed by that time a clear idea of their own learning processes in introductory French.

Data-Analysis Procedures

For each group the collected data were subjected to a one-tailed t-test with two groups (G1 = females, G2 = males) and one variable per item (the response to each strategy description using the 1 to 5 scale shown above). Means, standard deviations, and levels of significance for each individual item and each strategy group were identified.

We chose to use $p < .10$ as the criterion for statistical significance in this study, meaning that if the study were repeated many times, the probability is nine out of ten that the observed difference between males and females would occur (thus, it could not have happened by random error). This rather liberal level of significance was chosen because this was a pilot study with a small number of students. Had we used a larger group, significance in many cases would have been ensured even at a more rigorous $p < .05$ or $p < .01$ level. We wanted to discover and report all the findings of interest that we could, so these results would lead to hypotheses for testing with larger numbers of French students in later studies.

With reference to the means, we adopted the same interpretation system as used for the SILL. Specifically, high strategy usage is considered to be 3.5–5.0; medium usage is 2.5–3.4; and low usage is 1.0–2.4.

Results

Results indicated that looking at item-level (specific-strategy) data was even more informative than just considering the overall strategy groups on the questionnaire. Let us first consider the findings for each of the nine strategy categories, setting the scene for the findings by specific strategies.

Results by Nine General Strategy Groups

As Table 3 shows, of the nine general strategy categories on the Romance Language Learning Strategy Questionnaire, four showed significant gender differences: Part C (Learning Conjugations: female mean 3.56, male mean 3.16), Part E (Learning Grammar Structures/Rules: female mean 3.33, male mean 3.24), Part F (Learning from Context: female mean 3.71, male mean 3.30), and Part G (Learning from Various Activities: female mean 3.30, male mean 3.32). Of these, three out of four (C, E, and F) favored women, and the other (G) favored men.

Let us look at these results more closely. Part C, Learning Conjugations, and Part F, Learning from Context, had a high use of strategies by females and a medium use by males. Part D, Learning Grammar Structures/Rules, and Part G, Learning from Various Activities, showed medium use of strategies by both females and males, although the small differences between males and females for both parts were enough to be significant.

Table 3

Means, Standard Deviations, and Significance Levels for the Four Parts of the Questionnaire Showing Significant Gender Differences

Part	Name	Female Mean	Female SD	Male Mean	Male SD	$p <$
C	Learning conjugations	3.56 (high)	0.85	3.16 (med.)	0.57	.10
E	Learning grammar structures/rules	3.33 (med.)	0.39	3.24 (med.)	0.51	.08
F	Learning from context	3.71 (high)	0.46	3.30 (med.)	0.29	.06
G	Learning from various activities	3.30 (med.)	0.26	3.32 (med.)	0.45	.03

Results According to Specific Strategies

Results by specific strategies showed interesting patterns (see Table 4): high use by both males and females; medium use by both; low use by both; medium use by females, high use by males; and low use by females, medium use by males.

High Use by Both Males and Females

Three strategies for which gender differences occurred were used at a high level in general. For two of the three, females surpassed males in strategy use. Strategy 32, *I accept rules at face value*, had a female mean of 4.31 and a male mean of 3.50. Strategy 57, *I review from the textbook material*, showed a female mean of 4.46 and a male mean of 4.17. However, the third strategy displayed a slightly higher male mean than female mean: 4.17 versus 4.15 for Strategy 43, *I look for the general meaning, idea, or theme*.

Medium Use by Both Males and Females

Three strategies fit into this pattern. Of these, one favored women as more frequent users—Strategy 22, *I use lists organized in grammatical classes*—with a female mean of 2.85 and a male mean of 2.50. Two others—both of which can be considered somewhat negative learning behaviors—exhibited higher means for males than females. Strategy 35, *I do not compare/accept rules as part of a separate system*, was used more often by males (mean 2.67) than by females (mean 2.46). Strategy 45, *Not knowing the meaning of a word impedes my thinking process or my progress*, had a male mean of 3.25 and a female mean of 3.15.

Low Use by Both Males and Females

Four strategies relating to color coding and flash cards had low use by both females and males, although gender differences proved to be significant and consistently favored women. Strategy 9, *I use color-coded cards for gender categories*, had a female mean of 1.85 and a male mean of 1.08. Strategy 10, *I use pink and blue cards for gender categories*, differed between females and males with means of 1.92 and 1.08, respectively. Strategy 11, *I use other colors for gender categories*, averaged 1.69 for females and 1.08 for males. Strategy 19, *I use flash cards to remember new words*, contrasted between females and males with means of 2.38 and 1.33.

Table 4

Means, Standard Deviations, and Significance Levels for the Specific Strategies Showing Significant Gender Differences

Strategy Number and Name	Female Mean	Female SD	Male Mean	Male SD	p <
9. I use color-coded cards for gender categories.	1.85 (low)	1.14	1.08 (low)	0.29	.001
10. I use pink and blue cards for gender categories.	1.92 (low)	1.32	1.08 (low)	0.29	.001
11. I use other colors for gender categories.	1.69 (low)	0.95	1.08 (low)	0.29	.001
19. I use flash cards to remember new words.	2.38 (low)	1.39	1.33 (low)	0.89	.07
22. I use lists organized in grammatical classes (verbs, nouns, adjectives, etc.).	2.85 (med.)	1.72	2.50 (med.)	1.00	.04
29. I concentrate more on oral communication than on structures.	3.38 (med.)	1.19	3.67 (high)	0.78	.08
32. I accept rules at face value.	4.31 (high)	0.63	3.50 (high)	1.09	.03
35. I do not compare/accept rules as part of a separate system	2.46 (med.)	0.78	2.67 (med.)	1.30	.04
43. I look for the general meaning, idea, or theme.	4.15 (high)	1.07	4.17 (high)	0.72	.09
45. Not knowing the meaning of a word impedes my thinking process or my progress.	3.15 (med.)	0.90	3.25 (med.)	1.42	.06
57. I review from the textbook material.	4.46 (high)	0.78	4.17 (high)	1.19	.07
60. I review from test material only (quizzes, exams, etc.).	2.08 (low)	0.64	3.17 (med.)	0.94	.10

Medium Use by Females, High Use by Males

Only one strategy fit this pattern: Strategy 29, *I concentrate more on oral communication than on structures.* The male mean was 3.67, compared with the female mean of 3.38. This might suggest that use of strategies for grammatical learning is less among males.

Low Use by Females, Medium Use by Males

Just one strategy matched this pattern. Strategy 60, *I review from test material only*, had a higher male mean (3.17) than female mean (2.08). Thus, more males than females restricted their reviewing to test material only, a strategy that is not considered positive.

Summary of Results of the Current Study as Related to Previous Research

General Contrasts

Three of the four gender-significant strategy groups (Learning Conjugations, Learning Grammar Structures/Rules, and Learning from Context) showed greater use of these particular strategy groups by women than by men. When separate strategies were considered, females surpassed males in seven of the twelve gender-significant strategies. All seven of these were considered positive strategies, that is, techniques useful for efficient language learning. These included using color-coded cards for gender categories, using pink and blue cards for gender categories, using other colors for gender categories, using flash cards, using lists organized into grammatical classes, accepting rules at face value, and reviewing from the textbook material.

Our results showed that men, when compared with women, reported using strategies more frequently in the general category called Learning from a Variety of Activities. This might reflect versatility in learning. However, men in this study showed deficiencies in strategy use, even as reported for the strategies they used significantly more frequently than women.

Of the five strategies that men used significantly more often than women, three (failing to compare/accept rules as part of a separate system, becoming impeded when a word's meaning is not known, and reviewing from test material only) were considered negative strategies. Another of the five strategies used by men more frequently than by women was the technique of concentrating on more oral communication than on structures;

this could be considered a positive, negative, or neutral strategy, depending on the nature of the language task and the goals of the student and the program. The final male-dominant strategy, looking for the general meaning, idea, or theme, could be positive for certain language tasks.

Color Coding and Flash Card Strategies

Our finding of significantly greater use of color coding (in three strategies related to grammatical gender) by American university women compared with men coincides with the findings of Nyikos (1987). Nyikos suggested that using color as a social attractor is favored by women and is a natural basis for women's L2 strategies. As in our study, use of flash cards was found more frequently among women than men in the Puerto Rican study by Green and Oxford (1993). We might note here that color-coding strategies and flash-card strategies are similar in that they use the visual mode and involve the processing of highly detailed data.

Grammatical Strategies

We found many instances in which women, compared with men, showed significantly greater interest in grammar and grammar-related strategies. For example, women displayed greater overall use of the two strategy categories of Learning Conjugations and Learning Grammar Structures/Rules. Women exhibited greater use of specific strategies such as using grammar-based lists and accepting rules, and lesser use of specific strategies such as failing to compare/accept rules as part of a separate system and concentrating more on oral communication than on structures. Taken together, these results suggest a greater interest in grammar strategies among women and a greater aversion to such strategies among men. These results are in line with previous research showing that in our culture women, when compared with men, might be generally more interested in grammatical distinctions, grammar rules, and grammar strategies (Kramarae 1981; Oxford and Nyikos 1989) because of educational expectations; other cultures might have different patterns (Bedell 1993).

Strategy for Looking for the General Theme

The male dominance we found in regard to the strategy of looking for the general meaning, idea, or theme is not directly reflected in previous studies. However, it does seem linked with a more global approach to language learning that avoids analysis. Eschewing analysis in language learning fits in with men's general avoidance of grammar strategies as described above. This seems at first a bit surprising, in that males are often thought to be more analytic than females (see Oxford 1993a, 1993b). Perhaps males in general, although often analytic in their learning of other subjects, do not recognize the need to use analysis in learning a new language; maybe they are taking what they see as an easy, nonanalytical route in a required class; or perhaps some other phenomenon is in play that is not fully understood.

Strategies for Reviewing

In the current study, men compared with women restricted their reviewing significantly more often to test material only, while women significantly more often than men reviewed the textbook material also. Men's restricted reviewing echoes the findings of previous investigations in which men were significantly less involved than women in reviewing and other designated "good study strategies" (Ehrman and Oxford 1989; Green and Oxford 1993; Oxford and Nyikos 1989). Perhaps men do not become as involved in a required language class for which they have little personal motivation.

Strategies for Learning from Context

Learning from the context—a general category in which women in this study excelled—involves use of compensation strategies such as guessing. In this sample, men significantly more often than women tended to feel blocked when they did not know a word (possibly because they did not know how to use the context to help themselves). Such results confirm findings in two previous studies (Bedell 1993; Ehrman and Oxford 1989) of women's significantly greater use of compensation strategies or strategies for finding meaning. However, among advanced learners of English in Russia, men used compensation strategies more than women, although in an average university group in Russia, this was not the case (Frumina et al., forthcoming).

A Word about "Negative" Strategies

Several of the strategies in the questionnaire were considered to be less useful or less positive than others. For example, reviewing only from test materials, not comparing/accepting rules as a separate system, and being impeded by not knowing the meaning of a word were all seen as somewhat dubious strategies. This judgment was based on informal, albeit professional, observations that these strategies often seemed to lead to lower language performance. We need greater study of which strategies are really negative and of whether this holds for all students.

Summary of Results

As we can see, the results of this study upheld the findings of a number of previous studies, both published and unpublished, concerning gender differences in L2 strategy use. Most of the strategies in the current questionnaire did not show gender differences, but a large minority did. Overall, women in the present investigation surpassed men in the use of several strategy categories and of many strategies that might be viewed as effective for language learning. Less effective strategies were chosen more often by men. Women more frequently than men used strategies involving visual details, grammar, reviewing, and contextualized learning. This study showed that men more often than women looked for the main theme, thus underscoring a potentially (and perhaps surprisingly) global approach for men in language learning. Certainly such a finding needs much more study.

Implications

Like a number of previous studies, this investigation showed that females used many language learning strategies more frequently than males. Of course, in this study not all males learned in the same way, and not all females learned in the same way. Yet there were so many significant differences that we must consider the question: What does this mean for instruction in French and other languages?

The first implication for teachers is that knowing how our students function can help us tailor instruction for them. Knowing how students of both genders learn can help us improve our teaching by causing us to develop workable instructional strategies for both groups. Strategy questionnaires, diaries, observations, think-aloud procedures, and interviews might have great value. The questions arise: Which assessment tool is the best for my students? How much information do I need about my students' strategies? How much information do the students need about their own strategies? Which assessment mode provides the necessary data without taking too much time? Often the answer is that a questionnaire provides the first and most comprehensive look at strategy use. After that, almost any other tool could be a useful supplement.

The second implication is that we can teach our students, female and male, to use more and better strategies (for details, see Oxford 1990b). We should optimize the strategies that males and females use appropriately and well, and we should encourage everyone to develop strategies that go beyond gender boundaries. More research is surely needed on the link between specific strategies and language learning outcomes. If continued research shows that males need help in certain strategies, such as techniques for learning rules or grammatical gender, or if subsequent investigations again indicate that males choose dysfunctional strategies, we can easily teach males useful strategies by weaving them into normal lessons. If later investigations show that females might benefit from more strategies for finding the main theme, such strategies can readily be taught to females. Any student can learn to compensate for strategy weaknesses and can build a larger repertoire of strategies. Questions remain: How far can students stretch themselves and compensate by learning new strategies? What is the best mode for strategy training?

A third implication is that teachers need training to adapt themselves to their students' strategies and learning needs. The teacher needs to know what his or her own general learning styles and specific learning strategies are. To become the best facilitator of learning possible, the teacher must discover the strategies he or she is sharing with the students and then can consciously expand this strategy range. We might ask: Can and should teachers discuss their own styles and strategies with their students? To what degree can teachers train students to use strategies that are not traditionally in the teachers' own favored set of techniques?

A fourth implication deals with textbooks. We can start to consider who writes our language textbooks and what strategies these authors include. We can ask these questions: Do the authors purposefully target a wide range of strategies that work with all four language skills? Do they consider the strategy needs of both females and males? Do the strategies in their textbooks consciously or unconsciously reflect one gender? Would it make a difference to the writing of a textbook if the author had both males and females in mind?

A last implication concerns causes of gender differences in strategy use. We can easily see influences of socialization—especially educational and family effects—on language learning strategy use. Certainly, socialization appears to play a powerful role, but brain hemisphericity (roughly reflecting an analytic vs. a global contrast) might also have an influence. We might ask: What is the role of the corpus callosum in movement of information between the two hemispheres of the brain, and how does this differ by gender? Is it true that females in general have a thicker corpus callosum than males, allowing more interchange between the two halves of the brain? Does this help create greater flexibility in language learning? Why do females often surpass males in ability to learn foreign languages and in native language achievement as well? Does this relate to hemisphericity? From an instructional viewpoint, is strategy training a possibility for helping integrate the work of the two hemispheres in normally functioning people? If so, what would be the best age and stage for this to occur?

Many tantalizing questions remain about gender differences in L2 strategy use. This chapter has shared the most recent findings from relevant research and has described a new study of strategies of French language students. More investigation is needed to answer the remaining questions.

Works Cited

Associated Press. 1992, August 1. Study Shows Brains Differ in Gay, Heterosexual Men: Anterior Commissure Area Larger in Homosexuals. *Washington Post,* p. A2.

Bedell, David. 1993. Crosscultural Variation in the Choice of Language Learning Strategies: A Mainland Chinese Investigation with Comparison to Previous Studies. Master's thesis, University of Alabama at Tuscaloosa.

Belenky, Mary F., Blythe M. Clinchy, Nancy R. Goldberger, and Jill M. Tarule. 1986. *Women's Ways of Knowing: The Development of Self, Voice, and Mind.* New York: Basic Books.

Brecht, Richard, Dan Davidson, and Ralph Ginsberg. 1990. The Empirical Study of Proficiency Gain in Study Abroad Environments among American Students of Russian. In *American Contributions to the VII International Congress of MAPRIAL,* edited by Dan Davidson, 123–52. Washington, DC: American Council of Teachers of Russian.

————. 1991. On Evaluating Language Proficiency Gain in Study Abroad Environments: An Empirical Study of American Students of Russian (A Preliminary Analysis of Data). In *Selected Papers Delivered at the NEH Symposium in Russian Language and Culture,* edited by Zita D. Dabars, 101–30. Baltimore: CORLAC/Friends School of Baltimore.

Cahn, Lorynne D. 1988. Sex and Grade Differences and Learning Rate in an Intensive Summer Reading Clinic. *Psychology in the Schools* 25: 84–91.

Chamot, Anna U., and Lisa Kupper. 1989. Learning Strategies in Foreign Language Instruction. *Foreign Language Annals* 22: 13–24.

Chang, Shiang-Jiun. 1991. A Study of Language Learning Behaviors of Chinese Students at the University of Georgia and the Relation of Those Behaviors to Oral Proficiency and Other Factors. Ph.D. diss., University of Georgia at Athens.

Cohen, Andrew D. 1990. *Language Learning: Insights for Learners, Teachers, and Researchers.* New York: Newbury House/Harper and Row.

Crawford, Mary, and Margaret Gentry, eds. 1989. *Gender and Thought: Psychological Perspectives.* New York: Springer-Verlag.

Dreyer, Carisma. 1992. Learner Variables as Predictors of EFL Proficiency. Ph.D. diss., Potchefstroom University, South Africa.

Dunn, Rita. 1991. Do Students from Different Cultures Have Different Learning Styles? *InterED* 15: 12–16.

Eccles, Jacquelyne S. 1989. Bringing Young Women to Math and Science. In *Gender and Thought: Psychological Perspectives,* edited by Mary Crawford and Margaret Gentry, 36–58. New York: Springer-Verlag.

Ehrman, Madeline E., and Rebecca L. Oxford. 1989. Effects of Sex Differences, Career Choice, and Psychological Type on Adults' Language Learning Strategies. *Modern Language Journal* 73: 1–13.

Eisenstein, Miriam. 1982. A Study of Social Variation in Adult Second Language Acquisition. *Language Learning* 32: 367–91.

Elias, Marylin. 1992, August 3. Difference Seen in Brains of Gay Men. *USA Today* p. 8D.

Farhady, Hossein. 1982. Measures of Language Proficiency from the Learner's Perspective. *TESOL Quarterly* 16: 43–59.

Frumina, Yelena, Boris Khasan, Betty L. Leaver, and Rebecca L. Oxford. Forthcoming. Conflicted and Tolerant Educational Mind-Sets and Language Learning Strategies. In *Learner Awareness of Strategies,* edited by Rebecca L. Oxford and Betty L. Leaver. Cambridge, UK: Cambridge University Press.

Gage, Nathaniel L., and David C. Berliner. 1975. *Educational Psychology.* Chicago: Rand-McNally.

Gass, Susan M., and Evangeline M. Varonis. 1986. Sex Differences in NNS/NNS Interactions. In *Talking to Learn: Conversation in Second Language Acquisition,* edited by Richard Day, 327–51. Rowley, MA: Newbury House.

Gilligan, Carol. 1982. *In a Different Voice: Psychological Theory and Woman's Development.* Cambridge, MA: Harvard University Press.

Green, John M. 1991. Language Learning Strategies of Puerto Rican University Students. Paper presented at the annual meeting of Puerto Rico Teachers of English to Speakers of Other Languages, San Juan, PR.

Green, John M., and Rebecca L. Oxford. 1993. Learning Strategies: Patterns of Use by Gender and Proficiency. Paper presented at the annual meeting of International Teachers of English of Speakers of Other Languages, Atlanta, GA.

Halpern, Diane F. 1986. *Sex Differences in Cognitive Abilities.* Hillsdale, NJ: Erlbaum.

Hyde, Janet, and Marcia C. Linn, eds. 1986. *The Psychology of Gender: Advances through Meta-Analysis.* Baltimore: Johns Hopkins University Press.

Jacklin, Carol N. 1983. Boys and Girls Entering School. In *Sex Differentiation and Schooling,* edited by Michael Marland, 8–17. London: Heinemann.

Kimura, Diane. 1985. Left Brain, Right Brain: The Hidden Differences. *Psychology Today,* p. 85.

Kramarae, Cheris. 1981. *Women and Men Speaking.* Rowley, MA: Newbury House.

Lakoff, Robin. 1975. *Language and Women's Place.* New York: Harper and Row.

Larsen-Freeman, Diane, and Michael Long. 1991. *An Introduction to Second Language Acquisition Research.* London: Longman.

Lavine, Roberta Z., and Rebecca L. Oxford. Forthcoming. Language Learning Diaries as a Tool for Research and Self-Awareness. In *Learner Awareness of Strategies,* edited by Rebecca L. Oxford and Betty L. Leaver. Cambridge, UK: Cambridge University Press.

Maccoby, Eleanor E., and Carol N. Jacklin. 1974. *The Psychology of Sex Differences.* Stanford, CA: Stanford University Press.

Moir, Anne, and David Jessel. 1991. *Brain Sex: The Real Difference between Men and Women.* New York: Stuart/Carol.

Naiman, Neil, Maria Fröhlich, and Angie Todesco. 1975. The Good Second Language Learner. *TESL Talk* 6: 58–75.

Noguchi, T. 1991. Review of Language Learning Strategy Research and Its Implications. B.A. thesis, Tottori University, Japan.

Nyikos, Martha. 1987. The Effect of Color and Imagery as Mnemonic Strategies on Learning and Retention of Lexical Items in German. Ph.D. diss., Purdue University.

———. 1990. Sex-Related Differences in Adult Language Learning: Socialization and Memory Factors. *Modern Language Journal* 74: 273–87.

O'Malley, J. Michael, and Anna U. Chamot. 1990. *Learning Strategies in Second Language Acquisition.* Cambridge: Cambridge University Press.

Oxford, Rebecca L. 1989. Use of Language Learning Strategies: A Synthesis of Studies with Implications for Strategy Trainings. *System* 17: 235–47.

———. 1990a. Language Learning Strategies and Beyond: A Look at Strategies in the Context of Styles. In *Shifting the Instructional Focus to the Learner,* edited by Sally S. Magnan, 35–55. Middlebury, VT: Northeast Conference on the Teaching of Foreign Languages.

———. 1990b. *Language Learning Strategies: What Every Teacher Should Know.* New York: Newbury House/Harper and Row.

———. 1993a. Instructional Implications of Gender Differences in L2 Learning Styles and Strategies. *Applied Language Learning* 4: 65–94.

———. 1993b. *La différence continue . . .:* Gender Differences in Second/Foreign Language Learning Styles and Strategies. In *Exploring Gender,* edited by Jane Sutherland, 140–47. Englewood Cliffs, NJ: Prentice-Hall.

Oxford, Rebecca L., and Judith A. Burry. 1993. Evolution, Norming, and Psychometric Testing of Oxford's Strategy Inventory for Language Learning. Paper presented at the annual meeting of the National Council on Measurement in Education, Atlanta, GA.

Oxford, Rebecca L., and David Crookall. 1989. Language Learning Strategies: Methods, Findings, and Instructional Implications. *Modern Language Journal* 73: 404–19.

Oxford, Rebecca L., and Martha Nyikos. 1989. Variables Affecting Choice of Language Learning Strategies by University Students. *Modern Language Journal* 73: 219–300.

Oxford, Rebecca L., Martha Nyikos, and Madeline Ehrman. 1988. *Vive la différence?* Reflections on Sex Differences in Use of Language Learning Strategies. *Foreign Language Annals* 21: 321–29.

Oxford, Rebecca L., Young Park-Oh, Sukero Ito, and Malenna Sumrall. 1993a. Factors Affecting Achievement in a Satellite-Delivered Japanese Language Program. *American Journal of Distance Education* 7: 10–25.

———. 1993b. Learning Japanese by Satellite: What Influences Student Achievement? *System* 21: 31–48.

Politzer, Robert L. 1983. An Exploratory Study of Self-Reported Language Learning Behaviors and Their Relation to Achievement. *Studies in Second Language Acquisition* 6: 54–68.

Rigney, Joseph W. 1978. Learning Strategies: A Theoretical Perspective. In *Learning Strategies,* edited by Harold F. O'Neil, Jr., 165–285. New York: Academic Press.

Rubin, Joan. 1975. What the "Good Language Learner" Can Teach Us. *TESOL Quarterly* 9: 41–51.

Skehan, Peter. 1989. *Individual Differences in Second-Language Learning.* London: Edward Arnold.

Slavin, Robert E. 1988. *Educational Psychology: Theory in Practice.* 2d ed. Englewood Cliffs, NJ: Prentice-Hall.

Springer, Sally, and Georg Deutsch. 1989. *Left Brain, Right Brain.* New York: Freeman.

Stern, Hans H. 1975. What Can We Learn from the Good Language Learner? *Canadian Modern Language Review* 31: 304–18.

———. 1983. *Fundamental Concepts in Language Teaching.* Oxford: Oxford University Press.

Tannen, Deborah. 1986. *That's Not What I Meant!* New York: Morrow.

———. 1990. *You Just Don't Understand: Women and Men in Conversation.* New York: Ballantine Books.

Thorne, Barrie, Cheris Kramarae, and Nathaniel T. Henley. 1983. *Language, Gender, and Society.* Rowley, MA: Newbury House.

Tran, Thanh V. 1988. Sex Differences in English Language Acculturation and Learning Strategies among Vietnamese Adults Age Forty and Over in the United States. *Sex Roles* 19: 747–58.

Vann, Roberta, and Roberta Abraham. 1989. Strategies of Unsuccessful Language Learners. Paper presented at the annual meeting of Teachers of English to Speakers of Other Languages, San Francisco.

Wenden, Anita, and Joan Rubin, eds. 1987. *Learner Strategies for Language Learning.* Englewood Cliffs, NJ: Prentice-Hall.

Willing, Ken. 1988. *Learning Styles in Adult Migrant Education.* Adelaide, Australia: National Curriculum Research Council.

Yang, Nae-Dong. 1992. Second Language Learners' Beliefs about Language Learning and Their Use of Learning Strategies: A Study of College Students of English in Taiwan. Ph.D. diss., University of Texas at Austin.

———. 1993. Understanding Chinese Students' Language Beliefs and Learning Strategy Use. Paper presented at the annual meeting of International Teachers of English to Speakers of Other Languages, Atlanta, GA.

Appendix

Romance Language Learning Strategy Questionnaire: Initial Draft

Finding out about your language learning strategies can help your instructors design better and more efficient teaching methods. Please read the following items and choose a response (1 through 5) according to the this scale:

1. Never or almost never true of me

2. Generally not true of me

3. Somewhat true of me

4. Generally true of me

5. Always or almost always true of me

A. DEVELOPING LEARNING STRATEGIES

1. I am aware of my learning strategies.

2. I am capable of developing a learning strategy.

3. I use different strategies for different activities.

4. My learning strategy use varies according to the subject material.

5. I invent mnemonic devices such as bangos, Dr. and Mrs. Vandertramp, House of *être*, etc.

6. I have a favorite strategy.

7. I do not have any strategies.

B. LEARNING GENDER

8. I memorize gender randomly.

9. I use color-coded cards for gender categories.

10. I use pink and blue cards for gender categories.

11. I use other colors for gender categories.

12. I associate gender with my own gender.

13. I associate gender with left and right notions, for instance, masculine in the right column and feminine in the left column (or vice versa).

14. I memorize only one gender (feminine for instance) and assume other words are masculine.

15. When memorizing only one gender, I memorize whichever gender I identify with.

C. LEARNING CONJUGATIONS

16. I identify conjugation patterns.

17. I consider conjugations to be more vocabulary to memorize.

18. I distinguish fundamental principles of conjugations from pure mechanics.

D. LEARNING NEW WORDS

19. I use flash cards to remember new words.

20. I use random lists of words.

21. I use alphabetical lists of words.

22. I use lists organized in grammatical classes (verbs, nouns, adjectives, etc.).

23. I use word lists with opposites (petit/grand).

24. I associate words with a context or situation (function, action, theme, physical world, etc.).

25. I relate the new word to something I am familiar with.

26. I memorize the new word in a sentence.

27. I use rhymes or "sounds like" devices to remember new words.

E. LEARNING GRAMMAR STRUCTURES/RULES

28. I try for grammatical accuracy.
29. I concentrate more on oral communication than on structures.
30. I create my own grammar tables.
31. I reorganize the material my own way.
32. I accept rules at face value.
33. I question most rules.
34. I compare rules with the ones found in my native tongue.
35. I do not compare/accept rules as part of a separate system.
36. I draw parallels with my native tongue.
37. I look for similarities with my native tongue.
38. I identify similarities in my native tongue.
39. I use grammatical information I already know.

F. LEARNING FROM CONTEXT

40. I avoid dangerous comparisons such as word-for-word translations.
41. I make good use of cognates.
42. I use context for intelligent guesses.
43. I look for the general meaning, idea, or theme.
44. I answer all four WH-questions: who, what, where, when?
45. Not knowing the meaning of a word impedes my thinking process or my progress.
46. I look up every word in a dictionary.

G. LEARNING FROM VARIOUS ACTIVITIES

47. I retain information better from written exercises.
48. I retain information better from oral work.
49. I retain information better from recorded material.
50. I prefer/perform better in comprehensive exercises, such as essays.
51. I prefer/perform better in fill-in-the-blank exercises.
52. I prefer/perform better in reading comprehension exercises.
53. I prefer/perform better in listening comprehension exercises.

H. LEARNING FROM ERRORS

54. I identify most of my errors.
55. I distinguish between recurrent errors and occasional slips.
56. I understand why I make a certain type of error.

I. REVIEWING

57. I review from the textbook material.
58. I review from my class notes.
59. I review from my personal cards, index, summaries, etc.
60. I review from test material only (quizzes, exams, etc.).

Language Anxiety and Gender Differences in Adult Second Language Learners: Exploring the Relationship

Christine M. Campbell,
Defense Language Institute
Victor M. Shaw,
Defense Language Institute

Introduction

Most foreign language teachers at the postsecondary level are aware that a certain percentage of their students suffer from debilitating anxiety that impedes successful learning. In some cases, its effects are visible to the teacher: the student looks unduly apprehensive, tends to avoid eye contact by staring down at the top of the desk, and so on. Some students may even seem to resist learning: they have a "bad attitude" and refuse to fully participate in class. In other cases, the effects of debilitating anxiety are not visible to the teacher: the student appears to be learning, engages in communicatively oriented activities, and the like. But after two or three weeks of class, usually just before the semester deadline for dropping courses, the student drops the course. The most typical reason a student gives is "I'm afraid of getting a low final grade in the course and upsetting my GPA."

Over the past fifty years researchers in the language learning field have attempted to determine whether the worry, nervousness, or "blanking" experienced by some language students are manifestations of anxiety. Traditionally, psychologists have used the term "anxiety" to describe an unpleasant emotional state or condition. In the early 1960s, Cattell (1966;

Cattell and Scheier 1961, 1963) introduced the concepts of state and trait anxiety. Today, psychologists view the two types of anxiety as related yet quite different constructs. Spielberger (1983) offers the following explanation of the difference between the two in the introduction to the manual accompanying the highly reputable anxiety instrument he created, the *State-Trait Anxiety Inventory:*

> In contrast to the transitory nature of emotional states, personality traits can be conceptualized as relatively enduring differences among people in specifiable tendencies to perceive the world in a certain way and in dispositions to react or behave in a specified manner with predictable regularity. . . . Trait anxiety (T-Anxiety) refers to relatively stable individual differences in anxiety-proneness, that is, to differences between people in the tendency to perceive stressful situations as dangerous or threatening and to respond to such situations with elevations in the intensity of their state anxiety (S-Anxiety) reactions. . . . The stronger the anxiety trait, the more probable that the individual will experience more intense elevations in S-Anxiety in a threatening situation. (p. 1)

According to Phillips (1992), test anxiety and math anxiety are well-known types of state anxiety. Is the anxiety felt by some students in the language learning classroom another type of state anxiety or is it a separate construct? MacIntyre and Gardner (1991a) have attempted to answer this question. In their study, they identified language or "situational" anxiety as one of three factors obtained in an analysis of a factor structure underlying twenty-three scales assessing language anxiety and other forms of anxiety. The other two factors obtained were state anxiety and social evaluation anxiety. While this study indicates that language anxiety and state anxiety are separate constructs, more evidence in support of this hypothesis is needed before it can be accepted.

Phillips (1992) provides an overview of the anxiety literature over the past fifty years in her article "The Effects of Language Anxiety on Students' Oral Test Performance and Attitudes." Dividing the research into three areas, trait anxiety, state anxiety, and language anxiety, she cites six studies dealing with the first,[1] five dealing with the second,[2] and twenty-eight dealing with the third.[3] (See also Young, this volume.)

In the past, language anxiety researchers have investigated issues such as the definition of language anxiety per se (Lalonde and Gardner 1984; Gardner 1985; Horwitz 1986; Horwitz, Horwitz, and Cope 1986; Young 1986; Gardner, Moorcroft, and MacIntyre 1987; MacIntyre and Gardner 1988a, 1988b, 1989, 1991a, 1991b; Phillips 1990a, 1990b, 1991, 1992; Horwitz and Young 1991), competitiveness and anxiety in adult language learning (Bailey 1983), and anxiety felt by adult second language learners about speaking, listening, reading, and writing in the target language in a classroom setting (Campbell and Ortiz 1988, 1991a, 1991b). To date, however, no one has focused on the relationship between language anxiety and gender differences in adult second language learners. This chapter describes a study that examined anxiety felt by male and female postsecondary students about using the target language in a classroom setting at two key points in their language program: immediately before beginning a foreign language course and after fourteen days or sixty hours of classroom instruction. The authors will discuss the results and their methodological implications without putting forth a hypothesis about the reasons why levels of anxiety between male and female students differ. Presumably, the reasons for these differences are rooted in socialization factors. It is not within the scope of this chapter to examine the role of these factors.

Research Background

A review of the research on the relationship between anxiety and second language learning reveals inconsistent, and often contradictory, research results. The conflicting reports suggest that anxiety is a complex, multifaceted construct. As stated above, Phillips (1992) found that the studies on anxiety in second language learning over the past fifty years focused on trait anxiety, state anxiety, and language anxiety. Before reviewing the literature on language anxiety, this chapter will examine research done in the areas of trait anxiety and state anxiety in language learning.

Studies on trait anxiety have explored the relationship between performance in second language learning and trait anxiety. Some of the researchers found performance inversely related to trait anxiety (Dunkel 1947; Bartz 1975; Swain and Burnaby 1976); others did not (Pimsleur, Sundland, and McIntyre, 1964; Brewster 1971; Westcott 1973). Swain and Burnaby, for example, found a negative correlation between trait anxiety and only one of several measures of French proficiency for English-speaking children in a French immersion program.

Research on state anxiety has examined the relationship between performance in second language learning and state anxiety. In these studies, performance was inversely related to state anxiety (Wittenborn, Larsen, and Mogil 1945; Chastain 1975; Steinberg 1982; Scott 1986; Young 1986).[4] Young, for example, found significant negative correlations between anxiety and the *ACTFL Oral Proficiency Interview* (*ACTFL OPI*, to be distinguished from the *Interagency Language Roundtable OPI*).

However, the correlations were no longer significant after the effects of foreign language ability were taken into account.

Studies on language anxiety focusing specifically on the relationship between performance in second language learning and language anxiety reveal that performance is inversely related to language anxiety (Gardner et al. 1976; Horwitz 1986; Tucker, Hamayan, and Genesee 1976; Phillips 1990a, 1992). Tucker, Hamayan, and Genesee (1976), for example, found a negative correlation between scores on a standardized achievement test and language anxiety. Backman (1976), in contrast, did not find a relationship between performance and language anxiety. She did observe, however, that the two worst Spanish-speaking ESL students in her study received, respectively, the highest and the lowest score on an anxiety measure.

As the literature review indicates, considerable research on state, trait, and language anxiety in second language learning has been done. One aspect of language anxiety yet to be explored is the relationship between language anxiety and gender differences. Recognizing that individual or learner differences constitute a complex, multifaceted variable made up of variables such as gender differences, attitudes toward the target language and culture, learning style, and beliefs about language learning, the authors chose to focus on gender as one aspect of individual differences. Nyikos (1990) used this approach to research in her studies on socialization and memory as factors relating to gender differences in adult language learning. She described the approach this way:

> Learner differences are disparate and complex. The type of learner who may benefit from the instructional sequence or variables under investigation may vary widely. Each individual approaches a learning task with a unique set of expectations and assumptions and a preferred mode of learning. These variables must be accounted for in any psycholinguistic study if the results of investigations into learning are to be validly extrapolated to similar situations. One recognized approach to understanding individual variation is to investigate successful task performance by identifiable groups, namely men and women, and account for gender-related differences and beliefs that are in consonance with data and theory. (p. 273)

This chapter describes a study that investigated anxiety felt by male and female postsecondary students about using the target language in a classroom setting. The authors do not attempt to determine whether language anxiety is a form of state anxiety or a separate construct; they merely describe the study and discuss the implications of the results for the classroom. They will, however, refer to the anxiety observed as "language anxiety."

Using an instrument especially designed to measure anxiety about using the target language in a classroom setting—the *Survey of Attitudes Specific to the Foreign Language Classroom* (*SASFLC*; Campbell and Ortiz, 1986) (see Appendix)—the authors surveyed 177 students at two key points in their language program: immediately before beginning a foreign language course and fourteen days or sixty hours of classroom instruction later. The authors decided on sixty hours because they deem that students who are exposed to this number of contact hours—approximately the number of contact hours in a college semester course—can provide meaningful commentary about their language learning experience.

The authors wanted to determine:

1. whether the level of language anxiety in male students in Survey 1 differed significantly from the level of language anxiety in female students in Survey 1;

2. whether the level of language anxiety in male students in Survey 2 differed significantly from the level of language anxiety in female students in Survey 2;

3. whether the level of language anxiety in male students in Survey 1 and Survey 2 differed significantly;

4. whether the level of language anxiety in female students in Survey 1 and Survey 2 differed significantly.

Hypotheses 3 and 4 were aimed at determining whether the levels of language anxiety in males and females, respectively, change over time.

Method

Subjects

All the subjects were military personnel who were students at the Defense Language Institute (DLI), San Francisco branch. The majority of the subjects were high-school graduates between eighteen and twenty-one years of age who had enlisted in the service immediately after high school. Prior to assignment to DLI, all the subjects had taken the *Defense Language Aptitude Battery* (*DLAB*; 1977), a standardized test of foreign language aptitude developed by DLI to use for personnel placement.

One hundred seventy-seven students learning four different languages participated in the study—twenty-one Spanish, sixty-three German, sixty-six Russian, twenty-seven Korean—from five consecutive cohorts of students at DLI, San Francisco branch. The four languages mentioned were the only languages taught at the site of the study.

Although the language courses mentioned differed in length—Spanish lasted twenty-five weeks; German, thirty-four weeks; Russian, forty-seven weeks; Korean, forty-seven weeks—all students had thirty hours of team-taught classroom instruction per week. The teams were made up of four or five male and female teachers in different combinations—three males and two females, one male and three females, and the like—who were native or near-native speakers of the target language. One team taught each course of twenty-five to thirty students. All teachers purportedly used a learner-centered, communicative approach to promote language proficiency. (When teachers first arrive at DLI, they attend a two-week instructor's workshop in which they discuss the proficiency movement in language education, the design of a learner-centered curriculum, and ways to promote meaningful communication in the classroom.) They integrated the four skills in their lesson plans, used authentic material, and developed personalized, meaningful activities for students to do in pairs and groups.

The authors eliminated subjects who (1) were fluent in a foreign language and (2) had successfully completed one or more college semesters of foreign language because the authors assumed that fluent speakers and subjects who had passed a college foreign language course would be relatively comfortable, and not anxiety ridden, in the foreign language classroom. The authors also eliminated subjects without *DLAB* scores. The distribution by language of the 163 subjects who were included in the final analyses was as follows: twenty Spanish, fifty-eight German, sixty Russian, twenty-five Korean. (The authors will examine the role of language difference in a separate article.)

To determine whether the two groups of subjects—males and females—were homogeneous in terms of degree of aptitude for foreign language learning, the authors used *DLAB* scores to run a t-test. The results showed no significant differences at the .05 level between males and females ($t = -1.79$, $p = .076$). (See Table 1.)[5] Although the differences were not significant, the females tended to score higher than the males.

Materials

The authors used the *Survey of Attitudes Specific to the Foreign Language Classroom* (*SASFLC*) (see Appendix) to measure language anxiety about using the target language in a classroom setting among male and female

Table 1

T-Test on DLAB Scores

Sex	N	M	SD	t	p
Male	119	101.96	11.369		
				−1.79	0.076
Female	44	105.64	12.458		

students. The *SASFLC* has sixteen statements which subjects react to using a 5-point Likert-type scale ranging from 1 = strongly agree to 5 = strongly disagree. Eleven statements in the *SASFLC* center on communication apprehension as it specifically applies to the four skills (e.g., "I fear not understanding what the teacher is saying in a foreign language when I am in a foreign language classroom"); five statements deal with commonly held beliefs about foreign language study (e.g., "It is necessary to have a special 'ear' in order to learn a foreign language well").

Although the statements in the *SASFLC* and in the *Foreign Language Classroom Anxiety Scale (FLCAS)* developed by Horwitz (1983) both deal with communication apprehension, they differ in emphasis: as described above, the *SASFLC* statements specifically focus on the four skills and, separately, on commonly held beliefs about foreign language study; the *FLCAS* statements refer to communication apprehension in general (e.g., "In language class, I can get so nervous I forget things I know"), test anxiety, and fear of negative evaluation in the foreign language classroom. Horwitz later rewrote five items from the *French Class Anxiety Scale* created by Gardner, Clement, Smythe, and Smythe (1979) to make them generic and added them to the *FLCAS* item pool. Before constructing the *SASFLC*, Campbell and Ortiz studied instruments for measuring anxiety from other fields such as psychology, consulted with professionals in the foreign language field, and asked students to respond to questions about language anxiety. A panel of one statistician, one foreign language measurement expert, and one foreign language instructor well versed in testing examined the *SASFLC* and concluded that it was a valid measure of language anxiety in the classroom setting. Work is underway to establish its construct validity. To date, over five hundred postsecondary foreign language students have taken the *SASFLC*.

Using Cronbach's alpha coefficient, reliability analysis for internal consistency for the *SASFLC* is .89 for the eleven items in the survey that deal directly with foreign language anxiety and .61 for the five items that deal with misconceptions about foreign language learning. It can be argued that the rather low reliability coefficient for the five items mentioned is due to the small number of items involved. An instrument with a small number of items can yield a small reliability coefficient.[6] It can also be argued that the five items deal with a construct different from language anxiety, that is, commonly held beliefs about second language learning.

Procedures

After arriving at DLI, San Francisco, each cohort of students took Survey 1 immediately before starting the intensive course in Spanish, German, Russian, or Korean. Two weeks later, or after sixty hours of instruction, students took Survey 2, which was identical to Survey 1 except for item order.

Results

The authors performed a two-way repeated measures ANOVA on the results of Surveys 1 and 2 with gender and time of survey administration as the two independent variables. Results:

1. The interaction between gender and time of survey administration is significant ($F = 4.81$, $p = .030$). (See Table 2 and Figure 1.) (To enhance data readability, the Likert Scale values for the survey

Table 2

Repeated Measures Analysis of Variance

Source of Variation	SS	DF	MS	F	p
Within cells	19180.24	161	119.13		
Gender	222.90	1	222.90	1.87	.173
Within cells	6041.98	161	37.53		
Time of survey	5.43	1	5.43	.14	.704
Gender by Time of survey	180.38	1	180.38	4.81	.030

Figure 1

Anxiety Change over Time

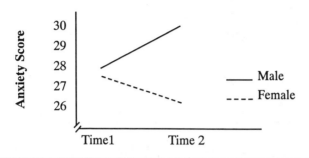

responses were converted. For example, whereas in the original survey 1= Strongly Agree [indicating high anxiety], after the conversion this value of 1 became 5.)

2. The results of Survey 1, which was administered to subjects the first day of the course, *before* the students entered class, revealed no significant differences in the level of language anxiety between male and female students ($t = .13$, $p = .90$). (See Table 3.)

3. The results of Survey 2, which was administered to the subjects on the fourteenth day of the course, after sixty hours of instruction, showed significant differences in the level of language anxiety between male and female students ($t = 2.15$, $p = .03$). (See Table 3.)

Table 3

T-Test on Anxiety Scores: Gender Difference

Survey 1	Sex	N	M	SD	t	p
	Male	119	27.899	8.414		
					0.13	.899
	Female	44	27.712	8.246		
Survey 2	Sex	N	M	SD	t	p
	Male	119	29.866	9.294		
					2.15	.033
	Female	44	26.327	9.340		

Table 4

T-Test on Anxiety Scores: Time of Survey

Males	N	M	SD	t	p
Survey 1	119	27.899	8.414		
				-2.42	.017
Survey 2	119	29.866	9.294		

Females	N	M	SD	t	p
Survey 1	44	27.712	8.246		
				1.13	.264
Survey 2	44	26.327	9.340		

4. The results of a t-test comparing levels of language anxiety in male students in Survey 1 and Survey 2 revealed significant differences ($t = -2.42$, $p = .02$). (See Table 4.)

5. The results of a t-test comparing levels of language anxiety in female students in Survey 1 and Survey 2 did not show significant differences ($t = 1.13$, $p = .26$). (See Table 4.)

6. Table 5 shows the number of subjects who responded "Strongly Agree" and those who responded "Agree" to statements in the *SASFLC*. Although the *SASFLC* comprises sixteen items, Table 5 contains only those statements in the survey that deal specifically with language anxiety. For each statement in the table, a percentage was computed by dividing the total number of subjects who responded to the statement into the "pooled" number of those who responded "Strongly Agree" and those who responded "Agree."

7. Table 6 shows the pooled and averaged data for statements in the survey referring to a specific language skill. Survey 1 revealed that language anxiety afflicts approximately 19 percent of the male students and 22 percent of the female students when speaking, 31 percent of the males and 31 percent of the females when listening, 14 percent of the males and 16 percent of the females when reading, and 13 percent of the males and 14 percent of the females when writing.

Table 5

Percentages of Strongly Agree and Agree by Sex

Statements	Survey 1 (Course beginning)		Survey 2 (Two weeks later)	
	Males n/N*(%)	Females n/N*(%)	Males n/N*(%)	Females n/N (%)
3. I fear making a mistake when I speak in a FL classroom setting.	28/119 (24%)	11/44 (25%)	45/119 (38%)	10/44 (23%)
4. I become anxious when I am being spoken to in a FL in a classroom setting.	25/119 (21%)	11/43 (25%)	51/119 (43%)	16/44 (36%)
5. I fear failing this course.	49/119 (41%)	20/44 (46%)	68/119 (57%)	22/44 (50%)
7. I become anxious when I am asked to write in a FL in a classroom setting.	15/119 (13%)	6/44 (14%)	22/119 (19%)	6/44 (14%)
9. I fear making a mistake in writing in a FL in a classroom setting.	17/119 (14%)	6/44 (14%)	26/119 (22%)	5/44 (11%)
10. I fear making a mistake in reading in a FL in a classroom setting.	19/119 (16%)	7/44 (16%)	25/119 (21%)	3/43 (7%)
11. I become anxious when I have to speak in a FL in a classroom setting.	31/119 (26%)	12/43 (27%)	58/119 (49%)	17/43 (40%)
12. I fear receiving a low final grade (D or below) in this course.	49/119 (41%)	22/44 (50%)	66/119 (56%)	18/43 (42%)
14. I fear not understanding what the teacher is saying in a FL when I am in a FL classroom.	48/119 (41%)	16/44 (36%)	49/119 (41%)	19/43 (44%)

Table 5

Percentages of Strongly Agree and Agree by Sex

Statements	Survey 1 (Course beginning)		Survey 2 (Two weeks later)	
	Males n/N^*(%)	Females n/N^*(%)	Males n/N^*%)	Females n/N^*(%)
15. I feel silly when I have to speak a FL in a classroom setting.	10/119 (8%)	5/43 (11%)	11/119 (9%)	2/43 (5%)
16. I become anxious when I have to read in a FL in a classroom setting.	15/119 (13%)	7/44 (16%)	31/119 (26%)	5/43 (12%)

Note: Table 5 includes only those statements in the SASFLC that deal with language anxiety.
*n—Number of students who responded "Strongly Agree" or "Agree" to the statement.
N—Total number of students who responded to the statement.

Table 6

Pooled Percentages of Strongly Agree and Agree by Language Skill

Speaking (Item #3, #11, #15)		Survey 1	Survey 2
	Male	19.3%	31.9%
	Female	21.5%	22.3%

Listening (Item #4, #14)		Survey 1	Survey 2
	Male	30.7%	42.0%
	Female	31.0%	40.2%

Reading (Item #10, #16)		Survey 1	Survey 2
	Male	14.3%	23.5%
	Female	15.9%	9.3%

Writing (Item #7, #9)		Survey 1	Survey 2
	Male	13.4%	20.2%
	Female	13.6%	12.5%

8. Survey 2 revealed that language anxiety afflicts 32 percent of the male students and 22 percent of the female students when speaking, 42 percent of the males and 40 percent of the females when listening, 24 percent of the males and 9 percent of the females when reading, and 20 percent of the males and 13 percent of the females when writing. (See Table 6.)

Discussion

The authors recognize along with Scovel (1978), Bailey (1983), Oller (1979), and others that identifying and defining the role of affective variables such as language anxiety in language learning is complicated by the fact that affective variables are usually not directly observable. Oller (1979, p. 9) posits that the measurement of affective variables is "necessarily inferential and indirect." The authors attempted to minimize inferring by querying the subjects directly via a questionnaire; they could not, however, collect additional data through interviews and student diaries due to administrative constraints. The authors will exploit these other data sources in future research.

The data from the present study reveal a significant interaction between gender and time of survey administration with opposite trends in levels of language anxiety in male and female students over a two-week period. From the administration of Survey 1, before the course began, until the administration of Survey 2, two weeks after the start of the course or after sixty hours of classroom instruction, the level of language anxiety in male students rose significantly while the level of language anxiety in female students slightly dropped. (See Figure 1 and Table 4.) The authors can only speculate about the reasons for the opposite trends. Although it is clear that gender interacted with time of survey administration, it is not clear exactly why it did.

Undoubtedly, any number of variables could explain the significant rise in the level of language anxiety among male students. Most likely, the rise is due to the interaction of different combinations of variables such as teaching methodology, testing practices, individual or learner differences (with its subsets gender differences, attitudes toward the target language and culture, learning style, and beliefs about language learning), and teacher differences. Detecting the effect of one specific variable on the subjects would require further research. In this chapter, the authors will refrain from speculating about the reasons for the rise in the level of language anxiety in male students in Survey 2, and instead will summarize the data results and make suggestions about how the foreign language educator might deal with the issue of language anxiety and gender differences in the classroom.

A careful review of the data in Table 6 reveals gender-related differences as they pertain to the four language skills. According to Table 6, approximately the same percentage of male and female students felt anxious about speaking in the target language before the course began; two weeks later, however, a greater percentage of males felt anxious about speaking than females. The same held true for reading and writing. For speaking, the percentage of females in Survey 2 who felt anxious rose less than 1 percent, while the percentage of males who felt anxious rose almost 13 percent. For reading and writing, the percentage of anxious females fell by approximately 7 percent and 1 percent, respectively, while the percentage of anxious males rose approximately 9 percent and 7 percent. In the case of listening, approximately the same percentage of males and females felt anxious before the course began; two weeks later, the percentage difference between males and females was slight (less than 2 percent), while the percentage hike from Survey 1 to Survey 2 for either group was considerable (almost 12 percent for males and 9 percent for females). Overall, both males and females felt more anxious about listening than the other three skills both before the course began and two weeks later.

There are two possible explanations for the high levels of anxiety for listening. First, listening is more threatening than the other skills because the listener has such little control over what the other party might say at a given moment. In some circumstances, questions and answers by the other party can be quite predictable and simply expressed (e.g., "Hello. How are you?"); in others, the questions and answers can touch on most any aspect of a topic and involve complicated expression containing embedded clauses, esoteric terminology, unfamiliar references, and more (e.g., "Are you a recovering existentialist?"). Second, listening creates more anxiety in DLI students in particular because the majority of the students know that they should have particularly strong listening skills to succeed in their future work. This realization makes them feel especially apprehensive about not understanding what the teacher and other students say.

The data in Table 5 also provide some insight into gender-related differences. According to Table 5, a slightly greater percentage of female students—5 percent—feared failing the course before the course began (see question #5); two weeks later, the percentage of females fearing failure rose only 4 percent while the percentage of males rose 16 percent. Likewise, a greater percentage of female students—9 percent—feared receiving a low final grade in the course before the course began (see question #12); two weeks later, the percentage of females fearing receiving a low final grade in the course dropped by 8 percent, while the percentage of males rose 15 percent.

The results of this study, *grosso modo*, suggest the following about male and female postsecondary students learning the target language in an intensive course:

1. After sixty hours of instruction, a considerable number of males are significantly more anxiety ridden in the classroom than their female counterparts. This anxiety among the males, it seems, is directly connected to (a) language activities requiring the student to listen, speak, read, and write in the target language and to (b) a fear of academic failure.

2. Overall, both males and females are more anxious about listening than the other skills both before a course begins and two weeks later.

The authors recognize that in learning research certain factors inevitably limit the generalizability of the conclusions. One factor of particular interest in this study is the context. The authors readily admit that this data may not be generalizeable to contexts other than DLI. One might argue that the military context, which is inherently more structured and regimented than the academic context, is more stressful for the student. Another factor is student type. The profile of the DLI student is different from that of the typical college or university student: the DLI student is both a student and a professional. As such, he or she may feel more burdened than the typical college or university student. It must be stated here, though, that the DLI student has minimal military duties.

A third factor influencing the generalizability of the conclusions is the role the language course plays in the student's career. The DLI student might feel greater pressure to succeed in a language course that is directly connected to his or her future career than his college or university counterpart who is majoring in a subject other than language. As discussed earlier, the higher anxiety levels for listening among both males and females before the course and after sixty hours of instruction may be due to the importance listening has for the DLI student's future work.

A fourth factor limiting the generalizability of the conclusions is course type. Currently, all students in DLI's intensive courses have thirty-five contact hours per week. Postsecondary students at colleges and universities typically have three to five contact hours of language per week. Undoubtedly, intensive courses are more challenging to students. Presumably, these types of courses can exacerbate the anxiety students feel.

Given the factors above that limit the generalizability of the conclusions, what are the implications of the results for the foreign language classroom?

These results, combined with results from learner style tests[7] and first-hand teacher observation, could assist curriculum developers or teachers in adapting the curricula to meet students' particular needs. If, as the literature (Nyikos, 1990) indicates, gender differences are a subset of individual differences, the foreign language professional can look to the vast amount of work done in the area of individual differences for ideas about how to deal with gender differences in the classroom (see also Meunier, this volume). In this context, gender differences can simply be seen as tendencies in one group of students versus another. Just as what Oxford, Ehrman, and Lavine (1991) call "global" and "analytic" foreign language learners approach particular learning tasks in different ways, so it appears that adult male and female second language learners differ in how they react in the foreign language classroom.

Even the most seasoned language teacher may feel ill-prepared to deal with individual differences and its subset gender differences in the foreign language classroom. The authors recommend they use Oxford and Lavine's (1992) six-point plan for coping with teacher–student style conflicts as a working model for dealing with individual differences and its subset gender differences. The six-point plan follows:

1. Assess students' and teachers' styles and use this information in understanding classroom dynamics.
2. Change your behavior as a teacher.
3. Change students' behavior.
4. Change the way group work is done in the classroom.
5. Change the curriculum.
6. Change the way style conflicts are viewed. (pp. 42–44)

Of special interest here is point number 5, "Change the curriculum" (p. 44). If, as the results of the study described in this chapter indicate, a considerable number of males are significantly more anxiety ridden in the classroom than their female counterparts after sixty hours of instruction, the teacher could consider conducting a special course designed to help anxiety-ridden students become successful language learners. Although the females in the class might not benefit from the course as much as the males, they will at least learn ways to enhance their language learning. Two such courses for anxiety-ridden students, Horwitz, Horwitz, and Cope's (1986) "Support Group for Foreign Language Learning" and Campbell and Ortiz's (1988, 1991a, 1991b) "Foreign Language Anxiety Workshop," attempt to reverse students' negative attitudes toward foreign language study. In both courses, students discuss their past and current experiences with language learning, learn about language-learning strategies, study ways to cope with anxiety, and more. In Horwitz et al.'s course, students voluntarily participate in weekly sessions lasting one or more hours which they attend outside of classroom hours; in Campbell and Ortiz's course, students spend the first one to three hours of the language course itself working through special materials.

Teachers can create their own materials or adapt materials from the two courses described to suit their students' needs after determining their students' anxiety levels via the *SASFLC* or the *FLCAS* surveys. Teachers who have conducted these courses find that students bond into a cohesive community of language learners by the end of these sessions.[8]

Aside from conducting special courses of this sort, teachers can also help anxiety-ridden students by choosing those methodologies best suited to students of this type. If teachers are not already using Terrell's (1977, 1982) "Natural Approach," they can at least adopt one of its tenets: students can respond in the target language, their native language, or a combination of both. Perhaps male students will feel less anxious about speaking (this study indicates that approximately one-third of them feel extremely anxious about speaking after sixty hours of instruction) if they can rely on English as a crutch whenever they feel they need it.

In addition to allowing students to answer in English, teachers can focus more on reading comprehension and writing exercises and less on speaking and listening comprehension activities at the beginning of a course. As just pointed out, male students in particular seem to find speaking activities threatening. Furthermore, this study suggests that both male and female students feel more anxious about listening than any of the other three skills both before the course begins and after sixty hours of classroom instruction. Although a proficiency orientation stresses skill integration from the outset, teachers can ease their students into speaking and listening activities by first explaining to them how to use language learning strategies such as deducing meaning from context, listening for and using cognates, taking risks, learning to deal with uncertainty, understanding the gist of what is heard or read, and so on. Teachers can also postpone testing of speaking and listening until several weeks into the course. If, as Krashen (1982) has hypothesized, a low-stress language learning environment encourages acquisition, then teachers should search out ways to create a challenging, but nonthreatening, learning environment in the classroom.

Conclusion

Although each new study on language anxiety sheds light on yet another aspect of the phenomenon, more research needs to be done before we will have a clear understanding of how this complex variable operates in the second language classroom. This study explored the relationship between language anxiety and gender differences. This study suggests that after sixty hours of instruction a considerable number of male postsecondary students in intensive language courses are significantly more anxiety-ridden about using the target language in the classroom than their female counterparts. It further indicates that both male and female postsecondary students in intensive courses are more anxious about listening than the other skills both before a course begins and after sixty hours of instruction. These results must be seen in the light of the factors that limit the generalizability of the conclusions, namely, context, student type, role of the language course in the student's career, and course type. Further research is needed before the results can be considered conclusive. For example, this study should be replicated in the university milieu so the results can be verified in a different context. Future research should also track students throughout an entire language course to determine changes in anxiety levels over longer periods of time. Another study might explore differences in levels of language anxiety across languages to include the commonly taught and the less commonly taught ones.[9]

Studies such as the one described in this chapter indicate that individual differences and its subset gender differences play a critical role in the foreign language classroom. Teachers must be aware of the impact of individual differences on learning and adjust the curricula accordingly. This awareness can help teachers better understand student attitudes and student performance. More importantly, this awareness can help teachers identify early on those students who are having difficulty learning because of problems such as language anxiety or teacher–student style conflicts. Early detection of problems like these can make the difference between success and failure for a student in the proficiency-oriented foreign language classroom of today.

Notes

1. Dunkel 1947; Pimsleur, Sundland, and McIntyre 1964; Brewster 1971; Westcott 1973; Bartz 1975; Swain and Burnaby 1976.

2. Wittenborn, Larsen, and Mogil 1945; Chastain 1975; Steinberg 1982; Scott 1986; Young 1986.

3. Backman 1976; Gardner et al. 1976; Tucker, Hamayan, and Genesee 1976; Scovel 1978; Bailey 1983; Ely 1986; Horwitz 1986; Horwitz, Horwitz, and Cope 1986; Scott 1986; Young 1986; Foss and Reitzel 1988; MacIntyre and Gardner 1989; Ehrman and Oxford 1990; Lavine and Oxford 1990; Loughrin-Sacco 1990; Phillips 1990a, 1990b; Young 1990; Campbell and Ortiz 1991a; Cope Powell 1991; Crookall and Oxford 1991; Daly 1991; Horwitz and Young 1991; Koch and Terrell 1991; Madsen, Brown, and Jones 1991; Mejías, Applbaum, Applbaum, and Trotter, 1991; Price 1991; Horwitz and Sadow 1992.

4. Young's 1986 article was cited in the introduction as an example of a study on language anxiety because it was defined as such by Horwitz and Young (1991) in *Language and Anxiety*. Phillips (1992) includes Young's 1986 article as an example of a study on state anxiety.

5. For those readers concerned about the differing Ns in the t-tests performed on the *DLAB* scores and survey results in this study, the authors provide the following information: According to the bulk of the literature in educational statistics, the difference in the Ns is taken into account in the process to determine t values. Guilford and Fruchter, two psychologists renowned for their expertise in educational statistics, refer to differing Ns when using t tests in their germinal text *Fundamental Statistics in Psychology and Education* (1956). In the last line of the section entitled "When t Tests Do Not Apply," Guilford and Fruchter state: "On the whole, t is not markedly affected except by rather strong violations [of the assumptions of the t tests, such as the one establishing that Ns should be as similar as possible], unless N is very small" (p. 162). The differing Ns in the present study do not constitute a "strong violation" because the variances of the two groups are not significantly different ($F = 1.20$, $p = .439$). A strong violation, according to Guilford and Fruchter, would be differing variances. They posit: "The reader should also be warned that if the two samples have markedly differing variances, the t test is questionable" (p. 161).

6. For example, when an instrument consisting of five items has a Cronbach's alpha reliability coefficient of .61, doubling the number of items using the Spearman-Brown formula will yield a reliability coefficient of .76.

7. Some well known style instruments are *The Personal Style Inventory* (Thomas P. Hogan and Champagne), *The Keirsey Temperament Sorter* (David Keirsey and Marilyn Bates. 1978.), *Learning Styles Inventory* (David Kolb, Irwin Rubin, and James McIntyre. 1971), *Myers-Briggs Type Indicator* (Isabel Briggs Myers and Katharine Briggs. Palo Alto, CA: Consulting Psychologists Press, Inc.), *Learning Channel Preference Checklist* (Lynn O'Brien 1990. Research for Better Schools.), *Style Orientation Survey* (Rebecca Oxford. 1987), *Your Style of Learning and Thinking* (Paul E. Torrence, C. Reynolds, T. Riegal, and O. Ball. 1987). Consult the first author for more information on these instruments.

8. In a personal communication (1988), T. Critchfield, a professor of Japanese, described the atmosphere in the class immediately after the students had participated in a four-hour anxiety-reduction course using Campbell and Ortiz's materials: "[There is] good humor and trust among members of the class as well as the lack of formal distance between students and instructor. Such is not unusual in my classes but [this] is a very, very early phenomenon, and one that I believe will result in a lower level of classroom frustration and consequent higher rate of student survival in the class."

9. The authors are currently doing research on this topic.

Works Cited

Backman, Nancy. 1976. Two Measures of Affective Factors as They Relate to Progress in Adult Second-Language Learning. *Working Papers in Bilingualism* 10: 100–122.

Bailey, Kathleen. 1983. Competitiveness and Anxiety in Adult Second Language Learning: Looking At and Through the Diary Studies. In *Classroom-Oriented Research in Second Language Acquisition,* edited by Herbert W. Seliger and Michael H. Long, 67–102. Rowley, MA: Newbury House.

Bartz, Walter 1975. A Study of the Relationship of Certain Learner Factors with the Ability to Communicate in a Second Language (German) for the Development of Measures of Communicative Competence. *Dissertation Abstracts International* 35: 4852A.

Brewster, Elizabeth S. 1971. Personality Factors Relevant to Intensive Audio-Lingual Foreign Language Learning. *Dissertation Abstracts International* 33: 68A.

Campbell, Christine, and José A. Ortiz. 1986. *Survey of Attitudes Specific to the Foreign Language Classroom.* Presidio of Monterey, CA: Defense Language Institute.

———. 1988. Dispelling Students' Fears and Misconceptions about Foreign Language Study: The Foreign Language Anxiety Workshop at the Defense Language Institute. In *New Challenges and Opportunities: Dimension—Languages '87,* edited by T. Fryer and Frank Medley, Jr., 29–40. Columbia, SC: Southern Conference on Language Teaching.

————. 1991a. Toward a More Thorough Understanding of Foreign Language Anxiety. In *Focus on the Foreign Language Learner: Priorities and Strategies,* edited by Lorraine A. Strasheim, 12–24. Lincolnwood, NJ: National Textbook.

————. 1991b. Helping Students Overcome Foreign Language Anxiety: A Foreign Language Anxiety Workshop. In Horwitz and Young, 153–68.

Cattell, Raymond B. 1966. *Handbook of Multivariate Experimental Psychology.* Chicago: Rand-McNally.

Cattell, Raymond B., and Ivan H. Scheier. 1961. *The Meaning and Measurement of Neuroticism and Anxiety.* New York: Ronald Press.

————. 1963. *Handbook for the IPAT Anxiety Scale.* 2d ed. Champaign, IL: Institute for Personality and Ability Testing.

Chastain, Kenneth. 1975. Affective and Ability Factors in Second Language Acquisition. *Language Learning* 25: 153–61.

Cope Powell, Jo Ann. 1991. Foreign Language Classroom Anxiety: Institutional Responses. In Horwitz and Young, 169–76.

Crookall, David, and Rebecca L. Oxford. 1991. Dealing with Anxiety: Some Practical Activities for Language Learners and Teacher Trainees. In Horwitz and Young, 141–50.

Daly, John. 1991. Understanding Communication Apprehension: An Introduction for Language Educators. In Horwitz and Young, 3–14.

Defense Language Aptitude Battery. 1977. Presidio of Monterey, CA: Defense Language Institute.

Dunkel, Harold B. 1947. The Effect of Personality on Language Achievement. *Journal of Educational Psychology* 38: 177–82.

Ehrman, Madelaine, and Rebecca L. Oxford. 1990. Adult Language Learning Styles and Strategies in an Intensive Training Setting. *Modern Language Journal* 73: 311–27.

Ely, Christopher M. 1986. An Analysis of Discomfort, Risktaking, Sociability, and Motivation in the L2 Classroom. *Language Learning* 36: 1–25.

Foss, Karen A., and Armeda C. Reitzel. 1988. A Relational Model for Managing Second Language Anxiety. *TESOL Quarterly* 22: 427–54.

Gardner, Robert C. 1985. *Social Psychology and Second Language Learning: The Role of Attitudes and Motivation.* London: Edward Arnold.

Gardner, Robert C., R. Clement, P. Smythe, and C. Smythe. 1979. *Attitudes and Motivation Test Battery, Revised Manual.* Research Bulletin No. 5. London, Ontario: University of Western Ontario.

Gardner, Robert C., R. Moorcroft, and Peter D. MacIntyre. 1987. *The Role of Anxiety in Second Language Performance of Language Dropouts.* Research Bulletin No. 657. London, Ontario: Department of Psychology, University of Western Ontario.

Gardner, Robert C., P. C. Smythe, R. Clement, and L. Gliksman. 1976. Second Language Learning: A Social-Psychological Perspective. *Canadian Modern Language Review* 32: 198–213.

Guilford, J., and Benjamin Frutcher. 1973. *Fundamental Statistics in Psychology and Education.* 5th ed. New York: McGraw-Hill.

Horwitz, Elaine K. 1983. *Foreign Language Classroom Anxiety Scale.* Reprinted with permission. University of Texas at Austin.

———. 1986. Preliminary Evidence for the Reliability and Validity of a Foreign Language Anxiety Scale. *TESOL Quarterly* 20: 559–62.

Horwitz, Elaine K., Michael B. Horwitz, and Jo Ann Cope. 1986. Foreign Language Classroom Anxiety. *Modern Language Journal* 70: 125–32.

Horwitz, Elaine K., and S. Sadow. 1992. A Preliminary Exploration of the Relationship between Learner Beliefs about Language Learning and Foreign Language Anxiety. Unpublished manuscript.

Horwitz, Elaine K., and Dolly J. Young, eds. 1991. *Language and Anxiety.* Englewood Cliffs, NJ: Prentice-Hall.

Koch, April, and Tracy D. Terrell. 1991. Affective Reactions of Foreign Language Students to Natural Approach Activities and Teaching Techniques. In Horwitz and Young, 37–40.

Krashen, Stephen D. 1982. *Principles and Practice in Second Language Acquisition.* New York: Pergamon Press.

Lalonde, R., and Robert C. Gardner. 1984. Investigating a Causal Model of Second Language Acquisition: Where Does Personality Fit? *Canadian Journal of Behavioural Science* 16: 224–37.

Lavine, Roberta Z., and Rebecca L. Oxford. 1990. Dealing with Affective Issues in the Foreign- or Second-Language Classroom. Paper presented at the annual meeting of the Modern Language Association, Chicago.

Loughrin-Sacco, Steven J. 1990. Inside the "Black Box" Revisited: Toward the Integration of Naturalistic Inquiry in Classroom Research on Foreign Language Learning. *Polylingua* 1: 22–26.

MacIntyre, Peter D., and Robert C. Gardner. 1988a. *Anxiety Factors in Language Learning.* Research Bulletin No. 677. London, Ontario: Department of Psychology, The University of Western Ontario.

———. 1988b. *The Measurement of Anxiety and Applications to Second Language Learning: An Annotated Bibliography.* Research Bulletin No. 672. London, Ontario: Department of Psychology, University of Western Ontario. (ERIC Doc. No. FL017649).

———. 1989. Anxiety and Second-Language Learning: Toward a Theoretical Clarification. *Language Learning* 39: 251–75.

———. 1991a. Language Anxiety: Its Reliability to Other Anxieties and to Processing in Native and Second Languages. *Language Learning* 41: 513–34.

———. 1991b. Methods and Results in the Study of Foreign Language Anxiety: A Review of the Literature. *Language Learning* 41: 25–57.

Madsen, Harold S., Bruce B. Brown, and Randall L. Jones. 1991. Evaluating Student Attitudes toward Second-Language Tests. In Horwitz and Young, 65–86.

Mejías, Hugo, Ronald L. Applbaum, Susan J. Applbaum, and Robert T. Trotter, II. 1991. Oral Communication Apprehension and Hispanics: An Exploration of Oral Communication Apprehension among Mexican American Students in Texas. In Horwitz and Young, 87–97.

Nyikos, Martha. 1990. Sex-Related Differences in Adult Language Learning: Socialization and Memory Factors. *Modern Language Journal* 74: 273–87.

Oller, John. 1979. *Research on the Measurement of Affective Variables: Some Remaining Questions.* Paper presented at the Colloquium on Second Language Acquisition and Use Under Different Circumstances, 1979 TESOL Convention, Boston.

Oxford, Rebecca L., Madelaine Ehrman, and Roberta Z. Lavine. 1991. Style Wars: Teacher–Student Style Conflicts in the Language Classroom. In *Challenges in the 1990s for College Foreign Language Programs,* edited by Sally Magnan, 1–25. Boston: Heinle & Heinle.

Oxford, Rebecca L., and Roberta Z. Lavine. 1992. Teacher–Student Style Wars in the Language Classroom: Research Insights and Suggestions. *ADFL Bulletin* 23: 38–45.

Phillips, Elaine. 1990a. The Effects of Anxiety on Performance and Achievement in an Oral Test of French. *Dissertation Abstracts International* 51: 1941A.

———. 1990b. Anxiety and Oral Proficiency Tests. Paper presented at the annual meeting of the Modern Language Association, Chicago.

———. 1991. Anxiety and Oral Competence: Classroom Dilemma. *French Review* 65: 1–14.

———. 1992. The Effects of Language Anxiety on Students' Oral Test Performance and Attitudes. *Modern Language Journal* 76: 15–26.

Pimsleur, Paul, D. Sundland, and R. McIntyre. 1964. Under-Achievement in Foreign Language Learning. *International Review of Applied Linguistics in Language Teaching* 2: 113–50.

Price, Mary Lou. 1991. The Subjective Experiences of Foreign Language Anxiety: Interviews with Anxious Students. In Horwitz and Young, 101–8.

Scott, M. L. 1986. The Effect of Affect: A Review of the Anxiety Literature. *Language Testing* 3: 99–118.

Scovel, Thomas. 1978. The Effect of Affect on Foreign Language Learning: A Review of the Anxiety Research. *Language Learning* 28: 129–42.

Speilberger, C. 1983. *Manual for the State-Trait Anxiety Inventory.* Palo Alto, CA: Consulting Psychologists Press.

Steinberg, Faith S. 1982. The Relationship between Anxiety and Oral Performance in a Foreign Language. M.A. thesis, University of Texas.

Swain, Merrill, and Barbara Burnaby. 1976. Personality Characteristics and Second Language Learning in Young Children: A Pilot Study. *Working Papers in Bilingualism* 11: 115–28.

Terrell, Tracy D. 1977. A Natural Approach to the Acquisition and Learning of a Language. *Modern Language Journal* 61: 325–36.

———. 1982. The Natural Approach to Language Teaching: An Update. *Modern Language Journal* 66: 121–32.

Tucker, Richard, Else Hamayan, and Fred H. Genesee. 1976. Affective, Cognitive, and Social Factors in Second Language Acquisition. *Canadian Modern Language Review* 32: 214–26.

Westcott, D. B. 1973. Personality Factors Affecting High School Students Learning a Second Language. *Dissertation Abstracts International* 34: 2183A.

Wittenborn, J. R., R. P. Larsen, and R. L. Mogil. 1945. An Empirical Evaluation of Study Habits for College Courses in French and Spanish. *Journal of Educational Psychology* 36: 449–74.

Young, Dolly J. 1986. The Relationship between Anxiety and Foreign Language Oral Proficiency Ratings. *Foreign Language Annals* 19: 439–45.

———. 1990. An Investigation of Students' Perspectives on Anxiety and Speaking. *Foreign Language Annals* 23: 539–53.

Appendix

[For office use: WS—*Y/N*]
Course # _____ Survey# ____1____ Date _____ SS# _____ Age_____
Location _____

SURVEY OF ATTITUDES SPECIFIC TO THE FOREIGN LANGUAGE CLASSROOM (SASFLC)

Please answer parts I and II below honestly and carefully. As the results will be used to better the current foreign language curriculum, it is very important that you spend time thinking about each answer. Your answers are anonymous.

I. Experience with the foreign language

1. Were any of your immediate family members (father, mother, brothers, or sisters) born in a foreign country?_____
   Which one(s)?   Where?

   _____   _____
   _____   _____
   _____   _____
   _____   _____

2. Were you born in a foreign country? _____
   Where?_____

3. Do any of your immediate family members speak a foreign language *fluently* (*not* slightly)?_____
   Which family member(s)   Which language(s)

   _____   _____
   _____   _____
   _____   _____

4. Do you speak a foreign language *fluently* (*not* slightly)?_____
   Which one(s)   Did you learn it at home or
                                       in school?

   _____   _____
   _____   _____
   _____   _____

5. Below, fill in the number of years that you studied the foreign language(s) at school. *First, identify the language; then, place the number of years.*

	First foreign language (FL)	Second FL	Third FL
elementary school (grades 1-6)	_____	_____	_____
junior high school (grades 7-9)	_____	_____	_____
high school (grades 10-12)	_____	_____	_____
college	_____	_____	_____

Number of semesters of the first FL	Second FL	Third FL
_____	_____	_____

II. Attitudes Specific to the Foreign Language Classroom

Please respond to the statements below using the following scale:

1. strongly agree
2. agree
3. undecided
4. disagree
5. strongly disagree

Once again, please answer honestly and carefully. Spend time thinking about each answer. Your answers are anonymous.

1. It is necessary to have a special aptitude (i.e., an inborn talent) in order to learn a foreign language well.
   1 2 3 4 5

2. It is necessary to have a special intelligence (i.e., higher I.Q.) in order to learn a foreign language well.
   1 2 3 4 5

3. It is necessary to have a special "ear" in order to learn a foreign language well.
   1 2 3 4 5

4. I become anxious when I have to speak in a foreign language in a classroom setting.
   1 2 3 4 5

5. I feel silly when I have to speak in a foreign language in a classroom setting.
   1 2 3 4 5

6. I become anxious when I am spoken to in a foreign language in a classroom setting.
   1 2 3 4 5

7. I become anxious when I am asked to write in a foreign language in a classroom setting.
   1 2 3 4 5

8. I become anxious when I have to read in a foreign language in a classroom setting.
   1 2 3 4 5

9. I fear failing this course.
   1 2 3 4 5

10. I fear receiving a low final grade (D or below) in this course.
    1 2 3 4 5

11. I fear making a mistake when I speak in a foreign language in a classroom setting.
    1 2 3 4 5

12. I fear not understanding what the teacher is saying in a foreign language when I am in a foreign language classroom.
    1 2 3 4 5

13. I fear making a mistake in writing in a foreign language in a classroom setting.
    1 2 3 4 5

14. I fear making a mistake in reading in a foreign language in a classroom setting.
    1 2 3 4 5

Answer No. 15 only if you are a high school graduate:

15. I think that the standard foreign language high school course is more difficult than the standard "verbally oriented" high school course such as History.
    1 2 3 4 5

Answer No. 16 only if you are a high school graduate:

16. I think that the standard foreign language high school course is more difficult than the standard "numerically oriented" high school course such as Algebra I.
    1 2 3 4 5

Demographically Induced Variation in Students' Curricular Preferences

Monika Chavez
University of Wisconsin at Madison

Introduction

This chapter examines how the demographic variables of foreign travel, previous foreign language learning experience, chosen or intended major field of study, age, language learning success (as measured by the grade in the last German course), and gender affect students' curricular preferences. The chapter focuses on findings procured by an instrument of evaluation, a forty-eight-item questionnaire administered to first- and second-year students of German at the University of Wisconsin at Madison. The chapter summary outlines the choices afforded and the problems posed by those results and thus provides a framework for further discussions.[1]

The recognition of the language learner as an individual (see Wong-Fillmore 1983) has also included the perception of the language learner as a member of particular demographic groups with their own particular characteristics. With the help of questionnaire-style research instruments, learner characteristics, such as beliefs about language learning (see Horwitz 1987, 1988) and the use of language strategies (see Oxford's Strategy Inventory for Language Learning, 1990), have been explored.

A large body of more recent studies have focused on gender (e.g., Bacon 1992; Boyle 1987; Goldberg Muchnik, and Wolfe 1982; Oxford 1993a, 1993b). For example, Meunier (this volume) and Zoubir-Shaw and Oxford (this volume) describe a wealth of studies on the effects of gender on the use of learning strategies, which include the following findings: Female second language learners, as compared to their male counterparts,

(1) perform better in listening comprehension (Eisenstein 1982; Farhady 1982); (2) prefer activities and strategic behavior that involve social interaction and negotiation of meaning (Ehrman and Oxford 1989); (3) engage more in functional practice strategies (Ehrman and Oxford 1989); and (4) show greater conformity to academic and linguistic norms, that is, they rely to a greater extent on formal rule-based strategies (Oxford and Nyikos 1989). In addition, Zoubir-Shaw and Oxford (this volume) offer findings based on their own research, which reveal, among others, the following characteristics of females: (1) they rely more heavily on visual learning aides (e.g., color-coded cards for gender categories) and lists organized in grammatical classes; (2) they are more rule-oriented; and (3) they use contextualized learning strategies more frequently.

In addition, behavioral and attitudinal characteristics of successful language learners, mostly with regard to specific skills and motivation rather than to curricular preferences, have been explored by, among many others, Buonomo (1990), Corbeil (1990), Gillette (1987), Politzer (1983), Ramsay (1980), Rubin (1975), Stern (1975), and Wenden (1987). The most commonly described characteristics of successful language learners include top-down processing, desire for communication, ability to monitor, attention to meaning, and willingness to work with authentic materials.

The effects of the variable of age have mainly been explored in studies of hypothesized deficiencies, such as those targeting pre- versus postcritical age language learning and language learning in the elderly (e.g., Brown 1983, 1985; d'Anglejan and Renaud 1985; Wagner 1992). Little research has been conducted on age groups that are neither elderly nor of the age traditionally associated with undergraduate foreign language study (eighteen to twenty-three years).

The effects of other foreign language learning experience have been investigated primarily with regard to transfer of cognitive or strategic behavior (Ramsay 1980; Werker 1986; Zobl 1992).

The roles of travel abroad and of the learners' major field of study have thus far received little attention.

As valuable as the various studies described above are to the profession, they do not address two issues that are of particular relevance to language teachers and supervisors of foreign language programs: (1) they do not take into consideration the fact that each individual student represents a bundle of demographic characteristics, with the consequence that an exclusive focus on any one demographic variable prevents us from realizing which of the demographic variables contribute to more diverse and which to less diverse preferences, motivations, satisfaction, or behavior; and (2) they survey and determine (mostly strategic) behaviors and outcomes that (a) are often artificially separated from particular instructional settings and (b) do not address learners' overall curricular preferences.

Even though it is essential for everyone in the profession to be aware of specifically focused insights derived under research testing conditions, it is equally necessary for us to know how students react to the demands, challenges, and opportunities posed by particular programs. For example, Goldberg Muchnik, and Wolfe (1982) show an unexpected negative correlation between overall attitude toward the target language/culture and specific teachers/courses, which they tentatively explain by disenchantment with the learning environment on the part of students.

Thus, the following chapter will investigate divergence in curricular preferences and satisfaction according to multiple demographic variables (gender, travel abroad, age, success as measured by grades, other foreign language learning experience, and major field of study), in a questionnaire format that is tailored to the specific characteristics of the first- and second-year German sequences at the University of Wisconsin at Madison (UW).

Methodology

Subjects

The findings presented are based on a questionnaire survey administered to 277 subjects who were enrolled in the first four semesters of German at UW.

The data have been analyzed in two distinct, separate sets: one pool comprising students in the first year; the other, students in the second year. This was done because, in some respects, those two data pools reflect separate programs. That is, the first- and second-year sequences have differing curricular goals and accordingly, different content; they are supervised by two different faculty members, and they serve somewhat different student populations. While there are a few students with German language learning experiences from high school or another institution of higher learning (i.e., an institution other than UW) in the first-year sequence, the second-year sequence comprises students of various backgrounds: those who have completed the first-year German sequence at UW along with those who enter the program directly from high school and those who transfer from another institution of higher learning. The specific characteristics of both the first- and second-year programs are described below.

Although program-specificity is a distinctive feature of this chapter and by necessity will be present in ensuing studies at other institutions as well, this study can reveal general trends that may occur in different settings (interlinguistic as well as interinstitutional), and suggest alternative areas of investigation.

Characteristics of the First- and Second-Year German Sequences at UW

Before discussing the differences between the two sequences, I need to describe similarities between them. Both programs are taught in multiple sections, take a four-skills communicative approach, draw on the same pool of instructors (mainly graduate student teaching assistants), follow the same semester-based sequence, and are supervised through frequent coordination meetings and classroom visits so that a reasonable adherence to the program by all instructors can be assumed.

The First-Year Sequence

The goals of the first-year sequence include the introduction of basic concepts of the German language as they pertain to the functional and situational aspects of grammar and vocabulary. Paradigms (such as all the tenses of the passive) are not taught in their entirety but rather with a selective focus on frequency and functionality. While many of the structural explanations are derived from the book, some focused structural practice also takes place in class. Nevertheless, the major focus of in-class activities is on communicative exchanges (including group work and pair work) and practical applications of linguistic structures. The degree to which explicit instruction on pronunciation and intonation is provided in class varies by instructor.

While oral language, including its two associated skills of listening and speaking, constitutes a major component of the first-year sequence, writing and reading are also important. Students write short essays and journal entries. Reading selections include some short prose texts but mainly simple authentic materials such as advertisements and schedules.

Writing, reading, and structural knowledge are routinely tested in quizzes and departmental exams. Oral exams are also integral to testing although their format varies by instructor.

The Second-Year Sequence

While the second-year sequence includes aspects of grammar and vocabulary instruction, relatively little time is devoted to it in class. Rather, regular (daily) homework assignments attempt to accomplish the following: recycle existing knowledge that students bring with them; expand students' level and areas of knowledge so that all students reach a linguistic proficiency that is both more similar in terms of overall achievement (remember that students' enter the second-year sequence from diverse backgrounds) and more personalized in terms of the ability to express one's individual thoughts, wishes, and the like; and emphasize the functional aspects of language by showing the students that grammar and vocabulary are to be used as tools of communication rather than topics of instruction. Thus, students are asked to generate responses, questions, thoughts, and so on, in particular situations and contexts. Most situational homework activities are preceded by written explanations (in the L1), comprehension check activities, strategic instruction, and production activities that are more narrowly focused.

Besides those daily assignments, semesterly homework assignments include the following: prereading of longer authentic texts that will be used in class, two one-week (each) periods of daily diary entries, five essays that involve different writing styles and objectives (opinion pieces, creative writing, retelling stories, descriptions of hypothetical events, etc.), and peer corrections (both for accuracy and for style).

In class, grammar explanations and more structured activities in general occur only when requested by the students or deemed necessary by the instructor, usually as a consequence of low accuracy in communicative and functional performance. Instead, most class time is devoted to interactive, situational activities, improvement of intonation and pronunciation, and work with a mix (literary, informational, etc.) of oral and written authentic texts, which involves extensive discussion of cultural issues and the practice of reading and listening strategies.

All four skills and cultural knowledge are monitored periodically through written, oral, and reading tests. The written tests target listening comprehension and the ability to communicate in particular situations. In order to emphasize the fact that writing (composition) is a process rather than a product, the writing of lengthier and cohesive pieces is not tested in class.

Demographics of the UW-Madison German Program Respondents

The following section describes the demographics of the 277 respondents according to the variables and variable subgroups used in the analyses. The distribution of subject variables is reported in percentages, with the raw numbers given in parentheses.

The groupings are based on a combination of self-evident (e.g., gender), intuitive (e.g., traditional vs. nontraditional college age), and numerically sensible criteria (e.g., combining the majors of German and other languages into one category in order to achieve a reasonable number of subjects in that category). Summary tables (Tables 1a and 1b) follow.

First-Year versus Second-Year German

Of the 277 respondents, 69.7 percent (193) were first-year students, as compared to 23 percent (65) second-year students. Nineteen respondents (6.9 percent) did not report their level of enrollment and subsequently were excluded from further analyses. The total number of students surveyed was thus reduced to 258.

Age

With all 258 subjects reporting their age, the first-year population consisted of 37.8 percent (73) nineteen years or younger, 38.3 percent (74) twenty to twenty-two years, and 23.8 percent (46) twenty-three years or older. In the second-year population, 38.5 percent (25) were nineteen or younger, 43.1 percent (28) twenty to twenty-two years, and 18.5 percent (12) twenty-three years or older.

Perhaps most noteworthy is the fact that nearly one-quarter of the first-year and nearly one-fifth of the second-year students belonged in the category of *23 years or older*, which exceeds the traditional college age.

Gender

With two of the 258 subjects not reporting their sex, a total of 256 subjects were surveyed according to gender. Those 256 subjects comprised a total of 192 first-year students, of whom 41.1 percent (79) were female and 58.9 percent (113) were male, and of 64 second-year students, of whom 45.3 percent (29) were female and 54.6 percent (35) were male. Thus, in both, the first- and the second-year sequences, the majority of students were male.

Last German Grade in a UW-Madison German Course

Since the grading policies of various high school German programs vary greatly, it was decided to survey only the most recent UW-Madison German course grades, despite the fact than many students enter the program directly from high school. This decision has resulted in only 170 students being included in the survey according to the variable of last German course grade.

Of the 110 first-year students surveyed, 55.5 percent (61) reported a grade of A, 36.4 percent (40) a grade of B, and 8.2 percent (9) a grade of C or lower. Of the 60 second-year students 38.3 percent (23) reported a grade of A, 45 percent (27) a grade of B, and 16.7 percent (10) a grade of C or lower.

Evidently, second-year grades were lower than first-year grades, with the majority of first-year students receiving a grade of A, as compared to the majority of second-year students earning a grade of B, and the assignment of grades of C and lower doubling from first to second year.

Major Field of Study

Two hundred thirty-seven of the 258 subjects indicated their chosen or intended major field of study. Of the 180 first-year subjects, 8.3 percent (15) majored or planned to major in German or another language; 25 percent (45) in business, history, political science, or international relations; 16.7 percent (30) in engineering or chemistry; and 50 percent (90) in another or not yet decided field. Of the 57 second-year subjects, 12.3 percent (7) majored or planned to major in German or another language; 29.8 percent (17) in business, history, political science, or international relations; 14 percent (8) in engineering or chemistry; and 43.9 percent (25) in another or not yet decided field.

Overall, besides the undecided/other group, actual or intended majors in business, history, political science, or international relations comprised the largest subgroup in both first- and second-year German.

Previous Foreign Language Learning Experience

All 258 subjects reported their previous foreign language learning experiences. Of the 193 first-year subjects, 31.1 percent (60) had never studied another foreign language, 46.6 percent (90) had studied one, and 22.3 percent (43) two or more foreign languages besides German. By comparison, of the 65 second-year subjects, 49.2 percent (32) had never studied another foreign language, 33.8 percent (22) had studied one, and 16.9 percent (11) had studied two or more foreign languages besides German.

What seems most interesting is the fact that the first-year subjects seemed to have more extensive other foreign language learning experiences than their second-year counterparts. An explanation may be sought in the circumstance that many of the second-year students continue in the UW program after having started their studies of German in high school. They may have concentrated their foreign language learning efforts exclusively on German. In contrast, the first-year clientele may have been made up to a larger extent of students who had studied another foreign language in high school (perhaps Spanish, which is offered more frequently than German) and then switched to German in college. It must be noted that the study of foreign language in high school is a UW-Madison entrance requirement.

Travel to a German-Speaking Country

Two hundred fifty-seven out of 258 subjects reported on their previous travel experiences to a German-speaking country. Of the 192 first-year students surveyed, 67.2 percent (129) had never been to a German-speaking country, while 22.9 percent (44) had spent a total of two months or less in a German-speaking country, and 9.9 percent (19) had spent more than two months. Of the 65 second-year students, 61.5 percent (40) had never visited a German-speaking country, 15.4 percent (10) had spent two months or less in a German-speaking country, and 23.1 percent (15) had spent more than two months.

Two findings appear noteworthy. First, as may be expected, overall more relevant travel-abroad experiences were reported in the second than in the first year. Second, this increase in foreign travel manifested itself primarily in a larger percentage of students (more than double) who had spent more than two months in a German-speaking country, rather than in a smaller percentage of students (only 61.5 versus 67.2 percent) who had never been to a German-speaking country at all. These results imply a greater diversity with regard to exposure to natural language learning situations in the second-year population: while the majority of students (61.5 percent) lacked such exposure altogether, 23.1 percent had had intensive (more than two months) travel abroad experiences.

Instrument

The questionnaire consisted of forty-eight questions gauging the students' level of satisfaction with regard to (1) the instruction they were given in specific language skills (reading, writing, speaking, and listening) and the cultures of the German-speaking countries, (2) the associated tasks (creative vs. structural, peer vs. teacher-centered, oriented toward the classroom vs. oriented outside the classroom), and (3) monitoring/correction behavior (originating from self, peers, or teacher; directed at particular

Table 1a

Distribution of Demographic Variables in First-Year Students

Variable	Percentage	n (maximum n = 193)
Age		
19 or younger	37.8	(73)
20–22 years	38.3	(74)
23 or older	23.8	(46)
Gender		
female	41.1	(79)
male	58.9	(113)
Last grade		
A	55.5	(61)
B	36.4	(40)
C or lower	8.2	(9)
Major		
German or another lang.	8.3	(15)
business, history, etc.	25.0	(45)
engineering/chemistry	16.7	(30)
undecided/other	50.0	(90)
Previous FL experience		
no other FL	31.1	(60)
one other FL	46.6	(90)
two or more other FL	22.3	(43)
Travel to Germ. sp. country		
none	67.2	(129)
2 months or less	22.9	(44)
more than 2 months	9.9	(19)

skills). Response scores range from 1 to 5. Students had to indicate whether they were satisfied with the amount of attention paid to a particular skill or activity (a score of 3), wanted much more of it (a score of 5), or wanted much less (a score of 1) of it.

Table 1b

Distribution of Demographic Variables in Second-Year Students

Variable	Percentage	*n* (maximum n = 65)
Age		
19 or younger	38.5	(25)
20–22 years	43.1	(28)
23 or older	18.5	(12)
Gender		
female	45.3	(29)
male	54.6	(35)
Last grade		
A	38.3	(23)
B	45.0	(27)
C or lower	16.7	(10)
Major		
German or another lang.	12.3	(7)
business, history, etc.	29.8	(17)
engineering/chemistry	14.0	(8)
undecided/other	43.9	(25)
Previous FL experience		
no other FL	49.2	(32)
one other FL	33.8	(22)
two or more other FL	16.9	(11)
Travel to Germ. sp. country		
none	61.5	(40)
2 months or less	15.4	(10)
more than 2 months	23.1	(15)

The coefficient alpha reliability of the forty-eight items was .864 for the total population (258 subjects), .868 for the first-year population (183 subjects), and .857 for the second-year population (56 subjects). The questionnaire can be viewed in the Appendix.

Statistical Procedures

The data were analyzed in two separate sets: the respondents from the first year and those from the second year. Two different kinds of analyses were applied to each of the two sets of data:

1. General item analyses (means, mode, standard deviation [SD], kurtosis [degree of heavy or light tailedness]), as shown in Table 2;

2. Item analyses by demographic variables (first vs. second year, gender, age, intended or chosen major field of study, grade in last German course at UW, previous language learning experience, travel to a German-speaking country), based on contingency tables (chi-squares),[2] as shown in Tables 3a and 3b. The response scores were divided into three groups: (1) scores of 1 (much less) and 2 (less), (2) a score of 3 (just right), and (3) scores of 4 (more) and 5 (much more).

In addition, the forty-eight items were subjected to a factor analysis, based on three factors that had been extracted from fourteen originally generated factors. For this analysis it was necessary to use responses from as large a subject pool as possible. Therefore, the analysis was based on responses from the total population, as shown in Table 2.

Data Collection Procedures

Data were collected in the spring of 1993, at the end of the semester so that students were fully aware of all curricular characteristics. The respondents were told about the research purposes of the study and were informed that their responses were to be anonymous and would not affect their grade. Each respondent received a written copy of the questions. Responses were gathered during regular class time, under the supervision of the respective instructor, and had to be entered by the students into computer-readable answer ("bubble") sheets by blackening the assigned score (ranging from 1 to 5).

Results

General Item Analyses

Although mean scores per item were obtained, the mode (most frequent response) may be a more appropriate measure, because mean scores do not take into consideration the pattern in which scores are distributed. Items

Table 2

Responses to Questionnaire by Item and Subject Group

Item	First Year			Second Year		
	Mode	Mean	SD	Mode	Mean	SD
01	3*	3.53	.722	4	3.52	.911
02	3	3.54	.810	4	3.66	1.010
03	4	3.48	.842	3	3.59	.907
04	3	3.32	.812	3*	3.28	.841
05	3	3.22	.900	4	3.38	1.147
06	3	3.57	.769	4	3.79	.774
07	4	3.68	.932	4*	3.86	.915
08	3	3.41	.993	3	3.72	1.066
09	4	3.54	.997	4	3.45	1.056
10	3	3.46	.764	3	3.66	.670
11	3	3.42	.800	3	3.66	.721
12	3	3.48	.751	4	3.79	.620
13	4	3.62	.748	4	3.76	.689
14	3	3.41	.724	3	3.45	.736
15	3*	3.28	.719	3*	3.38	.622
16	3	3.17	.738	3	3.28	.797
17	3	3.30	.738	4	3.72	.797
18	3	2.81	.889	3	3.31	.806
19	3	3.15	.870	3*	3.55	.827
20	3	3.11	.780	3	3.35	.857
21	3	2.96	.929	3*	3.28	.702
22	3	3.11	.926	3	3.10	.939
23	3	3.16	.878	3	3.28	.702
24	3	3.24	.767	4	3.31	.891
25	3*	3.18	.750	3	3.21	.726
26	3*	3.05	.709	3*	3.21	.620
27	3	3.13	.758	3*	3.28	.882
28	3	2.78	.737	3*	2.86	.789
29	3	2.90	.866	3*	2.79	.940

Table 2 (cont.)

Responses to Questionnaire by Item and Subject Group

Item	First Year			Second Year		
	Mode	Mean	SD	Mode	Mean	SD
30	3	3.20	.831	3	3.10	.817
31	4	3.46	.861	4	3.38	.820
32	3	3.13	.849	3*	3.28	.797
33	4	3.77	.779	4	3.90	.557
34	3	2.92	.964	3	3.03	.944
35	3*	3.21	.701	3	3.21	.412
36	3*	3.22	.643	3*	3.10	.489
37	3*	3.18	.680	3*	3.10	.409
38	3*	3.09	.643	3*	3.14	.441
39	3*	3.08	.699	3	3.10	.557
40	3	3.14	1.100	3	2.86	1.268
41	3	3.31	1.074	4	3.21	1.197
42	4	3.54	.890	4	3.59	1.119
43	3	3.50	.737	3*	3.55	.870
44	3	3.07	.930	3*	3.00	.731
45	3	3.44	.705	3*	3.41	.867
46	3	2.99	.878	3*	3.00	.731
47	3	3.46	.784	3	3.52	.688
48	3	2.97	.852	3*	3.17	.848

that yield a level of kurtosis (light tailedness) above 1 are marked with an asterisk. Such items tend to show fewer frequencies at the extreme responses and more toward the center of the scale.

When surveying these scores, one must consider that scores of 3 reflect the highest level of satisfaction with a particular activity, while scores above 3 express a desire for more attention to the activity and scores below 3 indicate a wish for less attention to it.

When examining these scores, specifically the modes, we notice (1) the high frequency with which a score of 3 (reflecting the highest level of satisfaction) is reported and (2) the fact that deviations from the ideal score of 3 are restricted to scores of 4, which signal a desire for more focus on a particular activity.

The first finding suggests either that students are truly quite satisfied or that students are not willing or capable of quantifying accurately their needs through numbers, that is, by the assignment of scores. Although this question cannot be resolved here, it may be taken, at least tentatively, as a sign that we need to put more effort into training students in monitoring, evaluating, and expressing their curricular needs.

The second finding indicates that students believe that "more is always better than less." The desire for "more" specifically concerns for both subject groups learning about German music or literature (item 12), the practice of intonation and pronunciation (item 13), reading short stories outside the textbook (item 31), and working with authentic video materials (item 42). In addition, the first-year subjects wished for more application of grammar rules in situational contexts (item 3), learning about how people live (item 7), and reading authentic materials such as newspapers and magazines (item 33). The second-year subjects desired more explicit grammar instruction (items 1, 2, 24), more activities focused on the practice of vocabulary (items 5 and 6), learning more about German politics and the economic system (item 8), practice of intonation and pronunciation in reading (item 12), group work (item 17), reading longer pieces of literature (item 34), and listening to tapes with songs (item 41).

Finally, bunching phenomena (as indicated by the degree of kurtosis) occur for both groups mainly in the areas of writing (items 25 through 29) and listening (items 35 through 39), although individual items sometimes differ between the two groups. In addition, bunching can be observed in correction behavior (items 43 through 46) for the second-year group and in a few other apparently randomly distributed items for both groups.

Factor Analysis

An analysis of items by three factors (see Table 3), and based on responses from both subject groups, shows the following items to be related. Rounded communality values are reported in parentheses.

Factor 1

Based on the first extracted factor, the following areas appear related: grammar (items 1, 2, 3), pronunciation and intonation (items 10, 11, 12, 13), oral activities (comprising reading aloud and speaking; items 15, 19, 20), writing (items 23, 24, 25, 26, 27, 29), reading (items 30, 31, 33), listening to the teacher speak to other students (items 36 and 37), listening

Table 3

Three-Factor Analysis by Questionnaire Items

Factor 1	Factor 2	Factor 3
1 (.395)	8 (.374)	7 (.413)
2 (.449)	9 (.329)	16 (.331)
3 (.324)	18 (.395)	17 (.380)
10 (.455)	21 (.394)	38 (.410)
11 (.493)	28 (.459)	39 (.413)
12 (.474)	34 (.383)	41 (.320)
13 (.512)		
15 (.305)		
19 (.434)		
20 (.360)		
23 (.394)		
24 (.484)		
25 (.516)		
26 (.382)		
27 (.449)		
29 (.401)		
30 (.356)		
31 (.400)		
33 (.328)		
36 (.320)		
37 (.336)		
42 (.347)		
43 (.435)		
44 (.400)		
45 (.400)		
47 (.453)		
48 (.311)		

to authentic video materials (item 42), and correction behavior (items 43, 44, 45, 47, 48). Since so many of the curricular topics surveyed in the questionnaire appear related based on Factor 1, a discussion of which areas are not included seems more fruitful than one of which areas are.

Most notable is the absence of the areas of vocabulary (items 4 through 6), culture (items 7 through 9), and listening activities other than those directed by the teacher and authentic video materials (items 35, 38, 39, 40, 41). While the areas of listening and culture surface in the other two factors, vocabulary remains an isolated area throughout.

Factor 2

Based on Factor 2, "big-C Culture" (German politics, economic system, literature, and music; items 8 and 9), writing opinion pieces (item 21), writing for other students (item 28), and reading longer pieces of literature (item 34) are related. In sum, this indicates a connection between the desire to learn about specific cultural issues and an orientation beyond the classroom with regard to a preference for texts whose primary focus is nonpedagogical.

Factor 3

Based on Factor 3, there appears to be a connection among the areas of "small- c culture" (learning about how people live; item 7), group and pair work (items 16, 17), listening to other students (items 38 and 39), and listening to songs (item 41). In sum, an orientation toward peers seems related to an interest in "small-c culture," including recordings of songs.

Finally, Factors 2 and 3 may describe two contrasting student profiles, respectively: Factor 2 may perhaps be typical of more sophisticated learners who are confident about examining complex cultural issues and who look beyond the classroom, while Factor 3 may uncover characteristics of less sophisticated students who are more comfortable with everyday cultural issues and require peer support. However, in order to examine the validity of these assumptions, further research is necessary.

Item Analyses by Demographic Variables

Tables 4a and 4b show which demographic variables (first vs. second year, age, gender, last UW German course grade, major field of study, previous language learning experience, and travel) resulted in significantly different responses to each of the forty-eight-items.

Due to the small number of subjects in some demographic subgroups, two levels of significance had to be set: <.1 (reported as `) and <.05 (reported as ").

The remainder of this section will be devoted to reporting findings.

Table 4a

Significance of Demographic Variables: The First-Year Subjects

Item	Vs. Second Year	Age	Gender	Last Grade	Major	Other Foreign Language	Travel
1	**			**			
2	**		**	**			
3		**		**			*
4							
5							
6				**			
7		**					
8							
9							
10						**	
11					**		
12				*		**	
13					*		
14				*			
15				*			
16		*				**	
17			*			**	
18							
19		**		**			
20				**			
21	**						
22	*						
23							**
24	*						
25							
26							
27				*			*
28		**					
29							

Table 4a (cont.)

Significance of Demographic Variables: The First-Year Subjects

Item	Vs. Second Year	Age	Gender	Last Grade	Major	Other Foreign Language	Travel
30	*		**				
31							*
32							
33							
34						*	
35							
36							
37			**				
38		*	*				
39						**	
40		**					
41						*	
42	*					*	
43				**		*	
44	**		*	**			
45							
46	**					*	
47				*			
48			**	**			

The Relative Influence of Demographic Variables in the Two Subject Groups

In the first-year group, the last grade accounted for most of the significant differences in responses, followed by previous foreign language learning experience, age, gender, travel, and the major field of study. By comparison, in the second-year group, previous foreign language learning experience constituted the most powerful variable, followed by major, age, travel, gender, and last grade.

Table 4b

Significance of Demographic Variables: The Second-Year Subjects

Item	Age	Gender	Last Grade	Major	Other Foreign Language	Travel
1			**			
2						
3	*			*		
4						
5					**	
6		*	*			
7						
8						
9					*	*
10	*					
11						
12						
13	**		**			
14					**	
15				**		
16						
17						
18						
19						
20						
21						
22	**					
23						
24						
25						
26						
27						
28						
29						

Table 4b (cont.)

Significance of Demographic Variables: The Second-Year Subjects

Item	Age	Gender	Last Grade	Major	Other Foreign Language	Travel
30						
31					*	
32				**		*
33					**	
34		*				
35				*		
36						
37		*				
38		**		**		**
39				**		
40					**	
41						
42						
43						
44					*	**
45						
46						
47						
48						

In sum, previous foreign language learning experience and age represented influential variables with regard to the responses in both groups. The extent to which major field of study and last grade influenced curricular preferences varied greatly between the two groups: major field of study played a great role in the second-year group but a minor one in the first-year group. Conversely, the last German course grade exercised a strong influence on responses in the first year but quite little in the second-year group.

The diminished role of the last German UW course grade in the second year may have to do with the fact that the demands of the second-year curriculum are quite different from those in the first year (on which many second-year's students' last course grades are based), and that good as well as less successful students face the same challenges in their adjustment to university classes.

Similarly, the strengthened influence of the major field of study on curricular preferences in the second year may develop as students more clearly define their professional goals and subsequently begin to evaluate courses, perhaps especially those in foreign languages, with regard to how likely they are to contribute toward the achievement of these goals.

Areas of Divergence in Curricular Preferences between First- and Second-Year Students

The first- and second-year student groups distinguished themselves most clearly in the following areas: explanations of and exercises on specific grammar rules; writing essays, stories, and grammar exercises; reading stories from the textbook; listening to (watching) videos and films; and peer correction in speaking and reading.

Specifically, in the area of grammar, first-year students scored higher in their need for more grammatical explanations, while second-year students scored higher in their request for more practice of grammar rules. First-year students were divided about the writing of opinion pieces, invented stories, and for oneself, with approximately a quarter wanting more and a quarter wanting less. Second-year students generally were satisfied with the amount or wanted more. First-year students were more satisfied with reading stories from the textbook while second-year students, by comparison, wanted less. Second-year students appeared much more ready to watch authentic video materials than their first-year peers. Finally, with regard to peer correction behavior, second-year students were very satisfied, with about three-quarters assigning the ideal score of 3. In contrast, first-year students were more divided about the issues, with one-quarter wanting more, and another quarter wanting less.

In sum, first-year students, not surprisingly, are less ready to take on authentic reading or video materials and perhaps more extensive or complex writing assignments than second-year students. They are also more concerned with the explanation rather than the practice of grammar rules. Lastly, they are more divided among themselves on the issues of writing and peer correction.

Areas of Curricular Preferences Most and Least Likely to Be Influenced by Demographic Variables

In the first year, preferences with regard to grammar and correction behavior were most likely to vary according to demographic variables, followed by oral reading (reading aloud or reading for pronunciation and intonation), and oral interaction with peers. One area that was not affected by demographic variables was big-C Culture.

In the second year, pronunciation and intonation together with various listening activities were most subjected to the influence of demographic variation. Preferences with regard to grammar and vocabulary instruction and reading also varied. Various types of oral interaction including reading aloud, writing, and correction behavior were hardly affected by demographic variables.

Overall, variation in curricular preferences according to demographic variables was much greater in the first year (forty-four occurrences of statistical significance, of which twenty-five were significant at a probability level of less than .05) than in the second year (thirty-two occurrences of statistical significance, of which sixteen were significant at a probability level of less than .05). More specifically, preferences with regard to correction behavior and oral activities (both speaking and reading aloud), which showed great demographic variation in the first year, remained quite stable in the second year.

Association of Demographic Variables with Curricular Preferences

Age

In the first year, age affected preferences with regard to the application of grammatical rules in situational contexts, small-c culture, speaking with peers, reading aloud, writing for other students, and listening to recordings. In particular, the oldest age group, followed by the youngest, was most dissatisfied with the current amount of application of grammatical rules, generally wanting more. With respect to small-c culture, the two younger age groups wanted to learn more than the oldest age group, by a margin of nearly 100 percent more subjects reporting the desire for more in the younger groups than in the older one. Older students also reported a greater reluctance to engage in oral interaction with peers but were more interested in writing for other students than were the younger groups. The older students also expressed more faith in the benefits of reading aloud. Younger students also found more merit in listening to other students than did their older peers. Finally, the youngest age group wanted less listening to audio recordings of people speaking German.

In sum, older students appeared less inclined toward spontaneous oral peer exchanges and more satisfied with controlled language uses such as writing or reading aloud. Their cultural interests may be more focused (less small-c culture) than those of their younger peers. Also, the youngest and the oldest student groups, that is, those that represent subjects just beginning college or those older than the traditional undergraduate students, were least satisfied with the curricular offerings in general.

In the second year, age affected preferences with regard to the application of grammar rules as well as pronunciation, intonation, and creative writing. Specifically, twice as many subjects in the older student group (91 percent of the total) wanted more application of grammar rules in situational contexts than did subjects in either of the two younger groups. With regard to the practice of pronunciation and intonation, the older the students were, the more of it they wanted: while only 36 percent of the youngest group wanted more, 61 percent of the medium and 83 percent of the oldest group did. Similar proportions were found with regard to learning specific rules of grammar and pronunciation. Creative writing was much less popular with the older students. Contrary to the findings for the first-year group, in the second year it was the older subjects who wanted to focus more on listening to peers.

In general, students in both groups shared age-related feelings about the application of grammar rules in situational contexts and to a lesser extent, students' preferences with regard to intonation and pronunciation activities, such as reading aloud.

Another noteworthy finding is the shift of attitude toward oral language in the older population, which occurs between the first and the second year. While in the first year older students appeared to shy away from oral exchanges, they were not any less inclined toward oral exchanges than their younger peers in the second year. To the contrary, their overall concern for rules and accuracy may have translated into a desire for more instruction concerning correct pronunciation and intonation. Perhaps after an initial adjustment period (the first year), older students began to subscribe to a true four-skills approach that they attempt to follow with as much accuracy as possible.

Gender

In the first year, gender influences preferences with regard to the practice of specific grammar rules, peer work, reading stories from the textbook, and listening to tapes. Specifically, females were more divided as a group with regard to the practice of specific grammar rules: while more females than males wanted more practice, fewer males than females wanted less. Surprisingly, because counterstereotypical, females were much less inclined to work in groups (and pairs, although not at a significant level) than males. Females were more divided as a group with regard to reading selections, with approximately one-quarter wanting to read more stories from the textbook and another quarter wanting to read fewer stories. By comparison, twice as many males as females wanted to read more stories from the textbook. However, with regard to stories from outside the textbook, more males than females wanted more as well. This indicates that females may be less inclined toward the reading of stories (no matter where they come from) in general and be more critical of textbook reading selections in particular. Males, on the other hand, appeared more critical of peer correction in speaking and writing, being divided quite evenly between those who want more and those who want less.

In the second year, feelings about the practice of vocabulary in situational contexts, reading longer pieces of literature, and listening to the teacher speak German appeared gender-related. In particular, 79 percent of females wanted more situational practice of vocabulary, as opposed to only 54 percent of males. As far as the reading of longer pieces of literature was concerned, females were much less enthusiastic than males, with only 10 percent of females wanting more, as compared to 31 percent of males, and 35 percent of females wanting less, as opposed to 20 percent of males. Females report less appreciation of listening to the teacher speak German.

In sum, preferences with regard to reading selections varied by gender in both groups, with the perhaps surprising finding that females appear to appreciate literature (stories inside and outside the textbook and longer pieces of literature) less than males. The reasons behind this phenomenon still require more extensive research. It could result from various causes, ranging from a simple lack of interest to a lack of self-confidence or a lack of willingness to tolerate ambiguity, both of which are necessary in dealing with foreign language texts.

Last Grade

In the first year, the last grade was a significant variable with regard to preferences in all areas of grammar, intonation and pronunciation, reading aloud, using vocabulary in situational contexts, some speaking activities, and correction behavior, especially that directed at speaking and that stemming from peers. Specifically, the lower the last grade of the student, the more explanation of grammar rules and the less practice of grammatical rules in situational contexts was desired. Moreover, students who had received a last grade of C or lower also were least satisfied and most divided as a group with the current level of practice of specific rules, with 56 percent wanting more and 22 percent wanting less. This low level of satisfaction and intragroup division with situational practice on the part of the low-achieving students was replicated in the area of vocabulary. Students who had received a grade of C or lower were also much more concerned with the practice of pronunciation and intonation in reading, with 67 percent wanting more and none wanting less. An identical result was found for focusing on pronunciation and intonation in listening and an even more extreme instance (although not statistically significant from the other groups) for practicing pronunciation and intonation in speaking, with 89 percent wanting more and none wanting less. Overall, poorer students appear much more concerned with pronunciation and intonation than their more successful peers. In contrast, low achievers appeared more divided on the issue of speaking German with the teacher in class. While more low than high achievers (45 percent vs. approximately 33 percent in each the A and the B groups) wanted more, more weaker students than strong ones (22 percent of the C or lower group, 8 percent of the B group, and none in the A group) wanted less speaking German with the teacher in the class.

In addition, poor students were much more divided as a group about reading aloud. While the general trend in the other two groups was toward more reading aloud, 33 percent of the students who had received a grade of C or lower in their last German course wanted less and 57 percent wanted more reading aloud alone; even more distinct, with regard to reading aloud in groups, 44 percent of poor students wanted more, with just as many wanting less.

Also, poor students were the most divided group with regard to writing for oneself, with 45 percent wanting less and 33 percent wanting more. The other two groups generally wanted more, but only about a quarter in each of the two high-achieving student groups (as opposed to a third in the low-achieving group).

Low achieving students were also divided on the issue of correction behavior in speaking; while 56 percent wanted more teacher correction, the same number wanted less peer correction. And while 22 percent wanted less teacher correction, 22 percent wanted more peer correction. Overall, the low achievers were most reluctant to be corrected by peers in speaking (56 percent of them wanting less as compared to 10–15 percent of better students, and only 22 percent of them wanting more as opposed to 28–38 percent of better students). While all student groups are generally more reluctant to be corrected by peers in writing than in speaking, poor students are much more so (45 percent as opposed to 15–21 percent in the better student groups). Conversely, teacher correction in writing is more popular than correction in speaking in all groups, with the poor students being slightly more divided on the issue (45 percent want more, 11 percent less). In general, the poorer the last course grade, the less teacher correction in writing students desired.

In sum, first-year low-achieving students desired more explicit instruction and less situational practice, were more concerned with pronunciation and intonation, preferred to rely on the teacher rather than peers for correction, and were less distinct as a group—that is, as individuals they reacted more divergently to different issues.

In the second year, in which the last grade played a much less distinguishing role, it accounted for variation in the explanation of grammar rules, using vocabulary in situational contexts, and the practice of pronunciation and intonation in speaking. More particularly, only 10 percent of low-achieving students were satisfied with the amount of attention directed to the explicit explanation of grammar rules. Generally, the lower the past grade, the more students desired explicit instruction on grammar rules. Thus, 70 percent of low achievers wanted more, as compared to 41 percent of B students and 35 percent of A students. However, quite similar to the A group (with 17 percent), 20 percent of low achievers wanted less instruction on grammar rules. Also, low-achieving students were least satisfied with the amount of attention paid to pronunciation and intonation in speaking. While they were second (behind the A group) in wanting more (60 percent of subjects), they were also the only groups that included subjects (10 percent) who wanted less. Finally, and very similarly to the first-year group, poorer students wanted less application of vocabulary in situational contexts.

In sum, preferences in the areas of grammar and to a lesser extent of pronunciation/intonation and vocabulary were affected by the last grade in both groups.

Major Field of Study

In the first year, where the major field study exercised relatively little influence on curricular preferences, the only area to be affected by this variable was the practice of pronunciation and intonation, both in specific exercises and in speaking in general. Specifically, students in the category "other" wanted more pronunciation and intonation exercises than those in any of the three other groups, which were (1) German or another language; (2) business, history, political science, international relations; and (3) chemistry and engineering. However, since it is not clear which chosen or intended major fields of study actually comprised the category "other," this insight is of little practical value. In addition, majors in German or another language were much more likely (73 percent of all subjects) to want more focus on pronunciation and intonation in speaking, followed by majors in chemistry and engineering (70 percent of subjects). Majors in business and so on were least likely (42 percent of subjects) to feel that way. This group also had the highest percentage (9 percent) of subjects who wanted less focus on pronunciation and intonation in speaking. While the preference for a stronger emphasis on pronunciation and intonation may be expected for majors in German or other languages, it is surprising with regard to the commonly (and apparently mistakenly) held beliefs about the objectives of chemistry and engineering majors.

By comparison, in the second year, curricular preferences varied in more areas according to the major field of study: in the application of grammatical rules in situational contexts, interaction in German with the teacher in class (speaking and listening), listening to peers, and reading brief authentic materials (advertisements, schedules, etc.). In particular, majors in German and other languages were least satisfied with the amount of attention paid to the application of grammar rules in situational contexts, with the majority of them (71 percent) wanting more. This number is much higher than that of any other group. By comparison, chemistry and engineering majors constituted the group with the most subjects (38 percent) wanting less of a focus on situational application of grammar rules.

With regard to speaking German with the teacher in class, business, history, political science, and international relations majors were most satisfied, with 100 percent of subjects assigning the ideal score of 3. Majors in German and other languages were the least satisfied, with the majority (57 percent) wanting more. Conversely, majors in German and other languages constituted the group most adamant about wanting to be able to listen more to spoken German (43 percent of subjects). Similarly, majors in German and other languages expressed a stronger need for focusing on listening to their peers (57 percent wanted more in response to item 38,

43 percent in response to item 39), while majors in business, history, political science, and international relations were the group that most strongly expressed a desire for less listening to other students. Obviously, both the productive and receptive aspects of spoken language are most important to majors of German and other languages.

Finally, majors in German and other languages expressed the strongest desire (86 percent of subjects) for the reading of short authentic texts (schedules, advertisements, etc.).

Apparently, with respect to curricular preferences, the first- and second-year groups shared few if any similarities.

Previous Foreign Language Learning Experience

In the first year, previous language learning experience influenced curricular preferences in the areas of pronunciation and intonation (learning rules as well as practicing in speaking), oral interaction with peers (group and pair work), reading longer pieces of literature, listening to peers, and audio recordings (both of people speaking and of songs), and some aspects of correction behavior (by the teacher in speaking, by peers in reading). Generally, the extent of previous language learning experience primarily affected preferences with regard to various aspects of spoken language and peer cooperation. Specifically, the more previous language learning experience students had, the more likely they were to want more instruction regarding the rules of pronunciation and intonation. The same held true for practicing pronunciation and intonation in reading. In contrast, the more experienced students were with regard to language learning, the more reluctant they were to see benefits in either group or pair work. Moreover, the more experienced language learners were, the more eager they were to read longer pieces of literature. Also, greater experience led to greater hesitation in recognizing listening to peers as beneficial. And while experienced learners overall wanted greater exposure to both audio and video recording, the 28 percent of experienced students who wanted less work with audio recordings shrank to 7 percent with regard to video materials. Conversely, while experienced learners exceeded less experienced learners and learners with no foreign language experience other than German only slightly in their desire for more audio recordings (49 percent of subjects as opposed to 43 and 44 percent, respectively), the distinction between the highly experienced and the no-experience groups was much greater for video materials (65 vs. 40 percent).

Finally, different preferences for correction behavior, although significant in two items (43 and 46), are difficult to interpret, with the possible exception of experienced learners' reluctance to tolerate peer correction when reading, which may echo the group's general skepticism toward peer cooperation.

In sum, experienced language learners were characterized by reluctance for peer cooperation, evidently preferring to rely on their own skills and judgment; greater readiness to cope with complex authentic texts (longer literary pieces as well as videos); and, finally, special concern for correct intonation and pronunciation.

In the second year, previous language learning experience yielded divergence in even more areas of curricular preferences, such as the memorization and repetition of vocabulary, focusing on pronunciation and intonation when listening, reading selections (stories outside the textbook, newspaper articles etc.), learning about German music and literature, listening to peers, and being corrected by peers. In particular, the greater the learners' experience was, the greater their desire for more memorization and repetition of vocabulary and to learn more about big-C culture (music and literature). The more experienced learners also were more concerned with pronunciation and intonation when listening. They were also more eager to read stories outside the textbook. The implications with regard to the reading of newspaper articles are less clear (with the no-experience and the high experience group sharing the most similarities), as are those with regard to listening to and being corrected by peers.

Thus, in both groups three areas were affected by previous language learning experience: (1) the willingness to venture beyond pedagogical materials and instead to tackle complex authentic materials; (2) the concern with oral language, including pronunciation and intonation and listening skills; and (3) peer cooperation.

Travel to German-Speaking Countries

In the first-year group, travel experience was associated mainly with curricular preferences for writing letters, perhaps the result of the opportunity or need to communicate with a German-speaking person across a distance. To a lesser extent, the desire for more practice of grammar rules in situational contexts, writing for oneself, and reading stories outside the textbook were also related to travel experience. However, while the desire for letter writing and reading stories outside the textbook clearly increases with the length of stay in a German-speaking country, the implications with regard to the other two points (situational grammar practice, writing for oneself) remain obscure in light of the score distribution.

In the second-year group, travel influenced students' preferences with regard to learning about German music and literature, reading short stories outside the textbook, listening to peers, and being corrected by other students when speaking. While the longer stay group was not the one in which the most subjects wanted to learn more about literature and music (the shorter stay group was), it was the group in which the fewest subjects wanted to learn less about these topics. Generally, the no-stay group was least interested in music and literature, with the lowest percentage of subjects wanting more and the highest percentage of subjects wanting less. Moreover, the longer the students had stayed in a German-speaking country, the more interested they were in reading brief authentic texts such as schedules and advertisements. The effects of the variable of travel on the students' reliance on peers (items 38, 44), although significant, remains unclear.

In short, travel was correlated mainly with the students' attitudes towards authentic and cultural materials.

Summary of Findings

Summing up the nature of the findings pertaining to the influence of demographic variables, I arrived at the following insights:

1. Some results were surprising, at least to this researcher, for example, the finding that females were less appreciative of literary texts and less willing to cooperate with peers than males, or the strong focus on pronunciation and intonation professed by chemistry and engineering majors. In hindsight, it seems that the related initial (and disproved) expectations may have been driven by unwarranted stereotypes. When conducting further research, care must be taken not to target selectively these apparently "counterintuitive" findings and to provide explanations that are not rooted in further stereotypical perceptions.

2. Other findings confirmed preconceived notions, such as, for example, the insights that majors in German or other languages are highly concerned with oral language or that older learners tend to shy away from spontaneous oral exchanges while gravitating toward opportunities to use language in a more controlled manner, such as in writing or reading. However, I must also caution that these empirical confirmations of commonly held beliefs should not be considered unalterable facts. For example, we have seen that the older learners' reluctance to engage in oral exchanges with their peers in the first year strongly declines in the second.

3. We must also distinguish between three effects that demographic variables can have at the level of significance. First, there is a proportional relationship in which an increase or decrease in variable strength (e.g., getting younger or older, having less or more language learning experience) produces a gradual increase or decrease in certain curricular preferences. For example, I found that the lower a student's last grade is, the more explanation of grammar rules he or she desires, and that with an increase in a student's language learning experience, the student becomes more reluctant to cooperate with peers. This type of finding lends itself well to practical applications in the classroom. Second, there are also divisions among the individuals in a particular demographic group. For example, I found that low achievers were divided on a variety of issues, among them, speaking German with the teacher, practice of specific grammar rules, and situational practice of vocabulary, and that females, as a group, were divided on the issues of reading selections. These kinds of findings are particularly problematic in terms of practical applications. Finally, there are results for which no clear patterns emerged. This was the case in many of the findings on how travel influences curricular preferences. These types of findings can have few if any practical applications and certainly require much additional research.

4. While many aspects of the curriculum are subject to variation by demographic variables, the instruction and practice of grammar and pronunciation and intonation, the selection of reading and listening texts, and oral language appeared most vulnerable.

Discussion

Although the findings arrived at in this study are too numerous to recapitulate, even in general terms, certain points deserve special attention:

First, the study's limitations need to be addressed. All insights gained here need to be compared to those based on data coming from a larger subject pool; this may be accomplished at a large German department or at an even larger program, which in turn may imply a program in a more commonly taught and studied language such as Spanish. The possibility of cross-linguistic variation in curricular preferences must also be taken into consideration, especially in languages with sound systems and/or writing systems very different from English (e.g., Chinese).

Second, the limitations of the practical applicability of these findings must also be considered:

a. Each learner represents a multitude of demographic variables; as such, one has to weigh shifts in curricular preferences based on one variable carefully against those stemming from another. While some variables (e.g., previous language learning experience and age) appear to have strong effects on almost all individuals, others (e.g., last grade, major field of study) do not.

b. As discussed above, some variables (e.g., low grade, being female) may result in remarkable within-group divisions with regard to curricular preferences in some areas. Thus, while it is always difficult to please everyone, it may be especially hard to please a majority of students in these cases.

c. Even if we could determine every single student's preferences, we have yet to decide how, and even to what extent, to respond as program coordinators. Specifically, we need to consider two issues: cohesion within the program (i.e., how individualized do we want our programs to become?) and cohesion beyond the program (i.e., how does the language program need to fit in with other classes and how does individualization of the curriculum affect these objectives?).

Third, the influence of demographic variables fluctuates over time. This may concern particular curricular areas such as that shown in the disappearance of the reluctance to engage in oral peer interaction on the part of older learners from the first to the second year. Or perhaps this may happen on a broader scale, as suggested by the finding that, overall, fewer instances of significant effects of demographic variables were found in the second than in the first year. This may be the result of the smaller second-year subject pool and needs to be investigated further, but it may also imply that an increase in proficiency level leads to greater learner homogeneity, perhaps the product of self-selection.

Fourth, as mentioned earlier, and based on the overall minimal deviation in the assigned scores from the ideal score of 3, we may need to train our students to evaluate more precisely their own curricular needs as well as our curricular offerings. Most departments administer course evaluations that seek to determine the students' satisfaction with the curriculum. In order to realize the full potential value of these surveys, students need to be able to assess and express their needs accurately.

Fifth, the finding that previous language learning experience constitutes a powerful variable in influencing students' curricular preferences should be of special interest to all program coordinators but especially to those employed by schools with a foreign language entrance requirement.

Programs in languages that are less commonly taught in high school may find that a large portion of their clientele has some experience in studying other foreign languages. Additional research is needed in order to determine whether previous experience in a different foreign language produces similar or varying effects.

Sixth, the finding that the correlation of the major field of study with curricular preferences increases in the second year of language study, or as students advance through their university studies, implies a need for foreign language departments to play an active role in interdepartmental cooperation and curricular planning.

Seventh, the vulnerability of and relationship among different curricular areas requires further investigation. For example, more research is needed to examine the finding through factor analysis that curricular preferences on vocabulary appear unrelated to those in any other area, or the somewhat confusing insight that both low-achieving (first-year) students and (first- and second-year) students with more language learning experience are more concerned with intonation and pronunciation than their high-achieving or less experienced peers.

In sum, demographic variables play an important role in students' curricular preferences, and while many relevant insights with immediate practical applications have been gained in this study, more research and discussion with respect to both theoretical and practical issues is still necessary.

Notes

1. The author wishes to thank Charles James, Carol Klee, Sally Magnan, and anonymous reviewers for their very helpful comments. She also would like to recognize Allan S. Cohen, Tae-Hak Park, and Charlene E. Tortorici of the University of Wisconsin at Madison Center for Testing and Evaluation for their invaluable assistance in collecting and analyzing these data.

2. I considered t- or F-tests inappropriate because the computation of mean scores does not reflect distributional patterns in responses.

Works Cited

Bacon, Susan. 1992. The Relationship between Gender, Comprehension, Processing Strategies, and Cognitive and Affective Response in Foreign Language Listening. *Modern Language Journal* 76: 160–78.

Boyle, Joseph P. 1987. Sex Differences in Listening Vocabulary. *Language Learning* 37: 273–84.

Brown, Cheryl. 1983. The Distinguishing Characteristics of the Older Adult Second Language Learner. Ph.D. diss., University of California at Los Angeles.

――――. 1985. Requests for Specific Language Input: Differences between Older and Younger Adult Language Learners. In *Input in Second Language Acquisition,* edited by Susan Gass and Carolyn G. Madden, 272–81. Rowley, MA: Newbury House.

Buonomo, Carol Lynn. 1990. The Successful and Unsuccessful Foreign Language Student: The Affective Domain. Ph.D. diss., Rutgers University.

Corbeil, Giselle. 1990. Successful and Less Successful Language Learners: Differences in How They Process Information. *Journal of Atlantic Provinces Linguistic Association* 12: 131–45.

d'Angeljan, Alison, and Claude Renaud. 1985. Learner Characteristics and Second Language Acquisition: A Multivariate Study of Adult Immigrants and Some Thoughts on Methodology. *Language Learning* 35: 1–19.

Ehrman, Madelaine E., and Rebecca L. Oxford. 1989. Effects of Sex Differences, Career Choice, and Psychological Type on Adults' Language Learning Strategies. *Modern Language Journal* 73: 1–13.

Eisenstein, Miriam. 1982. A Study of Social Variation in Adult Second Language Acquisition. *Language Learning* 32: 367–91.

Farhady, Hossein. 1982. Measures of Language Proficiency from the Learner's Perspective. *TESOL Quarterly* 16: 43–59.

Gillette, Barbara. 1987. Two Successful Language Learners: An Introspective Approach. In *Introspection in Second Language Research,* edited by C. Faerch and G. Kasper, 268–79. Clevendon, UK: Multilingual Matters.

Goldberg Muchnik, Arlene, and David E. Wolfe. 1982. Attitudes and Motivation of American Students of Spanish. *Canadian Modern Language Review* 38: 262–81.

Horwitz, Elaine K. 1987. Surveying Student Beliefs about Language Learning. In *Learner Strategies in Language Learning,* edited by Anita Wenden and Joan Rubin, 119–29. Englewood Cliffs, NJ: Prentice-Hall.

————. 1988. The Beliefs about Language Learning of Beginning University Foreign Language Students. *Modern Language Journal* 72: 283–94.

Oxford, Rebecca L. 1990. *Language Learning Strategies: What Every Teacher Should Know.* New York: Newbury House/Harper and Row.

————. 1993a: Instructional Implications of Gender Differences in L2 Learning Styles and Strategies. *Applied Language Learning* 4: 65–94.

————. 1993b: *La différence continues . . .*: Gender Differences in Second/Foreign Language Learning Styles and Strategies. In *Exploring Gender,* edited by Jane Sutherland, 140–47. Englewood Cliffs, NJ: Prentice-Hall.

Oxford, Rebecca L., and Martha Nyikos. 1989. Variables Affecting Choice of Language Learning Strategies by University Students. *Modern Language Journal* 73: 219–300.

Politzer, Robert L. 1983. An Exploratory Study of Self-Reported Language Learning Behaviors and Their Relation to Achievement. *Studies in Second Language Acquisition* 6: 54–69.

Ramsay, Ruth. 1980. Language Learning Approach Styles of Adult Multilinguals and Successful Language Learners. In *Studies in Child Language and Multilingualism,* edited by Virginia Teller and Sheila J. White, 73–96. New York: New York Academy of Sciences.

Rubin, Joan. 1975. What the "Good Language Learner" Can Teach Us. *TESOL Quarterly* 9: 41–51.

Stern, Hans H. 1975. What Can We Learn from the Good Language Learner? *Canadian Modern Language Review* 31: 304–18.

Wagner, Elaine. 1992. The Older Second Language Learner: A Bibliographic Essay. *Issues in Applied Linguistics* 1: 153–71.

Wenden, Anita. 1987. How to Be a Successful Language Learner: Insights and Prescriptions from L2 Learners. In *Learner Strategies in Language Learning,* edited by Anita Wenden and Joan Rubin, 103–17. Englewood Cliffs, NJ: Prentice-Hall.

Werker, Janet F. 1986. The Effect of Multilingualism on Phonetic Perceptual Flexibility. *Applied Psycholinguistics* 7: 141–55.

Wong-Fillmore, Lily. 1983. The Language Learner as an Individual: Implications of Research on Individual Differences for the ESL Teacher. In *On TESOL '82: Pacific Perspectives on Language Learning and Teaching,* edited by Mark A. Clarke and Jean Handscombe, 157–73. Washington, DC: Teaching of English to Speakers of Other Languages.

Zobl, Helmut. 1992. Prior Linguistic Knowledge and the Conservatism of the Learning Procedure. In *Language Transfer in Language Learning,* edited by Susan Gass and Larry Selinker, 176–96. Amsterdam: Benjamin.

Appendix

Questionnaire:

Please answer the following questions 1–48 in the order they appear on the *numbered* section on your bubble sheet (lighter and larger area):

How would you evaluate the amount of attention that is being paid to the following activities and issues in THE CURRENT SEMESTER:

I would like much less of it = 1

I would like somewhat less of it = 2

The amount is just right = 3

I would like more of it = 4

I would like much more of it = 5

1. explanation of grammar rules
2. exercises on specific grammar rules
3. applying grammar in situational context (e.g., role play, group work in which you get to use new grammar rules)
4. introducing new vocabulary items
5. memorization/repetition of vocabulary items
6. using vocabulary in a situational context (e.g., role play, group work in which you get to use new vocabulary items)
7. learning about how people live in Germany
8. learning about German politics or economy
9. learning about German music or literature
10. learning about rules of pronunciation/intonation
11. practicing pronunciation and intonation in exercises

12. practicing pronunciation and intonation in reading
13. practicing pronunciation and intonation in speaking
14. focusing on the pronunciation and intonation of German when listening
15. speaking German with the teacher in class
16. speaking with other students in a pair-situation
17. speaking with other students in a group-situation
18. giving presentations
19. reading aloud alone
20. reading aloud in groups
21. writing essays which state my opinion
22. writing stories I invent
23. writing letters
24. writing in grammar exercises
25. writing in vocabulary exercises
26. writing for the teacher
27. writing for myself
28. writing for other students
29. writing for others outside the class
30. reading stories from the textbook
31. reading short stories outside the textbook
32. reading advertisements, schedules, etc.
33. reading current newspapers and magazines
34. reading longer pieces of literature (dramas, novels, etc.)
35. listening to the teacher when s/he speaks German to me
36. listening to the teacher when s/he speaks German to other students
37. listening to the teacher when s/he speaks German to the class
38. listening to another student when we speak with each other
39. listening to other students speak to each other
40. listening to tapes with recordings of people speaking German
41. listening to tapes with German songs
42. listening to voices in films, videos, etc.

43. being corrected by the teacher when I speak
44. being corrected by other students when I speak
45. being corrected by the teacher when I read
46. being corrected by other students when I read
47. being corrected by the teacher when I write
48. being corrected by other students when I write

Part III

Policy and Curricular Implications

Making Learning Strategy Instruction a Reality in the Foreign Language Curriculum

Susan J. Weaver,
University of Minnesota
Andrew D. Cohen,
University of Minnesota

Introduction

During the last few decades there has been a marked shift in the focus of language instruction, a shift toward a focus on the needs of individual learners. Language teachers have begun to accommodate individual learners in the classroom by attempting to meet the differing linguistic, communicative, and sociocultural goals of their students, choosing instructional materials appropriate to these goals, and adapting different methodologies and approaches to learning to meet their students' differing needs. In general, the philosophy of foreign language instruction has changed from a static and teacher-centered orientation to one that is more interactive and communicative. The "domain" of language teaching has thus been broadened (Tarone and Yule 1989, p. 20).

Inherent in this shift in focus is also a shift in the responsibilities of both teachers and students in the foreign language classroom. No longer does the teacher act as the locus of all instruction, controlling every aspect of learning to ensure successful language acquisition. Rather, the learners themselves now, more than ever, are sharing the responsibility of achieving success, and in doing so are becoming less dependent on the language teacher for meeting their individual language learning needs. By giving the students more responsibility for learning, we are asking them to become more autonomous, to diagnose some of their own learning difficulties, and to self-direct the language learning process.

Given these changes, should language learners be left to their own devices or should they receive some form of training in how to learn the language under study? Our point of view is that learning will be facilitated if students become more aware of the range of possible strategies that they could use successfully throughout the language learning process. With learning strategy instruction, students can "learn how to learn" a foreign language when they are provided with the necessary tools to self-diagnose their learning difficulties, become aware of what helps them learn the language they are studying most efficiently, develop a broad range of problem-solving skills, experiment with both familiar and unfamiliar learning strategies, understand how to organize and use strategies systematically and effectively, make decisions about how to approach a language task, monitor and self-evaluate their performance, and learn how and when to transfer their strategies to new learning contexts. The process is one of taking responsibility for their own learning. The language instructor thus assumes the role of supporting the learners as they reach their personal learning goals so that language learning truly becomes a team effort.

Foreign language program administrators can contribute to this effort by offering learning strategy instruction to students as part of the foreign language curriculum. Strategies instruction (sometimes called "strategy training" or "learner training") can enhance students' efforts to reach language program goals because it encourages students to find their own ways to learn a foreign language successfully, and thus it promotes learner autonomy and self-direction. Considerable research has indicated that both good and poor learners at any level of proficiency can learn how to improve their comprehension and production of a foreign language[1] through the development, application, and transfer of language learning strategies. In this chapter we will examine several aspects of explicit learning strategy instruction that can be applied to the context of university-level foreign language programs. We will:

1. describe the goals of language learning strategy instruction;

2. discuss insights from L1 and L2 research regarding strategy instruction;

3. outline eight options available for student-directed learning strategy instruction;

...udent awareness of the purpose and rationale of strategy use, to give
...ts opportunities to practice the strategies that they are being taught,
...help students understand how to use the strategies in new learning
...ts. Each of the following sequences encourages conscious and pur-
...l strategy use and transfer, and allows students to monitor their per-
...nce and evaluate the effectiveness of the strategies they are using.
...Oxford et al. (1990) outline a useful sequence for the introduction of
...gies that emphasizes explicit strategy awareness, discussion of the
...ts of strategy use, functional and contextualized practice with the
...gies, self-evaluation and monitoring of language performance, and
...nstrations of how to transfer the strategies to new language tasks.
...sequence is not prescriptive regarding strategies that the learners are
...sed to use, but rather descriptive of the various strategies that they
...use for a broad range of learning tasks. The sequence they suggest is
...llowing:

...sk learners to do a language activity without any strategy training;

...ave them discuss how they did it, praise any useful strategies and
...elf-directed attitudes that they mention, and ask them to reflect on
...ow the strategies they selected may have facilitated or hindered the
...anguage learning process;

...suggest and demonstrate other helpful strategies, mentioning
...expected benefits, as well as the need for greater self-direction, making
...sure that the students are aware of the rationale for strategy use.
...Learners can also be asked to identify those strategies that they do not
...currently use, and consider ways that they could include new strate-
...gies in their learning repertoires;

...allow learners plenty of time to practice the new strategies;

...demonstrate how the strategies can be transferred to other tasks;

...provide practice using the techniques with new tasks and allow learn-
...ers to make choices about the strategies they will use;

...help students understand how to evaluate the success of their strategy
...use and to gauge their progress as more responsible and self-directed
...learners.

...Pearson and Dole (1987) have suggested a different approach to the
...ence of first language strategy training that can also be applied to the
...y of foreign languages. This model targets isolated strategies by includ-

4. present suggestions for developing in-service strategy training seminars for foreign language instructors; and

5. conclude with a step-by-step approach to the design of strategy training programs.

Goals of Language Learning Strategy Instruction

Language learning strategies are the specific actions taken to enhance one's
own learning, through the storage, retention, recall, and use of new information about the target language. They are the special thoughts and
behaviors students use to facilitate the completion of language learning
tasks. If students can learn to plan, monitor, and evaluate their own language learning through the systematic application of language learning
strategies, as well as perceive and know how to deal with difficulties they
encounter during the learning process, they will be able to take more
responsibility for self-directing the learning process and thus can more
fully benefit from classroom language instruction. Strategies, as defined
here, are at least partially conscious; they can range from cognitive and
metacognitive applications to social and affective functions; they can be
transferred to new language tasks; and they can be used by learners in
unique and creative ways to personalize the language learning process.

In other words, learners can develop language learning repertoires
that include cognitive strategies to practice and manipulate the target language; affective strategies to gauge their emotional reactions to learning
and lower anxieties; compensatory strategies to overcome limitations in
target language skills;[2] memory strategies to increase their ability to acquire
and use the language they have learned; and social strategies, such as cooperation with other learners and seeking opportunities to interact with
native speakers, in order to enhance learning. Learners can also become
versed in using the so-called metacognitive strategies for managing and
supervising their strategy use. Essentially, this means they can learn to ask
themselves what they will do, think about what they are doing, and then
evaluate what they have done. On the basis of this evaluation, they may
then extend their strategy use by transferring the strategies to new learning
tasks. In sum, these various types of strategies facilitate the language learning process by promoting successful and efficient completion of language
learning tasks by allowing students to develop their own individualized
approaches to learning.

For example, given the task of orally retelling a story read in the foreign language, Learner A may prepare for the task by visualizing the story, either mentally or by drawing pictures in sequence, while Learner B may prefer to remember the key words and phrases of the story. Learner C may use her background knowledge of a similar story that she has read and apply this knowledge when attempting to retell the new story. Learner D may focus on rehearsing what he will say (mentally, orally, or in writing) and try to relax by using positive self-talk or deep-breathing exercises. Learners E, F, and G may choose to collaborate with each other by pooling their resources, and Learner H may self-monitor his performance throughout the task, perhaps paying careful attention to his use of the past tense or new vocabulary items. The specific strategy chosen is not the issue here; rather, the issue is that the learners can successfully complete the task by using strategies that they themselves find useful.

Although early research focused on the strategies selected by "good" language learners,[3] strategies should not be labeled as inherently "good" or "bad," but rather evaluated in terms of their effectiveness for the individual learner and the completion of the language task at hand. Choosing an effective strategy depends on many factors, including the nature of the language task (its structure, purpose, demands), individual learner differences (such as learning style preferences, language learning aptitude, prior experience in learning other foreign languages, and personality characteristics), and the level of language proficiency. No single strategy will be appropriate for all learners or for all tasks, and individual learners can and should apply the various strategies in different ways, according to their personal language learning needs.

One goal of strategies instruction (i.e., explicitly teaching students how to develop individualized strategy systems) is to help learners recognize which strategies they already use and then work to develop a wider range of strategies, so that they can select appropriate and effective strategies within the context of particular language tasks. Ellis and Sinclair (1989, p. 2) describe this aim as one of providing learners with "the alternatives from which to make informed choices about what, how, why, when, and where they learn." A further goal of strategies instruction is to promote learner autonomy and learner "self-direction" by allowing students to choose their own strategies and do so spontaneously, without continued prompting from the language teacher. Learners should be able to monitor and evaluate the relative effectiveness of their strategy use, and more fully develop their problem-solving skills. The classroom teacher can

provide instruction and opportunities for practice gies, but ultimately the responsibility for choosi appropriate strategies is with the individual studen (1989, p. 2) note, "Learner training aims to help lea tors that affect their learning and discover the learn them best. It focuses their attention on the process emphasis is on *how* to learn rather than *what* to lear 201) further emphasizes that "the general goals of [st help make language learning more meaningful, to e tive spirit between learner and teacher, to learn about learning, and to learn and practice strategies that facil

Insights from Research Regarding Expli Strategy Instruction

Explicit instruction in the use of a broad range of stra grammar, reading, writing, listening, and speaking ski language vocabulary, has become a prominent issue i tion research. Efforts in strategy instruction have be researched for some time in first language pedagogy, es to reading strategies (e.g., Belmont and Butterfi Campione, and Day 1980; Duffy, Book, and Roehler Levin 1983; Brown, Palinscar, and Armbruster 1984; parallel efforts in assessing foreign language strategy trai appear in the literature (see Wenden and Rubin 19 O'Malley and Chamot 1990; Oxford 1990, 1993; Wen and Leaver, forthcoming).

Most of the research in the area of foreign language has focused on the identification, description, and class learning strategies.[4] This research has been aimed at lear fully or unsuccessfully used their knowledge of learning plete various language tasks or to describe their own le Although researchers have demonstrated that language le greatly from learning how to apply a wide range of stra guage skills and learning tasks, what remains to be detern effective way to conduct strategies instruction.

While no empirical evidence has yet been provided best overall framework for strategy training programs, at le ual training sequences have been identified. They have b

raise s
studen
and to
conte
posef
forma

strate
benef
strate
demo
This
supp
coul
the f

1.
2.

3.

4.
5.
6.

7.

seq
stu

ing explicit modeling and explanation of the benefits of applying a specific strategy, extensive functional practice with the strategy (ranging from highly structured practice to independent strategy selection and use), and the eventual transfer of the strategy to new learning contexts. Students may better understand the applications of the various strategies if they are first modeled by the teacher and then practiced individually. Their sequence includes:

1. initial modeling of the strategy by the teacher, with direct explanation of the strategy's use and importance;

2. guided practice with the strategy;

3. consolidation whereby teachers help students identify the strategy and decide where it might be used;

4. independent practice of the strategy; and

5. application of the strategy to new tasks.

After a range or set of strategies have been introduced and practiced, the teacher can further encourage independent strategy use and promote learner autonomy by encouraging learners to take responsibility for the selection, use, and evaluation of the various strategies they have been taught.

Chamot and O'Malley's (1994) sequence for facilitating the completion of language learning tasks includes four stages:

1. *Planning:* The instructor presents the students with a language task and explains the rationale behind it. Students are then asked to plan their own approaches to the task, choosing strategies they think will facilitate its completion. For example, they can activate prior knowledge by recalling their approaches to similar tasks and predict potential difficulties.

2. *Monitoring:* During the task the students are asked to "self-monitor" their performance by paying attention to their strategy use and checking comprehension.

3. *Problem solving:* As they encounter difficulties, the students are expected to find their own solutions. For example, they can draw inferences or ask for clarification.

4. *Evaluation:* After the task has been completed, the learners are then given time to "de-brief" the activity, that is, to evaluate the effectiveness of the strategies they used during the task. They can also be given

time to verify their predictions, give summaries of their performance, and reflect on how they could transfer their strategies to similar language tasks or across language skills.

Each of these sequences emphasizes discussions about the use and value of strategies, self-evaluation, and the transfer of strategies to new tasks, which are all necessary components of explicit strategies instruction. They can be used in various combinations to complement each other and to add variety to a strategy training program. During strategies instruction, teachers should be encouraged to provide suggestive, rather than corrective, feedback to allow students to consider alternative ways of approaching different learning tasks and allow them to focus on self-evaluation of the effectiveness and efficiency of their strategy applications.

Options Available for Student-Directed Learning Strategy Instruction

A number of different instructional models for foreign language learning strategy programs have already been developed and put into practice in various educational settings. The following eight options bring strategy instruction directly to the students and range from general study skills development separate from the language course to strategy training integrated into foreign language classes. Each differs in the level of explicitness of the instruction, the level of student awareness of the practical applications and transferability of the strategies, and the level of integration into the foreign language curriculum.

General Study Skills Courses

Most universities offer programs that help students to develop general study skills, to clarify their educational goals and values, and to diagnose individual learning preferences. These programs are sometimes intended for students who are on academic probation, but they can also target successful students who want to improve their study habits. Many of these general academic skills, such as using flashcards, overcoming anxiety, and developing good note-taking skills, can be transferred to the process of learning a foreign language. The courses are sometimes designed to include language learning as a specific topic of focus in order to highlight how learning a foreign language may differ from other types of academic coursework. Foreign language students can be encouraged to participate in these courses to develop general learning strategies.

These kinds of programs are especially helpful for more motivated students, who have experience transferring learning skills across class subjects, and can also assist learners in the development of a general awareness of the learning process. Participating students may become more efficient language learners even though the training is not provided within a contextualized language learning setting. However, general study skills courses may not be sufficient training for the task demands of learning a foreign language, although they may be the answer for universities without the funding necessary to provide specialized learning strategy instruction for students enrolled in foreign language classes.

Peer Tutoring

TANDEM programs began in the 1970s in Europe and have begun to flourish in many universities across the United States. Henri Holec (1988) describes this system as a "direct language exchange" program that pairs students of different native language backgrounds together for mutual tutoring sessions. Thus, for example, an American student of Italian would be paired with a student from Italy who is studying English as a second language. The principle requirements of the tutoring sessions are that the students have regular meetings, that they alternate the roles of both learner and teacher, and that the two languages be practiced separately and in equal amounts. Often, the students exchange suggestions about what kinds of language learning strategies they typically use, thus providing an ad hoc form of strategy training. Holec reports that feedback from participating students has been very positive, noting that the majority found the meetings to be less stressful than regular class sessions, a welcome change from more academic sources of language learning, and excellent opportunities to take more responsibility for learning. However, negative reactions have been primarily caused by the lack of structured learning materials, since the meetings can often be quite informal and thus do not provide the students with an organized approach to improving target language skills.

Another way to structure peer tutoring sessions is to encourage students who are studying the same language (at the same or different levels of proficiency) to organize regular target-language study groups. Students who have already completed the language course may also be invited to attend these meetings to maintain their fluency in the language. The less proficient students can benefit from the language skills of the more advanced students and ask for examples of the kinds of strategies they could use. The advanced students will benefit from the extra language practice and can become more aware of how they apply strategies to their language learning. In addition, the students themselves may have more insights into the particular difficulties of the target language than their own language teachers.

The peer tutoring approach to strategies training is very inexpensive and easy to organize, although, in terms of the strategy training itself, few students have the background necessary to provide each other with suggestions for systematic strategy use. Further, students may not be aware of how to transfer strategies across language skills and tasks. However, if the students are also receiving another form of strategy training, the peer tutoring sessions could be devoted to discussions of the students' reactions to the various learning strategies.

Research-Oriented Training

This kind of training is usually associated with empirical research. Researchers at several major universities are developing projects designed to assess the results of strategy instruction on student performance. Generally, an experimental group of foreign language students receives some kind of treatment (i.e., strategy instruction) and is compared with one or more control groups. Often, it is the researcher, and not the regular classroom teacher, who provides the training, although researchers are beginning to provide the regular classroom teacher with the necessary instructional materials to carry out the training programs (see, e.g., Weinstein and Underwood 1985; Chamot and O'Malley 1994).

While the experimental groups quite often show marked improvement in language performance, Oxford (1990) reports that the results have been mixed because there are several problems associated with strategy training for research purposes. First, not all students get to participate, and thus only a limited number of students benefit from the strategies instruction. However, on the plus side, the research project(s) may provide the impetus for implementing full-scale training programs and thus provide program administrators with research-based models that show how the strategy training might fit into a particular foreign language curriculum. Second, the strategy training is not always contextualized, so students often do not learn how to transfer the new strategies to other learning contexts. Because the transferability of strategies is an important aspect of any training program, students will not fully benefit from the strategies instruction until they are able to use the strategies effectively across language tasks. In this case, the more "aware" students will benefit most from the instruction. Third, researchers often choose to focus only on certain strategies for specific language skills, rather than conduct extensive training across both tasks and language skills. Again, this does not provide the learners with sufficient strategy training, although some students may be able to develop new strategy applications of their own.

Despite the problems, research-oriented training provides university foreign language program administrators and strategy researchers with empirical data related to the effectiveness of strategy training in authentic language classrooms. (For a comprehensive review of classroom studies, see Derry and Murphy 1986; O'Malley and Chamot 1990.)

Videotaped Minicourses

Joan Rubin developed an interactive videodisk program and accompanying instructional manual designed for adults (high school and above) to use before beginning an introductory-level foreign language course. The one-hour *Language Learning Disc* was designed to raise students' awareness of learning strategies and of the learning process in general, to show students how to transfer strategies to new tasks, and to help students take charge of their own progress while learning the language. Using authentic language situations, the instructional program includes twenty different foreign languages, and students can select the language, topic, and level of difficulty they wish to focus on. The materials are structured to expose language students to various strategies in many different contexts, and the videodisk is divided into three main sections: (1) an introduction, (2) general language learning strategies, and (3) strategies related to reading, active listening, or conversation.[5]

Although the benefits of this highly interactive and individualized program are considerable, several problems are associated with the videodisk. Unfortunately, it has had very limited circulation and thus has not been widely available to university-level foreign language programs. In addition, it requires very specialized technical equipment to operate. The necessary equipment is expensive to buy and has limited applications apart from the videodisk. However, students can use the multimedia package to explore several different aspects of the language learning process to prepare them for the study of a foreign language.

Awareness Training

Also known as consciousness-raising or familiarization training, this kind of training is often provided apart from regular language classroom instruction, and is usually the learners' first introduction to the concept of learning strategies. Oxford (1990, p. 202) describes awareness training as a program in which "participants become aware of and familiar with the general idea of language learning strategies and the way such strategies can help them accomplish various language tasks. In awareness training, however, participants do not have to use strategies in actual, on-the-spot language tasks." Dickinson (1992) emphasizes two kinds of learner awareness necessary for effective foreign language learning strategy instruction: language awareness (knowledge that makes it possible to talk about and describe language) and language learning awareness (knowledge about some of the factors that influence the learning process). Oxford and Cohen (1992, p. 13) refer to the latter as "strategy" awareness: "When one talks about strategy awareness, one is referring to the learner's understanding of his or her own strategy applications—how he or she takes in new language material, encodes it, and transforms it to make it usable for actual communication." This kind of awareness training should preferably take place within the individual classroom setting, but it can also be provided by language learning "experts" for large numbers of students.

For example, first-year language students at Carnegie Mellon University are required to participate in a set of activities that account for 15 percent of the grade in the language course. The students must attend three lectures on language learning, read one article on language learning strategies, complete Oxford's Strategy Inventory for Language Learning (SILL), complete a short questionnaire on their language learning background and motivation, and write three 250-word papers, reflecting on the behaviors and strategies discussed in the lectures, reading, and class discussions. The syllabus explains the rationale for this training: "In the course of this class, you will be asked to reflect on how you are learning and whether you are using the most appropriate strategies for your own learning styles and needs" (Harrington, Freed, and Tucker 1994). Feedback from student diaries seems to indicate benefits from the enhanced awareness of learning that this approach has encouraged.

Another example of general awareness training was provided during the Foreign Language Learning Strategy Symposium at the University of Minnesota in April 1994. The two featured speakers, Anna Uhl Chamot and Rebecca L. Oxford, gave a joint lecture entitled "Foreign Language

Learning Strategies: Practical Ways to Enhance the Language Learning Process." Current language learners from various language programs learned about the historical development of strategy training, current theoretical and research contexts, comprehension and production strategies, and ways to learn vocabulary. Chamot and Oxford also gave the participants a hands-on activity that included several learning strategies and thus provided firsthand experience with practicing the strategies. The lecture served as a general introduction to the variety of strategies that can be used when learning a foreign language, and the brief question-and-answer session that followed the lecture gave students opportunities to address issues related to their particular language learning needs.

Although awareness-raising is a crucial aspect of strategy training, it may not provide the learners with enough information and strategy practice to allow them to self-direct the learning process fully. Because this training is often not contextualized or related to the particular language tasks the students will be asked to perform in their own classrooms, many students may have difficulty knowing how and when to use the strategies to which they have been exposed, organizing and planning their strategy use, finding language-specific strategies, and transferring strategies across skills or tasks.

On the other hand, some students may find that this kind of training is sufficient to encourage independent (and appropriate) strategy use, and they seem to intuitively grasp the broader applications of language learning strategies. This option provides students with a general introduction to strategy applications, does not take time away from classroom language instruction, and can allow foreign language programs to collaborate in the development of general strategy training because it does not require language-specific strategy instruction.

Strategy Workshops

Short workshops can also be devoted to increasing overall learner awareness of learning strategies through various consciousness-raising and strategy assessment activities. They can be organized as a series of events to address the improvement of specific language skills (e.g., speaking, writing, vocabulary, etc.) or for learning a specific foreign language. These courses can be offered as noncredit classes for anyone interested in language learning, whether or not enrolled in a language course, or can be required as part of a language or academic skills course. Often these workshops offer a combination of lecture, hands-on practice with specific strategies for various language tasks, and discussions about the general effectiveness of systematic strategy use, in addition to awareness training.

An example of this method is the "Workshop Series in Language Learner Training" offered in consultation with the Learning and Academic Skills Center at the University of Minnesota. All university students were invited to attend one or more of the sessions, each of which focused on distinct aspects of the language learning process. The series included topics such as "Vocabulary Learning," "Attending to Ensure Learning and Speaking to Communicate," and "Reading for Comprehension." These workshops provided students with theoretical and empirical bases for learning strategy use, hands-on activities using general and specific strategies, and a bibliography of resources for further self-study. The participants also had opportunities for extensive small group discussions concerning problems that students often face in university-level language classrooms, ways to improve overall strategy use, the transfer of strategies to other language tasks, and goal-setting suggestions. Response to these workshops was overwhelmingly positive, and the students themselves have requested that more workshops be provided on a regular basis. The students were able to work with specific language skills, practice the strategies with direct feedback from the workshop leader, and ask for advice about improving strategy use.

The main advantage of this option is that each workshop can be devoted to a specific topic or skill and offered on an ongoing basis. Although a single workshop may be the only available option, a series of workshops may best meet the needs of a particular institution. If these workshops are provided over a period of time, they can reinforce the strategy training by serving to remind students on an ongoing basis of the importance of strategy applications. In addition, students may want to attend only those sessions related to the language they are studying or those that address their immediate language needs. As with general awareness training, these workshops can be offered to address general strategy applications, and thus be useful across language programs, although they can also be tailored to the needs of a particular language program.

Strategies Inserted into Language Textbooks

Many foreign language textbooks have begun to appear that (implicitly or explicitly) "embed" learning strategies into the class activities and thus into the language curriculum. When the strategies are implicit and thus not explained, modeled, or reinforced by the classroom teacher or the textbook itself, it does not provide for contextualized strategy training, and students may not be aware that they have been using the strategies at all. Sometimes the rationale for these activities is only explained in the teacher's manual and the teacher does not have sufficient training to explain the strategies' importance or value as language learning tools. Or a strategy may be described briefly in English (e.g., an explanation of how reflecting on the title of a reading to activate background schemata can aid target language comprehension), but is not reinforced by other activities in the book. Experienced language learners may recognize the usefulness of these strategies and find ways to transfer them to similar tasks, but the average or beginning student may not understand that these strategies can be transferred to new tasks or they may simply forget to use them. Thus, the language instructor will have to explicitly debrief and reinforce the strategies in the textbook, making sure that the students are aware of the purpose of systematic strategy use, in order to take advantage of the benefits of these strategies.

There are also a few textbooks that are expressly devoted to overt strategy instruction and "spiraling" (or progressive reinforcement) of the strategies as part of the language course itself. These books have strategy-embedded activities as well as explicit explanations of the benefits and applications of the various strategies they address. Because the focus of the activities is contextualized language learning, learners can develop their learning strategy repertoires at the same time they are learning the target language. Although most of the activities have been written for English as a second language (e.g., the *Tapestry* and *In Contact—On Target—In Charge* series), foreign language textbooks are also now becoming available (e.g., *¿Sabías Que . . . ?: Beginning Spanish*).

There are several advantages to using textbooks with explicit strategy instruction, the most obvious of which is that students will not have to undergo extracurricular training because the strategies are already included as part of the regular language course. In addition, these textbooks reinforce strategy use across both tasks and skills, and thus encourage students to continue applying the strategies on their own. However, the teachers themselves may still require strategy training in order to use the materials appropriately. This can be accomplished by providing in-service foreign language teacher development programs specifically designed to allow teachers to become aware of the applications of learning strategies and promote extensive strategy use in their classes. (See "Suggestions for Developing In-service Strategy Training Seminars," below.)

Strategies Integrated into the Foreign Language Classroom

Whether or not strategies are included in the textbooks, classroom teachers can integrate the strategy training into the regular language coursework, thus providing the students with contextualized strategy practice. Students will be able to see the direct applications of the various strategies to the language they are studying, have opportunities to share their strategies with the other students in the class, and increase their strategy repertoires within the context of the typical language tasks they are asked to perform. The teachers can individualize the strategy training, suggest language-specific strategies, and reinforce the strategies as they present the regular course content.

Although empirical research has not yet confirmed whether strategy training is most effective when woven into the regular language curriculum or when it is provided through separate, content-independent sessions (O'Malley and Chamot 1990, p. 184), researchers tend to agree that integrated strategy training is the preferred approach "in order to demonstrate to students the specific applications of the strategies and to promote the transfer of strategies to new tasks." Strategies that are presented as part of the regular course content, embedded into activities from the students' own textbooks and materials, provide for contextualized strategy practice and reinforcement. For large foreign language programs, this option is an efficient and highly cost-effective way to provide explicit strategy training to a great number of students.

Suggestions for Developing In-service Strategy Training Seminars

Foreign language program administrators can develop in-service strategy training seminars for classroom teachers in order to train teachers in the "techniques for delivering effective learning strategy instruction to students" (O'Malley and Chamot 1990, p. 154). The participating language instructors can gain a better sense of the individual needs of their students and positively reinforce effective strategy use during the course of the regular language curriculum, learn how to embed the strategies into everyday class activities, and overtly work with strategies related to specific curricular guidelines. Teacher training in learning strategies can also prepare the instructors for the spontaneous introduction of strategies in their classes, thus providing individualized and contextualized strategies instruction for a large number of students. In addition, these teachers then become "strategy experts" themselves and thus can offer valuable feedback on the effectiveness of integrated strategies instruction.

As with strategy training for students, there are several different options that program administrators can choose from, ranging from general awareness training to full-scale training seminars. For example, individual language programs could offer short awareness-raising workshops and lectures; language instructors could be asked to attend any of the numerous presentations, colloquia, and workshops given at professional conferences; or they could take part in an inservice strategy training seminar.

Of these options, seminars provide the most extensive (and most individualized) strategy training for teachers. These seminars could be offered as part of the preservice orientation program for incoming foreign language instructors within specific language departments or be organized as inservice training programs through the collaboration of several language departments. This kind of training would ideally include several different methods of instruction: lectures, outside reading assignments, pair and small-group discussions, hands-on strategy activities, journals describing learning/teaching experiences and issues, observations of classes taught by teachers who have already implemented strategy training with their students, interactive sessions to practice the development of strategy-integrated lesson plans, and peer/student microteaching.

Lectures and readings concerning the theoretical and research contexts in which strategy training has developed can provide the necessary foundation for more specialized and detailed strategy training. In addition, they can be tailored to the individual needs of the participants and thus enhance the effectiveness of the training program. In the case of reading assignments, the more that the participating instructors can learn about strategies instruction outside of class, the better time will be spent in the training classroom.

Discussions could include the emergence of strategy training as a means of integrating diverse teaching philosophies, methodologies, and learning styles/preferences, as well as address the various philosophical and methodological issues concerning the process of learning/acquisition. These discussions (in pairs or small groups) can serve to set the context for which the instructors will eventually use their training: the authentic foreign language classroom. The teachers-in-training should have numerous opportunities to reflect on the information being presented in the seminar, as well as to discuss their own language learning and teaching experiences, in order to prepare them for their future roles as facilitators of their own students' reactions to learner training. In addition, if this part of the training program emphasizes the role of the learner as a source of strategy and language learning knowledge, the instructors may feel more comfortable with these kinds of discussions in their own classes since they will have already had experience sharing similar ideas and suggestions.

A practical hands-on approach, where the participants themselves actively experiment with the strategies presented, will help to prepare the instructors to train their own students and allow them to practice implementing the strategies at the same time. For example, they could take diagnostic surveys (e.g., learning style/personality inventories and strategy assessment surveys), reflect on ways that they may differ from other language learners (e.g., think about and discuss their own language learning experiences and how individual style differences can affect strategy choice), actively participate in learner training activities (e.g., learn new vocabulary with different mnemonic devices, answer general comprehension questions after skimming a text, rehearse short speeches, selectively attend to short listening passages), and engage in problem-solving or metacognitive discussions (e.g., in small groups or pairs, discuss various ways to approach a particular task, isolate potential difficulties, make strategy choices, implement the selected strategies, and evaluate their effectiveness). After actively engaging in and reacting to authentic strategy use, the teachers-in-training can gain a better understanding of what to expect from their own students, as well as develop firsthand practice with generating multiple problem-solving techniques (i.e., choosing their own strategies). Thus, the instructors would *experience* the strategies before actually teaching them.

Participants may also find it useful to keep journals of their experiences during the training sessions to use as a resource when later called upon to present strategy training themselves. These journals could include affective reactions to the training, as well as ideas for the integration of strategies into various kinds of activities. Excerpts from these journal entries could later be compiled into a resource handbook for the teachers to use as support after the training program has ended.

Another useful resource for the teachers is the opportunity to observe authentic class sessions conducted by other language instructors who have already undergone the strategy training program. The teachers can meet to exchange ideas about specific aspects of the presented lessons and discuss how the strategy training fits into the overall language curriculum. If possible, the teachers-in-training should also have a chance to talk with the students in the class to discuss their reaction to the use of strategies. It is the learners themselves who can provide some of the most significant and insightful comments about the realities of classroom strategy training. If there are not enough language classrooms to observe, teachers could also watch videotapes of class sessions taught by colleagues who regularly provide explicit strategy instruction. These teaching demonstrations of strategies taught to students in authentic contexts can be especially helpful to show the teachers how the strategies are being embedded into a particular course curriculum.

Another important component of a teacher-training seminar of this type is providing the teachers with opportunities to practice integrating strategies into everyday lesson plans and developing strategy-based teaching materials. If the teachers only receive preprepared strategy materials to use with their students, they may have difficulty adapting the strategy instruction to their own students' needs. The seminar could provide the teachers with opportunities to generate their own ideas about how the strategies could be incorporated into their current language curricula by having them create new teaching materials. This can be accomplished by having the teachers bring in actual lessons that they have already prepared, and then in pairs or small groups they could work together to brainstorm ways in which different strategies could be inserted into the activities, create new materials to fill in any gaps, and finally share their ideas with the rest of the class. As a group, the participants could next generate several possibilities for presenting each activity, and by sharing these lesson plans, they would have access to a wide variety of ideas for strategy integration that they could later incorporate into future lessons. In addition, lesson-plan-integration activities can also serve as a feedback mechanism for both the training coordinator (to assess the effectiveness of the strategy training) and for the teachers themselves (to gauge their ability to apply the content of the seminar in practical ways).

Finally, after the teachers have had opportunities to create new materials, as well as to integrate strategy training into typical lesson plans, they should be able to present short strategy/language lessons to their peers in order to practice strategy training techniques before introducing them into their own classrooms. They would get further receptive practice with strategies from these presentations, as well as get essential productive practice with teaching various strategies. These microteaching sessions can also be extended to small groups of current language students for additional teaching practice. This would provide authentic responses to strategy training from actual language learners, allowing the teachers to experience a simulated classroom atmosphere much like what they will eventually face. If possible, these sessions could be videotaped, be used to generate discussions about the effectiveness of the lessons, and allow the teachers to reflect on their teaching skills, as well as provide the training coordinator with additional insight into the teachers' needs within and beyond the training sessions (e.g., to adjust the current training curriculum, for follow-up support after the "official" training has ended, or for future training sessions).

Anna Uhl Chamot at Georgetown University and her colleagues from the Washington, D. C., area school districts have offered training seminars for same-language teachers as part of an ongoing series of research projects. The teachers who participate in these projects receive prepackaged lesson plans, as well as instruction in creating their own materials, in order to provide students with strategy-integrated activities as part of the regular language curriculum. The teachers have opportunities to observe their same-language colleagues and are encouraged to begin conducting the class sessions without further materials from the research team (see O'Malley and Chamot 1990; Chamot and O'Malley 1994).

On the other hand, the teacher-training seminar at the University of Minnesota was created for teachers from different foreign language programs and no prepackaged teaching materials are provided. The seminar focuses on training the teachers to create their own instructional materials from the very beginning of the program. The teachers are thus responsible for applying the strategies to their own curricular needs, and, when possible, are paired with teachers from their own language department to share lesson plan ideas. For the less commonly taught languages (e.g., Hebrew, Hindi, Irish, Norwegian, Portuguese, etc.), the teachers are asked to form cross-language strategy support teams. Teaching suggestions are shared throughout the different foreign language programs and teachers thus have contact with a wide variety of instructional materials, teaching philosophies, and performance criteria.

Both of these teacher-training methods have been successful in bringing fully integrated strategy instruction to a great number of students by way of the regular classroom language teachers. The administrative decisions made for the different formats of these seminars were based upon the needs of the individual institutions, as well as the need to provide students with systematic strategy training that has been integrated into everyday classroom activities. The goal of this kind of seminar is to train classroom language teachers (who will eventually train their own students) in the identification, practice, reinforcement, and transfer of language learning strategies.

A Step-by-Step Approach to the Design of Strategy Training Programs

The options outlined above provide language program administrators with several choices for providing strategy training for large numbers of students. Based on the needs, resources, and time available to an institution, the next step is to plan the instruction the students will receive. Many considerations must be taken into account when designing explicit strategy training programs for foreign language learners. The following seven-step approach is largely based on suggestions for strategy training by Oxford (1990). This model is especially valuable because it can easily be adapted to the needs of various groups of learners and the resources available to a particular institution, as well as to programs for both short- and long-term strategy instruction. It can be used to prepare short workshops and awareness-training lectures for students and/or serve as a guideline for teachers who have attended strategy training seminars.

Determine the Learners' Needs and the Resources Available

The first step in designing any foreign language curriculum is to assess the needs of the learners. This is an especially crucial step when designing a curriculum that will integrate strategy training. The factors involved in this kind of needs assessment include: the level of proficiency of the learners, their experience with strategy use or with learning other languages, their beliefs and attitudes about language learning, their expectations regarding the roles of both the classroom teacher and the individual language learner, and the reasons why they have chosen to study a particular foreign language.

Next, the amount of time to be allotted to the training program must be considered. Will the program consist of short-term intervention or extensive strategy instruction? How many hours can be dedicated to this kind of instruction? Scheduling when the strategy training will take place within the particular foreign language curriculum should also be considered in this step.

How much funding is available for the training program? Should individual language programs sponsor the training or should it be a collaboration among several departments? Will the training be language-specific or more general in nature? Which kind of training program will be most cost-effective and thus reach the greatest number of students? Can the training be offered only once a year, or will it be offered on an ongoing basis throughout the year?

Finally, who will conduct the training itself? Does the sponsoring institution have resident "experts" who can carry out the program(s) and/or develop the materials needed, or will outside lecturers/trainers need to be brought in? (For further description of decisions related to materials development, see "Prepare the Materials and Activities" below.)

Select the Appropriate Strategies

First, determine the strategies that the learners already use and select strategies that are appropriate to the characteristics and needs of the learners. In addition to questionnaires and student interviews, a popular assessment tool is Oxford's (1990) Strategy Inventory for Language Learning (SILL), which has been translated into several foreign languages and has undergone extensive reliability and validity testing. (For a detailed description of methods of strategy assessment, see Cohen and Scott, forthcoming.) Learner characteristics to keep in mind during the selection process include learning style preferences, cultural or educational background, levels and types of motivation,[6] previous language study, and needs-related factors, such as proficiency goals and the kinds of tasks learners will be asked to perform in the language classroom.

Also, consider the transferability of the strategies to other language learning tasks. For example, the strategy of relating new language information to a meaningful visual image (e.g., a picture of an object or activity, or a mental representation of a word or phrase) can not only be extended to learning new vocabulary, but can also be useful for reading, writing, speaking, listening, and grammar tasks. Most strategies can be generalized in this way, although some (such as rote memorization) may have more limited benefits across language tasks.

Finally, decide whether the training will have a broad or a narrow focus. In other words, will the training focus on multiple clusters of strategies or will it include just a few? Or will the training consist of a combination of these approaches by first providing the learners with a wide range of strategies and then focusing exclusively on those which the learners themselves have chosen? Because one of the primary goals of strategy instruction is to encourage the learners to use strategies on their own, the latter approach may be more beneficial. By providing the learners with a broad range of strategies, the learners could thus select those which they find most useful. (See Dansereau 1985 for a description of these different approaches.) This decision may be affected by the amount of time available for strategy training and the proposed structure of the training program, as well as by the immediate and long-term needs of individual learners.

Consider the Benefits of Integrated Strategy Training

As noted above, there are significant benefits from providing strategy training as part of the regular class curriculum. Integrated strategies training is contextualized, can be individualized according to the needs of a particular group of learners, and provides hands-on practice with the strategies during authentic language learning tasks. Wenden (1987b, p. 161) notes that integrated strategy training "enables the learner to perceive the relevance of the task, enhances comprehension, and facilitates retention."

However, Wenden also notes that fully integrated strategy instruction may not encourage learner autonomy nor the spontaneous (unprompted) application of strategies by individual learners, may not be possible due to time or institutional constraints, or may not adequately meet the learners' objectives. She (1987b, p. 161) remarks, "In such cases, a course that focuses exclusively on helping students develop the skills necessary to learn the language on their own would appear to be the more appropriate, although less integrated, alternative." Thus the decision to integrate the strategies into daily classroom activities, using the course content to stimulate explicit strategy instruction and to reinforce the use of specific strategies, may not be feasible, but would provide the learners with contextualized strategy practice and would further allow students to actively apply the strategies they have been learning in class.

Consider Motivational Issues

Will students be graded on their efforts and/or receive course credit for participation in the strategy training program, or will they be motivated to learn the strategies simply because they want to become more effective language learners? As Oxford et al. (1990, pp. 206–7) point out, "[I]f learners have gone through a strategy assessment phase, their interest in strategies is likely to be heightened, and if you explain how using good strategies can make language learning easier, students will be even more interested in participating in strategy training." However, inducements such as extra credit may substantially increase enthusiasm in the college classroom, whether the strategy training is integrated in the daily activities or not.

Training programs can also be required for students as part of their regular language coursework, using special grading systems.

In addition, motivation can also be increased if the learners have at least some control over the strategies they will learn. The students themselves may prefer to choose the strategies that will be included in the training program, and because the learners will eventually be expected to select their own strategies when performing language tasks, their input early in the training process can facilitate the transition from explicit instruction and guided practice to self-directed strategy use.

Another factor to be considered is the relative level of resistance to strategy training. Some students may be reluctant to try out new strategies, preferring to rely on the strategies that they already employ, or may not be convinced of the benefits that accompany systematic strategy use. Other learners may have negative reactions to the training because of very strong cultural or personal beliefs about the teacher's role in the classroom and may resist the increased responsibility for learning that accompanies strategy training.

Prepare the Materials and Activities

First, it must be determined who will develop the instructional materials. Will teachers receive prepackaged training materials (from a textbook, curriculum coordinator, or researcher) or will they be expected to produce their own materials (perhaps by adapting the activities in the current curriculum to include strategies)? Will the learners themselves contribute to the development and collection of materials, thereby becoming even more involved in and having more control over the instructional program, or will the trainer (teacher, coordinator, or researcher) alone make decisions regarding the course materials and activities?

Next, will the strategy training be "flexible" and allow for the spontaneous introduction of new strategies as needed during a classroom activity or will there be a fixed training curriculum? While the latter may offer convenience and consistency across training programs, the former allows for more individualized strategy instruction. However, in order to conduct spontaneous strategy training in the classroom, the language teachers themselves need to undergo some form of in-service training to ensure that they have received appropriate and sufficient preparation for this kind of strategy instruction. If the goal is to provide the greatest number of students with individualized, contextualized strategy training, the teachers must also be trained.

Finally, the focus of instruction and the types of tasks that the learners will be asked to perform also need to be addressed during this preparatory phase. For example, does the course focus on oral production of the target language, does it emphasize the development of reading skills, or does it consist of an integrated skills approach? What kinds of activities do the teachers present during the classroom sessions and assign for homework? The types of strategies chosen should vary according to the skills that are emphasized and the typical kinds of learning activities that are included in the curriculum. Another possibility is to expand the types of activities typically found in the language classroom to make them more "strategy-friendly." Examples of this are cooperative learning tasks and small group discussions that focus on learner reactions to the training sessions. As Oxford et al. (1990, p. 209) wisely remark, "Activities must be interesting, varied, and meaningful, and they should deal not just with intellectual aspects of language learning, but with the affective side as well."

Conduct Explicit Strategy Training

Learners should be fully informed of what strategies they are being taught, the value and purpose of employing these strategies, and ways that they can transfer the strategies to other learning tasks. Learners should also be explicitly trained to select, monitor, check, and evaluate the strategies that they use (Brown, Campione, and Day 1980). This kind of explicit strategy training (sometimes called "direct" strategy training) differs from "blind" strategy training in one important aspect. While both kinds of training can include activities in which strategies are embedded (i.e., structured to elicit the use of specific strategies), the latter approach to strategy training does not provide the learners with explicit information about what strategies are being used or why they are useful. In other words, the students may not be aware that they are using the strategies that the activity has been designed to elicit, and thus may not be able to generalize the strategies to other learning contexts. Oxford (1990) cites several studies in which blind strategy training has resulted in improved performance on a particular language task, but in which learners did not continue to employ the strategy when faced with new language tasks. Wenden (1987a, 1987b, 1991) points out that when students are given information about the function, usefulness, and transferability of the strategies they are practicing, they will be more likely to use them spontaneously in other contexts. Since one of the primary goals of strategy instruction is to foster learner independence and autonomy, O'Malley and Chamot (1990, p. 184) conclude that "strategy training should be direct in addition to being embedded. In other words, students should be apprised of the goals of strategy instruction and should be made aware of the strategies they are being taught."

Evaluate and Revise the Strategy Training

Ongoing evaluation and revision of the training program is necessary to ensure its success. The learners themselves can provide some of the most insightful feedback for the teacher-trainer. Examples of criteria that can be used to evaluate the program include improved student performance across language tasks and skills, general learning skill improvement (including enhanced problem-solving skills), maintenance of the new strategies over time, the effective transfer of strategies to other learning tasks, and a positive change in learner attitudes toward the training program and the language course itself (Wenden 1987b; Oxford 1990). Tarone and Yule (1989) emphasize that ongoing needs assessment, based on feedback from the learners themselves, is an important part of any language program. If the focus of instruction is indeed on the learner, then learner input is essential to the successful evaluation and revision of the training.

As noted above, some strategy instruction may be unplanned and spontaneous, based on the immediate needs of learners who are having difficulties with a particular language task. These on-the-spot revisions can provide the learners with highly individualized strategy instruction, as well as additional practice using specific learning strategies. However, flexible strategy instruction requires that the teacher trainer (or the classroom teachers themselves) also undergo some sort of strategy training to facilitate strategy discussions with students.

Finally, the training program should also be revised after it has been completed, based on both teacher trainer and student feedback, before it is presented to the next set of learners. This last step naturally leads back to the first, in which the learners' specific needs are taken into consideration, thus fully completing the instructional cycle.

Conclusion

These options and guidelines for implementing foreign language learning strategy instruction allow program administrators who are interested in incorporating learning strategies into their foreign language curricula to tailor the training to suit the needs of their various numbers of students, as well as the needs of the individual institution or language program. The most important considerations when designing a strategy training program are the students' needs, the available resources (including time, the costs associated with developing a training program, materials, and the availability of teacher-trainers), and, ultimately, the feasibility of providing this kind of instruction.

As this chapter has described, the overall goal of any strategy training program is to help learners become more successful in their attempts to learn a foreign language. The task when considering the inclusion of learning strategies in a foreign language curriculum is to choose an instructional model that introduces the strategies to the students; teaches them to identify, practice, evaluate, and transfer strategies to new learning situations; and promotes learner autonomy so that students can continue their learning after they leave the language classroom. Students can be given more responsibility for learning and make informed choices about how they will learn the target language, thus becoming actively involved in the learning process.

There are several advantages of conducting strategy training programs for language instructors so that strategy training can be integrated into foreign language classes. These programs can be the most efficient and effective way to provide explicit strategies instruction to a large number of students. They can allow teachers to develop the skills necessary to conduct contextualized strategy training with their own students, give teachers a clearer understanding of how to encourage their students to use the strategies in and out of class, allow for flexible and highly individualized strategy training, provide students with opportunities to learn the strategies at the same time they are learning the language, and provide an arena for further research on the effectiveness of strategies instruction. When graduate teaching assistants receive strategy training, the benefits of their training can spread to other institutions after they graduate, and they can thus begin the movement to provide explicit and integrated strategies instruction for all foreign language students at all American colleges and universities. It is these teachers who will be the driving force behind making learning strategy instruction a reality in the foreign language classroom.[7]

Notes

1. See, for example, Hosenfeld (1977), Rubin (1981), O'Malley, Chamot, Stewer-Manzanares, Küpper, and Russo (1985), Abraham and Vann (1987), Chamot, O'Malley, Küpper, and Impink-Hernandez (1987), Bacon and Finnemann (1990), Ehrman and Oxford (1990).

2. Although Oxford (1990) includes in her learning strategy taxonomy the category of "compensatory" strategies, Tarone (1980, 1981) clearly differentiates between communication and learning strategies (based on the learner's intended purpose for using a particular strategy). Faerch and Kasper (1983) have dedicated an entire book to a discussion on this issue. Oxford and Cohen (1992) and Ellis (1994) provide additional distinctions and definitions of the various strategies.

3. See Naiman, Fröhlich, and Todesco (1975), Rubin (1975), Stern (1975), and Naiman, Fröhlich, Stern, and Todesco (1978), often collectively known as the "good language learner" studies, as well as Hosenfeld (1976). Nation and McLaughlin (1986) have addressed the difficulties associated with this approach to strategies research.

4. For reviews of research articles dealing with the description, identification, and classification of strategies, see Dansereau (1985), Oxford and Cohen (1992), Oxford (1993), and Oxford and Leaver (forthcoming).

5. For more information about the videodisk, contact Joan Rubin, 2011 Hermitage Avenue, Wheaton, MD 20902.

6. See Larsen-Freeman and Long (1991) or Ellis (1994) for discussions of the relationships among levels and types of motivation, strategy use, and language learning.

7. For more information on learning strategies, see Appendix 1 (Informational Computer Networks) and Appendix 2 (Annotated Bibliography of Learning Strategy Books). For a more detailed description of a sample teacher training curriculum, see Weaver (1994).

Works Cited

Abraham, Roberta, and Roberta Vann. 1987. Strategies of Two Language Learners: A Case Study. In *Learner Strategies in Language Learning*, edited by Anita Wenden and Joan Rubin, 85–102. Englewood Cliffs, NJ: Prentice-Hall.

Bacon, Susan, and Michael Finnemann. 1990. A Study of the Attitudes, Motives, and Strategies of University Foreign Language Students and Their Disposition to Authentic Oral and Written Input. *Modern Language Journal* 74: 459–73.

Belmont, John M., and Earl C. Butterfield. 1977. The Instructional Approach to Developmental Cognitive Research. In *Perspectives on the*

Development of Memory and Cognition, edited by Robert V. Kail, Jr., and John W. Hagen, 437–81. Hillsdale, NJ: Erlbaum.

Blanche, Patrick, and Barbara J. Merino. 1989. Self-Assessment of Foreign-Language Skills: Implications for Teachers and Researchers. *Language Learning* 30: 313–40.

Brown, Ann L., Joseph C. Campione, and Jeanne D. Day. 1980. Learning to Learn: On Training Students to Learn from Texts. *Educational Researcher* 10: 14–21.

Brown, Ann L., Annemarie S. Palinscar, and Bonnie B. Armbruster. 1984. Instructing Comprehension-Fostering Activities in Interactive Learning Situations. In *Learning and Comprehension of Texts,* edited by Heinz Mandl et al., 255–86. Hillsdale, NJ: Erlbaum.

Brown, H. Douglas. 1989. *A Practical Guide to Language Learning: A Fifteen-Week Program of Strategies for Success.* New York: McGraw-Hill.

————. 1991. *Breaking the Language Barrier: Creating Your Own Pathway to Success.* Yarmouth, ME: Intercultural Press.

Chamot, Anna Uhl, and J. Michael O'Malley. 1994. *The CALLA Handbook: Implementing the Cognitive Academic Language Learning Approach.* Reading, MA: Addison-Wesley.

Chamot, Anna U., J. Michael O'Malley, Lisa Küpper, and M. V. Impink-Hernandez. 1987. *A Study of Learning Strategies in Foreign Language Instruction: First Year Report.* Washington, DC: InterAmerica Research Associates.

Cohen, Andrew D. 1990. *Language Learning: Insights for Learners, Teachers, and Researchers.* Boston: Heinle & Heinle.

Cohen, Andrew D., and Kimberly Scott. Forthcoming. Approaches to Assessing Language Learning Strategies. In *Learner Awareness of Strategies,* edited by Rebecca L. Oxford and Betty Lou Leaver. Cambridge, UK: Cambridge University Press.

Dansereau, Donald F. 1985. Learning Strategy Research. In *Thinking and Learning Skills: Relating Learning to Basic Research,* edited by Judith W. Segal, Susan F. Chipman, and Robert Glaser, 209–40. Hillsdale, NJ: Erlbaum.

Derry, Sharon J., and Debra A. Murphy. 1986. Designing Systems that Train Learning Ability: From Theory to Practice. *Review of Educational Research* 56: 1–39.

Dickinson, Leslie. 1992. *Learner Autonomy 2: Learner Training for Language Learning.* Dublin, Ireland: Authentik Language Learning Resources.

Duffy, Gerald G., Cassandra Book, and Laura R. Roehler. 1983. A Study of Direct Teacher Explanation during Reading Instruction. In *Searches for Meaning in Reading/Language Processing and Instruction,* edited by Jerome A. Niles, and Larry A. Harris, 295–303. Rochester, NY: National Reading Conference.

Ehrman, Madeline, and Rebecca L. Oxford. 1990. Adult Language Learning Styles and Strategies in an Intensive Training Setting. *Modern Language Journal* 74: 311–27.

Ellis, Gail, and Barbara Sinclair. 1989. *Learning to Learn English: A Course in Learner Training.* Glasgow, Scotland: Cambridge University Press.

Ellis, Rod. 1994. *The Study of Second Language Acquisition.* Oxford: Oxford University Press.

Faerch, Claus, and Gabriele Kasper. 1983. *Strategies in Interlanguage Communication.* New York: Longman.

Garner, Ruth. 1987. *Metacognition and Reading Comprehension.* Norwood, NJ: Ablex.

Harrington, Michael, Barbara Freed, and G. R. Tucker. 1994. Learning about Language Learning: Its Role in Foreign Language Instruction. Paper presented at the annual meeting of the American Association of Applied Linguistics, Baltimore, MD.

Holec, Henri. 1988. *Autonomy and Self-Directed Learning: Present Fields of Application.* Project No. 12: Learning and Teaching Modern Languages for Communication. Strasbourg, France: Council for Cultural Co-operation.

Hosenfeld, Carol. 1976. Learning about Learning: Discovering Our Students' Strategies. *Foreign Language Annals* 9: 117–29.

———. 1977. A Learning-Teaching View of Second-Language Instruction: The Learning Strategies of Second Language Learners with Reading-Grammar Tasks. Ph.D. diss., Ohio State University.

Larsen-Freeman, Diane, and Michael H. Long. 1991. *An Introduction to Second Language Acquisition Research.* New York: Longman.

Naiman, Neil, Maria Fröhlich, H. H. Stern, and Angie Todesco. 1978. *The Good Language Learner.* Toronto: Ontario Institute for Studies in Education.

Naiman, Neil, Maria Fröhlich, and Angie Todesco. 1975. The Good Language Learner. *TESL Talk* 6: 58–75.

Nation, Robert, and Barry McLaughlin. 1986. Novices and Experts: An Information-Processing Approach to the "Good Language Learner" Problem. *Applied Psycholinguistics* 7: 41–45.

O'Malley, J. Michael, and Anna Uhl Chamot. 1990. *Learning Strategies in Second Language Acquisition.* The Cambridge Applied Linguistics Series. New York: Cambridge University Press.

O'Malley, J. Michael, Anna Uhl Chamot, Gloria Stewer-Manzanares, Lisa Küpper, and Rocco P. Russo. 1985. Learning Strategies Used by Beginning and Intermediate ESL Students. *Language Learning* 35: 21–46.

Oxford, Rebecca L. 1990. *Language Learning Strategies: What Every Teacher Should Know.* New York: Newbury House/Harper and Row.

———. 1993. Research on Second Language Learning Strategies. *Annual Review of Applied Linguistics* 13: 175–87.

Oxford, Rebecca L., and Andrew D. Cohen. 1992. Language Learning Strategies: Crucial Issues of Concept and Classification. *Applied Language Learning* 3: 1–35.

Oxford, Rebecca L., David Crookall, Andrew Cohen, Roberta Lavine, Martha Nyikos, and Will Sutter. 1990. Strategy Training for Language Learners: Six Situational Case Studies and a Training Model. *Foreign Language Annals* 22: 197–216.

Oxford, Rebecca L., and Betty Lou Leaver, eds. Forthcoming. *Learner Awareness of Strategies.* Cambridge, UK: Cambridge University Press.

Pearson, P. David, and Janice A. Dole. 1987. Explicit Comprehension Instruction: A Review of Research and a New Conceptualization of Learning. *Elementary School Journal* 88: 151–65.

Pressley, Michael, and Joel R. Levin, eds. 1983. *Cognitive Strategy Research: Educational Applications.* New York: Springer Verlag.

Rubin, Joan. 1975. What the "Good Language Learner" Can Teach Us. *TESOL Quarterly* 9: 41–51.

———. 1981. Study of Cognitive Processes in Second Language Learning. *Applied Linguistics* 2: 117–31.

————— 1989. How Learner Strategies Can Inform Language Teaching. In *Proceedings of LULTAC,* edited by V. Bickley. Hong Kong: Institute of Language in Education, Department of Education.

Rubin, Joan, and Irene Thompson. 1994. *How to Be a More Successful Language Learner.* 2d ed. Boston: Heinle & Heinle.

Scarcella, Robin C., and Rebecca L. Oxford. 1992. *The Tapestry of Language Learning: The Individual in the Communicative Classroom.* The Tapestry Series of Language Learning. Boston: Heinle & Heinle.

Stern, H. H. 1975. What Can We Learn from the Good Language Learner? *Canadian Modern Language Review* 31: 304–18.

Stevick, Earl W. 1989. *Success with Foreign Languages: Seven Who Achieved It and What Worked for Them.* Cambridge, UK: Prentice-Hall International.

Tarone, Elaine. 1980. Communication Strategies, Foreigner Talk, and Repair in Interlanguage. *Language Learning* 30: 417–32.

—————. 1981. Some Thoughts on the Notion of "Communication Strategy." *TESOL Quarterly* 15: 285–95.

Tarone, Elaine, and George Yule. 1989. *Focus on the Language Learner.* Oxford: Oxford University Press.

Weaver, Susan J. 1994. Language Learning Strategies Instruction: Considerations in the Design of a Teacher Training Curriculum. Master's paper, University of Minnesota, Minneapolis.

Weinstein, Claire E., and Veronica L. Underwood. 1985. Learning Strategies: The How of Learning. In *Thinking and Learning Skills: Relating Learning to Basic Research,* edited by Judith W. Segal, Susan F. Chipman, and Robert Glaser, 241–59. Hillsdale, NJ: Erlbaum.

Wenden, Anita. 1987a. How to Be a Successful Language Learner: Insights and Prescriptions from L2 Learners. In *Learner Strategies in Language Learning,* edited by Anita Wenden and Joan Rubin, 103–17. Cambridge, UK: Prentice-Hall International.

—————. 1987b. Incorporating Learner Training in the Classroom. In *Learner Strategies in Language Learning,* edited by Anita Wenden and Joan Rubin, 159–68. Cambridge, UK: Prentice-Hall International.

—————. 1991. *Learner Strategies for Learner Autonomy: Planning and Implementing Learner Training for Language Learners.* Language Teaching Methodology Series. Cambridge, UK: Prentice-Hall International.

Wenden, Anita, and Joan Rubin, eds. 1987. *Learner Strategies in Language Learning*. Language Teaching Methodology Series. Cambridge, UK: Prentice-Hall International.

Willing, Ken. 1989. *Teaching How to Learn: A Guide to Developing ESL Learning Srategies. Teacher's Guide and Activity Worksheets*. Sydney: National Centre for English Language Teaching and Research.

VanPatten, Bill, James F. Lee, Terry L. Ballman, and Trisha Dvorak. 1992. *¡Sabías que . . . ?: Beginning Spanish*. New York: McGraw-Hill.

Appendix 1
Informational Computer Networks

Several informational networks that deal with issues related to foreign and/or second language learning and teaching are accessible by electronic mail. These computer lists and other electronic services allow foreign language students, instructors, researchers, and program administrators a forum for sharing and requesting up-to-date information about a variety of language-related issues, including learning strategy programs and research projects that are in progress throughout the world. There are also networks that deal with the instructional issues of individual foreign languages, as well as provide curricular recommendations for foreign language program administrators. Because all of the sharing is done electronically, these networks are a highly cost-efficient means of accessing information regarding learning strategies instruction. The following computer networks are a sample of the many electronic forums available for obtaining more information about foreign language learning strategies and foreign language learning strategies instruction:

1. *The NeSSLA Report (Network of Styles and Strategies in Language Acquisition)*. First published in 1992 as the Consortium for Research on Adult Language Learning and Acquisition (CORALLA) Newsletter by Rebecca Oxford, the new version of this informational newsletter is provided through the Center for Advanced Research on Language Acquisition (CARLA) at the University of Minnesota. It includes reports of ongoing research projects, updates on learning strategy programs, lists of current publications, ongoing professional conferences, and other information related to learning styles and strategies, both nationally and internationally. It is distributed electronically through Internet, and hard copies are also available upon request. To subscribe, post the message: SUBSCRIBE NeSSLA <your name> to CARLA@MAROON.TC.UMN.EDU or send a letter of inquiry

to *The NeSSLA Report*, c/o CARLA, 1313 5th Street SE, Suite 105, Minneapolis, MN, 55414.

2. *FLASC-L (Foreign Language Supervisors and Coordinators)*. This is an unmoderated list for those who direct/coordinate/supervise multisection foreign language programs. Its purpose is to foster discussion of issues related to the development and coordination of multisection programs and to provide a community of professorial discussion and support. It is intended as an open, supportive collegial forum where diverse views can be expressed and discussed in a spirit of mutual respect. Possible topics for discussion include: TA training, supervision, and evaluation; materials and methodologies; the role of course supervisors in language departments; and articulation among different levels of instruction. To subscribe, post the message: SUBSCRIBE FLASC-L to LISTSERV@UCI.EDU.

3. *FLTEACH (Foreign Language Teaching Forum)*. This list was formed to serve as a forum for communication among foreign language teachers at the high school and college levels. The aim is to improve communication among the professionals involved in training student teachers for certification in language teaching in New York State (NYS) and beyond. Its audience includes methodologists, university supervisors, cooperating teachers in junior high and high school, student teachers, and anyone involved in developing or implementing the NYS curriculum or engaged in the certification process. Although the initial focus is on language teaching in NYS, this list is developing a broader national base. To subscribe, post the message: SUB FLTEACH <your name> to LISTSERV@UBVM or LISTSERV@UBVM.CC.BUFFALO.EDU.

4. *SCOLT (Southern Conference on Language Teaching)*. This list is intended as a general service for foreign language educators to disseminate professional announcements, presentations, special programs, questions, inquiries, informal article reviews, and so on. To subscribe, post the message: SUBSCRIBE SCOLT <your name> to LISTSERV@ CATFISH.VALDOSTA.PEACHNET.EDU.

5. *SLART-L (Second Language Acquisition, Research, and Teaching Discussion)*. This list is intended to allow those interested in research into second language acquisition and the teaching of second languages to share their professional experiences and research. To subscribe, post the message: SUB SLART-L <full name> to LISTSERV@CUNYVM or LISTSERV@CUNYVM.CUNY.EDU.

6. *LINGUIST.* This list is an e-conference that serves as a place of discussion for those issues that concern the academic discipline of linguistics and related fields. The e-conference is international in orientation, and hopes to provide a forum for the community of linguists as they exist in different countries. There is no specific ideological or theoretical focus; discussion of any linguistic subfield is welcomed. To subscribe, post a message to: LINGUIST-REQUEST@UNIWA.UWA.OZ.AU or LIST-SERV@TAM VM1.TAMU.EDU.

7. *TESL-L (Teachers of English as a Second Language).* This list provides an electronic forum for teachers of English as a second or foreign language (ESL/EFL) around the world to exchange questions and ideas. The list is international in scope and is supported by a grant from the U. S. Department of Education's Fund for the Improvement of Post-Secondary Education (FIPSE) to build an extensive database of materials relevant to the field. TESL-L also has a large database of Computer-Assisted-Language-Learning (CALL) materials and programs. To subscribe, post the message: SUB TESL-L <your first name> <your last name> to LIST-SERV@CUNYVM.CUNY.EDU.

Other lists include:

8. *EDSTYLE (Learning Styles Theory and Research)*
LISTSERV@SJUVM.BITNET or LISTSERV@SJUVM.STJOHNS.EDU.

9. *TEACHEFT (Teaching Effectiveness)*
LISTSERV@WCU.BITNET.

10. *FLAC-L (Foreign Language Across Curriculum)*
LISTSERV@BROWNVM.

11. *LLTI (Language Learning Technology International Information Forum)*
LISTSERV@DARTCMS1.

12. *LTEST-L (Language Testing Research and Practice)*
LISTSERV@UCLACN1.

13. *MULTI-L (Language and Education in Multilingual Settings)*
LISTSERV@BARILVM.

14. *TESLFF-L ("Fluency First" and Whole Language Pedagogy)*
LISTSERV@CUNYVM.

15. *NLRC (National Language Resource Center: University of Minnesota)*
NLRC-LIST-REQUEST@MAIL.UNET.UMN.EDU.

Appendix 2
Annotated Bibliography of Learning Strategy Books

Several excellent books have been written in this area. Some are intended specifically for students and others are written for teachers and researchers. All of them address awareness training, as well as provide useful guidelines for applying learning strategies to the study of a foreign language. Results from second language research on learning strategies, as well as practical materials, make these books important resources for the development of strategy training programs. The books can also be used to supplement foreign language course textbooks or be used in teacher training programs. Several of them list additional sources of information about learning strategies and learning strategies instruction.

Books Aimed Directly at Learners:

1. *A Practical Guide to Language Learning: A Fifteen-Week Program of Strategies for Success,* by H. Douglas Brown. New York: McGraw-Hill, 1989 (75 pp.).

This learner-directed strategies manual helps to prepare students for the process of learning a foreign language by using practical exercises. Based on empirical research, each chapter highlights strategies that students need to pay attention to while they are studying a foreign language. The strategies include: goal setting, developing self-confidence, calculated risk taking, cooperative learning, and resisting direct translation to L1. The book can be used to supplement any foreign language course.

2. *Breaking the Language Barrier: Creating Your Own Pathway to Success,* by H. Douglas Brown. Yarmouth, ME: Intercultural Press 1991 (184 pp.).

The practical guidelines presented in this book are an excellent introduction to learning strategies for any current language learner. Using a series of short assessment tools, learners can begin to self-diagnose their learning style preferences, language learning attitudes, and language processing skills. The book provides real-world examples to describe the language learning process in an informal way.

3. *Learning to Learn English: A Course in Learner Training,* by Gail Ellis and Barbara Sinclair. Glasgow, Scotland: Cambridge University Press 1989 (teacher's book, 154 pp.; learner's book, 118 pp.)

Developed to supplement existing course materials, this book is designed for learners of English as a second or foreign language. Learners have opportunities to reflect on their current strategies, develop new strategies, assess short-term learning goals, organize their learning, and self-evaluate the language learning process for each of the four skills (reading, writing, speaking, and listening), as well as for grammar and vocabulary. The book is very practical and learner-centered, and authentic examples of student responses are provided.

4. *How to Be a More Successful Language Learner*, by Joan Rubin and Irene Thompson. Boston: Heinle & Heinle, 2nd ed., 1994 (120 pp.)

The second edition of this popular book for language learners stresses learner autonomy. It provides concrete suggestions for how learners can become more independent, effective, and successful in their attempts to learn foreign languages. Divided into two parts, this useful reference guide introduces learners to the nature of the language learning process and then provides step-by-step suggestions on how to improve vocabulary, grammar, reading, writing, listening, and speaking skills. Easy to read, the book is an excellent resource for beginning, as well as advanced, language learners.

5. *Teaching How to Learn: A Guide to Developing ESL Learning Strategies*, by Ken Willing. Sydney: National Centre for English Language Teaching and Research, 1989 (teacher's book 151 pp.; learner's book, 120 pp.)

Written for ESL learners, this teacher/student guide provides extensive hands-on practice with ten different strategies. The book is divided into two parts: managing the learning process and managing information. Examples of the strategies include categorization, inferencing, and selectively attending. The flexible activities can be used individually or to supplement a language course, and can easily be adapted for use with foreign language curricula.

Books Aimed at Teachers and Researchers:

1. *The CALLA Handbook: Implementing the Cognitive Academic Language Learning Approach*, by Anna Uhl Chamot and J. Michael O'Malley. Reading, MA: Addison-Wesley, 1994 (340 pp.).

The primary scope of this book is the incorporation of learning strategies into content-based curricula. It is a very practical volume that helps the language or content teacher to develop lesson plans that integrate explicit strategies instruction. By providing numerous examples of lesson plans and activities across many subject areas, the authors provide a clear and practical approach to strategies instruction and assessment.

2. *Language Learning: Insights for Learners, Teachers, and Researchers*, by Andrew D. Cohen. Boston: Heinle & Heinle, 1990 (217 pp.).

This volume is useful for anyone interested in the applications of learning strategies. Each of the first six chapters provides numerous examples for the reader to practice the strategies presented (for vocabulary, speaking, reading, and writing), and the rest of the book consists of a survey of the language learning strategy research. Especially useful for researchers, current language learners and teachers will also find many helpful suggestions for enhancing the learning process.

3. *Learner Training for Language Learning,* by Leslie Dickinson. Dublin, Ireland: Authentik Language Learning Resources, 1992 (67 pp.)

Intended for language teachers, this volume condenses several years of strategy research by reviewing the background to learner training and examining the key ideas involved. It provides excellent summaries of awareness training theory and technique, as well as suggestions for classroom activities. It is an excellent resource for the strategies teacher-trainer.

4. *Learning Strategies in Second Language Acquisition,* by J. Michael O'Malley and Anna Uhl Chamot. New York: Cambridge University Press, 1990 (340 pp.)

This book is especially useful for learning strategy researchers. A complete review of the literature is provided, and the authors describe, classify, and explain the rationale behind systematic strategy applications. Various instructional models are presented, providing the reader with numerous examples of how learning strategy instruction is being conducted at the national and international levels. Theoretical and practical approaches to strategies instruction make this book an important source for both language teachers and language researchers.

5. *Language Learning Strategies: What Every Teacher Should Know,* by Rebecca L. Oxford. New York: Newbury House/Harper and Row, 1990 (342 pp.).

The most famous of the strategy books, Oxford's text is the source of the Strategy Inventory for Language Learning (SILL), which has been translated into several foreign languages and provides learners with a hands-on method to self-diagnose their language learning strategies. The book contains extensive examples of how the different strategies presented can be applied across language skills and tasks. This would be an excellent textbook for a teacher training seminar as it presents learning strategies instruction in a systematic, practical format, while also providing the theoretical foundations of strategy applications.

6. *Learner Awareness of Strategies,* by Rebecca L. Oxford and Betty Lou Leaver, eds., Cambridge, UK: Cambridge University Press, forthcoming.

This volume will encompass various aspects of learner awareness of strategies through strategy assessment techniques, as well as through direct instruction in strategy use. It incorporates the works of several of the most prominent researchers and teacher trainers in the field. The focus of the book is on the individual learner, combining both research- and teaching-oriented perspectives. Because of its vast applicability to a broad range of interests in learning strategies, this book will be an important resource for both teachers and researchers.

7. *Success with Foreign Languages: Seven Who Achieved It and What Worked for Them,* Earl W. Stevick. Cambridge, UK: Prentice-Hall International, 1989 (157 pp.).

Based on extensive interviews with "successful" learners, Stevick's book provides the reader with an authentic account of learner differences. Each of the seven learners details a unique approach to the learning process. The book summarizes each of the interviews by providing descriptions of the students' learning patterns and strategies, and suggests ways for both learners and teachers to facilitate the language learning process. Theoretical, personal, and practical approaches to language learning are the main ingredients of this one-of-a-kind book.

8. *Learner Strategies for Learner Autonomy: Planning and Implementing Learner Training for Language Learners,* Anita Wenden. Cambridge UK: Prentice-Hall International, 1991 (172 pp.).

This book provides teachers with a step-by-step approach to the systematic design of language learning curricula intended to encourage and facilitate learner autonomy. Beginning with theoretical foundations, Wenden provides the reader with practical, research-based suggestions on how to train learners to develop strategies in order to become more independent and effective learners. Especially helpful to teachers and teacher trainers are the several assessment tools presented throughout the book.

9. *Learner Strategies in Language Learning,* by Anita Wenden and Joan Rubin, eds. Cambridge, UK: Prentice-Hall International, 1987 (181 pp.).

Combining the work of several authors, Wenden and Rubin address three main areas in their book: the conceptual frameworks of learning strategies, research-based insights into strategies and strategies instruction, and ways to promote learner autonomy. The book provides an overall perspective of the issues related to studying learning strategies in the foreign language classroom. Many of the chapters have provided a starting point for those interested in strategies research. The book is especially useful as an introduction to the concept of learning strategies, as well as a resource for both language researchers and educators.

Students Labeled Learning Disabled and the Foreign Language Requirement: Background and Suggestions for Teachers

Ann Sax Mabbott
University of Minnesota

Introduction

In general, students labeled learning disabled (LD) have had serious problems with one or more aspects of language processing in their first language. It is understandable, then, that such students might encounter difficulties in a college foreign language (FL) class, which requires the student to process a second language. When teachers today sense that they are facing increasing numbers of students with serious language learning problems, they are probably right. Better remedial programs in elementary schools and a greater emphasis on the importance of a college education in the last twenty years have led more students labeled LD to seek higher education (Demuth and Smith 1987).

attending college for a long time. Dinklage (1971) first addressed the issue in a paper that related the stories of numerous Harvard undergraduates who were never able to obtain their degrees because they could not pass the FL requirement despite repeated, sincere attempts to do so. At that time, he made an impassioned plea to grant LD-labeled students waivers from the FL requirement so that their academic and professional careers would not be ruined because of an inability to perform well in a FL class.

In addition to students who have been officially labeled LD through psychological testing, there is another group of students who exhibit characteristics that make them very similar to students labeled LD, but who have never been tested or labeled. These students often have serious difficulties with some aspect of language processing, but may have been able to compensate for their weaknesses because of their intelligence and diligence (Dinklage 1971). Like the students who have been labeled LD, such students often find that their compensatory strategies start to break down when they are faced with the demands of a foreign language class.

There is evidence, however, that LD-labeled and comparable students can be successful language learners in an immersion setting (Bruck 1982; Curtain 1986; Mabbott 1994; Schultz 1991) or if they are given extra support in the classroom (Bilyeu 1982; Demuth and Smith 1987; McCabe 1985; Myer, Ganschow, Sparks, and Kenneweg 1989; Sheppard 1992; Sparks, Ganschow, Kenneweg, and Miller 1985). This would lead one to believe that it may be inappropriate or inadequate pedagogy, rather than student inability, that may be the cause of LD student failure in FL classes.

Although most teachers would sincerely like to help students with any kind of disability, it often is not clear to them what a learning disability is or how such a disability might affect performance in a second language class. Many do not know how a teacher can help such students in their efforts to learn a second language, or whether such students should be granted foreign language requirement exemptions, which are becoming increasingly popular.

This chapter provides some of the information that college teachers need to deal better with students who are labeled LD. It consists of: (1) a definition of LD and information about how one is tested for LD, (2) suggestions for improved pedagogical practice for LD-labeled students, and (3) arguments for alternatives to exemption from the foreign language requirement for students who are labeled LD. In the Appendix, this chapter also provides material that can be used during teacher education workshops or seminars that deal with the topic of assisting students who are labeled LD to learn a foreign language.

Definition of Learning Disability

It is extremely difficult to define what a learning disability is, and to determine who is actually afflicted with one. Learning disabilities have been viewed from four different perspectives: medical, psycho-educational, information-processing, and social (Wixson and Lipson 1984). Experts from each of the four groups define differently the etiology, basic issues, and directions for remediation. In addition, researchers from all perspectives agree that there is a great deal of variability among the subjects whom they define as LD, making it virtually impossible to arrive at a definition that is satisfactory to all. The resulting confusion has led to a legal definition that is exclusionary in nature. Public Law 94-142, which provides funding for remedial services for learning disabled children, defines a learning disability in the following way:

> a disorder in one or more of the basic psychological processes involved in understanding or in using language, spoken or written, which may manifest itself in the imperfect ability to listen, think, read, write, spell, or do mathematical calculations. The term does not include children who have learning problems which are primarily the result of visual, hearing, or motor handicaps, of mental retardation, emotional disturbance, or environmental, cultural or economic disadvantage. (*Federal Register* 1977, p. 65083)

Although this definition is imprecise, the FL educator should note the major issues that emerge in it. The first is that learning disabilities are usually related to difficulties in performing linguistic tasks. It is not surprising, then, that a learning disability may interfere with second language acquisition. Problems with linguistic tasks for students labeled LD can be exacerbated by or caused by attention deficits, memory dysfunction, sequential disorganization, and/or weaknesses of verbal cognition (Levine 1987).

The rest of the definition tells us what learning disabilities are not. Learning disabilities are not the result of any visual, hearing, or motor handicaps. Students labeled LD generally have normal vision, hearing, and mobility. The third is that, by definition, students labeled LD are not below average in intelligence, and may, in fact, have very high IQ's. It is very important that teachers not assume that students with learning disabilities are any less bright than other students in the class. Finally, one should also remember that the learning problems of students labeled LD are not caused by socioeconomic factors or by poor academic backgrounds.

The official definition of LD tells educators what does not cause LD, but it does not explain what the basic problem is that keeps relatively bright people from developing strong literacy skills. This issue is a complex one, but in recent years LD reading research has been able to isolate the apparent cause of the reading problems that also can have consequences for spelling, writing, and speaking. Research summarized by Liberman and Liberman (1990) and Stanovich (1991) indicates that the individual's degree of phonological awareness is the greatest predictor of reading problems associated with learning disabilities. They argue that the fundamental problem for people who cannot read is associating verbal labels with visual symbols; such individuals have a deficit in the ability to encode and retrieve phonological information. Reading-impaired children may also suffer from oral language deficits (poor vocabulary, problems with morphology or syntax, and problems with comprehension of syntactic structures), but many display normal oral language (Catts and Kamhi 1987). Non-LD learners may have problems that are very similar to ones that LD learners have; the difference is one of degree. To determine whether a weakness is severe enough to warrant LD labeling, a student must undergo extensive testing.

Testing for Learning Disabilities

Testing for LD is a long, difficult, and expensive process. In the elementary and secondary schools, testing is paid for by the school district if a professional team in the school determines that testing is warranted by a child's performance in school. Some universities and colleges provide testing for students; others do not, and the prohibitive cost of testing keeps some students from seeking it.

There is no single test that indicates the presence of a learning disability. Instead, a wide battery of tests is given, including an IQ test (often the WISC-R) and achievement measures such as the Woodcock-Johnson Psychoeducational Battery (W-J) and the Woodcock Language Proficiency Battery (WLPB). Diagnosis is made on the basis of discrepancies between IQ and achievement measures. Sometimes discrepancies between subtests of either the IQ test or the achievement test are used as a basis of diagnosis. If the discrepancy is large enough, students are labeled as having a learning disability because they are not performing up to their potential. Such students generally have problems processing either written language or oral language or both. (See Mercer 1987, pp. 119–151, for a review of assessment issues.)

It must be noted here that students are sometimes inappropriately labeled LD, either consciously or unconsciously by psychologists. In order to get federal funding for special education in the public schools, children sometimes must be labeled LD rather than just as slow learners or socioeconomically deprived. As a result, school psychologists will stretch definitions in order to provide extra help to children who they feel need it. In other cases, the inappropriate use of testing instruments with students whose first language is not English leads them to be labeled LD. One study (Ortiz and Yates 1983) indicates that Hispanics are overrepresented in LD classes by 300 percent as a result of the misuse of such instruments. Another study by Miramontes (1987) of oral reading miscues of Hispanic students with a LD found that many of the labeled students (on the basis of their inability to read in English) could read in Spanish and therefore were not LD at all. Finally, there is currently much anecdotal evidence among college foreign language professionals about how students who do not care to learn a foreign language can "buy" testing and evaluation from private psychologists stating that they are incapable of learning a second language. Such evaluations allow them to be excused from the second language requirement.

The serious problems associated with labeling suggests that educators could better spend their time looking for appropriate pedagogy for all students who are struggling with the foreign language requirement, rather than worrying about who is correctly or incorrectly labeled. Since so many students have questionable labeling attached to them, and since there may be many others who may legitimately have a LD but have never been tested, it could be that alternative methods of teaching and assessment rather than exemptions from the foreign language requirement may be the better way to help students who are struggling in their attempts to learn a second language. The exemption issue will be discussed in greater depth later in this chapter, after a discussion of the consequences of LD in the FL learning setting.

Learning Disabilities and Foreign Language

It has been assumed for quite some time (Levine 1987) that students who have learning difficulties with spelling, reading, writing, or listening comprehension in their first language will encounter similar difficulties when studying a second language. Several researchers indicate that this is the case. Work done by Gajar (1987) and Sparks, Ganschow, and Pohlman (1989) indicates that college students who have trouble learning a second language may exhibit three types of linguistic coding deficits in their first language: phonological, syntactic, and semantic. In subsequent work, Sparks, Ganschow, Javorsky, Pohlman, and Patton (1992) and Sparks and Ganschow (1993a) have shown that, as in findings from LD reading research, a weakness in phonological processing is the major problem underlying both first language reading disabilities and problems with foreign language learning. Sparks and Ganschow (1991) have introduced the term *linguistic coding deficit hypothesis* to explain this situation. The linguistic coding deficit hypothesis states that difficulty with one's first language, rather than any affective factors, is a major factor in foreign language learning problems. According to these researchers, poor performance resulting from low aptitude may result in negative affective responses, such as anxiety. Thus, contrary to much reported research on anxiety in the FL class (Horwitz, Horwitz, and Cope 1986; MacIntyre and Gardner 1991; Madsen, Brown, and Jones 1991), their work postulates that anxiety may be the result of poor performance in the foreign language class rather than a cause of poor performance (Ganschow et al. 1994; Sparks and Ganschow 1993b). Although Sparks and Ganschow may be overstating the case, they are bringing up issues that have not been considered adequately in FL anxiety research.

Use of the *Modern Language Aptitude Test* to Predict Foreign Language Learning Problems

If one accepts the existence of a *linguistic coding deficit*, it is natural that one would want a test to distinguish students who have a linguistic coding deficit from those who do not. In addition to a battery of English language tests, Sparks et al. (1992) suggest using Carroll and Sapon's (1959) Modern Language Aptitude Test (MLAT). This test includes a measure of phonological processing ability, and, according to Sparks et al. (1992), can help predict who would have problems learning a foreign language so that teachers can be notified of potential problems. Such notification would enable teachers to take steps to help remediate FL learning problems in a timely fashion, before students are completely lost.

It is not clear, however, whether the MLAT is an appropriate measure of language aptitude when one considers the communicatively oriented goals of foreign language education and the conceptual framework with which progressive foreign language educators tend to view second language acquisition today (see Ellis 1985 and Larsen-Freeman and Long 1991 for more information on second language acquisition theory). A brief discussion of the problematic nature of this test is warranted here, because almost all of the research in this area to date involves using the MLAT (see all Sparks and Ganschow references in the bibliography).

The MLAT has been proven to be a reliable measurement tool for the federal government to use to distinguish people with a high potential for rapidly learning a language for intelligence-gathering purposes (Parry and Stansfield 1990). However, the fact that FL educators rarely use the MLAT for diagnostic purposes indicates that they may not feel it is appropriate for the educational context. The MLAT was developed at a time when FL educators were attempting to understand the language learning process according to the positivist paradigms of the social sciences. Such a view of language learning lacks any social, cultural, political, or historical context, and reduces language to a system for transmitting messages rather than the exchange of significant ideas that shape the world as we understand it (Pennycook 1990). Instead of seeking an elite group of rapid language learners (which is the government's purpose), most FL educators see their role as making second language learning universally available. They want to empower students by facilitating an expansion of their ability to communicate, to construct personal meaning, and to interact reflectively. Instead of considering second language learning a behavioral science, educators see FL acquisition as a constructivist-oriented field relating to communication within a cultural framework.

Although Ehrman (in this volume) confirms that the MLAT continues to be a good predictor of performance at the Foreign Service Institute, other research indicates that the MLAT may be a poor predictor of success in college foreign language classes. When Goodman, Freed, and McManus (1990) administered the MLAT to a large number (586) of students at the University of Pennsylvania, they found that there was very little relationship between the MLAT and grades in FL classes as determined by regression and ANOVA analyses. When discrepancies between SAT scores and the MLAT were computed, they also turned out not to distinguish good from poor students. It is tempting to use a test like the MLAT as an easy solution for determining who will not be able to learn a second language, but, as this study shows, the results may not be valid. Even Carroll and Sapon (1959) argue, in the manual for the MLAT, that the best predictor of student success in foreign language is the actual opportunity for the student to learn. Ehrman (in this volume) also indicates that the best predictor of foreign language learning success is previous experience learning foreign languages. Rather than trying to find a way to predict failure, a better course of action would be to find ways to help all students labeled LD in their attempts to learn a FL, so that they can obtain the experience that is essential for subsequent success. Suggestions for better pedagogy will follow a discussion of what currently is typical of the LD-labeled students' experiences with FL.

332 *Faces in a Crowd: The Individual Learner in Multisection Courses*

What Happens to LD-Labeled Students in High School and College FL Classes?

Ehrman (in this volume) argues that the best predictor of FL learning success is previous experience with FL. It is precisely a lack of experience that so often characterizes the situation of LD-labeled students in college. Both Levine (1987) and Bruck (1982) have indicated that LD-labeled students, just like all other students, are most likely to be successful language learners if they start very young. Beginning FL study in the elementary school is not typical in the United States, however, so this discussion will start with an examination of what happens in junior and senior high schools.

Although the situation is changing, many LD-labeled students never take a foreign language in junior and senior high school. At the junior high level, students are often prohibited from taking a foreign language unless they get a recommendation from an English teacher or a counselor. Since these students often have weak literacy skills, they are not likely to be recommended for FL study. In high school, they are often counseled out of FL because it is felt that it will be difficult for them (for a case study describing such a situation, see Mabbott 1994).

In other situations, the LD-labeled students may attempt FL and fail, or go "language shopping," where they desperately try different languages hoping that they can find one in which they can be successful. Sometime these students find sympathetic teachers who help them succeed. Generally, these students do not go abroad on exchange or travel programs that would support their language study, because it is students with stronger academic records who are chosen for such programs.

When these students go to college, their experiences are similar. Some find sympathetic instructors who help them, but many fail, go "language shopping," do not go abroad, and/or finally take majors that do not have FL requirements. The problems that they have with their learning disability, of course, are exacerbated by the fact that they are competing in classes with students who have a background in studying FL. Most students in a beginning-level college Spanish class, for example, have either studied Spanish or some other FL before. Therefore, LD-labeled students in effect have a double handicap: their LD and a lack of background knowledge about learning an FL. Understandably, such students are often very frustrated in their attempts to succeed in the FL language and thus they seek exemptions from the foreign language requirement. Exemptions, however, do not solve the problem of how to help LD-labeled students learn an FL.

It would be more productive to review the literature that describes successful FL acquisition and instruction on the part of LD-labeled students and to draw conclusions for sound pedagogical practice from that literature.

Successful Language Acquisition on the Part of LD-Labeled Students: Immersion Settings

Just as is the case for non-LD students, the best way for LD students to learn a second language is to start as early as possible (Levine 1987), preferably in an immersion setting (Curtain 1986). Professionals in the field of FL education are well aware of the numerous multilingual societies on the earth where everyone, unless he or she suffers from some extremely serious physical or psychological handicap, *speaks* more than one language. The immersion setting that a multilingual society provides appears to be one where an LD is little impediment to second language learning, when one is considering basic oral communication skills.

There is also evidence that LD-labeled students can learn an FL when they are purposely placed in an immersion setting. In the Canadian French immersion school context, Bruck (1982) completed a carefully designed study that showed that children labeled LD in French immersion schools made just as much cognitive and linguistic progress in their academic subjects as their peers, also labeled LD, who were taught in their first language. At the same time, they were learning a second language, albeit not as quickly as their non-LD classmates. Mabbott (1994) has shown that older students (high school and college) labeled LD also manage to learn a foreign language when they are given an opportunity to learn that language in an immersion setting. For instance, Colby College in Maine has used its semester-long language programs abroad (in Cuernavaca, Mexico, and Lübeck, Germany) as an option for LD students who were struggling with the foreign language requirement. Students who first failed or did poorly in the classroom have been quite successful in those immersion settings, and some have even come back to campus to major in an FL (J. Olivares, personal communication 1994).

Unfortunately, these cases are not typical of LD-labeled students' experiences. Due to a predominant view that FL is not a part of the basic, essential curriculum in the United States, educators and parents have not put forth a great deal of effort to provide immersion experiences for students, and especially not for students who have academic weaknesses. This practice stands in sharp contrast to Western Europe, where student exchanges between countries with different languages are the norm and are funded by the governments. If FL educators in the United States could convince educational policy makers and parents that FL study should be made available to more students, and not just to an elite, strides could be made in providing more immersion experiences for all students. Such immersion experiences appear to be the best way to promote FL acquisition among students who are labeled LD. They do not guarantee, of course, that the students will become fluent in all four skill areas (reading, writing, listening, and speaking). Students will continue to be weak in areas where they are weak in their first language, but immersion experiences have enabled many students who failed in FL language classes to develop skills that enable them to function in the FL (see Mabbott 1994, for case studies of such students).

Foreign Language Classroom Instruction

Although LD-labeled students seem to succeed with FL acquisition in immersion settings, they tend to do less well in the classroom. Since FL acquisition seems to be possible in immersion settings, it appears to be that classroom practice is not conducive to learning for these students. The difference between the immersion setting and the typical classroom setting is that acquiring the language in the immersion setting relies largely on oral language presented in a rich context, while classroom learning often relies more on printed text that is often out of context. Even when classroom instruction is oral and contextualized, assessment remains largely written and decontextualized. It could be that what is so difficult for LD-labeled students is the way that foreign languages are taught and tested in the classroom rather than the task of actual acquisition.

It is not surprising that LD-labeled students would have problems in the FL class. By definition, such students have had trouble with literacy skills. Although they may be doing well in other content area classes, it is because they have learned appropriate compensatory strategies, either on their own or with the help of their teachers. Among the compensatory strategies that LD-labeled students commonly take advantage of are studying longer than other students, getting help from tutors, using computer spell and grammar checks, having a friend or parent proofread papers, taking extra time to complete assignments and tests, completing alternative assignments, and obtaining information through conversation or videotapes rather than from books. If those compensatory strategies are not allowed in the FL class, students will do poorly in their areas of weakness, and may fail the class. Intensive studying on the part of the student may help, but it must be remembered that no amount of studying is going to turn a poor speller in English, for example, into a good one in the FL.

FL teachers need to consider what compensatory strategies they deem appropriate for their classes. Here are some strategies they can consider. (1) Allow students extra time to complete coursework. For students with mild disabilities, extra time for tests and assignments is often the only help that they need. Students with more severe disabilities may choose a slower-paced class or choose to audit a course before taking it for credit. (2) Provide reading texts on tape. Listening to a tape while reading can be invaluable for students with decoding and/or reading comprehension problems. (3) Teach students how to use schemata-related reading activities to help reading comprehension (Melendez 1985). (4) Use a process approach to writing where students do multiple drafts while getting feedback on their writing from their peers and their teacher (Dvorak 1986). Process writing is invaluable to students who have problems with syntax and spelling. (5) Adopt an outcome-based approach to FL education where students can retake tests on which they do poorly. (6) Allow students to use reference materials during tests. The University of Minnesota German language program routinely allows first and second year students to use grammar charts and verb lists during written tests. Since the students are required to do large amounts of writing, they gradually internalize the rules and forms and gradually become less reliant on the reference materials. (7) Provide alternative assignments. If a student performs well orally but has trouble with spelling, for example, the teacher may allow the student to complete extra oral assignments to compensate for poor grades on tests which require accurate spelling. (8) Weigh grades differently so that a student's strengths may count more heavily than his/her weaknesses.

In addition to allowing compensatory strategies, some teachers have modified their practice to help LD-labeled students succeed. Some teachers attempt to mimic immersion settings in the classroom as much as possible. They have found that students who may have trouble with certain aspects of language learning (e.g., learning the rules about language) or with reading may be able to acquire a second language orally if it is presented in a context that allows ample negotiated interaction. Likewise, students who have trouble processing oral language will be aided by a context-rich environment that provides many visual clues to support the oral message. McCabe (1985), working in a junior high setting, suggests that LD-labeled students can be successful if there is an emphasis on conversation rather than on the rules of grammar. She also stresses a well-organized classroom routine and frequent repetition. Bilyeu (1982), working in higher education, supports McCabe's suggestions, but also stresses the need for a context-rich environment with a variety of learning modalities and the use of repeated experiences with similar, yet varied materials. She feels that a focus on content and communication is necessary, and also stresses that the teaching techniques that helped her LD-labeled students the most were also the most effective for all of her students.

Other instructors and researchers have found that LD-labeled students benefit from linguistics instruction, slower paced classes, and extensive tutoring. Demuth and Smith (1987) conducted a study where students were given specially tailored linguistics lessons designed to familiarize them with how languages in general, and the target language in particular, work. The researchers show that the students who underwent their particular treatment improved their scores on the MLAT. Myer, Ganschow, Sparks, and Kenneweg (1989) and Sparks, Ganschow, Kenneweg, and Miller (1991) promote using an Orton-Gillingham multisensory approach (Orton 1966) to teach phonetic features of the FL in the foreign language class. Miller (1985) suggests using mentor students from more advanced classes as tutors. Sheppard (1992) developed a special Spanish course for LD-labeled students that had reduced pace and content and also used tutors.

According to published teacher experience, successful remediation has gone in two separate directions that should probably be merged. One is an emphasis on the phonological and syntactic aspects of language (Demuth and Smith 1987; Myer et al. 1989), areas where students labeled LD are often weak. The other is an emphasis on context-rich communicative aspects of language that will give students multiple paths toward comprehension and learning (Bilyeu 1982; McCabe 1985; Sheppard 1992). The former approach may be quite useful as a means of improving limited production aspects of second language learning, such as spelling, decoding, and grammar, aspects that are often the basis for assessment in introductory language courses, but it addresses only a very small part of language learning. These productive aspects need to be connected to the expressive functions of language that Bilyeu, McCabe, and Sheppard address. It seems, then, that a context-rich class with the support of compensatory strategies and intensive tutoring on the phonological and syntactic aspects of language might be the most successful teaching approach for students labeled LD.

One last consideration is the setting in which such instruction should take place. As mentioned earlier, it is clear that the immersion setting, with instructional support, is the most likely to lead to successful FL acquisition. If that is not an option for students, one should consider whether small classes designed just for students with language learning problems may be a better option than mainstreaming students and giving them extra support. One can make arguments for both approaches. Small, slower paced classes may provide badly needed affective support and individual attention for students who have had poor language learning experiences in the past. On the other hand, a regular class may provide a student with more competent interlocutors, and thus a richer language learning environment. In the workshop section of this chapter (see the Appendix), more specific suggestions for classroom instruction are given.

Alternative Languages

Along with seeking extra help with their FL learning, students can also consider taking alternatives to the modern languages that they usually choose to fulfill their FL requirement. Some students who have problems with aural processing and struggle with conversational approaches to language instruction can do well in ancient language classes. Latin, ancient Greek, or biblical Hebrew, which do not require oral/aural skills, may be good options for them. Students who have good oral/aural skills but have trouble with written texts may find studying Native American languages, which generally rely on oral/aural tradition more than on written texts, a satisfactory option.

American Sign Language (ASL), commonly used by the deaf community in the United States and some other countries, may also be a good option for some LD-labeled students. ASL has been recognized by many colleges and universities as a legitimate second language, representing a culture that differs from mainstream American culture. Students at the University of Minnesota, for example, may choose to study ASL to fulfill their foreign language requirement. It stands to reason that students who have serious problems with decoding printed text or with phonological processing may not be handicapped seriously in the study of ASL, which requires kinesthetic memory.

However, it would not be pedagogically sound to coerce students with learning problems to choose ancient languages, Native American languages, or ASL as easier routes toward fulfilling the foreign language requirement. These alternatives may not fulfill students' personal and career goals. These courses should also not become a dumping ground for students with language learning problems. Accommodations to ensure the possibility of studying any language that the LD-labeled student chooses is the ideal form of support, and it is a responsibility that all FL teachers should share.

Exemptions from the Foreign Language Requirement

Since Dinklage made his impassioned plea in 1971 to help college students struggling with FL requirements by providing them waivers, exemptions from the FL requirement have become more common. Most colleges and universities have some kind of exemption policy today (Ganschow, Sparks, Myer, and Roeger 1989). Freed (1987) summarizes the proceedings of the 1985 Modern Language Association on the topic and explains in detail the policy at the University of Pennsylvania. Some schools grant waivers to any student who can produce appropriate documentation from a psychologist, while others require that the students also make a concerted effort with FL before a waiver will be granted. Most institutions require a substitution of the foreign language requirement by culture or linguistics courses for students who are granted a waiver.

One issue that seems to receive no attention in this discussion is that exemptions may have the effect of unofficially creating policies that run counter to the intention of public law. Section 504 of the Federal Rehabilitation Act of 1973 states that no otherwise qualified handicapped individuals (including those labeled LD) shall be excluded from participation in any program receiving federal funding. Most colleges and universities receive federal funding of some kind. When administrators encourage college students to take an exemption from the foreign language requirement, they are in effect denying those students the opportunity for an equal education. When the advisors of high school students labeled LD discourage them from taking a foreign language in high school, they make it especially difficult for those students to start a language in college because they compete in classes with students who have a background in FL learning that they never had. The LD-labeled college students also must deal with teachers who assume that all students have studied some foreign language in high school. This policy of exemptions further makes it possible for foreign language departments and teachers not to address the needs of those students who truly want to learn a foreign language for personal reasons or need to learn a foreign language for career purposes. In effect, it cuts the students off from many jobs that require some foreign language proficiency, and, as Fisher (1986) mentions, excludes students from social acceptance by educated people. As Levine (1987) and Dinklage (1971) point out, no one's academic career should be ruined because of an inability to learn a foreign language; but at the same time, no one's personal or career aspirations should be thwarted because of a lack of opportunity to study a foreign language. If educators are to serve their students well, they must find ways to help all students who are interested to learn a second language rather than abandon them.

One consideration that has not been examined in any depth by American FL educators is how other countries deal with FL requirements for students who are labeled LD. Learning disabilities are not an exclusively American phenomenon. A cross-cultural study done by Stevenson, Stigler, Lucker, and Lee (1982) established that reading disability, for example, exists among Japanese and Chinese children in approximately the same proportions as it does among children in the United States. A perusal of second language education literature in Germany indicates that foreign language teachers in Germany have also recognized that LD-labeled students have problems in FL classes (Jung 1981, 1985; Reisner 1978).

The difference between Germany and the United States, however, is that granting exemptions from the FL requirement is not even a consideration in Germany. All German students must pass a foreign language requirement to graduate from high school because FL proficiency is considered essential for the economic and intellectual well-being of all citizens. Similarly, a doctoral dissertation written by Rodriguez de Vidal (1983) reveals that some teachers in Puerto Rico are also trying to find ways to teach LD-labeled students English as a second language because of the economic necessity for Puerto Rican citizens to be able to speak English.

Although FL proficiency does not seem to be as immediately necessary for English-speaking North Americans as it does for Germans and Puerto Ricans, most FL educators agree that proficiency in a second language is an essential trait of an educated citizen. It also seems to be the only college requirement caught in this debate. No one is considering waiving college English requirements because of the challenges they provide poor readers. Math is another area that is often difficult for students labeled LD, but exemptions from math requirements at colleges that have them are generally not considered (S. Zurek, personal communication 1994). Instead, colleges find ways to teach math to students with special needs. It may be that it is in the best interest of some students that they be

given a waiver for the FL requirement, but it surely would be more beneficial to most if FL educators would try to accommodate their disabilities
and help them to progress toward proficiency in a FL of their choice as
much as they can.

Conclusion

The issue of FL learning on the part of LD-labeled students in the college
classroom is one that is going to increase in prominence. Unmotivated students, whether they have a disability or not, will try increasingly to convince school officials that they are incapable of learning an FL and petition
for exemptions. Motivated students, on the other hand, who truly have an
LD but still want to learn an FL for personal or professional purposes, will
demand better services.

The best solution for both situations is to have the expectation that all
students can learn an FL. One look at other cultures shows that societies
that have the expectation that all people will learn more than one language
are largely successful in achieving that goal. Since FL learning for virtually
everyone is not an impossible goal, LD support services and FL departments should move away from the questionable practice of testing for FL
learning disabilities to grant exemptions and move toward pedagogical
practice that will help all students.

First and foremost, it would behoove all foreign language professionals
to push for early language learning for all students. Since past experience
with FL is the greatest predictor of success for adult FL learners, such a policy would probably help LD-labeled students more than anything else.
That will not happen right away, so other forms of support need to be
found in the meantime. For students who start their FL learning later in
life, the most successful setting for that learning is immersion with instructional support. Education professionals need to encourage LD-labeled students to take part in such programs rather than to discourage them, as is
currently often the practice. Finally, teachers need to realize that it may not
be the actual acquisition that is difficult for LD-labeled students, but rather
some of the specific tasks that students are faced with in FL classes. If teachers take the broader view of FL communication and see it more as a way to
expand students' ability to communicate, to construct personal meaning,
and to interact reflectively, and less as correct grammar and spelling, then
they will not find it difficult to incorporate appropriate pedagogical support
in their instruction. A context-rich learning environment, extensive tutoring, and allowing compensatory strategies will help the goal of true com-

munication in the FL. These strategies do not guarantee perfect, or even good, acquisition of all communicative skills, but with a change in attitude and goals, an imperfect acquisition of skills, or a slower acquisition of skills will no longer be an impediment to continued FL learning.

Works Cited

Bilyeu, E. E. 1982. Practice Makes Closer to Perfect: Alternative Techniques for Teaching Foreign Languages to Learning Disabled Students in the University. Eric Doc. No. ED234558.

Brod, Richard, and M. Lapointe. 1989. The MLA Survey of Foreign Languages and Degree Requirements 1987–88. *ADFL Bulletin* 20: 17–41.

Bruck, Margaret. 1982. Language Impaired Children's Performance in an Additive Bilingual Education Program. *Applied Psycholinguistics* 3: 45–60.

Carroll, John. B., and Stanley M. Sapon. 1959. *Modern Language Aptitude Test.* Chicago: Psychological Corporation/Harcourt Brace Jovanovich.

Catts, Hugh W., and Alan G. Kamhi. 1987. Relationship between Reading and Language Disorders: Implications for the Speech-Language Pathologist. *Seminars in Speech and Language* 8: 377–92.

Curtain, Helena A. 1986. The Immersion Approach: Principle and Practice. Eric Doc. No. ED267626.

Demuth, Katherine A., and Nathaniel B. Smith. 1987. The Foreign Language Requirement: An Alternative Program. *Foreign Language Annals* 20: 67–77.

Dinklage, Kenneth T. 1971. Inability to Learn a Foreign Language . In *Emotional Problems of the Student,* edited by G. B. Blaine, 185–205. New York: Appleton-Century-Crofts.

Dvorak, Trish. 1986. Writing in the Foreign Language. In *Northeast Conference on the Teaching of Foreign Languages: Listening, Reading, Writing. Analysis and Application,* edited by Barbara H. Wing, 145–67. Middlebury, VT: Northeast Conference Reports.

Ellis, Rod. 1985. *Understanding Second Language Acquisition.* Oxford: Oxford University Press.

Fisher, Elissa. 1986. Learning Disability Specialist Looks at Foreign Language Instruction. *Hill Top Spectrum* 4: 1–3.

Freed, Barbara F. 1987. Exemptions from the Foreign Language Requirement: A Review of Recent Literature, Problems, and Policy. *ADFL Bulletin* 18: 13–17.

Gajar, Anna H. 1987. Foreign Language Learning Disability: The Identification of Predictive and Diagnostic Variables. *Journal of Learning Disabilities* 20: 327–30.

Ganschow, Leonore, and Richard Sparks. 1986. Learning Disabilities and Foreign-Language Difficulties: Deficit in Listening Skills? *Journal of Reading, Writing and Learning Disabilities International* 2: 305–19.

———. 1987. The Foreign Language Requirement. *Learning Disabilities* 2: 116–23.

Ganschow, Leonore, Richard Sparks, Reed Anderson, James Javorsky, Sue Skinner, and John Patton. 1994. Differences in Language Performance among High, Average, and Low-Anxious College Foreign Language Learners. *Modern Language Journal* 78: 41–55.

Ganschow, Leonore, Richard Sparks, James Javorsky, Jane Pohlman, and Angela Bishop-Marbury. 1991. Identifying Native Language Deficits among Foreign Language Learners in College: A "Foreign" Language Learning Disability? *Journal of Learning Disabilities* 24: 530–41.

Ganschow, Leonore, Richard Sparks, Bettye Myer, and Kathy Roeger. 1989. Foreign Language Policies and Procedures for Students with Specific Learning Disabilities. *Learning Disabilities Focus* 5: 50–58.

Goodman, John F., Barbara Freed, and William J. McManus. 1990. Determining Exemptions from Foreign Language Requirements: Use of the Modern Language Aptitude Test. *Contemporary Educational Psychology* 15: 131–41.

Hewins, Catherine P. 1986. Writing in a Foreign Language: Motivation and the Process Approach. *Foreign Language Annals* 19: 219–23.

Horwitz, Elaine, Michael B. Horwitz, and Joanne Cope. 1986. Foreign Language Classroom Anxiety. *Modern Language Journal* 70: 125–32.

Jung, Udo. 1981. The Grammatical Abilities of German Dyslexics in English as a Foreign Language. *System* 9: 223–33.

———. 1985. Contrastive Patholinguistics: The Acquisition of English Grammatical Morphemes by German Dyslexics in a Foreign-Language Teaching Context. In *Papers and Studies in Contrastive Linguistics* 19, edited by Jacek Fisiak, 5–27. Arlington, VA: Center for Applied Linguistics.

Larsen-Freeman, Diane, and Michael H. Long. 1991. *An Introduction to Second Language Acquisition Research.* London: Longman.

Levine, Melvin. 1987. *Developmental Variation and Learning Disorders.* Cambridge, MA: Educators Publishing Service, Inc.

Liberman, I. Y., and A. M. Liberman. 1990. Whole Language vs. Code Emphasis: Underlying Assumptions and Their Implications for Reading Instruction. *Annals of Dyslexia* 40: 51–76.

Mabbott, Ann Sax. 1994. An Exploration of Reading Comprehension, Oral Reading Errors, and Written Errors between English and a Second Language by Subjects Who Are Labeled Learning Disabled. *Foreign Language Annals* 27: 293–324.

McCabe, Lenora. 1985. Teaching the Slower Student. *New York State Association of Foreign Language Teachers Bulletin* 36: 5–6.

MacIntyre, Peter, and Robert C. Gardner. 1991. Investigating Language Class Anxiety Using the Focused Essay Technique. *Modern Language Journal* 75: 296–304.

Madsen, Harold, Bruce Brown, and Randall Jones. 1991. Evaluation Attitudes toward Second-Language Tests. In *Language Anxiety: From Theory and Research to Classroom Implications,* edited by Elaine K. Horwitz and Dolly J. Young, 65–68. Englewood Cliffs, NJ: Prentice-Hall.

Melendez, E. Jane. 1985. Applying Schema Theory to Foreign Language Reading. *Foreign Language Annals 18*: 399–403.

Mercer, Cecil D. 1987. *Students with Learning Disabilities.* Columbus, OH: Merrill.

Miller, Jeff. 1985. Foreign Language for Special Education Students: A Special Education Teacher Speaks. *New York State Association of Foreign Language Teachers Bulletin* 36: 9–10.

Miramontes, Ofelia 1987. Oral Miscues of Hispanic Students: Implications for Assessment of Learning Disabilities. *Journal of Learning Disabilities* 20: 627–32.

Myer, Bettye, Leonore Ganschow, Richard Sparks, and Silvia Kenneweg. 1989. Cracking the Code: Helping Students with Specific Learning Disabilities. In *Defining the Essentials for the Foreign Language Classroom,* edited by D. McAlpine, 112–20. Lincolnwood, IL: National Textbook.

Ortiz, A. A., and J. R. Yates. 1983. Incidence of Exceptionality among Hispanics: Implications for Manpower Planning. *NABE Journal* 7: 41–54.

Orton, June L. 1966. The Orton-Gillingham Approach. In *The Disabled Reader*, edited by J. Money, 119–46. Baltimore: Johns Hopkins University Press.

Parry, Thomas S., and Charles W. Stansfield. 1990. *Language Aptitude Reconsidered.* Englewood Cliffs, NJ: Prentice-Hall/Regents.

Pennycook, Alastair. 1990. Critical Pedagogy and Second Language Education. *System* 18: 303–14.

Reisner, Helmut. 1978. Englischunterricht und Leserechtschreibschwäche [English instruction and dyslexia]. *Der Fremdsprachliche Unterricht* 12: 49–60.

Rodriguez de Vidal, Eloina. 1983. Evaluation of the Appropriateness of a Developmental Conception and Sequence in Teaching Some English Grammar Structures to Spanish Speaking Children with Learning Disabilities. Ph.D. diss., University of Wisconsin at Madison.

Schultz, Renate A. 1991. Second Language Acquisition Theories and Teaching Practice: How Do They Fit? *Modern Language Journal* 75: 17–25.

Sheppard, Marie. 1992. *Pilot Alternative Spanish Course.* Paper presented at the Conference on Learning Disabilities at the College Level, University of Colorado, Boulder.

Sparks, Richard, and Leonore Ganschow. 1991. Foreign Language Learning Difficulties: Affective or Native Language Aptitude Differences? *Modern Language Journal* 75: 3–16.

———. 1993a. Searching for the Cognitive Locus of Foreign Language Learning Difficulties: Linking First and Second Language Learning. *Modern Language Journal* 77: 289–302.

———. 1993b. Perceptions of Low and High Risk Students and Students with Learning Disabilities about High School Foreign Language Courses. *Foreign Language Annals* 26: 491–510.

———. 1993c. Identifying and Instructing At-Risk Foreign Language Learners in College. In *The Dynamics of Language Program Direction*, edited by David P. Benseler, 173–99. Boston: Heinle & Heinle.

Sparks, Richard, Leonore Ganschow, James Javorsky, Jane Pohlman, and John Patton. 1992. Test Comparisons among Students Identified as

Low-Risk, High-Risk, and LD in High School Foreign Language Courses. *Modern Language Journal* 76: 142–59.

Sparks, Richard, Leonore Ganschow, Silvia Kenneweg, and Karen Miller. 1991. Use of an Orton-Gillingham Approach to Teach a Foreign Language to Dyslexic/Learning-Disabled Students: Explicit Teaching of Phonology in a Second Language. *Annals of Dyslexia* 41: 96–118.

Sparks, Richard, Leonore Ganschow, and Jane Pohlman. 1989. Linguistic Coding Deficits in Foreign Language Learners. *Annals of Dyslexia* 38: 179–95.

Stanovich, Keith E. 1991. Cognitive Science Meets Beginning Reading. *Psychological Science* 2: 70–81.

Stevenson, Harold W., James W. Stigler, G. William Lucker, and Shin-ying Lee. 1982. Reading Disabilities: The Case of Chinese, Japanese, and English. *Child Development* 53: 1164–81.

U.S. Office of Education. 1977. Assistance to States for Education of Handicapped Children: Procedures for Evaluating Specific Learning Disabilities. *Federal Register* 42: 65082-85. Washington, DC: U.S. Government Printing Office.

Weschler Intelligence Scale for Children, Revised. Weschler, D. 1974. *Weschler Intelligence Scale, Revised.* New York: Psychological Corporation.

Wixson, Karen, and Marjorie Youmans Lipson. 1984. Perspectives on Reading Disability Research. *Handbook of Reading Research* 2: 539–70.

Appendix

Workshop on Learning Disabilities for Foreign Language Teachers

In this section I give, in outline form, some of the information that I present at workshops on FL instruction for students labeled LD. After my presentation, I divide the teachers into groups to work on scenarios depicting typical students with language learning problems. After discussing a scenario as a small group, each group should present their ideas for appropriate remediation to the larger group. The scenarios are found at the end of this Appendix.

III. Definition of Learning Disability:

    A. "Specific Learning Disability" means a disorder in one or more of the basic psychological processes involved in understanding or in using language, spoken or written, which may manifest itself in an imperfect ability to listen, speak, read, write, spell, or to do mathematical calculations. The term includes such conditions as perceptual handicaps, brain injury, minimal brain dysfunction, dyslexia, and developmental aphasia. The term does not include children who have learning problems that are primarily the result of visual, hearing, or motor handicaps, of mental retardation, or emotional disturbance or of environmental, cultural, or economic disadvantage (*Federal Register*).

B. Associated Terms
  1. *Dyslexia:* severe difficulty in learning to read
  2. *Attention deficit disorder:* inability to pay attention for more than a very short period of time
  3. *Hyperactivity:* excess of nonpurposeful motor activity, trouble sitting still

C. Exclusions: academic problems that are not learning disabilities
  1. Mentally retarded
  2. Emotionally behaviorally disturbed
  3. Visually or hearing impaired
  4. Culturally or economically disadvantaged

D. Diagnosis: through psychological testing which finds a discrepancy between intelligence and achievement. There is no test for a FL disability, but learning disabilities in the first language are likely to have consequences for FL.

II. The Nature of Learning Disabilities: problems with auditory processing of language, visual processing of language, or both, often caused by difficulty in associating verbal labels with visual symbols or difficulty discriminating sounds. Some students who have never been tested or labeled may exhibit the same characteristics. Non-LD students can exhibit similar problems, but generally not to the same degree.

A. Typical Visual Processing Problems
  1. Can't distinguish "b" from "d," "was" from "saw"
  2. Sees first letter of word and just the configuration of the rest
  3. Sees one letter at a time
  4. Spacing appears different and punctuation isn't seen

     5. Longer words can be easier than shorter ones (recognized by shape)

     6. Concrete objects like "computer" are easier than filler words like "the," "their," "each," "other"

     7. Short-term memory—looks up phone number and forgets it when dialing

     8. Figure/ ground difficulties (confused by too much visual stimuli; doesn't know what to look at on a crowded blackboard, for example)

B. Typical Auditory Processing Problems

     1. Can't distinguish "glue" from "glow"

     2. Can't tell where one word ends and the next starts

     3. Can't focus on one auditory signal in a noisy room

     4. Hears narrative and mixes up sequence

     5. Forgets oral directions

C. Other Related Problems

     1. Abstraction: trouble understanding abstract ideas

     2. Long-term memory: studies and forgets by next day

     3. Difficulty responding even when she or he knows the answer—can't verbalize what she or he knows

     4. Poor handwriting—some handwriting problems are genuine, sometimes students write poorly on purpose to hide inability to spell

     (Adapted from information presented at the 1991 Upper Midwest Branch of the Orton Dyslexia Society Spring Conference)

III. What Happens to LD Students in High School and College FL Classes?

A. High School

     1. Often advised not to take foreign language

     2. Fail

     3. Go "language shopping"—try one language after another in a desperate attempt to find one in which he or she can be successful

     4. Sympathetic teacher helps them

     5. Generally do not go abroad

B. College
1. Fail
2. Take majors that do not require FL
3. Go "language shopping"
4. Get an exemption from the FL requirement
5. Sympathetic instructors help student
6. Generally do not go abroad

C. Consequences of High School and College Policies
1. LD-labeled students are not starting languages early, and therefore not getting the background they need to succeed
2. Since over 25 percent of colleges and universities have FL entrance requirements and over 50 percent of colleges and universities have FL exit requirements (Brod and Lapointe 1989), the opportunities, both academically and professionally, are limited for LD students who are not allowed to succeed in foreign language classes.

IV. Helping Students with Learning Problems: Suggestions for Foreign Language Teachers

A. Recognizing a Problem—On the first day of class, tell the students to see you
1. If they had serious difficulties in high school foreign language classes.
2. If they have never studied a foreign language before.
3. If a student does not come forward, but is obviously floundering at the end of the first week. It's crucial that students receive support from the beginning of the semester.

B. Determining the Nature of the Problem
1. Through an interview, try to find out if the student is really trying to learn or is just not putting forth any effort.
2. If the student seems to be trying, question him or her about past problems with English and foreign languages. Ask if she or he had problems with reading, spelling, grammar, or writing in grade school.
3. School records may indicate whether the student was ever labeled LD. Bright students often manage to get by undiagnosed, however.

C. Remediation
1. If the student has language learning difficulties, start tutoring him or her right away. Do not wait for the first exam, for it may be too late then.
2. Go over the day's lesson ahead of time with the student. Explain in English what is going on. Explain grammar in English.
3. Language features that are obvious to most students (like letter/sound correspondence) may not be clear to students with learning problems. Point these out and help the student practice them.
4. Use lots of contextual clues such as acting, pictures, objects, charts, and diagrams in your teaching.
5. Students who have problems reading may be better at listening comprehension. Consider taping the readings for the students, and let them listen as they read. Consider using films instead of literary texts.
6. Focus on what the student can do rather than on what she or he cannot do. You may have to give the student alternative assignments.

D. Testing and Grading—Modify the Testing Situation to Allow the Student to Succeed.
1. Giving more time to complete the test may be enough.
2. LD students are often easily distracted. Allow them to take exams alone in a quiet room.
3. Give the student an alternative test that emphasizes his or her strengths rather than weaknesses.
4. Consider an outcomes-based approach, where students can retake different forms of the same test until they pass.
5. Consider letting the student use grammar charts or dictionaries.
6. Use a process approach with multiple drafts for writing assignments.
7. These students may just need more time to learn than others. Consider not grading the students at all until they have an idea what language learning entails. Allow them to audit a course before they take it for credit.

E. Support for the Student
1. Encourage the student to go abroad to the target language country and live with native speakers.

2. Students with learning problems are quite sensitive about these problems. Continually remind the students that you know that they are intelligent people who happen to have a problem with foreign language learning. Point out something that they can do better than you.

V. Determining a Need for Adaptation—If you are not sure whether a student who has never been labeled LD is not doing well because of a lack of effort or because of a learning disability, try to answer the following questions. If most of the answers are yes, you may decide to try to accommodate the student, or recommend him or her for testing.

Checklist to Determine Need for Adaptation

Yes   No

1. Does the student want to learn a foreign language?
2. Does the student attend class regularly?
3. Does the student try to do the homework assignments?
4. Does the student have a history of problems with foreign language learning?
5. Did the student have problems learning how to read, spell, or write in elementary school?
6. Does the student do well in other classes?

Scenarios

The following scenarios are based on real students encountered by college foreign language teachers. After considering the information given in this chapter, groups of teachers or teaching assistants should be able to brainstorm possible approaches to each student's problems.

Instructions

For each of the following scenarios, think of how you as an instructor would handle the situation in and out of class. How might you help the student achieve as well as possible in the foreign language that you teach? (Possible answers are provided in parentheses.)

1. You start teaching your first-semester Spanish class with lots of communicative activities. Tim does all right with the oral exercises, but when

you ask students to start reading what they have learned to say out loud during the second week of class, Tim is not able to do it. After a while he admits that he was in special education classes for a learning disability all through elementary and high school.

(Tim could benefit from tutoring on letter/sound correspondence in Spanish. The tutor might consider the Orton-Gillingham approach. See Myer et al. 1989, Sparks et al. 1991, and Orton 1966 for more information about this approach.)

2. Laura is having trouble writing compositions and comes to you for help. She has spent some time abroad, and her oral skills far exceed those of her peers. She tells you that she is frustrated with her writing ability and is ready to give up on the class. In her compositions it is not uncommon that one word will be spelled two or three different ways, and she often leaves words out.

(Laura might find a process approach to writing beneficial. Instead of just turning in a final copy of her essays, let her do several drafts. Teach all students how to do peer editing, or give her feedback on the drafts yourself. See Dvorak 1986 or Hewins 1986 for directions on how to implement process writing in the FL class.)

3. Susan is a very bright third-year student who plans to go to medical school. She has tried to get a waiver for the foreign language requirement because of a learning disability that was diagnosed her senior year in high school, but was denied by the college because she received passing marks in high school French. She has trouble with letter/sound correspondence, and with understanding grammar. She has heard that you are a sympathetic teacher, and has decided to enroll in your German class. She tells you that she passed French in high school only because her teacher gave her credit for trying hard. She wants to succeed in your class, and asks you for advice.

(Susan should start working with a tutor from the first day of class. The tutor should concentrate on letter/sound correspondence and explaining grammar in English, but also provide some FL oral practice for Susan. The tutor should explain what will be covered in class ahead of time, so that Susan can develop some background knowledge that will help her understand what is going on during class.)

4. Eric comes from a high school foreign language program that did not require much oral work. In that setting, he did all right because he was good at memorizing vocabulary lists and verb forms. Your class requires a lot of speaking and listening comprehension. Eric tells you that he really can't understand anything you say.

(You may have to modify your instruction to provide Eric with more visual and contextual support. Use drama, pictures, objects, charts, and diagrams in your teaching. Write key words on the board while you are talking with the students. Suggest to Eric that he make use of audio and video tapes to help reinforce the correspondence between the sound and the written words.)

5. Elena admits to you that she is a very slow reader. Usually she avoids reading as much as possible. She gets most of her information from lectures rather than textbooks. Your class requires about two hundred pages of reading in the foreign language, and Elena does not know how she can possibly read more than fifty pages in one semester.

(Provide Elena with a tape of the text or a tutor who can read out loud to her. Suggest that she listen and read at the same time. If a movie version of the text is available, suggest that she watch that before reading the text, so that she has some background knowledge of the plot when she reads. Use schemata-related reading activities to help her comprehension. See Melendez 1985 to learn more about using schema theory for teaching FL reading comprehension.)

6. You have noticed that one of your first-year students, Ben, has trouble sitting still in class. He sits in the back of the class, and often stares out the window. When you try to draw his attention to something on the blackboard, he doesn't seem to know where to look. He is not failing, but his quiz grades are not good, and his handwriting is extremely difficult to read. Ben admits to you that he has a very hard time memorizing new vocabulary words even though he spends a lot of time on it.

(Ben has trouble concentrating and does not have good study habits. It would help him if you gave some suggestions. Ask Ben to sit in the center front of the classroom where it will be easier to pay attention to what you are doing. Keep the blackboard uncluttered; it might help Ben if only what he needs to pay attention to at the time were on the board. Give students an outline of the lesson each day and draw attention to it as you complete different activities so that he is not as likely to get lost. Find out how Ben is studying. He may need you to suggest some different strategies, such as writing down words he needs to learn or making flash cards that he can carry around and practice with. See if he can study together with a more successful classmate until he develops better study habits.)

A Student-Centered Spanish-for-Native-Speakers Program: Theory, Curriculum Design, and Outcome Assessment

Cecilia Rodríguez Pino,
New Mexico State University
Daniel Villa,
New Mexico State University

Introduction

Methodology in Spanish-for-Native-Speakers (SNS) programs has undergone a transformation over the last two decades, moving from a normative approach aimed at "correcting" the variety of speech spoken in the student's community, to a comprehensive approach based on developing communicative competency through literacy. However, as Faltis (1990) points out, although these two approaches differ in significant ways, they share two common characteristics: promoting learning *about* language before using it for authentic purposes and employing a teacher-centered knowledge base, the "banking" concept identified by Freire (1970). The alternative that Faltis proposes employs both Freirian and Vygotskyan constructs of learning; in these, the student assumes a central position in the learning process, becoming in effect both teacher and student, instead of playing a passive role in the classroom.

The synthesis of Freirian and Vygotskyan concepts of learning is particularly suited to an SNS program because the students who enter such programs possess widely varying degrees of language skills, from the

355

English-dominant speaker who understands only a few words and phrases in Spanish to the Spanish-dominant speaker who has had little or no formal education in Spanish. Continued immigration from Spanish-speaking countries and the tendency toward intergenerational language loss serve to increase the variance in the degree of language skills of the student. Focusing on the individual learner in a multisection SNS program takes into account this continuum of language skills and facilitates the accommodation of instruction to the individual's needs and capabilities. Thus, in designing a student-centered SNS program it is necessary to: (1) establish a theoretical base for program development, (2) suggest a curriculum that meets the individual needs of native speakers, and (3) measure the results of changes in the curriculum.

One Student-Centered SNS Program: Background and Theoretical Perspectives

At New Mexico State University (NMSU) a student-centered SNS program is currently being developed that aims to classify the individual speaker's knowledge of Spanish, to identify his or her instructional needs, and to design a curriculum that recognizes the diverse language abilities of all students and enriches those abilities. Faltis (1990, pp. 117–18) observes that a normative view of the Spanish a native speaker brings to class holds that it is somehow "deficient" or "substandard," and that a principal goal of an SNS class is to "correct" such varieties of language. This attitude is reflected in the titles of SNS classes offered at NMSU since their inception in 1945. The SNS course offered from 1945 to 1960 was labeled "Corrective Spanish"; the catalog description states that this course is "for Spanish American students only. Especially designed for those who speak Spanish, but who need drills in grammar, reading and diction *to correct errors common to New Mexican Spanish.*" In 1962 the SNS course title changed to "Remedial Spanish," with the course description now reading: "For Spanish speaking students only. Especially designed for those who can speak Spanish but need drills in grammar, reading and diction." In 1968 "Spanish for Spanish Speaking Students" appeared, with the corresponding description: "For Spanish speaking students only. Exercises in grammar, speech correction and vocabulary building." It is not until 1975 that "speech correction" was dropped from the course description.

The recent changes in course title and description (and course content) reflect the implementation of the comprehensive approach, as suggested by Valdés-Fallis (1978). However, despite the growing awareness among language teachers that the Spanish a native speaker brings to a class is a valuable asset, advocates of the comprehensive approach persist in the attitude that some spoken norm, often not that of the student, must be achieved. This attitude conflicts with Freire's (1970) suggestion for resolving the teacher–student contradiction because the student must accept a passive role in assimilating the "standard" variety. Hidalgo (1990), while examining the question of what variety of language to employ for teaching Hispanic college students, presents a traditional view of the use of a "standard":

> Changing the status of Spanish from a vernacular to a semiofficial language will not only institutionalize it but create the appropriate use domains that will guarantee its preservation. Until this happens, we should be committed to teaching the standard, to discovering the areas of major morphosyntactic discrepancies between standard and dialect, and to transmitting the most practical orientation for the acquisition of the former and the retention of the latter. (p. 123)

In the NMSU program, we go beyond the idea that some external spoken "standard" must be imposed on the learner in order to increase his or her oral language skills. We hold the view that the retention of the spoken language by the individual, reflecting the speech of the community of which that individual forms a part, is a central and valuable goal in and of itself, and must play a central role in any SNS program. This corresponds to Faltis's (1990, p. 119) idea that "a reconciliation of set roles for students and teacher can occur only if there is an opportunity for dialog." He continues by quoting Freire, who states that "[in] an encounter among men who name the world, it must not be a situation where some men name on behalf of others" (1970, p. 66). Similarly, Fishman (1991, p. 342) writes that "the standard variety need not be as obligatory in speech as in writing. Indeed, all dialects should remain valid in speech, particularly in informal and intimate speech within their [native speakers'] own traditional speech networks and communities."

We do not suggest that the study of a formal written variety of a language be excluded—a point to which we will return—but that the basic foundation of a culturally and linguistically appropriate SNS program should contain a positive emphasis on the language of the community in which it exists. Fishman (1991), while discussing the role of Spanish language programs in U.S. universities, observes that

> Spanish is taught and offered as both a graduate and an undergraduate major in hundreds of institutions of higher education throughout the USA. Although many Hispanic students attend these courses and constitute the bulk of the country's Spanish majors . . . this entire realm is not linked to Hispanic community life and generally is not designed to (and does not) produce individuals who are committed to or involved in either language maintenance or RLS [reversing language shift]. (p. 215)

In order to avoid this situation, we seek to establish a connection between our SNS program and the Spanish-speaking community (specific methodology is discussed below).

Another assumption that appears to have driven the design of SNS programs is that the student controls the language variety of the community; it is this variety that is to be "corrected" or used as a bridge to some standard form. We do not find this to be the case for many students in our SNS program. Various researchers have documented the shift from Spanish to English among U.S. Hispanics, including López (1978), Veltman (1988), Solé (1990), and Bills, Hernandez-Chávez, and Hudson (1993), among others. We observe this trend among students in our program; a recent survey of self-reported Spanish language use indicates a general pattern of language shift from Spanish to English (Villa 1993). As a result, one student may have only a vaguely receptive capability, being able to produce but a few words or phrases, while another may communicate in Spanish only in restricted domains, such as concrete, "day-to-day" family matters.

Hence, the SNS program faces a general pattern of language shift. There is a growing recognition of this phenomenon in the literature on SNS programs that indicates a concern for maintaining the student's home language (see Valdés 1981). Following our assertion that maintaining the community's spoken language should be a goal in and of itself, we emphasize that the variety to be reacquired is that of the individual's own community.

We base this conclusion on Fishman's (1991) observation that in order to maintain a language, there must exist a pattern of intergenerational maintenance. He employs what he calls a "Graded Intergenerational Interruption Scale" (GIDS) that measures varying degrees of language loss or maintenance, with stage 8 representing the greatest degree of interruption and stage 1 the least (pp. 87–109). Fishman considers stage 6 to be a crucial point, in that "the lion's share of the world's intergenerationally continuous languages are at this very stage and they continue to survive and, in most cases, even to thrive, without going on to subsequent ('higher') stages" (p. 92). The student's community-language variety—that spoken by parents, relatives, friends, and other community members—in effect establishes the standard to be acquired. With regards to defining what this standard might be, the student becomes his or her own researcher and teacher, investigating the linguistic norms of his or her community, and communicating this information to peers and the instructor in the classroom setting.

Finally, with regards to Hidalgo's (1990) assertion that we must wait until the student's language variety is validated with some "semiofficial" status before implementing it in instruction, Fishman (1991, p. 111) asserts that "the most crucial ameliorative steps that are undertaken are and must be those that pro-RLS [Reversing Language Shift] 'forces' can reasonably support and attempt by dint of their own time, funds and devotion." It is unclear when, if ever, the varieties of Spanish spoken in the United States will be extended semiofficial status. The amount of time, effort, and funds needed to bring about the social, political, and economic changes for the "legitimizing" of U.S. Spanish are beyond the grasp of those involved in working with the SNS program at NMSU. However, changes in SNS theory and curriculum are possible; it is here that language shift can be affected, to whatever degree that might be. Therefore, we do not believe it necessary for some external consensus to "legitimize" the variety of Spanish that the student brings to the classroom. It is we ourselves who legitimize it.

In summary, the SNS program at NMSU is based on the following precepts:

1. The program has as a principal goal the reversing of language shift. Doing so will enrich a student's language skills in a culturally and linguistically appropriate manner.

2. The student is both learner and teacher, assuming an active role in language enrichment.

3. The spoken standard of the classroom reflects that of the students' community.

Recognizing the Bilingual Continuum: Placing the Student in the SNS Program

The first step in matching instruction to the individual's language abilities is placing the student in an appropriate level of study. In order to facilitate this process, the Spanish Component administers the University of Texas at El

Paso Department of Languages and Linguistics Spanish Placement Exam, developed by Armando Armengol, Richard Teschner, and Richard Ford at UTEP, to all incoming students before registration in their first Spanish class in the lower-division sequence. The placement instrument includes sections on elementary and advanced grammar, elementary and advanced vocabulary, orthography, and grammar theory. In addition, there are ten native-speaker indicators; Teschner (1990, p. 817) describes these as "colloquial words or expressions that are characteristic of Mexican-origin Spanish, and that seldom if ever make their way into Spanish-as-foreigner-second-language textbooks." If a student who has acquired Spanish in a native-speaking environment employs six of the ten native-speaker indicators correctly, he or she is automatically placed in the SNS program. Further analysis of other sections of the evaluation help in determining specifically what level of the SNS sequence the student should enter. A student who identifies fewer than six indicators is scheduled for an interview, in order to form a more accurate assessment of that student's language skills. The placement evaluation was first applied on a programwide basis at NMSU in the fall semester of 1993 and resulted in 106 students placing in the first-semester SNS class, with 65 entering the second semester of the current sequence.

Background information on students in the program shows that they may be broadly classified as follows: (1) immigrant and first-generation students who are Spanish-dominant, (2) second-generation bilinguals fluent in English and Spanish to varying degrees, and (3) third- and fourth-generation students who prefer to speak English, using Spanish only with monolinguals or in limited domains on limited topics (e.g., greeting a grandparent in Spanish). We believe that this last group of students, those with varied receptive skills and "lost" Spanish language productivity, merits as much attention in the SNS program as do the first and second groups, who are able to communicate in the target language. These students, in spite of the lack of oral productivity, bring cultural and linguistic knowledge to the classroom, knowledge that is not shared by the nonnative speaker studying Spanish as a second language.

As Valdés (1992) points out, there may be many differences in language abilities even within the same generation due to numerous factors such as the amount of access to both English and the immigrant language and the lack of opportunities for reading and writing in Spanish, among others. Therefore, it is absolutely essential that bilingual students who are misplaced in the nonnative track be given guidance to build their confidence in a program that will help them develop at their own pace with other students who have had similar experiences with the heritage language.

The importance of this last observation lies in the fact that many students with limited productive capabilities are reluctant to enroll in "native-speaker" classes, as they do not consider themselves "native speakers." We find that most second-generation students whose language experiences at home are predominantly in Spanish feel quite secure in registering in the SNS track. However, there are a few second- and many third-generation bilinguals who feel uncomfortable entering the SNS class because they are English-dominant and lack sufficient Spanish language experiences to produce the language. These students tend to register for first-year Spanish in the nonnative track. When their exam results indicate placement in the native track, their responses are varied: "I don't speak good Spanish," "I speak a lot of Spanglish," "My parents don't speak Spanish to me very often," or "I don't know how to speak it correctly." Such responses show that the students feel that their heritage language has little value or use in society, that only "correct" Spanish merits usage, and that one must have a good command of the language to be able to enroll in an SNS program.

This receptive bilingual population has traditionally been lost in the crowd. They do not belong in the nonnative track or in a traditionally grammar-based SNS program at the university level. Due to this situation, the SNS program at NMSU is focusing attention on these students after the language placement and assessment is administered. Such students answer four or five native indicators and have average scores on the elementary grammar and advanced vocabulary sections. An oral interview given by the director indicates that many of these receptive bilinguals have good listening skills because there is a monolingual relative in the home environment or a fluent bilingual who consistently uses Spanish to interact with them. Many of these receptive bilinguals have had limited opportunities to listen in a wide variety of contexts and topics in the Spanish language environment and few opportunities to produce their heritage language. This population, with its limited productive abilities and varied receptive skills, offers a special challenge to the profession to design much-needed instruction in the area of language maintenance and retrieval. In order to integrate these individuals into the SNS program at NMSU, the program itself has been redesigned; the following section sketches the new program and offers a brief description of the foci of different class levels.

A Suggested Curriculum for a Student-Centered SNS Program

Since its inception in 1945, the SNS program has consisted of a two-semester sequence. However, we do not feel that such a sequence adequately addresses the wide variety of language skills that the students bring to the classroom. Therefore, the program is being expanded to meet the linguistic diversity found among native speakers. This expanded curriculum includes an entry-level course for students who have not maintained their heritage language and need to develop their receptive and productive skills and to expand their active vocabulary. The second and third semesters in the sequence continue this process while promoting reading and writing skills. The fourth semester emphasizes study of the structure of Spanish, both prescriptively and descriptively; this class corresponds to what has been traditionally called a "grammar" class.

The first-semester course devotes class time to activities that stimulate students' pride in their cultural heritage and language. Classroom instruction for this course has been designed to create a nonthreatening context with language and cultural activities that provide: (1) the opportunity for students to use the variety of the heritage language found in their community, emphasizing its inherent legitimacy so that it forms a solid foundation on which further language skills may be built; (2) authentic tasks to improve their varied receptive skills, such as the use of videos, audiotaped narratives, and dialogues; (3) interaction with other bilinguals outside the classroom with various authentic activities designed in class groups that guide them through basic speaking tasks they can successfully accomplish. Upon completion of this first course, students have had numerous language experiences with their class peers, the instructor, and immediate community members, as well as a variety of contextualized listening opportunities that expand their vocabulary range and functional skills, in preparation to expand contacts in the nonimmediate community. We define "immediate community" as the extended family and close friends; the "nonimmediate community" comprises those who share linguistic and cultural experiences similar to those of the student's immediate community, but who are minimally acquainted with the student, if at all.

In the second semester of the sequence students are encouraged to expand their functional range in the heritage language through a variety of activities. Those oriented toward development of vocabulary and oral productivity are discussed below. At this level, students are exposed to listening activities in a wide range of contexts, some of which are not heard in the home domain. In line with Fishman's (1991) assertion that intergenerational communication is a key to language maintenance, native speakers of the community language are invited to the class to give presentations. Valdés (1992) states that for language maintenance to take place, students who have strong receptive and productive skills require access to a wide and full range of domains and functions. She suggests monolingual contexts such as television, radio, video materials, and other genres for which English may also be used in the language community. Since there are numerous radio and television stations in Las Cruces, El Paso, and Juárez that offer a wide variety of monolingual contexts, we are exploring Valdés's suggestions for designing instructional activities for multiple levels of language use. Regular access to the monolingual resources found in the community allows students to listen to voices other than that of their instructor. Students develop their community variety by exposure to authentic speech that is beyond their productive skills in a variety of domains and contexts. Hence, upon completion of the second course, students have continued language experiences with their class peers, instructor, and immediate community members, and in addition have begun to expand receptive capabilities to include the nonimmediate community. Reading skills are introduced, using authentic Spanish materials from the United States.

In the third course of the sequence, in addition to expanding their communicative skills, students increase their writing abilities. Students begin to express themselves in a nonformal written context. Organization, transitions between ideas, and the expression of affective themes, among others, are developed in this level. Increased attention is paid to prescriptive norms of orthography, with the exception of texts written for affective expression (poetry, journals or diaries, short stories, etc.). The basic use of a metalanguage is also introduced at this level. Community-based communication is integrated into the development of writing skills. In short, this level places an increased emphasis on the reading and writing areas of the four skills. Upon completion of the third level of the sequence, the students have developed ties with the nonimmediate as well as the immediate community, and have continued to broaden their awareness of the community language as it exists in literary form. They also develop the ability to express themselves, both affectively and instrumentally, with the written form of the language.

The fourth-semester class is designed to closely study metalanguage introduced in the second and third semesters, and to learn how it is applied to an understanding of both written and spoken language. A traditional component of prescriptive grammar, contextualized in written exercises, is intended to focus the student on skills needed to employ Spanish in formal written contexts. At the same time, the metalanguage is studied as a linguistic tool that can be used to better understand the community language. For example, the concept of person and number markers can be used to analyze the second-person singular variants *-tes* or *-stes* (e.g., *hablates* or *hablastes*) in the preterite. The study of verb morphology helps in understanding how items such as *puchar*, *espeletrear*, *monquear*, and *tichear* form a legitimate part of the community's language variety. Additionally, such concepts as the dynamics of lexical borrowing and codeswitching are introduced, so that the student is given the opportunity to recognize that what he or she has often heard labeled as "Spanglish," "slang," "pocho," or "mocho" forms part of the dynamic that occurs whenever two (or more) languages come in contact. A historical component illustrates the truth that even "proper" Spanish is a product of certain developmental tendencies and that what is observed in the heritage language community in fact represents the evolution of the Spanish language in general.

We note here that the validity of the community language variety is asserted at all levels of the SNS program. As Grosjean (1982, p. 192) observes, a language minority may internalize the negative opinions of the language majority toward the minority's language variety. The students in our SNS program have had a lifetime of hearing their community language variety referred to disparagingly. Such entrenched negative opinions must be carefully weeded out, a task that requires constant repetition at all levels in the sequence.

Thus, the design of the program aims to develop the productive and receptive abilities of the receptive bilingual and to expand the language skills of the productive bilingual, enriching whatever language skills are brought to the program and encouraging positive attitudes toward the heritage language, while encouraging analytical skills that aid the student to better understand the dynamics of the linguistic community of which he or she forms a part. Upon finishing the sequence, the student may elect further studies in Spanish language and/or literature, all of which fall outside the SNS program, or may discontinue the classroom study of the language; in either case, the foundations that provide a better understanding of and respect for the heritage language will have been created.

These foundations are important for career opportunities for native speakers of Spanish. The SNS program is presently working with the Department of Social Work at NMSU to train students to work with the local Spanish-speaking community. There is a dearth of social workers who can address the needs of this community in its language variety, and those who can do so have an advantage in the job market. Similarly, there is a need for those who speak the local variety of the language in a variety of careers, for example, in the banking industry, health care, law enforcement, court systems, food services, and, most significantly, bilingual education in the public school systems.

Common wisdom has held that students must master a "good" variety of Spanish in order to obtain a good job; perhaps those who adhere to this view perceive "good" jobs to be those working with corporate executives in Mexico City or some other metropolis in Latin America or Spain. While these types of jobs do exist, it is much more probable that the students who study in the SNS program at NMSU will look for employment in the regional economy, where there is a strong demand for bilinguals. We have not yet tracked the careers of those who have studied in the SNS program, but we can offer anecdotal evidence of this demand. A student enrolled in the fourth-semester "grammar" class during spring semester 1994 was hired at the end of the semester as an administrative assistant for an attorney who handles public defense for the federal court system. The job entails interpreting for the monolingual English-speaking attorney who defends monolingual Spanish-speaking clients; it goes without saying that the language variety encountered among these clients is not of a literary type. In sum, the local language variety may well be advantageous to the student in the search for employment after finishing university studies. This is another area that demands further research; at present, no studies suggest what "real-world" Spanish language skills are needed in the private and public sectors.

Strategies for Connecting the SNS Program with the Spanish-Speaking Community

Many strategies have been proposed for instructional purposes in SNS programs, yet few have been included in textbooks with the goal of connecting the student with the heritage language and culture in contextualized and interactive activities in the community. Many of the instructional techniques proposed by researchers in the field of SNS, and the steps needed to achieve positive results, have not been sufficiently elaborated in the professional literature to establish their effectiveness. We seek here to suggest relevant techniques; detailed elaboration of step-by-step implementation falls outside the scope of this chapter.

We find that successful exercises in the NMSU program center on a high degree of interaction between students, teacher, and community. Instructional materials do not attempt to "lump" a diverse population of native speakers in the SNS classroom into one level of language ability or another. Each student has opportunities to develop individual strengths. The ethnographic interview is an effective technique that focuses on student/teacher/community interaction, the "four skills," and heritage culture. Other techniques, such as the sociolinguistic survey, the oral history interview, and the dialogue journal, also give students opportunities to explore their language and culture in the community context. These techniques also address the multiple levels of proficiencies of the native-speaker student population and offer interesting and challenging avenues to retrieve and maintain the heritage language, while developing the four skills at the individual's level.

Ethnography, the work of describing a culture or a way of life from the native point of view, has been effectively used by the social sciences to obtain cultural information. With regards to the implementation of this type of study, Trueba (1993) states that language must be included since language and culture are inseparable and intertwined: one cannot be acquired without the other. Robinson (1988, pp. 73–84) observes that ethnography takes place in a "real-world" environment, not in a laboratory setting, and therefore must use techniques that do not prestructure or pre-categorize what is to be observed. She also notes that we do not have any good ethnographies of cultures commonly taught in American schools and universities; the cultural studies that have been collected and interpreted by ethnographers describe exotic cultures rather than those that would be relevant to local communities and societies. Merino and Samaniego (1993) suggest that the ethnographic interview is an instructional strategy that has not been explored in SNS classes; they go on to say that the bilingual community's cultural resources can become the focus for a SNS course.

Thus we consider ethnographic studies an excellent starting point in the SNS program (Rodríguez Pino 1994). Students begin to interact in the classroom and participate in structured activities in their immediate communities with the goal of studying their local culture and its language variety. There exists in Las Cruces and the surrounding communities a rich linguistic research environment for the study of social and cultural topics relevant to students in the SNS programs. During the past academic year, SNS classes at NMSU have been exploring the use of the ethnographic study to learn about their own native language and culture by using community resources.

Rodríguez Pino states in her newsletter (funded by the National Endowment for the Humanities) that in implementing the ethnographic interview students should first be introduced to the definition of the study of ethnography and what role it plays in researching their native language and culture. The notion that ethnography is a useful method for obtaining cultural information from the native's point of view and that its purpose is to explore how people within the target culture group their experiences and prioritize them are stressed. The selection of topics for the ethnographic research project can be taken care of in various ways. The class can "brainstorm" in groups or as a whole class after the instructor provides a brief overview of the historical, social, and cultural background of Las Cruces and the surrounding areas.

Students are asked to volunteer family members to speak on several topics. In addition, the instructor provides a list of potential consultants in order to facilitate contacts in the community. We note here that immediate community members are preferred when beginning an ethnographic study, but if an individual identifies someone in the extended community with whom he or she can comfortably work, no attempt should be made to discourage such contact. Indeed, it is at such a juncture that the instructor must be aware of each individual's level of confidence in his or her language competency, so that an appropriate community member (or members) is identified. Strategies for carrying out the ethnographic interview are then discussed in class among students, and sample interviews with peers are conducted as a "priming" activity. Students then conduct the interview in the community; resulting data are analyzed in class.

We have found that this process provides a tremendous amount of material for both class-internal and class-external study. Ethnography works well as a first step in retrieving language; students record accounts about their heritage culture so that they may describe, interpret, and evaluate events that have not been recorded or documented anywhere else in rich and vivid detail from the native speaker's point of view. It is at this point that students assume their role as teachers. The ethnographic interview is an important tool for obtaining information about the cultural diversity of the Hispanic population's language and culture, reclaiming heritage, and interpreting accounts of relevant topics with background data from native speakers' accounts to native speaker student researchers. This occurs in a nonthreatening setting, when students who have minimal productive abilities can focus on the "task at hand" rather than on language production. At the same time, they are exposed to an increased amount of the community's language variety, providing them with the opportunity outside the classroom to enrich their language skills.

An extension of the ethnographic interview is the oral history. This activity is aimed at the student's re-creation of a personal or family history, a "microhistory," within a broader historical context, the "macrohistory." With regards to language skills, the student is encouraged to conduct the oral history interview while using as much of the target language as possible. In-class background discussion provides a macrohistory of the area, including such topics as the Tratado de Guadalupe Hidalgo, the Mexican Revolution, indigenous populations, and economic development, among others. In addition, methods for conducting interviews are discussed to avoid problems such as closed questions. In-class interviews are held to develop interviewing skills. Students then conduct an initial interview in order to begin gathering data from a community member or members. Again, in light of the goal of developing oral productivity, students are encouraged to work with members of the immediate community.

A third activity for developing an awareness of a student's community language norms, in this case through defining the standard of the community, is the linguistic survey. The use of such an approach has been suggested by Solé (1981), Gutiérrez-Marrone (1981), and Merino (1989). Solé suggests providing students with print and visual media to observe the usage of "standard" and "nonstandard" varieties of language so that they may distinguish between the two; Gutiérrez-Marrone proposes techniques for students to discover differences in standard lexical variants in specific semantic domains through print media or interviews with consultants. Merino's interview techniques in the design of the linguistic survey includes questions on lexical items by semantic category and individual word listing by domain, activities carried out *in the classroom*.

We suggest a different approach. We ask our students to go out into the community, both immediate and nonimmediate, in order to establish what the community norms are in a variety of domains, some of which are chosen so as to be out of the student's day-to-day contact with the heritage language. For example, we have noticed that lexical items usually not included in students' vocabularies concern the flora and fauna commonly found in the area. In discovering these terms, students not only enrich their vocabulary, but do so with words used commonly in the community, rather than in other variants of Spanish, thereby recognizing the importance of one group not naming the world for another group.

The basis for this survey is the instrument developed at the University of New Mexico by Garland Bills and Neddy Vigil (1992) for the New Mexico/Colorado Spanish Survey. This is an extensive collection of photos and realia designed to elicit lexical items in a wide range of domains. The instrument is too extensive to be employed in its entirety by the student/researcher, so collaboration in class between students and instructor is essential for designing a workable instrument. Following the techniques developed by Bills and Vigil, a portion of the interview consists of free conversation, so that the student does not simply elicit a list of items, but must interact with the consultant on a personal basis, thereby developing his or her communicative skills and increasing social interaction in the community. Again, the goal of this activity is to establish a standard variety that corresponds to that with which the students are in contact, be they from Las Cruces, Española, El Paso, Silver City, or Clovis; we do not wish our local variety to be converted into some sort of overarching standard.

Outcome Assessment of the SNS Program

The principal goal of the SNS program at NMSU is to enrich the native speaker's language abilities. We have suggested a theoretical base, a curriculum, and activities that can be used to achieve that end. However, we recognize that such a program cannot be implemented strictly as a result of a priori musings based solely upon anecdotal experience. Steps must be taken that measure the impact of theory and methodology so that the program benefits from "real-world" data for further programmatic refinement. That is, we do not view the program as a finished product, but instead as a work in progress that demands concrete data to support its validity.

However, on choosing a means of outcome assessment, problems immediately arise. One could possibly use some type of oral language proficiency instrument, such as the ACTFL-ETS oral proficiency interview; a dramatic increase in measurable oral proficiency would surely be a hallmark of success. Unfortunately, Barnwell (1989) eloquently points out fundamental flaws in the ACTFL-ETS instrument that call into question its validity. Furthermore, even if these problems could be satisfactorily resolved in the near future, it would not be clear whether the ACTFL-ETS interview could be used to measure SNS students' oral proficiency, as Valdés (1989) points out. She proposes three alternatives:

> (1) we can attempt to change the language attitudes of the [ACTFL-ETS] testers and to modify their notions of "correctness" by launching a profession-wide campaign; (2) we can present our evidence to ACTFL and insist that it be made clear that existing standards and guidelines cannot be used validly with ethnic native speakers; or (3) we can design an oral proficiency rating scale for bilingual speakers that differs, not only in the way in which the rating scale is applied, but which is based on an entirely different set of assumptions about the developing ability of bilingual native speakers as they progress through direct instruction in their first language. (p. 400)

For the purposes of assessing the progress students make in our program, any one of the three alternatives suggested above is not a viable solution for *short-term* program assessment. We cannot wait some undetermined length of time until an ideal assessment becomes available; our program demands immediate evaluation.

The alternative proposed here, and the one that is currently being implemented at NMSU, is twofold. One assessment is the use of a sociolinguistic instrument that measures the student's self-reported use of the heritage language, using a Likert-type scale. The instrument also elicits data on intergenerational communication in Spanish, if the student considers that he or she is using more Spanish than before entering the program, and affective and instrumental attitudes toward the community variant, among other variables. We feel that if an increase in self-reported language use and intergenerational communication can be established, that in itself would provide important support for our program design. If this is not the case, then our theory, instructional techniques, and measures must be reviewed and revised, in order to improve them. Toward this assessment goal, the sociolinguistic instrument itself is undergoing revision and refinement, in conjunction with the Department of Experimental Statistics at NMSU, in order to create as statistically reliable a measure as possible.

However, we do not wish to rely solely upon statistics, which can never present a complete picture of that which is being analyzed. Included in our program evaluation are written comments of students who have participated in the program. We feel that if the student is to be recognized as a central, active figure in the learning process, then that student must of necessity participate in the outcome assessment. In order to achieve this goal, written comments are elicited from the students in every level at the end of each semester and analyzed qualitatively and quantitatively with regard to both positive and negative comments about class activities, fieldwork, readings, and more. These results are then compiled into a single document that records both successes and failures in the program. We stress that these comments form an integral part of outcome assessment and are not something to be elicited and then archived in the "round file."

Finally, we recognize that these assessments do not directly measure the progress of a student in the program. However, faced as we are with the need to refine the program each semester, we employ what assessment tools we have until a well-researched, culturally, and linguistically appropriate system is available. There is indeed much work to be done in this area.

Conclusion

The teaching of Spanish to native speakers at New Mexico State University has experienced dramatic changes since its inception in 1945. Changes in the program reflect the advances in the field during the last two decades, both in theory and in practice. It is our intent to continue the development of New Mexico State's SNS program by examining the theory that underlies this effort, refining class internal and class external activities that encourage the reacquisition and maintenance of heritage language skills, and measuring the effectiveness of the program in meeting its stated goals. Dedicated researchers have invested tremendous amounts of time and energy toward improving SNS programs, and so far have made impressive strides. Researchers and educators at New Mexico State will continue to contribute to the growing body of knowledge in the field, to whatever degree possible, so that SNS programs in general will continue to become more oriented toward the students they serve.

Works Cited

Barnwell, David. 1989. Proficiency and the Native Speaker. *Hispania* 20: 42–46.

Bills, Garland D., Eduardo Hernández-Chávez, and Alan Hudson. 1993. The Geography of Language Shift: Distance from the Mexican Border and Spanish Language Claiming in the Southwestern United States. *University of New Mexico Working Papers in Linguistics* 1: 15–30.

Bills, Garland D., and Neddy A. Vigil. 1992. *Data Collection Handbook for the Linguistic Atlas of the Spanish of New Mexico and Southern Colorado.* Albuquerque: Department of Linguistics, University of New Mexico.

Faltis, Christian. 1990. Spanish for Native Speakers: Freirian and Vygotskian Perspectives. *Foreign Language Annals* 23: 117–26.

Fishman, Joshua. 1991. *Reversing Language Shift: Theoretical and Empirical Foundations of Assistance to Threatened Languages.* Multilingual Matters no. 76. Clevendon, UK: Multilingual Matters.

Freire, Paolo. 1970. *Pedagogy of the Oppressed.* New York: Herder and Herder.

Grosjean, François. 1982. *Life with Two Languages: An Introduction to Bilingualism.* Cambridge, MA: Harvard University Press.

Gutiérrez-Marrone, Nila. 1981. Español para el hispano: Un enfoque soci-olingüístico. In *Teaching Spanish to the Hispanic Bilingual: Issues, Aims and Methods,* edited by Guadalupe Valdés, Anthony G. Lozano, and Rodolfo García-Moya, 69–80. New York: Teachers College Press.

Hidalgo, Margarita. 1990. On the Question of "Standard" versus "Dialect": Implications for Teaching Hispanic College Students. In *Spanish in the United States: Sociolinguistic Issues,* edited by John J. Bergen, 110–26. Washington, DC: Georgetown University Press.

López, David E. 1978. Chicano Language Loyalty in an Urban Setting. *Sociology and Social Research* 62: 267–78.

Merino, Barbara. 1989. *Techniques for Teaching Spanish to Native Spanish Speakers.* Davis, CA: Español Para Triunfar/Spanish for Success: A Summer Institute for High School Spanish Teachers of NSS Students at the University of California at Davis.

Merino, Barbara J., and Fabián A. Samaniego. 1993. Language Acquisition Theory and Classroom Practices in the Teaching of Spanish to Native Spanish Speakers. In *Language and Culture in Learning: Teaching Spanish to Native Speakers of Spanish,* edited by Barbara J. Merino, Henry T. Trueba, and Fabián A. Samaniego, 115–23. London: Falmer Press.

Robinson, Gail L. 1988. *Crosscultural Understanding.* New York: Prentice-Hall.

Rodríguez Pino, Cecilia. 1994. Ethnographic Studies in the SNS Classroom. *Teaching Spanish to Southwest Hispanic Students Newsletter* (New Mexico State University) 1, no. 1: 4–5.

Solé, Yolanda. 1981. Consideraciones pedagógicas en la enseñanza del español a estudiantes bilingües. In *Teaching Spanish to the Hispanic*

Bilingual: Issues, Aims and Methods, edited by Guadalupe Valdés, Anthony G. Lozano, and Rodolfo García-Moya, 21–29. New York: Teachers College Press.

————. 1990. Bilingualism: Stable or Transitional? The Case of Spanish in the United States. *International Journal of the Sociology of Language* 84: 35–80.

Teschner, Richard V. 1990. Spanish Speakers Semi- and Residually Native: After the Placement Test Is Over. *Hispania* 73: 816–22.

Trueba, Henry T. 1993. Culture and Language: The Ethnographic Approach to the Study of Learning Environments. In *Language and Culture in Learning: Teaching Spanish to Native Speakers of Spanish,* edited by Barbara J. Merino, Henry T. Trueba, and Fabián A. Samaniego, 26–44. London: Falmer Press.

University of Texas at El Paso. 1993. University of Texas at El Paso Department of Languages and Linguistics Spanish Placement Exam.

Valdés, Guadalupe. 1981. Pedagogical Implications of Teaching Spanish to the Spanish-Speaking in the United States. In *Teaching Spanish to the Hispanic Bilingual: Issues, Aims and Methods,* edited by Guadalupe Valdés, Anthony G. Lozano, and Rodolfo García-Moya, 3–20. New York: Teachers College Press.

————. 1989. Teaching Spanish to Hispanic Bilinguals: A Look at Oral Proficiency Testing and the Proficiency Movement. *Hispania* 72: 392–401.

————. 1992. The Role of the Foreign Language Teaching Profession in Maintaining Non-English Languages in the United States. In *Languages for a Multicultural World in Transition,* edited by Heidi Byrnes, 29–71. Lincolnwood, IL: National Textbook.

Valdés-Fallis, Guadalupe. 1978. A Comprehensive Approach to the Teaching of Spanish to Bilingual Spanish-Speaking Students. *Modern Language Journal* 62: 102–10.

Veltman, Calvin. 1988. *The Future of the Spanish Language in the United States.* New York: Hispanic Policy Development Project.

Villa, Daniel. 1993, 8–10 October. Distance from Mexico: The Impact on Language Shift in a Border Region. Paper presented at the Conference on El Español en los Estados Unidos 14 at the University of Texas at San Antonio.

Contributors

M. Mahdi Alosh (Ph.D., The Ohio State University) is Assistant Professor of Arabic at the Ohio State University, where he teaches courses in Arabic and Arabic instructional methodology. In addition, he is coordinator of the Arabic Language Program and supervises graduate teaching associates. He is a tester of Arabic proficiency certified by ACTFL. His primary research interests are in curriculum design, materials development, learning and reading strategies, CALL, and assessment of language abilities. He is author of a series of instructional textbooks for Arabic entitled *Ahlan wa Sahlan* and is completing revisions of a new edition that will be published by Yale University Press in 1995.

Christine M. Campbell (Ph.D., Purdue University) is Test Project Director in the Directorate of Evaluation and Standardization at the Defense Language Institute, Monterey, California. Her primary duty is to supervise an international team of test developers who write proficiency tests in a variety of foreign languages. She has published on language anxiety, motivation in language learning, and testing. She is Chair of The International Language and Culture Foundation and the Director of Test Development of the National Spanish Examination. Recently, she was named 1994 Distinguished Education Alumnus by Purdue University.

Monika Chavez (Ph.D., University of Texas at Austin) is Assistant Professor of German at the University of Wisconsin at Madison, where she directs the second-year German program and supervises teaching assistants. She teaches graduate courses in applied linguistics. Her research interests focus on language processing.

Andrew D. Cohen (Ph.D., Stanford University) is Director of the Institute of Linguistics and Asian and Slavic Languages and Literatures, Full Professor in the Department of English as a Second Language, and member of the Graduate Faculty in Linguistics at the University of Minnesota. He is also Director of the University of Minnesota's National Language Resource Center. He has published numerous research articles on bilingual education, language testing, and language learning strategies. The second edition of his testing textbook, *Assessing Language Ability in the Classroom* (1994), has recently appeared.

Robert M. DeKeyser (Ph.D., Stanford University) is Assistant Professor of Linguistics at the University of Pittsburgh, where he teaches courses in second language acquisition, applied linguistics, and research methodology. His main research interests are in the cognitive psychology of foreign/second language learning, individual differences and their interaction with teaching methods, and interlanguage variation. He has published in journals such as *The Modern Language Journal, TESOL Quarterly, AILA Review, Language Testing,* and *Hispania.*

Madeline Ehrman (Ph.D., The Union Institute in Cincinnati, OH) is Director of Research Evaluation and Development in the School of Language Studies, Foreign Service Institute, U.S. Department of State. She holds advanced degrees in both linguistics and clinical psychology. Her research emphasizes the role of personality factors in intensive language learning. In recent years, she has published and spoken on the subject of individual differences in adult language learning in a variety of fora.

Charles J. James (Ph.D., University of Minnesota) is Professor of German and of Curriculum and Instruction at the University of Wisconsin at Madison, where he is coordinator of German TAs, director of the first-year language program, and adviser for secondary education in German. He teaches courses in German at all levels, as well as methods courses, both for undergraduate and graduate students of German. He is a founding member of the AAUSC and served as the organization's first treasurer and first editor of its Newsletter. A life member of the AATG, he is also a member of ACTFL and MLA. His research interests include language testing strategies and the educational systems of Germany. He has published articles and reviews in *Foreign Language Annals, Die Unterrichtspraxis, The Modern Language Journal,* and *Polylingua.*

Carol A. Klee (Ph.D., University of Texas at Austin) is Associate Professor of Hispanic Linguistics and Director of the Spanish and Portuguese Language Programs at the University of Minnesota, Twin Cities Campus, where she supervises TAs and teaches courses on foreign language pedagogy, second language acquisition, sociolinguistics, and Latin American dialectology. Her research interests include bilingualism, language contact, and second language acquisition. She is currently coordinating several research projects on immersion education in the National Language Resource Center at the University of Minnesota. She was recently elected to the Executive Council of the AATSP and is currently serving as vice-president of the AAUSC.

Ann Sax Mabbott is a Ph.D. candidate in the Department of Curriculum and Instruction at the University of Minnesota. Her primary research interest is second language acquisiton on the part of learners who are labeled learning disabled. She has also been active in second language teacher education, German language education, and teaching English as a second language. She is on the editorial board of the *MinneTESOL Journal*.

Sally Sieloff Magnan (Ph.D., Indiana University) is Professor of French at the University of Wisconsin at Madison, where she teaches courses in French language and teaching methodologies and supervises teaching assistants. Her primary research interests are foreign language methodologies, error analysis, and proficiency testing. She is the editor of *The Modern Language Journal* and edited the 1990 Northeast Conference Reports, *Shifting the Instructional Focus to the Learner* and the first volume of this AAUSC series, *Challenges in the 1990s for College Foreign Language Programs*. She is also a past President of the AAUSC.

Lydie Meunier (Ph.D., University of Arizona) is Assistant Professor of French at The University of Tulsa, Oklahoma. Her responsibilities include French language, teacher education, applied French linguistics, coordination of the elementary French program, content-based French courses in preparation for business and translation certificates, as well as courses in the Women's Studies program. Her primary research interests are in second language acquisition and pedagogy. She is particularly interested in the use of technology and its role in efficient language learning, as well as in gender and personality differences in a foreign language instructional environment. She has published pedagogical materials for Heinle & Heinle and DC Heath, as well as software reviews in the Northeast Conference Newsletter. She has also published in the *French Review* as well as in *CALICO Journal*.

Rebecca L. Oxford (Ph.D., University of North Carolina) is Professor of Language Education and Area Head of Teacher Education, College of

Education at the University of Alabama. She is a well-known author on the topics of language learning styles, strategies, methods, and testing. She holds a Ph.D. from the University of North Carolina, a M.Ed. from Boston University, and two degrees in Russian (Yale and Vanderbilt). She is now co-editing the *Tapestry Program*, an ESL/EFL series of over forty books, published by Heinle & Heinle..

Cecilia Rodríguez Pino (M.A., New Mexico State University) is Assistant Professor of Spanish at New Mexico State University, Department of Foreign Languages, where she is Director of the Spanish for Native Speakers Program. Her research interests are in language pedagogy with emphasis on Spanish for native speakers instruction. Currently she is Project Director of a National Endowment for the Humanities grant on "Teaching Spanish to Southwest Hispanic Students." She has co-authored articles in *Foreign Language Annals* and *The Modern Language Journal* and several first year Spanish ancillaries for Heinle and Heinle Publishers. This year she is on the Executive Board of the Southwest Conference on Language Teaching (SWCOLT) and serves as Assistant Program Chair.

Victor M. Shaw (M.S., Univ. of Southern California) is Senior Researcher in the Research and Analysis Division of the Directorate of Evaluation and Standardization at the Defense Language Institute (DLI), Monterey, California. As Senior Researcher, he analyzes and interprets data from a variety of DLI research projects in second language learning. His research interests include language anxiety and motivation in language learning.

Daniel Villa (Ph.D., University of New Mexico) is Assistant Professor at New Mexico State University, Department of Languages and Linguistics, where he is Director of the Intermediate Spanish for Non-Native Speakers' Program. His research interests include dialectal variations in New Mexico Spanish and issues in language loss, reversing language shift, and acquisition of Spanish by non-native speakers. Currently he is researching Spanish discourse structure for machine translation purposes.

Susan J. Weaver (Ph.D. Candidate, University of Minnesota) is a Teaching Assistant for the L2 Learning Strategies Project at the University of Minnesota's Center for Advanced Research on Language Acquisition. She has designed and conducted strategy training seminars for university-level foreign language teachers, teaches English as a Second Language to graduate and undergraduate students, and is an active member of several

University of Minnesota administrative committees. Her research interests include learning style preferences and their relationship to learning strategies, language processing, and English for Special Purposes.

Dolly Jesusita Young (Ph.D., The University of Texas) is Associate Profesor of Spanish at the University of Tennessee at Knoxville, where she teaches courses in Spanish language, second language acquisition, foreign language teaching methodologies, and in addition supervises teaching assistants. Her research and publication areas include language anxiety, second language reading, and cognition and learner perspectives on language learning. She has co-edited a volume entitled *Language Anxiety* by Prentice Hall and co-written an intermediate level Spanish reader by Holt.

Sadia Zoubir-Shaw (Doctorate, University of Provence, Aix-en-Provence, France) is Assistant Professor of French at the University of Alabama, where she directs the Elementary French Language Program and supervises teaching assistants. Her research interests include experimental phonetics, applied linguistics, pedagogy, and second language acquisition. She regularly teaches French in the Middlebury Summer Language School.

AAUSC STYLE SHEET FOR AUTHORS

In-Text Citations

The *AAUSC Issues in Language Program Direction series uses the author-date citation system described in The Chicago Manual of Style,* 14th ed. *(Note that here and elsewhere a number of these references do not refer to a real work; they are for illustration purposes only.)*

1. Basic reference: If, from the context, the author is clear, use only the date within parentheses. If not, use the last name of an author and the year of publication of the work, with no punctuation between them. Note that no designation of "ed." or "comp." is used.

   (VanPatten 1993)

   Benseler and Cronjaeger (1991) provide the first comprehensive listing on the topic of TA development in foreign languages in their extensive bibliography.

   Although exhortations to the contrary are easily found (Allwright 1981), the textbook, particularly the introductory textbook . . .

2. For a reference with page numbers, use a comma to separate date and page number. Precede the page number(s) with p. or pp.

   (Byrnes 1990, p. 42)

3. For a reference with volume and page numbers use arabic number for volume, colon, and arabic number for page:

   (Weinberg 1952, 2: p. 129)

4. For a reference to volume only, add volume number to avoid ambiguity:

   (Weinberg 1952, vol. 2)

5. Works by two or three authors, use this form:

   (Smith and Jones 1991)

   (Smith, Jones, and North 1993)

6. For works by more than three authors, use "et al." If there is another work of the same date that would also abbreviate to "et al.," use a short title identifying the work cited.

   (Mitchell et al. 1992)

   (Mitchell et al., Writing Space, 1992)

7. For a work by an association or agency without a specific author, use the organization name in full. If the name is particularly long, you may abbreviate but be sure that the reader will be able to easily find it in the works cited and that it is used consistently throughout the text.

   (ACTFL 1994)

8. For two or more references, separate them by using a semicolon. Add a comma for page numbers.

   (Smith 1991; Jones 1992; Light 1990)

   (Smith 1991, p. 6; Jones 1992; Light 1990, pp. 72–74)

9. For multiple works by same author, do not repeat name and separate by comma if there are no page numbers. If there are page numbers, separate by semicolons and use commas for page numbers:

   (Kelly 1896, 1902a, 1902b)

   (Kelly 1896, p. 4; 1902a, pp. 120–22; 1902b, p. 45)

10. For a new edition of an older work; put the original date of publication in square brackets:

    (Piaget [1924] 1969, p. 75)

11. For a personal communication, do not include the reference in the Works Cited section. Write the prose of the text to indicate personal communication, with the year given in parentheses:

    *In a personal communication (1994), Tucker indicated that . . .

Works Cited Section

The AAUSC series uses *The Chicago Manual of Style* (14th ed.) "B" reference style. Consult chapter 16 of *Chicago*.

Order of Entries:

Always alphabetize by last name of principal author; for questions of alphabetization, see *Chicago* chap. 17.

1. If an author has both individual and coauthored works, all individual works precede coauthored ones.

   a. By date: oldest first

   b. If more than one work in the same year, order by alpha and add a lowercase a, b, c, etc.: 1993a, 1993b

2. Coauthored works:

   a. cluster together groups containing the same coauthors. Groups of 2 precede groups of 3, which precede groups of 4, etc.

   b. within each group, organize by date (oldest first)

   c. if more than one work with same date, organize by alpha using a, b, c.

Clément, Richard. 1980. Ethnicity, Contact and Communicative Competence in a Second Language. *In Language: Social Psychological Perspectives,* edited by H. Giles, W. P. Robinson, and P. M. Smith, 147–54. Oxford: Pergamon.

Clément, Richard, and Bastian G. Kruidenier. 1983. Orientations on Second Language Acquisition: 1. The Effects of Ethnicity, Milieu, and Their Target Language on Their Emergence. *Language Learning* 33: 273–91.

―――. 1985. Aptitude, Attitude and Motivation in Second Language Proficiency: A Test of Clément's Model. *Journal of Language and Social Psychology* 4: 21–37.

Clément, Richard, Zoltán Dörnyei, and Kimberly A. Noels. Submitted for publication. Motivation, Self-Confidence, and Group Cohesion in the Foreign Language Classroom.

Three-em Dashes (―――) for Repeated Names:

Do not use when a coauthor is first added. If the same author is used again, add 3-em.

Dörnyei, Zoltán. 1990a. Analysis of Motivation Components in Foreign Language Learning. Paper presented at the Ninth World Congress of Applied Linguistics, Greece.

―――. 1990b. Conceptualizing Motivation in Foreign-Language Learning. *Language Learning* 40: 45–78.

Dörnyei, Zoltán, and Sarah Thurrell. 1992. *Conversation and Dialogues in Action.* Hemel Hempstead: Prentice-Hall.

―――. 1994. Teaching Conversational Skills Intensively: Course Content and Rationale. *ELT Journal* 48: 40–49.

Special Notes

1. Personal names beginning with "Mc" or any abbreviated forms of "Mac" should be indexed under "Mac" as though the full form were used.

2. For all state abbreviations, consult Chicago 14.17.

3. There is always a comma separating the names of authors, even if there are only two authors:

   Bernhardt, Elizabeth, and JoAnn Hammadou. 1987.

4. There are no quotation marks around article titles. Use quotes only when there is a title within a title. Books are in italics.

5. Abbreviate page-number spans according to 8.69

Journal Article: One Author (16.104)

Note that identification of the issue is used *only* when each issue is paginated separately (in contrast to the common practice of consecutive pagination throughout a volume).

> Lange, Dale. 1986. The MLA Commission of Foreign Languages, Literatures, and Linguistics: Comments and Advice. *ADFL Bulletin* 17: 28–31.

Journal Article: Two or More Authors (16.104)

> Allen, Wendy, Keith Anderson, and Léon Narváez. 1992. Foreign Languages Across the Curriculum: The Applied Foreign Language Component. *Foreign Language Annals* 25: 11–19.

Organizations, Associations, or Corporations (16.52)

If a publication issued by an organization bears no personal author's name on the title page, it should be listed by the organization, even if the name is repeated in the title or in the series title or as the publisher.

> American Council on the Teaching of Foreign Languages. 1986. *ACTFL Proficiency Guidelines.* Hastings-on-Hudson, NY: ACTFL.

Edited Book (16.46):

Byrnes, Heidi, and Michael Canale, eds. 1987. *Defining and Developing Proficiency: Guidelines, Implementations, and Concepts.* Lincolnwood, IL.: National Textbook.

Article in an Edited Book

James, Dorothy. 1989. Reshaping the "College-Level" Curriculum: Problems and Possibilities. In *Shaping the Future: Challenges and Opportunities,* edited by Helen S. Lepke, 79–110. Burlington, VT: Northeast Conference.

Book in a Series (16.86)

Magnan, Sally Sieloff, ed. 1991. *Challenges in the 1990s for College Foreign Language Programs.* AAUSC Issues in Language Program Direction. Boston: Heinle & Heinle.

Johnson, Carl L. 1944. *Professor Longfellow at Harvard.* Studies in Literature and Philology, vol. 5. Eugene: University of Oregon Press.

Article in Edited Book that Is Part of a Series

Lee, James F., and Bill VanPatten. 1991. The Question of Language Program Direction Is Academic. In *Challenges in the 1990s for College Foreign Language Programs,* edited by Sally Sieloff Magnan, 113–27. AAUSC Issues in Language Program Direction. Boston: Heinle & Heinle.

An Edition (16.79)

Pedhazur, Elazar J. 1982. *Multiple Regression Behavioral Research: Explanation and Prediction.* 2d ed. New York: Holt, Rinehart, and Winston.

Publisher's Information Implies a Special Publishing Division

Light, Richard J. 1992. *Harvard Assessment Seminars Second Report.* Cambridge: Harvard University, Graduate School of Education.

Unpublished Thesis (16.132, if published see below)

Tucker, Holly. 1994. Echo in the Text: Rewriting in Charles Sorel's *Berger Extravagant.* Ph.D. diss., University of Wisconsin-Madison.

Published Thesis (16.96 if microform; treat as normal book if otherwise. Note use of italics.)

Jones, Mildred. 1962. *Il Pastor Fido: Sheep and Their Shepherds.* Chicago: University Microforms.

Papers Read at a Meeting (16.133)

Magnan, Sally Sieloff. 1990. Preparing Inexperienced TAs for Second-Year Courses: Are Our Orientations and Methods Courses Adequate? Paper presented at the annual meeting of the American Council on the Teaching of Foreign Languages, Nashville.

Forthcoming or In press (16.57)

Knight, Susan. Forthcoming. Dictionary: The Tool of Last Resort in Foreign Language Reading. A New Perspective. *Modern Language Journal.*

Waldman, Lila. In press. Bilingual Adminstrative Support Personnel in United States Corporations. *Modern Language Journal* 78.

Eric Docs

Rubin, Joan, and Irene Thompson. 1992. Material Selection in Strategy Instruction for Russian Listening Comprehension. Eric Doc. No. ED349796.